THE SPARTAN SUCCESSION

(Sequel to *The Team the Titans Remember*)

VOLUME 1:
THE GENESIS (1972–1985)

MARK A. O'CONNELL

Copyright © 2020 Mark A. O'Connell
All rights reserved
First Edition

PAGE PUBLISHING, INC.
Conneaut Lake, PA

First originally published by Page Publishing 2020

ISBN 978-1-64628-849-6 (pbk)
ISBN 978-1-64628-850-2 (digital)

Printed in the United States of America

To Dale Foster: a guiding force then—and now.

CONTENTS

Foreword by Billy Miles 7
Acknowledgments 11
Introduction..15

Chapter 1:   The Last Years of Joyce 19
    Part 1: Cementing a Legacy..19
    Part 2: The Fall from Grace 38
Chapter 2:   A Legend's Successor 61
    Part 1: Extra Large Shoes to Fill..61
    Part 2: 1975 69
    Part 3: The Last Wolverines (1976) 86
Chapter 3:   Fire Left 99
Chapter 4:   One Tribe of Salemites 111
    Part 1: The Resistance 111
    Part 2: We Shall Be One..125
Chapter 5:   Kucer Named King of the Spartans 132
Chapter 6:   The First Two Battle Waves 138
    Part 1: 1977 138
    Part 2: 1978 159
Chapter 7:   Can Thompson Rally the Spartans?.........................176
Chapter 8:   His Trio...190
    Part 1: The Beleaguered (1979) 190
    Part 2: The Nearly Crushing Blow (1980) 204
    Part 3: Little Fun in Eighty-One 224
Chapter 9:   A Secession of Sorts...235
Chapter 10: 1982: We Shall Not Kick 266

Chapter 11: 1983...285
    Part 1: An Effective Trap Block...285
    Part 2: A Country Boy Named Willie................................297
    Part 3: Now That Was the Right Call! 315
Chapter 12: 1984: The Last in the Snake Pit......................333
Chapter 13: 1985...356
    Part I: A Stadium of Their Own 356
    Part 2: The New Era Is Complete 371
Chapter 14: Lest We Forget 393

Sources for The Spartan Succession 401
Index..405
Notes 415

FOREWORD

"Salem is a state of mind." These words, uttered by Salem's late mayor Jim Taliaferro, best describe the feelings held by so many of the citizens who live in our small city. This Salem "state of mind" is exhibited in so many ways but never more so than on Friday nights, lit up by the glow of the Salem stadium lights, illuminating our football team running on to the field to face yet another opponent. Salem is uniquely ours, but no more so than hundreds of other small cities and towns across this great country that count the days until the beginning of another football season. Towns that hold dear the young folks who play the game. I have been both privileged and blessed to count myself as a former player and as a long-time football coach in this wonderful story.

Mark O'Connell—sportswriter, broadcaster, historian and writer—has produced yet another riveting book that will lead the reader on a journey. A journey that takes us into the locker room and onto the playing field, giving us a keen view of the making and the continuation of a high school football dynasty. I had the pleasure of getting to know Mark as he began his writing of *The Team the Titans Remember*. It was this book that provided the doorway for stepping back in time, as O'Connell led us through the trials, tribulations, and utter joy of creating a football dynasty. O'Connell's passion for his subject and attention to detail are found throughout his work, as he interweaves the first-hand accounts of the many players, coaches, and fans that have provided the fuel for generating the magnetic hold over the hearts of a town and its people.

This book, *The Spartan Succession*, showcases O'Connell's love for sports combined with his steadfast pursuit of historical accuracy. His story of the evolution of Salem's football dynasty is a world that I am not only familiar with, but also a world that has been an integral part of my life since 1961. The fight song, sung during the games of Andrew Lewis High School, remains the same today for Salem High School. "Salem-born and Salem-bred and when I die, I'll be Salem dead." These words combine a bond that connects not only the players and coaches throughout the years, but also a bond between a high school and the fans that have remained loyal through the decades.

For me, 1961 will forever remain a turning point in my life. On the first day of my eighth-grade year, and after having attended the eighth-grade convocation and eager to get back home and savor the remaining few days of summer vacation, I was stopped in the exit lines of students by the eighth-grade football coach. His words to me, as best as I remember, were to report to football practice the very next day! I never questioned that directive and reported for practice the next day as ordered. That coach, Herbert Copenhaver, redirected my whole life.

Many of those who had a profound effect on my life can be found within the pages of this book and will forever have my eternal gratitude and deep admiration. Coaches, Eddie Joyce and Willis White, gave me more than I could ever give them. Although they had their distinctly different styles of coaching, they both held fast to the one common denominator that distinguishes and separates the great coaches from others. They were teachers. Coaching is teaching, and teaching is coaching! They imparted their wisdom and leadership not only on their players, but also on their assistant coaches and the community of Salem as well. Coach Dale Foster, to whom this book is dedicated, also strongly influenced me as a player and later as a coach. His quiet demeanor and thoughtful style of coaching provided a solid foundation from which the "slanting monster" defense became so effective in the success of Andrew Lewis High School. Dale Foster's leadership as Salem High's athletic director also played a significant role in the continuation of a football dynasty that remains strong to this very day. To these men, past teammates, the multitude of players I've been blessed to coach and so many others I give my eternal gratitude. Thank you!

Finally, to Mark O'Connell, I am humbled and honored to have been asked by you to write this foreword. The story that unfolds in the following pages brings back to life so many memories and times that Salem cherishes and holds dear. This story has a universal appeal and will also bring back traditional memories and images that many others hold for their communities in which they live. For me, the "sound of cleats" on the pavement, as we made our way to battle under the lights, still rings deeply in my soul and will forever remain in my heart.

Billy Miles
Andrew Lewis High School class of 1966

ACKNOWLEDGMENTS

First, and foremost, I'd like to acknowledge my wife, Diana. She was the first person I asked about the idea of this book, and she immediately supported the idea. Though she is only recently familiar with the Salem sports culture, she really "gets" the whole concept of "Salem born and Salem bred." It is truly fair to say that she is a Spartan fan by marriage.

Next on my list of go-to people was Charlie Hammersley. A 1969 alumnus of Andrew Lewis High, he was one of the most gifted athletes to have ever played in Salem. He recently retired after a career as the director of Salem's Parks and Recreation. Despite his athletic and vocational accomplishments, he has remained humble and a friend to many. He is, in my estimation, a class act. He agreed that writing this book was a good idea, which ignited my enthusiasm. In the previous book, *The Team the Titans Remember*, he was the first former Lewis player I interviewed. Afterward, he helped guide me through the list of prominent people to meet with. When it came to this book, he mentioned the necessity of getting Dale Foster on board. Without so, this ship would not have sailed.

Dale Foster served as the fact-checker for the manuscript of *The Team the Titans Remember*. A former assistant football coach at Andrew Lewis High School during its glory days, he remains a devoted Wolverine and intent upon protecting the legacy of Andrew Lewis football under the late Eddie Joyce Sr. Initially, he resisted the idea of a book about the success of the Spartans for fear it would diminish the Lewis legacy. He later acquiesced, conditioned upon the Lewis legacy remaining intact. I committed to both protecting the legacy and honoring the Spartans for their unique accomplishments. Once on board, Foster immediately began making his contributions to the completion of this book and was the first person officially interviewed for this book.

I knew I needed a research specialist, someone willing to do the grunt work for this project—i.e., the reviewing of countless newspaper articles on microfilm. Previously my daughter, Bekah, served in this capacity but was not available for this project. Stepping up in her place was the very devoted Michelle Capozzoli (PhD graduate, clinical psychology, University of Nebraska-Lincoln). She proved dedicated and diligent; however, her time was limited. She relocated to the Boston area to work in her profession.

About midway into this project, I assumed the role as research specialist and spent countless hours at the Alderman Library at the University of Virginia in Charlottesville. My sincere thanks to the entire staff, all of whom were very helpful. I especially came to enjoy the interaction and communication with three members: Eva Letterner, Olivia Dupont, and Stephen Hoyle, all of whom were working on their graduate degrees at the time. It was always nice to be greeted with a smile and interact with them before the tedious business of looking at microfilm!

Tony Wirt, a longtime teacher and coach at Andrew Lewis Middle School, eagerly made school yearbooks available to me.

Katie Lewis, an English teacher and yearbook advisor, eagerly made Salem High School yearbooks available to me.

The staff at the Salem Museum eagerly supported the mission. They included Fran Ferguson and Alex Burke. Upstairs in the Logan Library, Connie Kerfoot Stone and Mary Ann Sesler Hollandsworth assisted in the project as well.

Ms. Dorothy Hurt, newsroom assistant at the *Bristol Herald Courier*, provided a copy of an obituary pertaining to one of the former Salem football coaches.

Mr. Roger Christman of the Library of Virginia assisted me with locating online records of clemency.

Brian Hoffman of the *Salem Times-Register* was very gracious in his willingness to share any information, including photographs, to include in this book. He has written for the newspaper since 1974 and has followed the sports programs in the area as closely as anyone. Even after forty-four years on the job, his enthusiasm and dedication have never waned.

My son, Ethan O'Connell, spent several hours developing a website for me, which enables me to promote this book and the ones before it. Further, he assisted in the review of the *Salem Times-Register* newspapers on microfilm at the Roanoke County Library. His reviews covered the years 1983, 1984, and 1985.

Special thanks to my mother, Jan O'Connell of Salem, who has always believed in my abilities much more than I. She is an alumnus of Andrew Lewis High, where she was a majorette. Since this book and the previous one is about football, it is fitting to say that it would be impossible for me to have a bigger "fan" than she.

INTRODUCTION

It's nice when the natural sequence of events is clearly known.

Such is the case with this book, the sequel to *The Team the Titans Remember*, which was written to set the record straight about what *really* happened in 1971 during Virginia's Group AAA state football championship when the Titans of T. C. Williams High of Alexandria played the Wolverines of Andrew Lewis High of Salem.

Contrary to what was depicted in the highly acclaimed film *Remember the Titans*—which portrayed Williams defeating its archrival, George C. Marshall High, in a nail-biter of a game decided on the last play (using some trickery, no less)—*The Team the Titans Remember* tells the true story of the Williams-versus-Lewis game played on a sunny and unseasonably warm Saturday afternoon on December 4, 1971, in Roanoke's Victory Stadium, where Williams won by shutout, 27–0.

Well beyond that championship game, the book chronicles the glory days of Wolverine football that took place during what former Lewis assistant coach Dale Foster described as "the best years of [Coach Eddie] Joyce," or 1962–1971. During those ten illustrious seasons, the Wolverines won two state titles and were runner-up three times. That means in literally half of those ten seasons, the Wolverines were in contention for a state crown. To those he coached and to those who served as his assistants, especially Foster, Coach Joyce became a legend. And in recent years, former Lewis players honored Foster with the sobriquet the Man Behind the Legend.

The book also asserts that the '71 Lewis team was an extension of and a final segment to a lasting legacy that had begun in 1962 when the team won the first of its two state championships.[1]

Under the late Eddie Joyce Sr., who took over the Lewis program in 1960, a major change occurred.

Prior to 1960, the Lewis football team had been average; it literally had won about half of its games and lost the other half each season. Further, the foregone conclusion each season was that it would likely lose to Roanoke's Jefferson High, the local power that competed for state titles and claimed its most recent—and what would turn out to be its last—title in 1957.

Three years into his tenure, Joyce led the Wolverines to their first state title in 1962 and, two years later, added their second—and last—in 1964. After that, Lewis claimed the honor of runner-up three times: 1966, 1967, and 1971.

Joyce, who coached for a total of sixteen seasons at Andrew Lewis (fifteen of those as the head coach), coached his last Lewis team in 1974.

Mike Stevens succeeded Joyce and coached the Wolverines during the '75 and '76 seasons, which represented Lewis's last years as a high school.

Lewis's last graduating class was in 1977.

That's because during the 1977–1978 school year, Salem High School was opened by the Roanoke County Public Schools to consolidate the student bodies of both Andrew Lewis and Glenvar High Schools, which then became middle schools.

The school colors chosen for Salem were maroon and silver, and the nickname selected was Spartans. The colors and mascot chosen were clearly neutral considering that Lewis's school colors were blue and white and Glenvar's green and gold, and their school's mascots were Wolverines and Highlanders, respectively.

The city of Salem established its own school system, which officially began during the 1983–1984 school year. The previous

---

[1] The 1962 Lewis team had to forfeit the state title due to an ineligible player.

year, in 1982, Glenvar reopened and remained under the auspices of Roanoke County.

To this day, Andrew Lewis continues to operate as a middle school.

The basic premise of this book is that the Spartans have brought back the winning football tradition in Salem that Andrew Lewis originally established there, hence the title of this book, which reflects that the Spartans have succeeded to the throne once held by the Wolverines.

While it will be tempting for people to make comparisons between the Wolverines and Spartans, here are some helpful reminders of the dangers thereof. Comparisons can prove both tricky and touchy and can lead to unproductive and controversial discussions.

To be fair—and this is critical—the Wolverines and Spartans won, and have won, under different conditions and during a *very* different culture and time.

Current-day Salemites are familiar with the success of the Salem Spartans but may not be aware of how successful the Wolverines were. Like a skillful attorney in the courtroom, Dale Foster puts forth compelling evidence to prove the validity of the Lewis legacy.

Knowing human nature, however, comparisons will be inevitable. If there must be comparisons, I offer a few *safe* ones. First, both the Wolverines and Spartans were/are proven winners. Second, they were/are based in Salem, which has become known as Virginia's Championship City.[2]

---

[2] The community of Salem also has a large interest in athletics and has become known as Virginia's Championship City. It is home to the Salem Red Sox, a high class A affiliate of the Boston Red Sox, and the Amos Alonzo Stagg Bowl, the NCAA Division III Football Championship game, which is held at Salem Football Stadium. Salem's success in holding these events led the NCAA to also move the NCAA Men's Division III Basketball Championship and the NCAA Division III Volleyball Championship to the Salem Civic Center and the Women's NCAA Division II Softball Championship to the James I. Moyer Sports Complex. The city hosts several other statewide, regional, and national sporting events at its facilities. These events are attracted by the city's hospitality, modern facilities, and overall community support. (Source: www.visitroanokeva.com.)

Third, like the Lewis teams that experienced average seasons before Eddie Joyce took the reins, Salem's football team experienced its share of "growing pains." From 1977 to 1982, three different head coaches took their turns at establishing Salem as a winner. In 1982 the team was anything but a winner. But the pendulum was about to swing, and the decisive turning point came in 1983 when Willis White was hired as the fourth head coach of the Spartans.

It is my hope that this book will accomplish at least two goals: one, preserve the Wolverine legacy for all time, and two, honor the Spartans for their accomplishments.

Coach Foster is understandably protective of the Wolverine legacy and its integrity, but he also happens to be the common denominator in both Lewis's and Salem's football success. Not only was he a valuable assistant coach under Joyce and the author of *The Slanting Monster Defense in Football* (the defensive set used by the Wolverines beginning in 1963), but he was also the person most responsible for the hiring of Willis White.

Without Foster's influence, two things may have never occurred: one, the success of the Wolverine teams from 1962 to 1971, and two, getting the right coach at Salem to lead the Spartans to success.

In keeping with the natural sequence of events, it was only fitting to dedicate this book to him.

Chapter 1

THE LAST YEARS OF JOYCE

Part 1: Cementing a Legacy

"Band of Brothers": members of the 1966 Andrew Lewis state runner-up team seen here at the old Salem Municipal Field that Lewis players dubbed "the snake pit." From left to right: Freddie Amrhein, Bill Whitman, Gary Moore, Craig Stinnett, David Shelor and John Givens.

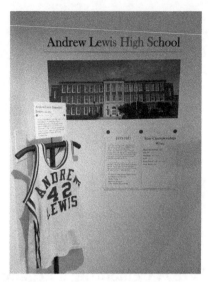

Andrew Lewis High School and its achievements. (Photo taken by author at Salem Museum which granted permission to print). Andrew Lewis High School and its record of achievements. The basketball jersey was worn by Charlie Hammersley, a member of the school's state championship team of 1968.

In my previous work, *The Team the Titans Remember*, the narrative provided the history of the Andrew Lewis High School Wolverines football teams predominantly through the legacy years of 1962 through 1971 under the head coach Eddie Joyce. For the most part, the narrative concluded with the Group AAA state championship game played on December 4, 1971, in Roanoke's Victory Stadium. Lewis's opponent, the Titans of T. C. Williams, won, 27–0.

Recall that the film *Remember the Titans* (released in 2000), and which immortalized the Titans, made no mention of Andrew Lewis, Coach Joyce, or even the Victory Stadium. Those omissions provided much of the inspiration to write *The Team the Titans Remember*.

Chapter 17 of that book is titled "1971: The Last of the Best." This chapter pertains to the '71 Lewis team that played in the state championship game. That season represented the last of the "best years of Joyce," which former assistant coach Dale Foster describes as the ten seasons spanning 1962 through 1971. For the record, the

THE SPARTAN SUCCESSION

1971 Lewis team was not the last good Wolverine team, but it was the last team that made it to the state finals.

That said, let's pick back up on the Wolverine trail following that famous '71 campaign. Coach Joyce returned to the helm for three more seasons, and the records are impressive.
In 1972, Lewis compiled a regular-season record of 8–2; in 1973, the Wolverines went 8–1–1; and in 1974 (Joyce's last season), Lewis finished at 7–1–2.[1]

Now let's consider Coach Joyce's season and grand totals after fifteen illustrious seasons:

- In 1960, it was 4–4–2. Even during his debut season, the team finished at 0.500.
- In 1961, it was 7–2–1. This included a win over Jefferson, the first for Lewis since 1940.
- In 1962, it was 10–0–0, including nine shutouts and a state championship.[3]
- In 1963, it was 7–2–1.
- In 1964, it was 10–0–0. It was an undisputed crown and a season during which Lewis handed nemesis E. C. Glass a shattering 53–12 defeat.
- In 1965, it was 8–2–0.
- In 1966, it was 10–1–0. It was a state runner-up season following a loss to Granby in the first-ever playoff game.
- In 1967, it was 10–1–0. It was another runner-up finish.
- In 1968, it was 6–3–1.
- In 1969, it was 8–2–0.
- In 1970, it was 7–3–0.
- In 1971, it was 12–1–0. It was the last state title game for Lewis.[2]
- In 1972, it was 8–2–0. This includes a win over Lane of Charlottesville, the 1963 state champion, and the first loss to Patrick Henry since 1963.[3]

---

[3] The 1962 Lewis team had to forfeit the championship due to an ineligible player.

- In 1973, it was 8–1–1. They played Culpeper County for the first time ever and won at 16–13; lost to Patrick Henry, which went on to win the AAA state championship; and tied Cave Spring at 12–12.[4]
- In 1974, it was 7–1–2. Lewis made its first appearance in the Group AA Blue Ridge District. The loss was to William Fleming (19–13), and the ties were with Franklin County (12–12) and Patrick Henry (6–6).[5]
- Total wins: 122.
- Total losses: 25.
- Total ties: 8.
- Winning percentage: 78.

It is also noteworthy that under Joyce, the Wolverines turned the tables on the Magicians of Roanoke's Jefferson High who, for years, had held sway over Lewis and many other opponents.

Prior to 1960, the Magicians had mesmerized the Wolverines. Of the forty-two games played between the two teams before 1960, Jefferson had won thirty-four, lost four, and tied four times, the most recent of which was in 1958.

During the Joyce years, Lewis and Jefferson met fourteen of his fifteen seasons. The Wolverines dominated the series with eleven wins against only three losses.

Jefferson won in 1960, and then Lewis rattled off seven-straight wins from 1961 through 1967. The Magicians won back-to-back games in 1968 and 1969, but the Wolverines finished strong with wins in 1970 (26–9), 1971 (21–6), 1972 (by the biggest margin ever, 51–0), and 1973 (46–28).

The two teams did not play in 1974.

The aforementioned history prompts this question: *how* good were the Joyce-led Wolverines, and how is their legacy cemented for all time?

THE SPARTAN SUCCESSION

Consider what former sportswriter/editor Bob McLelland of the *Roanoke Times & World-News* reported.[4]

In an article written in 1974, McLelland wrote: "Against the Roanoke Valley opponents, Joyce was 52–9–1. 11–3 against Jefferson; 12–3 against William Fleming; 9–2–1 against Patrick Henry; 7–0 against William Byrd; 7–1 against Cave Spring; 4–0 against Northside; and 1–0 against both Roanoke Catholic and Glenvar."[6]

Think about it: 52–9–1 against the local rivals? That's a winning percentage of 0.845! Another way of putting it is this: Lewis won at least eight out of every ten games against its Roanoke Valley opponents. Given the numbers against the locals, the Wolverines under Joyce were simply dominant.

The Salem fans were naturally appreciative.

Conversely, others were not.

There is a natural tendency for people to respond to someone's success in either one of two ways: one, they admire you for it and join you in support or, two, they resent you for it and want to see you toppled. This explains—I submit in large part—why highly successful programs, organizations, and individuals are either loved or hated.

As a current-day example, let's consider the New England Patriots of the National Football League.

---

[4] "Born, raised and educated in Roanoke, Virginia, Bob McLelland worked for the Roanoke Times & World News from 1949 to 1980 filling the shoes of sportswriter, sports editor and metro editor. His gifted writing and prize-winning columns earned him legendary status in the sports media profession, but it was his dedicated community involvement and passion for local sports that earned him hero status at home. For more than 45 years, McLelland coached community football, his teams winning an amazing 80 percent of their games and a national championship. Along the way, McLelland became a role model and mentor to generations of Roanoke's up and coming athletes, always emphasizing the importance of sportsmanship, ethics, hard work and the joy of competition. McLelland, honored both professionally and civically by such groups as Virginia Sportswriters and Sportscasters, Virginia High School Coaches Association, Sports Magazine and both the Roanoke and Virginia State Chambers of Commerce, was also a charter member of the Roanoke College Sports Hall of Fame. In 1989, the football field at Roanoke's Victory Stadium was named in his honor." (Source: www.vasportshof.com).

Hate them or love them, the indisputable truth is that they have been highly successful. As of the submission of this manuscript in 2019, the Patriots have played in eleven Super Bowls and won six and lost five.

They are neither short on fans or critics. I have met many people who hate them, and some have accused them of cheating, which is most attributable to the controversy known as Deflategate, and this began in January of 2015. The Patriots were accused of deflating game balls. (For the timeline of events and the findings of the investigation, please see www.espn.com, and search timeline of events for Deflategate.)

In contrast, supporters of the Patriots now sport T-shirts with these words: "They hate us 'cause they ain't us."

Could the Wolverines under Coach Joyce—who won fairly and squarely and were never accused of cheating but who dominated the local competition—have countered their critics with the same explanation: "They hate us 'cause they ain't us"? You decide.

In addition to McLelland's assessment, up next is Coach Foster's comprehensive and authoritative written analysis that sets forth just how special the Wolverines under Coach Eddie Joyce really were[7]:

> I dedicate this article to the memory of Coach Eddie Joyce.
>
> The Virginia High School League (VHSL) held its very first state championship football game in 1966. The game was played between two undefeated AAA schools, Andrew Lewis and Granby (of Norfolk). Here is a quote from the state championship game program: "Records speak for themselves. Thus, Eddie Joyce of Andrew Lewis High has to be ranked as one of the most successful scholastic football coaches ever to appear on the Virginia scene… Eddie is well-respected by his rival coaches and for good reason—his record tells the story."

THE SPARTAN SUCCESSION

Foster elaborated on "the story":

> It is important to understand the classification system used by the VHSL in the past and today.
>
> In 1966, if a school had an enrollment of 1,000 or more students, it was classified as AAA. Andrew Lewis's enrolment in 1966 was 1,200 students, which placed Lewis in the AAA classification. Because it was classified as AAA, Lewis had to play much larger schools, sometimes double or even triple its size—even playing a school with 5,000 students! The 1966 state championship program was correct with its analysis of Coach Joyce's record against that very TOUGH SCHEDULE.
>
> In 1986, the VHSL implemented changes in its classifications of schools by adding two divisions to each of the three previously-in-place classifications. Divisions 1 and 2 comprised Group A, Divisions 3 and 4 made up Group AA, and Divisions 5 and 6 were included among Group AAA. From lowest to highest enrollment, the sequence was Division 1, 2, 3, 4, 5, and 6.

Note: In more recent years, the VHSL implemented yet another change, which essentially changed the nomenclature of the classifications to 1A, 2A, 3A, 4A, 5A, and 6A. Foster's written submission underscores the significance of strength of schedule, records against quality opponents, the classification system, and some other significant numbers. He continues as follows:

> When you talk about Andrew Lewis football during the Eddie Joyce era, four numbers immediately come to mind: 18,000, 28, 43, and 1:46

[1 minute and 46 seconds]. For the very first time, in 1971, the VHSL held a state playoff which format included regional, state semi-finals and finals pairings to eventually determine a true AAA state champion. After 104 Group AAA teams played through the regular season and playoffs, there were only two teams still undefeated: Andrew Lewis and T. C. Williams of Alexandria.

On December 4, 1971, Andrew Lewis, with an enrollment of 975 students [by today's classification system, Lewis would be classified as 3A while its successor, Salem High, is currently classified as 4A] and T. C. Williams, which was the combination of the three triple A public high schools in Alexandria (Hammond, George Washington, and T. C. Williams) and which had an enrollment of 5,000 students, played for the AAA (Triple A) state championship in Roanoke's Victory Stadium before a crowd of 18,000 people. Compare this to Salem Stadium which seats 7,157. This crowd (18,000) of people could fill Salem Stadium two and a half times! This was probably the largest crowd to attend a single high school football game in the state of Virginia. This game, won by T. C. Williams, was the subject of the movie, "Remember the Titans." T. C. Williams was tied with Washington High School of Tulsa, Oklahoma as the No. 2 ranked team in the country. Andrew Lewis was ranked as the No. 25 team in the country.

During the first round of the 1971 AAA state playoffs with 15,000 in attendance at Roanoke's Victory Stadium, undefeated Andrew Lewis was trailing E. C. Glass (enrollment of 2,928 students) 14 to 0 with six minutes left in the game. Many of the 15,000 fans in attendance began to exit the stadium since Andrew Lewis would need to score three touchdowns in the final six minutes. Then the unbelievable happened. It didn't take six minutes but only the next 1 minute and 46 seconds for all-state quarterback Eddie Joyce Jr., who held several state-passing records, to pass for three touchdowns and a two-point conversion for the 20–14 win. And with the help of two fumble recoveries by the Lewis defense, the Wolverines ran out the final four minutes and 28 seconds remaining in the game to remain undefeated. Joyce ended his career as the state's all-time leading passer.

To quote Coach Joyce after the game, "This was my greatest win."

Quoting the *Roanoke Times*, "This would have to be one of the greatest athletic moments in the history of the Roanoke Valley."

And Billy Sample, who caught the winning touchdown pass, was quoted as saying, "This was my most exciting moment in my athletic career," which included a successful Major League Baseball career with the New York Yankees, Texas Rangers, and Atlanta Braves.

The number 28 represents the most points scored against Andrew Lewis by any of the 105 teams Lewis played between 1962 and 1971. William Fleming scored 28 points against Lewis in 1970 and T.C. Williams, the number 2 ranked team in the country, scored 27 points against Lewis in

1971. Most of the games were against teams that would be classified today as 6A, the largest of the current six classifications. One Lewis team, the undefeated 1962 AAA state champions, led the state in defense by allowing only 12 total points as they shut out 9 of 10 opponents.[5]

The 1966 AAA state championship runner-up team also led the state in defense and offense by outscoring their opponents, 345 to 39. This same team made history by playing Granby in the very first state championship game ever held in the state of Virginia. This game was televised live back home since it was played in Norfolk. During this time-period the VHSL recognized only one state champion, and that was the AAA (Triple A) state champion. At present the VHSL recognizes six state champions.

Garry Throckmorton, offensive guard and nose guard on defense, was voted the honorary captain of the 1966 AAA (Triple A) all-state team by receiving the most votes. This was only the second time in history that a lineman received that honor.

Jersey no. 43 was worn by two AAA 1st team All-State players. First, Russell Harris wore the number and was a member of Andrew Lewis's two undefeated AAA State Championship teams, 1962 and 1964. In 1964, he was selected to the AAA All-State 1st team as a running back and monster man on defense, and he was also voted

---

[5] The 1962 Lewis team had to forfeit the championship due to an ineligible player.

the most outstanding high school football player in the state of Virginia. Harris was a member of the 1964 Parade All American Team as a running back. This was the second year that the Parade Magazine selected the best high school players in the country at each position.

After Harris, Charlie Hammersley wore no. 43. He was a member of two AAA state championship runner-up teams, 1966 and 1967, as a running back and monster man on defense. In 1966, he became the first sophomore to be selected to the AAA All-State 1st team. He also made the AAA All-State 1st team as a junior. Charlie was certainly on his way to becoming the first player in Virginia to make the AAA All-State 1st team three years in a row until a serious automobile accident, between his junior and senior years, denied him that recognition.

Harris, Hammersley, Joyce, Throckmorton and their fellow Wolverines were a special group of players: a true band of brothers that competed at the triple A (AAA) level [the equivalent of 5A or 6A today] and were state champions in 1962 and 1964—both years undefeated—and was a runner-up in 1966, 1967, and 1971 with records of 10–1, 10–1 and 12–1, respectively. During this time, Lewis's record was 88 wins, 15 losses, and 2 ties.

For years, Lewis—with a student enrollment of 1200—975 had been a member of the Western District. (Andrew Lewis's enrollment dropped when Glenvar High School opened in 1966.)

These were Lewis's fellow district teams and their enrollments:

E. C. Glass—2500–3000 students
GW-Danville—2500–3000 students
Halifax County—2500–3000 students
Patrick Henry—2000 students
William Fleming—1800 students
Jefferson—1000 students after Patrick Henry opened in 1961.

Through the 1971 season, Lewis had established a history of playing the following eleven teams which had won multiple AAA state championships. They were: GW-Danville, E. C. Glass, Hampton, Graham, Lane (of Charlottesville), Douglas Freeman, Granby, T. C. Williams, Beckley and Charleston (of West Virginia) and Dobyns-Bennett (of Tennessee). All except one, Graham, had an enrollment between 2,000 and 3,000 students, and one had an enrollment of 5,000 students. Between 1962 and 1971, Lewis's record against those eleven triple A state championship teams—both in and out of state—was 22 wins, seven losses and two ties.

G.W.-Danville won two Group AAA state championships

E.C. Glass won three Group AAA titles. Glass was Lewis's biggest rival. There was only one high school in Lynchburg, a city of 75,000. Glass was a hotbed for college recruits. As an example, the 1965 Glass team had eight seniors sign a Division I scholarship. Even Paul M. "Bear" Bryant, who was the head coach at the University of Alabama at the time, and who won a total of six national championships, recruited Glass players because of their talent. E. C. Glass had a difficult time filling out its football schedule because schools refused to play them because of their outstanding talent, so the Virginia High School League gave Glass permission to play two nationally known prep schools, Fork Union and Staunton Military Academies. These two prep schools played college freshman teams when freshmen were ineligible to play varsity back in the '60s.

Two Heisman Trophy winners prepped at Staunton Military Academy: Howard "Hopalong" Cassady (Ohio State in 1955) and John David Crow (Texas A&M in 1957).

Lewis's record against Glass between 1962 and 1971 was 6 wins 1 loss and 2 ties. According to Coach Vince Bradford, the longtime coach at E. C. Glass, the 1964 undefeated state champion Andrew Lewis team gave him his worst defeat, 53 to 12.

And it wasn't just the big wins against Glass. Lewis also played these winning programs:

Hampton, to date, has won 17 Group AAA state championships and two national championships by being ranked the No. 1 team in the country. Hampton is the all-time winningest school in state history with 830 wins. Its coach, Mike Smith, is the fourth winningest football coach in the country and was twice named as National Coach of the Year. Andrew Lewis split with Hampton, winning 21–0 at home in 1966, and losing 20–0 at Hampton in 1967. Because of a late arrival of a Piedmont Airline charter plane which carried the Andrew Lewis team, game officials delayed the start of the game 15 minutes, so the Lewis players could warmup. (A normal warmup time is around 45 minutes.) This put Lewis at a great disadvantage against a state power like Hampton. This was Lewis's only loss that year, and cost the team a third triple A state championship in the last five years.

Graham of Bluefield won 1 AAA State Championship Lane 2 AAA State Championships Lane of Charlottesville had a 53-game winning streak, 1962–1967. (This is still a state record.)

Douglas Freeman of Richmond won one AAA State Championship

Granby of Norfolk won four AAA State Championships.

T. C. Williams of Alexandria won the Triple A title in '71 and was ranked the No. 2 team in the country.

So that there is less confusion, the AAA (Triple A) classification has been used throughout this analysis. The top classification in the state at one time was known as 1-A, then it became AAA (Triple A), and now it is known as 6A. To put matters in perspective, Salem High School, as of the writing of this analysis, has an enrollment of about 1300 students and is classified as 4A among the six classifications.

THE SPARTAN SUCCESSION

By today's classification system, Andrew Lewis would be classified as 3A.

Coach Herman Boone (played by Denzel Washington in the movie *Remember the Titans*) was asked in the movie "What kind of football do you play at T. C. Williams?" Coach Boone replied, "We play AAA (Triple A) football here at T. C. Williams." What he meant was they played in the top division in the state which included the largest schools and the best teams the state had to offer.

Those schools in Virginia, which were classified as AAA then, would be today's equivalent of 6A, which is the largest classification in the Virginia High School League.

Foster continued his case, citing evidence that Lewis even went outside the state in search of the biggest, and the best, competition.

Andrew Lewis had a record of 4–1 against three out-of-state teams that had won multiple AAA or AAAA state championships. Lewis had two wins against Woodrow Wilson of Beckley, West Virginia, and two wins against the winningest team in Tennessee: Dobyns-Bennett of Kingsport. The only loss was to the AAAA state champion Charleston of West Virginia and by the score of 7–0. The state championships these team won include; Charleston with three (and probably the largest high school in the state) and Woodrow Wilson also with three.

Dobyns-Bennett High had the most wins of any team in the state of Tennessee and won twelve

(12) state championships and was a member of the largest of all classifications.

The Wolverines did not have it easy. For example, Glass—in 1965—had eight seniors on that team that signed Division 1 scholarships. We played them during the last game of the season. I had the chance to scout them throughout the season because they played seven of their games on Saturday night.

And the attendance at some of the Lewis games? Unbelievable!

These were some of the crowds in attendance for the Lewis team in 1971: 18,000 for the championship game against T.C Williams, 15,000 for the Glass game, 13,000 at both the William Fleming and Patrick Henry games, and 10,000 at many other games.

We played the best teams in the state like GW-Danville, the 1968 AAA (Triple A) state champion, and this is not fake news; and the best team in West Virginia, AAAA state champion Charleston, both in the same season. Both games were fairly close, 14–6 and 7–0, respectively, and we only had about 1,000 students. This was the Glenvar effect.

On two different occasions Coach Joyce flew his team to northern Virginia and to Hampton, Virginia to play George Washington High School of Alexandria and Hampton High School.

THE SPARTAN SUCCESSION

> [Assistant] Coach [Wallace] Thompson and I graded game film before Monday's practices. It would take us all day. We graded every player on every play. The players knew they were being graded and couldn't wait until Monday to see their grades.
>
> Coach Joyce would put the results on the back of a "coke" (Coca-Cola) poster which hung on the wall of the locker room. The lowest percentage resulted in the "Baby Doll Award." Coach Joyce would have the doll and the pink shirt, and at Monday's practice he announced the (not-so-proud) recipient.

Foster explained that the grading process was tough and even the better players might find themselves in line to receive the dreaded Baby Doll Award.

One of the best such examples is that of Hammersley. Once, during the same week that the *Roanoke Times* named him as the Back of the Week, he was also the recipient of the Baby Doll Award.

Worthy of praise and derision at the same time? How was this possible?

In Foster's book *The Slanting Monster Defense in Football*, examples of the stringent grading process can be found beginning on page 214, and at some point, even Hammersley didn't make the grade![8]

Now, back to Foster:

> When Glenvar High School opened in 1966, Andrew Lewis—by today's standards—would have been classified as a 3A school. But the Wolverines played 6A schools, both in and out-of-state. There were three very important things that gave Andrew Lewis an edge against those bigger schools. 1): a two-week preseason football camp which was sponsored and paid for by

the Salem Sports Foundation; 2): strict game-film grading on each player, including the "Baby Doll" Award; 3): A 10–15-page scouting report on the team's next opponent was issued to each player before Monday's practice.

The legendary Eddie Joyce was Lewis's football coach, athletic director, assistant principal, and—for a time—the city's mayor. To quote an ex-Andrew Lewis player, who was a successful high school head-football coach for 40 years, including 38 years at one school: "People just don't understand how big Andrew Lewis football was during the Eddie Joyce-era. Friday night football was a way of life in Salem: you either went to the football game or you stayed at home by yourself. When there was a football game, the whole town shut down. All the stores in downtown Salem showed their support for Lewis with blue and white, the school's colors, as decorations in their windows. [At] the preseason football camp, which we had for two weeks at Camp Alta Mons, they worked us like dogs but fed us like kings. We had all you could eat—steak almost every night—all paid for. I will never forget the game nights when Lewis played at home. On Fridays, there was a 10-minute service at a church after school. We went to different churches each week. Then, we'd meet in a classroom where [Coach Joyce] would get us all whipped up in a frenzy. After that we walked over to the stadium and everyone was quiet except the sound of the cleats on the pavement. I can still hear the sound. People would line the street. It was a great atmosphere. Coach Joyce even flew the team on a charter flight for a game against GW-Alexandria. This was the second time Coach Joyce flew the team to an away game. This was my first flight. I'd say for most of us it was."⁹

Foster concluded his compelling and persuasive case with these words:

> Other coaches have won in the past, but if you checked their schedules, they played schools of equal size or smaller. Not so with Coach Joyce: he was unique—the only VHSL coach who played and won against schools double, or even triple, the size of Lewis, and still won two Group AAA state championships in 1962 and 1964, and three runner-up finishes in 1966, 1967 and 1971. No wonder he is considered a LEGEND!!!¹⁰

In addition to McLelland, Foster, and a well-known area coach, consider this succinct assessment from former Wolverine Donald "Boozie" Daulton (Andrew Lewis class of 1971): "In 1968, we played [GW-] Danville, the best team in the state of Virginia, and we played Charleston, the best team in the state of West Virginia. Both games were close."

Daulton was a sophomore on the '68 Lewis team and began his career as a lineman, but Coach Joyce decided to move him to running back.

"That was one of the best decisions we ever made," said Foster of the switch.

The '68 Lewis team fell to GW-Danville during the second game of the season by the score of 14–6. The Cardinals, as they were named then, were under fifth-year head coach Alger Pugh and claimed Virginia's state championship.

Lewis also lost to Dobyns-Bennett High of Kingsport, Tennessee, by a score of 7–0.

Daulton became a battering ram for the Wolverines and a crowd favorite. After graduation from high school, he played briefly in college before beginning a career in the automobile industry. In 2016, at the time of our interview for the previous book, Daulton had been in the industry for forty-four years and had co-owned a used-car lot trading as Freedom Auto Sales for twenty-four years. Over the years, he enjoyed Salem football and the University of Virginia sports, especially football and basketball.[11]

He retired in 2017, and his health soon failed him. He was diagnosed with liver cancer and succumbed on January 29, 2018, at the age of sixty-five.[6] Less than a week before his death, Charlie Hammersley and I had the opportunity to visit with Daulton at his home. Predictably, the subject of Wolverine football, including Coach Joyce, came up. During that discussion, Daulton emphatically gave Joyce the top mark of 10 on a scale of 1 to 10.

He, Foster, and Hammersley are just a few of the former Wolverines who will forever hold Coach Joyce in high esteem. With their help and loyalty, plus the indisputable record of wins and losses against high-caliber competition, the legacy of Coach Joyce has been cemented for all time.

Part 2: The Fall from Grace

Throughout the years, former Lewis coaches and players have opted to cherish the memories of Lewis's success under a man they revere as a legend—and understandably so.

His credentials, accomplishments, and profound influence on the young men he coached, the assistants he mentored, and the students he taught instilled values and life lessons that served them well then and throughout their lives.

---

[6] Donald Wayne "Boozie" Daulton was born on February 11, 1952, a son of the late Ruby and Willard Daulton. Originally from Cumberland County, Virginia, Daulton and his family moved to Salem in 1965. He told this author that his father nicknamed him "Boozie" He died on January 29, 2018. He is survived by his wife, Vicki, and their daughters Carrie Daulton and Brea Hatt and husband, Andrew; grandchildren Kylie, Blakely and Beckett. He was preceded in death by a daughter, Amy Daulton, and a brother, Ray Daulton, and his wife, Jenny. (source: obituary found online at www.johnoakey.com.)

But there was another chapter in Joyce's life that tarnished his reputation, and this cannot—objectively and accurately as part of the history—be overlooked or glossed over. Perhaps the earliest warning sign that there was trouble ahead for Eddie Joyce came in 1974 when Joyce, amid allegations of misuse of funds, resigned following the '74 campaign.

Joyce is no longer living, so his version of what happened is no longer possible to obtain. However, at least two people can "testify" as to what they remember about the events that unfolded and ultimately marked Joyce for life.

One of the two is Foster, his loyal and gifted assistant, who began coaching at Andrew Lewis in 1962 and continued through 1971. After that, he served in several different capacities within the school system and is arguably as authoritative as anyone in Salem when it comes to knowing the ins and outs of most decisions that were made.

He identified two events that left him feeling deeply hurt and disappointed. He began with Coach Joyce's fate.

"Mark, I have lived in Salem for fifty-five years and by far the biggest scandal during that time was when a Roanoke County Jury found Coach Joyce guilty of mishandling $3,800 of school funds. I attended that trial. He was sentenced to serve time in jail and he lost his teaching certificate."[12]

The second event which wounded him deeply is discussed in Volume 2.

Let's meet someone else highly attuned with the circumstances surrounding that first event.

* * *

Better Ask Deke

Born on December 11, 1943, in Newport News, Virginia, George Summers Jr. was four years old when his family moved to Salem. He has always been known to his family and friends as Deke.[13]

"I was named after two guys who my parents used to invite over for dinner," recalled Summers. "Both guys were single. One was named Decker and the other was Econ. They were shipped out for service, and they reportedly told my parents, 'Make sure you name your son after us.' So my parents put the two names together and came up with Deke."[14]

Summers graduated in 1962 from Andrew Lewis High, where he played both football and basketball. "I was accepted at the University of Virginia, where I planned to major in architectural engineering. But I weighed 140 pounds, and I wanted to play football. Fred Hoback was an assistant coach at Andrew Lewis and suggested I check out Hampden-Sydney. I didn't even know where it was. He took me, Richard Beach, and one other player down there. I got accepted, and the two of them got put on the waiting list.[15]

"My dad had been in either the active or reserves of the army, so I had grown up going to reserve officers' meetings and summer camps with him because he was a lieutenant colonel. At the time, they had a program where you could go on active duty for six months and then be in the reserves for six or six and a half years. Since I didn't really know anything about Hampden-Sydney, I told the admissions guy that I might just go in the army for six months and make sure this is what I want to do.[16]

"I was at Fort Jackson, South Carolina, and I knew that the [1962 high school state championship football] game was coming up [for Andrew Lewis] with [E. C.] Glass. Early Saturday morning, I took off hitchhiking to Roanoke [November 10, 1962]. I walked into Municipal Field in full uniform and right before the play when Cecil Blankenship broke loose and scored the winning touchdown."[17]

Like many in attendance, Summers derived much satisfaction watching the winning play unfold. He, too, had played at Lewis.

In the football program printed for the game of September 23, 1960, which was the second annual Sandlot Benefit Football Game, Summers was listed on the program's roster as a quarterback who weighed 140 pounds and below two other quarterbacks, Charles Bailey and Wayne Hall. This benefit game was played between Andrew Lewis and Blacksburg. As a sign of the times, consider this depiction:

on the front of the program was a football player pictured running the football, wearing jersey no. 72 and wearing a helmet similar in appearance to that worn traditionally by the Michigan Wolverines and without a face mask. The program sold for ten cents.[18]

That was Summers's junior year.

"My senior year, I started at safety," he said. "I played a little offense here and there, and I also punted."[19]

Next, it was on to Hampden-Sydney.

"I lied for four years [about my weight]," admitted Summers. "I didn't think they would think I could play at 160 pounds, so whenever I weighed in, I always added ten pounds to whatever I weighed. And there you played both ways, offense and defense, for the most part. I started at free safety for three years, and then my senior year, I played quarterback and punted."[20]

Summers majored in history and economics and graduated in 1967 and immediately embarked on a coaching career.[21]

"One day I was at Hampden-Sydney, and the next day, I was at Robert E. Lee Junior High [in Staunton], teaching ninth-grade math in a trailer in the parking lot. I had started out as a math major, so they let me teach math, and I coached baseball in the spring."[22]

Later that same year, he returned to Andrew Lewis and reunited with Coach Joyce.

"Eddie [Joyce] had told me that after I graduated [from college] and as soon as an opening was here that it would be me [who would get the job]."[23]

Summers was hired as a teacher, and he taught history and economics.[24]

During the first of his eight seasons on Coach Joyce's staff, the team went to preseason camp at Alta Mons, where Summers said he helped Coach Foster with the running backs. He soon began coaching both the offensive and defensive backs, and he served in this capacity for the duration of his time at Andrew Lewis.[25]

He would have gladly served longer, but serious trouble beset the head coach. Through it all, Summers—and so many other

Salemites—remained loyal to Joyce, whose fate would soon be in the hands of an impaneled jury.

* * *

In the August 15, 1974, edition of the *Roanoke World-News*, an article written by Jack Chamberlain, education writer, appeared under the headline "Joyce accepts blame for fund irregularities."[26]

An audit of the school's internal accounts had been conducted that summer. Mr. Bayes Wilson, assistant superintendent for business for the county schools, told Chamberlain that the irregularities in the Andrew Lewis athletic account were brought to the attention of school officials about mid-June, a week or ten days after the annual audit began.[27]

The auditors were Rothgeb, Miller & Sells of Roanoke, who asked for permission to audit the Lewis accounts for the past three years. Wilson indicated that permission had been granted.[28]

The discrepancies totaled nearly $4,000 over a period of three years. Joyce told Chamberlain that they were the result "of his administrative mistakes and not criminal intent."[29]

Prior to the publication of this article, Joyce had resigned from his school administration duties (i.e., athletic director and assistant principal) at Andrew Lewis to "stick to coaching football."[30]

Roanoke County and school board officials turned the matter over to Roanoke County Commonwealth's attorney John Lampros for investigation.[31]

Roanoke County school superintendent Arnold Burton told Chamberlain that Joyce had requested to be relieved from his administrative duties, that Joyce's request would be granted, and that Joyce would become a driver education teacher and retain his coaching job.[32]

Chamberlain interviewed Joyce and quoted him as saying, "My real interest is football. I have been for some time wanting to give up my administrative duties. I just got tired of it."[33]

Joyce told him that he had attended graduate school at Virginia Tech for over three years but had not completed the requirements for a master's degree required for school administration. He said he felt he was "pulling Lewis's accreditation ratings down."[34]

The audit, wrote Chamberlain, "firmed up his decision to retire from school administration."[35]

Consistent with his coaching philosophy to accept a loss without excuse or blame, Joyce told Chamberlain, "I felt, under the circumstances, that I hadn't done a real good administrative job. [The audit] bears this out."[36]

What exactly happened, and who else was involved?

Chamberlain reported that "he [Joyce] and the school ha[d] been doing business with CMT sporting goods of Roanoke for about four or five years and three different accounts were involved in the discrepancies... CMT had an account with the Lewis athletic department, the Virginia Coaches Association and Joyce personally, all administered by Joyce.[37]

"For convenience, Joyce said, CMT carried the address of Andrew Lewis High School for all three accounts, including his own personal account.[38]

"Joyce said some bills intended for the coaches' association or himself apparently were paid from the high school account and apparently little attention was given to it for the last three years..."[39]

"Joyce said CMT ha[d] already rectified the accounts by giving the school nearly $4,000 credit that the school erroneously paid on the other two accounts. He said the coaches' association ha[d] paid about $2,500 to CMT and Joyce personally ha[d] paid about $1,500 to CMT to rectify the accounts."[40]

After some additional questioning by Chamberlain, Joyce indicated that "he had a continuing or revolving account with CMT and, 'from time to time, I made some payments on it.'"[41]

In an article that appeared below this one, staff writer Dick Hammerstrom wrote that the evidence would probably be submitted to a Roanoke County Circuit Court grand jury.[42]

State police, Lampros, and Salem Commonwealth's attorney Charles B. Phillips had been asked to handle the investigation.[43]

The irregularities stemmed from posting unauthorized charges to the accounts.[44]

Jurisdiction of this case belonged to the county. Though Andrew Lewis High was in Salem, it was owned and operated by the Roanoke County school system, and the sporting goods store was also located in the county.[45]

In the next day's edition of the *Roanoke World-News*, staff writer Charles Stebbins reported, "Control of Salem city council will shift this month from Republicans to independents and council is expected to once again get a mayor who is not aligned with any political party."[46]

The relevance and importance of this article is this: Eddie Joyce, an independent, was a member of council and the city's former mayor. With the expected shift in control, it was speculated that Joyce might once again be elected mayor, though Stebbins indicated that the "possibility has diminished to some extent in the last 24 hours by the hint from Joyce that he would resign from council unless completely cleared of any wrongdoing in financial irregularities at Andrew Lewis High School."[47]

Here again, Joyce accepted responsibility for the irregularities but said they were the result of administrative errors.[48]

In what can now be viewed as foreshadowing, Stebbins reported, "If this controversy is not settled by Sept. 2 when council meets to elect a mayor, Joyce may not be the front-running candidate. In that case, the next leading candidate may be [Jim] Taliaferro, who has aligned himself with Joyce and often supports the same causes."[49]

Numerous articles pertaining to Joyce's pending case were published with various legal jargon used to describe what crime, exactly, he was charged with. Clarity came in an article published on August 7, 1975, which indicated that Joyce was indicted on one count each of embezzlement and obtaining money or goods by false pretense. (For additional clarity, embezzlement is considered as a larceny offense, and obtaining money or goods by false pretense is included among the various fraud crimes.)[50]

This same article indicated that his trial by jury was scheduled for August 27–28 with the Honorable Ernest W. Ballou presiding.[7] With no further continuances, the jury—comprised of eleven men and one woman—began hearing testimony on August 27 after Joyce had pleaded not guilty to the single charge of obtaining money or goods by false pretense. If, in fact, Joyce was ever indicted for embezzlement, no word followed as to the fate of that charge.[51]

Joyce was represented by Mr. Arthur Smith, whose opening remarks cited the flaws contained with the bookkeeping systems at both CMT and Andrew Lewis. Smith was quoted as saying, "We're going to try the system [of bookkeeping]. He [Joyce] was everything at Andrew Lewis High School, and they made him a bookkeeper."[52]

The Commonwealth saw things much differently.

Lampros told the jury that Joyce had "devised a scheme whereby he would submit pay vouchers to the school for payment of his personal account at CMT." The time period alleged was July 1, 1970, through May 30, 1974, and that fourteen checks were involved.[53]

The jury took less than an hour to impanel. During the process, Judge Ballou's questions to prospective jurors included this one: "Do any of you have any feeling with regard to victories or defeats by Andrew Lewis football teams?"[54]

---

[7] Ernest Wade Ballou was born on December 3, 1921. He was a US Navy veteran of World War II and the Korean conflict. The Roanoke native retried from the Naval Reserve in 1966 with the rank of commander. He graduated from the University of Virginia School of Law in 1949 and began practicing law in Roanoke. In 1969, he was appointed a state judge in the Twenty-Third Judicial Circuit, a position he held until his retirement in 1987. He was an original member of the Judicial Inquiry and Review Commissions, which investigated and disciplined judges for improper conduct and was instrumental in revamping the jury selection program in Roanoke. Throughout his career, Ballou mentored young lawyers. He died on January 6, 2004. He was preceded in death by his wife of forty-eight years, Ruth Sachers Ballou. The couple had four children, and Ballou was known as a true family man. (source: findagrave.com).

Assuming they answered honestly, this was the jury that would decide Joyce's fate, and they would hear much testimony about the accounting and bookkeeping methods at both CMT and Andrew Lewis.

* * *

The Trial

The prosecution's witnesses included two bookkeepers from CMT, plus another office worker, three office employees, and CMT president, Richard Trent. Their combined testimony conflicted at least twice with Smith's contention that Joyce's account was accidentally credited by the school.[55]

One witness, a salesman at CMT, testified that while he was employed as the manager of the watersports' department, he had helped pick out a scuba-diving outfit for the coach and that he had later taught one of Joyce's sons in a scuba-diving class.[56]

Another salesman testified that Joyce had come to him and asked for assistance picking out a scuba-diving outfit for his son.[57]

This testimony stood in sharp contrast to that provided by previous witnesses who testified that Joyce had purchased scuba-diving gear to use as a door prize for the Virginia High School Coaches Association Clinic held in Salem.[58]

Invoices from CMT also included an assortment of camping gear.[59]

When the prosecution rested, the defense made the motion to strike the evidence, which Judge Ballou denied.[60]

The defense then presented its case, which included calling Joyce to the witness stand, where he "emphatically denied" ever intending to defraud the school by charging personal items to the school's account at CMT.[61]

Further, he testified that over the four-year period in question, CMT never sent him record of his personal account there, nor had he ever received a bill from the firm. When asked what he thought of these omissions, Joyce said there were numerous things of a personal nature that stores would give to coaches. He was quoted as saying, "There are fifty different methods of making out invoices at CMT."[62]

Joyce's testimony about sporting goods stores giving personal items to coaches was somewhat corroborated by Deke Summers, who testified on behalf of the defense. However, on cross-examination, he could not recall when or by whom.[63]

In a recent interview with him, he recalled this about his testimony and the trial: "They called me as a witness because [Joyce's] attorney wanted me to testify that all of these sporting goods companies would give the coaches stuff: a hat, a shirt, whatever. CMT was the main sporting goods store in Roanoke. We didn't deal with them. We dealt with the Athletic House in Knoxville. Eddie [Joyce] bought almost everything of any significance from the Athletic House. That's the reason a couple of players went to [the University of] Tennessee. That was the Knoxville connection."[64]

In rebuttal, one of CMT's three partners testified that the company "had a policy of selling things to coaches at wholesale rates, but not of giving them gratuities."[65]

During the trial, the defense spent about an hour in its direct testimony, and then Lampros went back to work with his cross-examination.[66]

In counsels' closing arguments, Smith maintained his position that the bookkeeping methods at both Lewis and CMT were flawed, while Lampros countered with the argument that it was "inconceivable that a person could charge items for four years and never wonder why he wasn't getting billed for the goods."[67]

"When was he going to pay for this? When he retired at the age of 65? I could see where one or two or three or maybe five of these were accidental, but 75? You've got to be kidding!" he said as he waved a stack of invoices.[68]

Following the arguments by the counsel, Judge Ballou provided instructions to the jury.[69]

Soon, it would decide the fate of a beloved coach whose teaching and coaching career were unblemished up to this point.

* * *

The Jury's Decision

Given his high profile in the community, the court's actions were followed closely by the media and often made front-page news. The jury's decision was no exception.

In the August 30, 1975, edition of the *Roanoke World-News*, the headline for this case read, "Evidence convicts Joyce."[70]

The article indicated that the jury had "reviewed the evidence countless times" before convicting Joyce of obtaining money or goods by false pretense (nearly $4,000 in school funds) and had fixed his punishment at thirty days in jail and a fine of $1,000.[71]

The jury deliberated for six and a half hours before coming to a consensus. The jury's foreman, a certified public accountant, told reporters that he and the jury went through a vast amount of evidence—invoices, bills, checks, and ledgers—many times before arriving at a verdict. They quoted the foreman as saying, "It became too convincing after a while," but he also indicated that he agreed with Smith's contention that there was "evidence of sloppy bookkeeping on the part of both CMT and Andrew Lewis High School."[72]

What was Joyce's reaction to the verdict?

This same article reported that Joyce's face tightened but that he showed no emotion. He looked downward for a second and spoke briefly to Smith, who told the court he planned to appeal the decision.[73]

Judge Ballou allowed Joyce to remain on bond (personal recognizance) pending the outcome of the appeal and gave Smith two weeks to file any posttrial motions and Lampros one week to respond to those.[74]

Joyce, who had resigned in November of 1974 as the coach at Andrew Lewis, had become employed as a salesman by the Neese Mining Company.[75]

Before returning to more news surrounding the trial, consider the public's reaction several months before when Joyce had announced that he was resigning from his position as the head football coach at Andrew Lewis.

THE SPARTAN SUCCESSION

In an article in the *Roanoke Times*, dated November 15, 1974, and written by Bob McLelland, sports editor, the headline read: "Eddie Joyce resigns at Lewis."[76]

This was real—and sad—news.

McLelland quoted Joyce as saying, "This is something I have been considering for some time. It was an accumulation of things that led to my decision."[77]

The veteran sportswriter wrote of Joyce's great success at Lewis and added: "Joyce was also a leader in the formation of the Virginia High School Coaches Association and with the organization of the annual all-star football and basketball games and clinics." McLelland also quoted Joyce with saying this: "I have always intended to quit coaching at a time I could leave a solid program. We had an outstanding team this year and we do not have many seniors. I feel whoever takes my place will start with a solid foundation."[78]

What did other prominent citizens say in response to Joyce's decision?

In this same article, McLelland quoted Patrick Henry head football coach Merrill Gainer with this: "Our area and the entire state is losing an outstanding football coach. His record speaks for itself and the people of Salem should be in debt to him for what he has done for Andrew Lewis football… He has been a tremendous leader in area and state athletics."[79]

And this was from Robert "Bob" Lee Barnett: "There isn't enough good I can say for Eddie Joyce. He has done a lot more for Salem than Salem has done for him. He is a tremendous coach. He works hard and goes into the finer points of the game. I don't think he can ever be truly replaced."[8, 80]

---

[8] The late Bob Barnett served as a medic in the army during World War II. Before that, he was a graduate of Andrew Lewis High, where he had been a good athlete, especially as a football player. After his discharge from the service, Barnett returned to his native Salem and began a long coaching and officiating career. Dale Foster described him as "being the best at working out cramps" when the players had them. Barnett coached the ninth-grade team and contributed much to the sandlot football program in Salem. Many Salemites, including this author, recall fondly that Barnett served as an umpire for baseball games.

In an article written by Dan Smith of the *Roanoke Times*, under the headline "Players, coaching foes sorry to see Lewis's Eddie Joyce quit," he quoted players like Eddie Reed, a Lewis defensive back (and the starting safety on Lewis's 1971 team), with saying, "You played football for him. A lot of players play for the student body or for the town or for something. For us, it was always him... I am just glad I had four years under him. I would hate to have to come back with him not here."[81]

Smith reported that a couple of months prior to Joyce's resignation, the coach "began having problems because of the book-keeping for the athletic department. Accusations and rumors were followed by an investigation which [w]as continuing."[82]

Mike Brancati, another defensive back who moved to Salem from Waynesboro, reportedly told Smith this: "[Coach Joyce] had a little talk with us when that was going on. He said he didn't want all the fuss to bother us, that it was his problem and he would take care of it. We had faith in him and we knew he was behind us 100 per cent."[83]

Now back to Summers, who said he spent a lot of time with Coach Joyce. "By the time [Coach Joyce's case] went to trial, I was already at Robert E. Lee [High School of Staunton as the head football coach]. But those last four or five years that I was there [at Andrew Lewis], I was pretty much his right-hand guy. We would travel together, he and I and Eddie Jr., and put on clinics. If he planned to retire, he never told me. When all of this [the news of the misuse of funds] broke, we were still practicing. The newspaper reporters were there [at the practice field], and we had gone into the coaches' office after practice. One of the reporters tried to follow us in there. I was the last coach in, and I just turned around, put my hands up, and said, 'No, you can't come in here.' The reporter wanted to talk and ask questions about what was going on. I didn't push the guy. I didn't do anything. I just put my hands up and said, 'No, you're not coming in here.' Now whether he bumped into my hands or not, I don't recall.[84]

"When it was definite that Eddie wasn't coming back, he told me, 'I have told them that I have people on my staff who are capable of doing this job. What he meant was, I was capable of doing the job. I had been so much in his camp the whole time. During the last few years, he wanted Salem to have its own school system, and I was a big proponent of that, handing out fliers and everything else. Maybe that wasn't a good decision on my part because here I am saying I want a school system other than the one I'm working for. Right off the bat, I'm not the superintendent's favorite guy. Eddie pretty much told me that if he recommends me, 'It'll probably be the kiss of death, and you're not going to get [the job].'"[85]

* * *

Back to that day in court following his conviction, Joyce and his family quickly exited the courtroom and did not speak to reporters. Smith soon filed a motion to set aside the verdict, and the motion to be heard was scheduled for September 30.[86]

The basis for the motion were these five contentions: that the verdict of the jury was contrary to the law and the evidence, that the jury was misdirected by the court, that the court was without jurisdiction or venue to try the case, that Joyce was denied a trial by his peers, and that the indictment failed to charge a crime in that it did not allege ownership of the funds supposedly stolen by the defendant's false pretenses.[87]

On September 30, Judge Ballou considered the motion and denied it. He then proceeded to sentence Joyce in accordance with the punishment fixed by the jury—thirty days in jail and a fine of $1,000.[88]

Smith planned to appeal the case, and Joyce remained on bond pending the outcome of the appeal to the Virginia Supreme Court. Approximately one month later, Joyce submitted his resignation from the Salem City Council.[89]

Most recently a council member, Joyce had previously served as the mayor and had been the biggest vote getter in the last two elections. Who replaced Joyce on the council? A fellow independent by the name of Billy C. Shaw, a district sales manager for Harleysville Insurance Company.[90]

* * *

Two articles appeared in the *Roanoke World-News* that reported that Joyce began—and finished—his jail term *before* the Virginia Supreme Court had ruled on his appeal from the Roanoke County Circuit Court.

In the December 19, 1975, edition, the relevant headline read: "Joyce begins jail term." Its unnamed author reported that Joyce entered the Salem city jail on December 18 to begin serving a thirty-day sentence. His attorney, Arthur E. Smith, expressed surprise that Joyce had entered the jail. A spokesman for the Roanoke County Commonwealth Attorney's office said Joyce will complete his sentence in fifteen days if he works while in jail. If he chose not to work, he would be released in twenty days.[91]

An informed source said that Joyce chose to serve at this time because of his present unemployment and the effect that the unsatisfied jail sentence may have on future attempts to secure a job. Apparently, Joyce was no longer employed with the aforementioned mining company. Two weeks later, this same source reported that Joyce satisfied the jail term and was released on December 31, 1975.[92]

How did he spend those two weeks in confinement? As Deke Summers reported in a recent interview, Joyce worked in the kitchen and fixed breakfast every day for his fellow inmates.[93]

* * *

Reflections

While the jury's foreman, obviously well qualified in money matters as a certified public accountant, assured reporters that the jury had carefully reviewed the evidence before rendering its verdict, recall in previous narrative how Dale Foster considered the whole process: in a word, *scandalous*.

Foster believes that people in the county wanted Joyce toppled.

And consider this analysis of the political climate provided recently by Summers: "There were a couple of things that all came together. First, [Andrew Lewis] had beaten the hell out of everybody locally for so many years, so we were not everyone's favorite team. Secondly, there was the political issue (with wanting to establish our own school system), and third, CMT certainly didn't have any love for Eddie because we bought most of our football equipment from the Athletic House."[94]

Summers then opined, "They would welcome someone other than Eddie as head coach / athletic director at Andrew Lewis. That was a lot of revenue they were missing. When I was called [to testify], Eddie's attorney asked me if CMT had ever given me anything as a coach and I said, 'Yeah, they all do. Numerous times.' Then the prosecuting attorney asked me, 'What did they give you and when?' I said, 'I didn't know. I didn't write it down when they gave us something.'"[95]

Summers's take on the facts surrounding the criminal case is hearsay, and while a court of law often does not consider hearsay evidence, what Summers recalls is pertinent here for an understanding of the circumstances surrounding the case, especially since Coach Joyce is no longer living and cannot provide his version.

"I understood from Eddie that he had three accounts with CMT because, obviously, we had to buy some things there. If we needed a couple of chin straps, you're not going to go to Knoxville to get it."[96]

"He had three accounts at CMT: one for Andrew Lewis High School, a personal account, and an account for the all-star games. According to Eddie, Eddie Jr. had charged some scuba gear, snorkeling gear or something, at CMT, and they had sent the bill to the school. Testimony at the trial was that the bookkeeper at CMT put everything on one bill and sent it to the school. They didn't separate it: this is school, this is personal, and this is for the all-star games."[97]

"According to Eddie, he just gave it to the secretary to pay. It was paid, and so therefore the school paid for Eddie Jr.'s gear. That was the misappropriation of funds."[98]

This author then asked Summers this: "To this day, did he (Coach Joyce) know that it (his son's personal gear) was on the bill?"[99]

Summers replied, "Nobody but Eddie knows that."[100]

This author then asked Summers what he thought happened, and Summers replied, "He (Coach Joyce) had so much going on. I think he just passed the bill on to be paid."[101]

As for his opinion about Joyce's integrity and character, Summers one-lined it with this word: *impeccable*. He added, "Anytime we went anywhere, I never paid for anything. He always took care of his assistant coaches. Everybody thought the fix was in. If you didn't live in Salem, then you were in that camp. Anything they could do to bring Eddie Joyce down and Andrew Lewis down, they were going to do, especially with the idea of the separate school system."[102]

In consideration of all the circumstances and the options afforded to the jury, it is reasonable, on one hand, to contend that the jury—if thoroughly intent upon convicting Joyce—could have convicted him of a misdemeanor rather than the felony, as provided in the instructions given by the judge. That decision would have not, and should have not, been guided by Joyce's position of power and stature in the community but rather by the circumstances surrounding the case. Even the jury's foreman questioned the bookkeeping methods at both places, which provided reasonable doubt as to Joyce's criminal intent. In retrospect, there just wasn't enough doubt to sway the jurors.

Still, given Joyce's otherwise unblemished record in the community, a misdemeanor conviction would have sent enough of a message to a man who didn't have to be told anything twice. He had always been gainfully employed and, as Summers noted, "anyone in Salem would have been willing to help him out (financially)," which would have guaranteed that restitution would have been made in whole.[103]

Further, a misdemeanor conviction would not have resulted in his automatic dismissal from some of the positions he served in the community. Instead, the stigma of a felony conviction would be with him for the remainder of his natural life.

Could CMT have stopped things "in its tracks" before the matter became criminal in nature?

Yes. When Joyce presented checks to the company, its representative could have asked him to which accounts were the checks to be applied. On at least two occasions, Joyce sifted through the checks at CMT before payments were made, and it appeared he sorted them out. However, if he misapplied the checks to the different accounts, that could indicate the possibility of criminal intent, or it could indicate applying those simply in error. Recall that Smith told jurors that Andrew Lewis High School had made Joyce virtually everything—including a bookkeeper—and there is no doubt that bookkeeping was not Joyce's forte.

On the other hand (and as this same foreman noted), the evidence became too convincing. As Lampros pointed out (and which likely resonated with the jurors), the incidents of misuse and illegitimate postings on these accounts spanned a time period of nearly four years, and the occurrences were far too many to ignore or to consider as incidental. His assessment, which the jury considered, greatly reduced the likelihood that Joyce did not know what was going on. In fact, Lampros was insistent that Joyce *did* know what was going on.

Bottom line: it is not possible to know Joyce's motives. Was there criminal intent, or was it simple mismanagement? He is no longer with us to answer that inquiry. Neither is it possible to know the motives of the jurors who tried his case.

But what cannot be disputed is that the jury acted within the limits of the law, and its foreman assured everyone that he and his fellow jurors reviewed the evidence several times before making their decision—indeed, an unpopular one in Salem.

For Foster, Summers, and a host of other former assistants and players, the decision against Joyce proved a bitter pill that has never been easy to swallow.

To help put the matter into proper and lasting perspective, consider what F. LaGard Smith, author of *The Daily Bible*, wrote: "How often do men fall at the height of success, and the greater the height, the greater the fall."[104]

* * *

News of Joyce's case on appeal simply ceased to appear in the Roanoke newspaper. Did his attorney, at Joyce's request, withdraw the appeal? Did the Virginia Supreme Court consider the appeal and deny it? Or did the same court decline to even hear the appeal?

Searching for an official answer, this author contacted the Supreme Court of Virginia and was informed that records dating back to the 1970s could possibly be found in the archives section at the Library of Virginia.

Next, this author telephoned the library, and its representative researched the matter and indicated that a search of the databases of both the Supreme Court and the Court of Appeals, plus the published Supreme Court report (and even for boxes that contain the original jurisdiction cases), all failed to yield any findings of any case related to Joyce. Further—and more mysterious still—the Roanoke County Circuit Court has no actual record of Joyce's conviction, no file material pertaining to the case, and not even an index card with his name on it.

Nevertheless, in the July 9, 1976, edition of the *Roanoke World-News*, a small article appeared under the headline "School officials ask Joyce teaching ban."

Roanoke County school officials prepared a complaint against Joyce and sought the suspension or revocation of his teaching certificate. Reportedly, the state's Department of Education required local school officials to file a complaint against anyone holding a teaching certificate if he or she has been convicted of a crime.[105]

Not until 1979 did more articles report on Joyce's case.

In the January 9, 1979, edition of the *Roanoke Times & World-News*, an article written by John Witt under the headline "Joyce asks Gov. Dalton for pardon" revealed that Joyce had asked the then governor John Dalton for a full pardon.

Witt wrote that Joyce had declined comment on his pardon request, fearing that any public statement might jeopardize his request. Joyce's attorney, Roanoke County delegate Ray Robrecht, told Witt that Joyce hoped to clear his name so he can return to coaching and that several schools had expressed an interest in hiring Joyce.[9, 106]

But before Joyce could coach, protocol required that he renew his teaching certificate, which was previously revoked by the State Board of Education. However, even if Joyce was granted a full pardon, the board was not required to restore his teaching certificate.[107]

In his letter asking Governor Dalton to grant Joyce's full pardon and restore his constitutional rights, Robrecht cited the good influence Joyce had on his students and athletes and stated a belief that Joyce is best qualified for a career in teaching. The letter was accompanied by personal recommendations from at least thirty prominent Salem residents who wholeheartedly supported the pardon.[108]

What were Joyce's chances of a full pardon?

Witt indicated that since Dalton had taken office, forty-one requests for full pardons had been referred to the parole board but only ten had been granted.[109]

Dalton had several options; he could refuse clemency or offer one of the following: an absolute pardon (if he thought Joyce was innocent and a victim of a miscarriage of justice); a simple pardon (which would recognize that Joyce had paid his debt to society but not remove his conviction from his criminal record or alter his legal status); or simple restoration of Joyce's right to vote and hold office.[10, 110]

---

[9] Robrecht packed a resume as solid as he packed a punch. He was interviewed in Oct. 1984 by Mark Bradley, a news writer for the *Salem Times-Register*. Both Bradley and Robrecht had been boxing champions. Robrecht had been an attorney, a U.S. Marine, a county prosecutor, a five-time member of the Virginia House of Delegates and a champion boxer. In 1959 and 1962, he was Virginia's Golden Gloves champion in the 165-pound middleweight division. He retired from the ring in 1966 with a record of 14 wins and only one defeat. Date of publication Oct. 11, 1984.

[10] Currently in Virginia, there are three types of pardons. A simple pardon is a statement of forgiveness, which often serves as a means for a petitioner to advance in employment, education, and self-esteem. A conditional pardon is available only to people who are incarcerated and is usually granted for early releases from prison. An absolute pardon allows the convicted person to petition the court to have the conviction removed from his/her criminal record.

How long would Joyce, his attorney, and Joyce's family and friends have to wait for the governor's decision? Two and a half months.

But it wasn't what Joyce had asked for; instead, Governor Dalton granted Joyce only a simple pardon. The official language, as reported in Senate Document No. 2 (the list of pardons and other forms of clemency from January 6, 1979, to January 9, 1980) reads: "Sentenced August 29, 1975, in the Circuit Court of Roanoke County to thirty days in jail and a fine of $1,000 on a conviction of grand larceny. His fine has been paid. Subject was granted removal of political disabilities on March 30, 1979."[111]

Note that the document indicates that Joyce was convicted of grand larceny, whereas news articles reported that Joyce was convicted of obtaining money or goods by false pretense. If the Roanoke County Circuit Court—or any other entity—had written record of the conviction, absolute clarity would have been provided in this narrative.

Further, Witt reported in the April 3, 1979, edition of the *Roanoke Times & World-News* that a parole board spokesman refused to comment on the context of their report to the governor, who reviewed its report and a host of letters from Joyce's friends and supporters in Salem.

As a matter of protocol, when a case is submitted to the parole board for clemency, the commonwealth attorney who prosecuted the case and the judge who presided in the case have the options to agree to or oppose the petitioner's request. In this case, that meant John Lampros and Judge Ernest Ballou.

Both opposed Joyce's request for a full pardon.[112]

And even if Joyce had been granted a full or absolute pardon, there is credible reason to believe—and this is substantiated in later

---

This type of pardon is rarely granted because it is based on the belief that the petitioner was unjustly convicted and is innocent (source: www.virginia.gov,) Witt's use of the word *full* is synonymous with *absolute*.

narrative—that he would never coach again in the Salem or Roanoke County public schools.[11]

Throughout the years, Summers stayed in contact with his former head coach and lifetime friend.

"I saw him within months of his passing. When we got together, we usually talked about the sports world and his physical condition. We talked little about the past.[113]

"I had bought a home near Hilton Head, South Carolina, and whenever I would come home (to Roanoke), I would go up [Route] 220 and stop in Mayodan and spend time with Eddie. He was doing

---

[11] And yet his coaching days in other places were far from over. After a four-year hiatus from coaching (1974–79), he applied for the head coaching job at Salem High in 1979 but was not hired. That same year, however, he was hired as the head coach at Roanoke Catholic, and his assistants included Bill Winter, Kent Eastrom, George George, Paul Ripley, and Eddie Joyce Jr., the offensive coordinator. Later, Joyce would go on to coach at Natural Bridge High (located in Rockbridge County), beginning in 1984 through 1987, at Calvert High in Calvert, Maryland. He took over a football program that went 0–10 in 1983 and made it respectable. After four seasons there, he had compiled a record of 21–19 (source: Tom Tereshinski, former coach at Calvert for thirty-one years and retired in 2013; he coached with Joyce for one season).

He even coached at least one semiprofessional football team.

In early January of 1981, Joyce reportedly signed a two-year contract to coach the Virginia Hunters, members of the American Football Association (source: RTWN 01.10.81 Bob Teitlebaum).

Interestingly enough, the team's first player acquisition was Bruce Palmer, the former William Byrd High and University of Maryland star defensive lineman (source). Palmer was not only a successful high school and collegiate football player, but he was also an accomplished high school wrestler. While at William Byrd High, he won two individual state championships in the heavyweight division in 1973 and 1974 (source: personal knowledge and the VHSL record book, page 167).

In an article that appeared in the *Roanoke Times & World-News*, dated March 22, 1981, the headline read: "Virginia Hunters: Saturday was a first step." This article reported on the semiprofessional football team known as the Virginia Hunters and the tryouts for the team. Reportedly, 125 hopefuls showed up for tryouts at the Veterans Administration Medical Center field in Salem. Joyce's assistants included Ravis "Red" Stickney, Billy Miles Jr., George Miller, and—you guessed it—Deke Summers. Some of the players attending included former Lewis standouts Eddie Joyce Jr. and Roger Surber.

fine, but he lived on a very meager subsistence, nothing fancy. He had an old black and white TV. Don Russo and I would tell people that we were cousins, but we weren't. We were such good friends. Don and I bought him a flat-screen, color TV so he could watch football and basketball games. The home was nothing fancy. [His sons] Eddie Junior and Dennis were living with him, so he was supporting them.[114]

"While Eddie was in Mayodan, he was in a really bad car crash. He had been out playing poker with the guys and was on his way home, and whether it was a deer or whether he fell asleep, he ran off the road and hit a tree. He was in the hospital for weeks, and I went to see him numerous times. He was in really bad shape. He had some broken bones, and I think he developed an infection. It was a touch-and-go situation for a while at the hospital, but he was eventually released and went back home. We stayed in touch."[115]

Revered and admired by so many of his former players and assistant coaches, Eddie Milton Joyce Sr. died on October 14, 2012, at the age of eighty-three, two weeks shy of his eighty-fourth birthday.[116]

Notwithstanding the actions of the criminal justice system, to those who remember him fondly, neither his fall from grace nor the passage of time can undermine his reputation and legacy.

Chapter 2

A LEGEND'S SUCCESSOR

Part 1: Extra Large Shoes to Fill

While penning the words to this first part of the chapter, I couldn't help but think of the late George Jones, an iconic figure in country music. Coach Joyce liked country music, and the people of Salem aren't exactly averse to it.

Among the many popular songs that Jones sang, one was "Who's Gonna Fill Their Shoes?" Here is the chorus of that song taken from www.metrolyrics.com:

> Who's gonna fill their shoes
> Who's gonna stand that tall
> Who's gonna play the Opry
> And the Wabash Cannonball
> Who's gonna give their heart and soul
> To get to me and you
> Lord I wonder, who's gonna fill their shoes[117]

Without question, Joyce left extremely large shoes fill. Perhaps those shoes could only be tried on but not truly filled.

Who was the first to try them on for size?

Not Deke, and somewhat to his chagrin.

"When I went for the interview with the superintendent, the first thing he said was 'I understand you assaulted a member of the news media.' I pretty much knew right then I was not going to get the job. There wasn't much to the interview after that. That's when I applied for and got the job at Robert E. Lee [High School] in Staunton."[118]

The honor of coaching the Wolverines went to another long-time Lewis assistant, Mike Stevens.

And Summers did not begrudge him.

"Mike had been on the staff for a long time," recalled Summers. "He mainly coached the defensive backs. He had played defensive back at the University of Virginia. He knew what he was doing. I'm not sure that anyone else on the staff applied."[119]

Before we meet Mr. Stevens, Summers certainly made the most of his opportunities.

He debuted as the head coach of R. E. Lee in 1975. In 1977, he and Tom Peters of Fort Defiance were named Coaches of the Year by the *Daily News Leader*. Lee was competing at double A, went 8–2 during the regular season, and won the Region II title before losing to Southampton, the defending state champion. Fort Defiance was classified as single A.[120]

After another year at Lee, Summers decided to quit teaching and coaching. He started two businesses in Roanoke and did not attend a high school or college football game for the next fifteen years.[121]

But that couldn't last forever.

"I was working eighty hours a week," he recalled. "There was an article in the Roanoke paper about a camp that was asking for volunteers. This was in 2000, and Ronde and Tiki Barber (former Cave Spring High, University of Virginia, and NFL players) had come back to the area and planned to have this camp for kids, which they did for years.[122]

"They were looking for volunteers, and I called up and offered my services. I told them I hadn't coached for fifteen years but I'd be glad to come help with registration or whatever they needed me to do. On the first day, they didn't have enough coaches, so they asked me if I would help the coaches and run the kids through the drills. I agreed, and on the second day, Ben Foutz, who was the head coach at Cave Spring, said, 'You know as much as any of my assistant coaches. Would you be interested in joining our staff at Cave Spring?' I accepted, and (former Andrew Lewis assistant coach) Bill Winter helped me.[123]

"I was there for a couple of years until Hidden Valley High School opened, and I moved there as an assistant. I was there for two years as an assistant along with Burt Torrence, who got the head coaching job at Northside, so I went to Northside as his offensive coordinator for two years.[124]

"For personal reasons, I later decided I wasn't going to coach anymore, but I realized I had nineteen years of coaching and thought it would be neat to have twenty.[125]

"We had scrimmaged Brookville, and I knew Jeff Woody, the head coach. He had played at Hampden-Sydney, and I called him up and asked if he needed any help for the coming year. He said he would love to have me for now and to just 'scout the Roanoke teams.' I would prepare these ten and twelve-page scouting reports that were so detailed that he said, 'We need you to scout as many teams as you can, and we need you to come to practice during the week so you can go over the scouting reports with the team as we prepare for the games.'[126]

"By the end of that year, they said they wanted me on the staff the next year. For five years, I would leave work in Roanoke and commute back and forth to Lynchburg every day. During that era is when we won twenty-eight straight games and back-to-back state championships.[127]

"Jeff decided to take the job at Monticello High mainly because his wife was a nurse at UVA Hospital, was from Charlottesville, and had wanted to move back there. I went with him, and we were there for two years. Stuff went down at Monticello when the AD (activities director) had to resign, and Jeff decided to take the head coaching job at E. C. Glass High School.[128]

"I wasn't about to move again, so that's when I called it quits. My last year of coaching was in 2014."[129]

Summers still has a business in Roanoke, but for the past three years, he has resided in Hilton Head, South Carolina.[130]

* * *

The departure of Eddie Joyce and the hiring of Mike Stevens were a big woo in the Roanoke Valley.

To provide further flavor of the times, consider some of the other events that happened in 1975: the hit film *Jaws* had its theatrical release in June; newspaper heiress Patty Hearst became "Most Wanted" and was arrested for armed robbery after having been previously kidnapped in Berkeley, California; the Suez Canal reopened for the first time since the Six-Day War (1967); the unemployment rate in the US reached 9.2 percent, and President Gerald Ford recognized recession and also signed a $2.3 billion loan to enable New York City to avoid bankruptcy; in boxing, Muhammad Ali defeated Joe Frazier in their trilogy, often referred to as "The Thrilla in Manilla"; the top television programs included *The Six Million Dollar Man*, *Kojak*, *The Jeffersons*, *All in the Family*, *Maude*, *Good Times*, *M*A*S*H*, and *The Carol Burnett Show*.[131]

Some people born this year who would later become famous include Jimmie Johnson, college and NFL coach and commentator, golfer Tiger Woods, and actress Angelina Jolie.[132]

What were the top five songs of 1975?

- At number 1 was "Love Will Keep Us Together" by the Captain and Tennille.
- At number 2 was "Rhinestone Cowboy" by Glenn Campbell.
- At number 3 was "Philadelphia Freedom" by Elton John.
- At number 4 was "Before the Next Teardrop Falls" by Freddy Fender
- At number 5 was "My Eyes Adored You" by Frankie Valli.[133]

And clothing? This author was seventeen years old in 1975 and remembers all too well the bell-bottom jeans, wide-lapel shirts, leisure suits, white belts, platform shoes. Then there was the age of disco music, which some loved and others disdained.

For some additional flavor of the times, the reader is encouraged to watch *That 70's Show*, a comedy set in Wisconsin, which parodies many of the events, fads, and styles of the time.

Now let's get back to the business at hand and meet a legend's first—and technically only—successor.

***

Arguably, any one of the former assistants on Joyce's staff was qualified to assume the head coaching job. But the most obvious choice would have been Dale Foster, who had served under Joyce beginning in 1962 and was instrumental in several ways, including the implementation of the "slanting monster defense," which Lewis began using during the 1963 season. Folks in position of influence knew of Foster's credentials, and so it's no surprise that he was approached about this job.

Here's how he remembers it: "The first thing [Arnold Burton, the superintendent of Roanoke County Schools] said was, 'We want to offer you the job as the head football coach at Andrew Lewis High School.' I said, 'Mr. Burton, I haven't coached in six years and so much has changed. I don't think I can do a good job. I don't think I should take it.' Then he said, 'Well, then I want you to be an assistant principal, the athletic director, and an assistant football coach.'"[134]

Foster declined the offer to coach the football team, and ultimately, the honor went to Mike Stevens, who had joined the staff in 1963, the year the team implemented the monster defense.

Going into 1975, Stevens had been at Andrew Lewis for twelve years. He had done his job well, and he had paid attention to how Joyce coached a football team.

In a personal interview with Stevens on April 6, 2018, he offered much insight.

"Eddie [Joyce] always had his finger on the pulse of everything on the football field," said Stevens who always got along with his chief and with whom the relations were business rather than social.

"We didn't socialize. He ran with another group, and I had kids at home and tried to be with them when I could. It was mostly business, and I don't remember having any problems working with him. I recognized that he was the brains of the operation, and I tried to do my best at whatever was asked of me."[135]

In fact, Stevens was first asked to coach positions he had never played before.

"When I joined the staff in 1963, I coached the ends and the monster on defense and the offensive linemen. I had no experience with the offensive linemen, but I was learning all along. It's amazing that you can think you know the game until you have to put the whole game together."[136]

No, Stevens was never a lineman either in high school or in college. He played in the backfield on both sides of the football.[137]

Known as "Mike" to his family and friends, Michael Musgrove Stevens was born in Roanoke, Virginia on August 13, 1941. He attended schools in Roanoke City, including William Fleming High, where he graduated in 1959. He was a senior member of the Fleming team that beat Jefferson for the first time ever in 1958 and by the score of 27–20. By 1961, Fleming had managed just one win and two ties (in 1945 and 1956) in the nineteen games played against Jefferson.[138]

In that close victory over the Magicians, running back Stevens rushed for two touchdowns. Indeed, it was a proud moment for Stevens and his Colonel teammates.[139]

Stevens also wrestled at Fleming and, after graduation, attended the University of Virginia, where he continued his football career. He was a member of the freshman team, and then the following year, as a sophomore, he and his teammates had the dubious distinction of being members of a winless Cavalier team.[140]

"When I was there, you had to play both ways," said Stevens. "I played in the backfield on both the offense and defense."[141]

He graduated in 1963 with a bachelor of arts degree in biology, and he later earned a master's degree in education at the University of Virginia in 1968. Soon after receiving his undergraduate degree, he became a teacher and coach at Andrew Lewis.[142]

"It was funny," recalled Stevens. "I had a bachelor of arts degree, but it wasn't in education. I interviewed for jobs in pharmaceutical sales and with the federal government, but that meant moving out of Virginia, and my wife didn't want to do that. I decided to apply to schools in both Roanoke County and City. Roanoke County offered me a contract."[143]

Before moving into his coaching and teaching career, it is of importance to note that Stevens and his wife, Sharon Littreal Stevens, married in 1960 and, as of the preparation of this manuscript, have been married for fifty-eight years. The couple began dating when they were freshmen at William Fleming, and she, too, pursued a career in teaching. They retired at the same time in 1996.[144]

Back to Stevens's career, he began teaching biology and a ninth-grade chemistry class at Lewis in 1963. That year, he joined the football team's coaching staff and was assigned as mentioned.[145]

"Even though I was coaching the offensive line, Coach Joyce would tell you what he wanted you to do, which basically meant that you were following his directions. That's pretty much the way he operated. You learned what was expected following his direction. What we all knew about Eddie [Joyce] was that he was in charge. He knew what he wanted done, and we did it. That's why he was so successful.[146]

"At Lewis, we also had some great kids. They were manageable, coachable, and they were dedicated. The coaching interaction was always positive. In the classroom, you could get situations where it was not necessarily positive all the time. But on the field, we were winning, and you got the notoriety that came with it. The interaction with the players was the best part of it all."[147]

And Salem was a great place to coach, teach, and raise a family.[12]

---

[12] Mike and Sharon Stevens have two sons. Brian Stevens was born on July 23, 1961, and Todd Stevens was born on June 4, 1964. Both Brian and Todd played football at Cave Spring High and graduated from there. Brian earned a bachelor's degree in biology at the University of Virginia and recently retired from Air Traffic Control and lives outside Miami, Florida, with his wife and their two daughters. Todd graduated from Virginia Tech with a degree in civil engi-

"I liked the community," said Stevens. "My kids [sons, Brian and Todd] were growing up there when I was coaching at Lewis. Salem is such a great area. We never felt unsafe with our kids going to school."[148]

Stevens and others saw the proverbial writing on the wall that things were going to change drastically, a reference to Joyce's resignation that led to the coaching vacancy.

Looking back, Stevens said, "There were rumors that drifted through that we picked up on. When I saw that things were definitely going to change, I had to decide which direction I wanted to go. I was encouraged to apply for the job. I saw it as a good opportunity. I felt like I knew enough with my experience under Coach Joyce, and that probably had something to do with the encouragement people gave me."[149]

Stevens and Joyce never talked about the prospect of Stevens becoming the new head coach, but Stevens did recall running into Joyce after the first game of the 1975 season when Joyce congratulated him.[150]

---

neering and is currently employed as a construction engineer for VDOT in the Staunton, Virginia, district. He, too, is married and has two daughters.

THE SPARTAN SUCCESSION

Part 2: 1975

Head coach Mike Stevens surveys the Wolverines along with assistant coach Bill Winter on his left.

David Weeks (11) and Perry Nichols (15)

The versatile Bill Britts in action

What was Stevens's approach as the new head football coach at Andrew Lewis? One could describe it using the popular expression "If it ain't broke, don't fix it." Stevens said as much in the season preview written by the veteran Bob McLelland.[151]

He planned to use what he had learned under Coach Joyce for eleven seasons and to continue with the same offensive and defensive sets. It didn't hurt that Stevens would have twenty-three lettermen and a promising group of newcomers to catapult his head-coaching debut.[152]

Stevens expected the offense to continue as a passing team with the return of quarterbacks Perry Nichols and David Weeks. Their receiving targets would include Robbie Irvin, Larry Smith, and Mickey Reed.[153]

The running game would feature Charles Hopkins, Vernon Neese, Greg French, and Tommy Harrison. Up front their leading blockers would likely be Dale Tyree (guard) and Bobby Williams (center).[154]

Stevens had on defense hard-hitting safety Bill Britts and end Larry Marrazzo.[155]

Team-wise, defending Blue Ridge District champion Andrew Lewis along with William Byrd and Alleghany were expected to battle for this year's title.[156]

Lewis would open the regular season at home to Pulaski County.[157]

Game 1 (September 5):
Andrew Lewis 28, Pulaski County 0

Stevens not only made his head-coaching debut, but he made it at home against rival Pulaski County, and his quarterback made sure Stevens left Municipal Field feeling very good in his new role.[158]

Perry Nichols completed 17 of 20 passes for 278 yards and 3 touchdowns. It could be said that Nichols could have been perfect under different circumstances.[159]

Of his three incompletions, one pass was dropped, one was thrown away to avoid trouble, and the other was a "balloon ball" to end the first half. For his outstanding performance, Nichols was named by the *Roanoke World-News* as the first offensive player of the week for 1975.[160]

Who was the first defensive player of the week?

That honor was bestowed to linebacker Kurt Kreider of William Fleming, who helped lead the Colonels to an upset win over GW-Danville, 21–14. Kreider's team leading 7 solo and 5 assisted tackles included racing down a receiver and dropping him to the ground before he could score.[161]

Next, the Wolverines traveled to Rocky Mount to continue the series against the Eagles of Franklin County High, a rivalry that began in 1970.

Game 2 (September 12): Franklin County 22, Andrew Lewis 13

Not only did the Eagles win, but they broke a fifteen-game losing streak in the process. They also handed Coach Stevens his first career loss and edged closer toward tying the series with Lewis. After this win, the series record was 2–3–1.[162]

Tied 13–13 in the fourth quarter, Franklin County's Larry Brooks went over from the one to give the Eagles the lead they would not relinquish. The scoring drive included a 43-yard run by Clyde Smith. The Eagles went for 2 and converted when quarterback Gary Gilmore ran it over on a fake try at kicking the extra point.[163]

Perry Nichols completed 15 of 27 passes for 208 yards and 2 touchdowns to Larry Smith.[164]

Franklin County's 2 other touchdowns came on a 9-yard run by Smith and a fumble recovery by Steve Echols in the Lewis end zone.[165]

How did Stevens see it?

"We told the kids the history of this series. I don't know whether Franklin gets fired up, but they always play well against us. We turned the ball over at crucial times, but they played a good game. We had our opportunities."[166]

Next, the Wolverines made the short trip to Vinton to play the Terriers of William Byrd.

Game 3 (September 19): Andrew Lewis 14, William Byrd 0

With the offense sputtering, Lewis turned to its special teams for a lift.

And Larry Smith delivered.

Scoreless at the intermission, William Byrd kicked off to start the third quarter. Smith fielded the ball and ran 97 yards for 1 of the 2 Lewis touchdowns, as the visiting Wolverines turned back a determined bunch of Terriers.[167]

Byrd battled back and looked on its way to a game-tying touchdown before Lewis's David Weeks intercepted quarterback Mike Robertson to stop the Terrier bite. Though Byrd soon got the ball back after its own interception, a field goal attempt was blocked.[168]

Lewis then put together its only sustained drive of the night when quarterback Perry Nichols threw a 17-yard touchdown pass to Charles Hopkins. Harry Gaston connected on 2 point-after-touchdown kicks.[169]

It was an off night for Nichols, who entered the game having completed 32 of 47 passes in the 2 previous games. In Vinton, he completed just 4 of 15 and was intercepted 3 times.[170]

Lewis also committed 3 other turnovers. But Byrd had its share of miscues. The Terriers threw 4 interceptions. Weeks had 1, and Bill Britts collected 3.[171]

What did the head coaches say after the game?

Byrd's Don Oakes, an alumnus of Andrew Lewis, said, "We thought we could beat them. We worked hard all week on defense, but that one play [the kickoff return] made all the difference."[172]

Stevens felt some relief. "We needed this one," he said. "We have had some mental lapses and a little depression after what happened last week."[173]

Next, the Wolverines traveled to Roanoke's Victory Stadium to play the Colonels of William Fleming.

Game 4 (September 26): Andrew Lewis 22, William Fleming 21

The Wolverines engineered a come-from-behind victory, and Colonel head coach Don Lee once again showed how gracious he could be in defeat.[174]

Consider some of his comments told to Bob McLelland in the sports editor's write-up that appeared in the September 27 edition of the *Roanoke World-News*: "It's like I told the kids, Lewis has a winning tradition and when you have that you find ways to win. This isn't the first time they did something like that, and it sure as heck won't be the last. It's a tribute to Lewis and the whole city of Salem."[175]

Now that's classy.

The mathematical difference came down to two kicks: a successful one by Lewis and a missed one by Fleming.[176]

The Colonels squandered their halftime and third-quarter leads, and late in the game, they missed what would have been a game-winning field goal from 35 yards out. Larry Smith scored 2 touchdowns for the Wolverines—a 26-yard pass from Greg French and an 89-yard pass from aerial specialist Perry Nichols. French scored on a 1-yard run. Harry Gaston kicked 2 extra points, and Bill Britts converted one 2-point conversion.[177]

McLelland also interviewed Stevens, but he had to wait first.

He wrote: "It took nearly ten minutes for the excited Lewis dressing room to calm down enough for any conversation. But the Wolverines, to a man, said they never doubted the comeback."[178]

With the win, Lewis improved to 3–1 on the season, while Fleming fell to 1–2–1.

Up next, the Wolverines hosted the district-leading Cougars of Covington.

Game 5 (October 3): Andrew Lewis 35, Covington 7

This was supposed to be a tough district contest, but some big plays by the home team helped propel the Wolverines to a huge trouncing of the Cougars.[179]

Perry Nichols returned to form and led the offensive attack. The Lewis quarterback completed 9 of 17 passes for 220 yards and 2 touchdowns—both to Robbie Irvin, who hauled them in for 54- and 36-yard scores.[180]

Greg French led the rushing attack. He finished with 16 carries for 90 yards and 2 TDs. Larry Smith returned a punt for 65 yards for the team's other touchdown. Harry Gaston kicked 3 PATs, and French caught a pass from Bill Britts for a 2-point conversion. Covington avoided the doughnut loss in the fourth quarter when Ronnie Shue caught a 15-yard touchdown pass from Curtis Jordan. Teammate Dean Martin (not the former singer, actor, comedian, and film producer) kicked the extra point.[181]

Now, midway through the regular season, the Wolverines—under first-year head coach Mike Stevens—were an impressive 4–1.

French's efforts did not go unnoticed by local sportswriters. When the Football Stars of the Week were announced, he was named the scholastic offensive player of the week.[182]

What did his head coach say about him?

"Greg doesn't have blinding speed, but he is a tough and durable runner. He gets the tough yardage."[183]

The scholastic defensive player of the week honor went to a player named Dabo Noftsinger (yes, that's right), a 5'8", 180-pound junior lineman for North Cross, a private school in southwest Roanoke, whose nickname was Raiders.[184]

In the team's win over Warren Academy, Noftsinger was clearly the chief raider and pillager. He virtually did it all on defense; he made 10 solo tackles, was in on numerous assists, recovered 3 fumbles, and blocked an extra point.[185]

With a German-sounding name, might we say, "Sehr gut, Herr Noftsinger"?

Up next, the Wolverines make the short trek to Daleville to play the Cavaliers of Lord Botetourt High. (And for the record—for those readers not from the Roanoke Valley and its surrounding areas—the name of the school is pronounced Lord Bot-a-tot.)

Let's consider what was said about this matchup before the game was played.

Sportswriter Dan Smith noted that history favored the Wolverines, who had been members of the Blue Ridge District for two seasons now and had yet to lose a game to a district opponent. Meanwhile, the Cavaliers had not defeated a district foe in three years.[186]

Botetourt head Coach Otis Timberlake remained hopeful that the Lewis team might overlook his, especially since the Wolverines blasted the Cavaliers the year before by the score of 59–0.[187]

And Stevens wasn't about to let his players overlook Botetourt or anybody else. "We go under the impression that anybody can beat anybody. Because of our schedule and the points we need for the playoffs, every game is a district game for us and we can't afford to lose any of them."[188]

Game 6 (October 10): Wolverines 21, Cavaliers 0

The headline for this game story might have caused some readers to think of a popular song released a year and a half before this game was played. The song "Same Old Song and Dance" was released on March 19, 1974, by Aerosmith, a popular American hard rock band.

Under the headline "It's the same old story," sportswriter Jack Bogaczyk of the *Roanoke World-News* wrote of Botetourt's continuing woes in contrast to Lewis's continuing success.[189]

The two teams played on a soaked field and through a driving rain that slowed down some of the action, including the passing game of Lewis quarterback Perry Nichols. But Nichols scored on a 1-yard sneak after teammate Dale Tyree recovered a Cavalier fumble and the Wolverines led at halftime, 7–0. In the second half, running back Charles Hopkins went to work. During a 69-yard scoring-drive, Hopkins carried the ball 9 times and capped the drive with a 8-yard touchdown run. With less than 9 minutes to play, teammate Larry Smith scurried 55 yards with a punt return for TD.[190]

The Lewis defense held the Botetourt offense to just 3 first downs "and Wolverine punter Mark Williams kept the Cavaliers backed up in their own territory with four boots for a 47-yard average," wrote Bogaczyk.[191]

Now, just past the midway mark in his first season, the Stevens-led Wolverines were 5–1 with a big match-up ahead. Lewis was scheduled to play Roanoke's Patrick Henry, whose Patriots won the Group AAA state football championship in 1973. Often referred to simply as PH, the Patriots also had a 3-game winning streak in place against the Wolverines.

This match-up was big for another, and more important, reason. At that time, points were used to determine playoff teams and were governed by the rules set forth by the Virginia High School League (VHSL). Andrew Lewis and its fellow members of the Blue Ridge District were members of Region III, which also included the Seminole and Piedmont Districts.

Midway through the regular season, Appomattox and Rustburg were both undefeated in the Seminole and Martinsville was unbeaten in the Piedmont. It would take more than just winning the district to qualify for the playoffs; it would take points. And a surefire way of picking up a slew of points was for a team to beat a larger one.[192]

In this case, double-A Lewis would be playing against triple-A Patrick Henry.

And the Patriots were no fluke.

As one former member of the heralded 1971 Lewis team recently remarked when he reflected on the 1970s, "PH got pretty damn good."[193]

Before moving into those results, Dan Smith authored an interesting story about Lewis's passing tendencies with these features: The Lewis offense had switched from a pass oriented one to the ground game. Opposing defenses and, even the weather, were both contributing factors.[194]

Coach Stevens was quoted as saying, "People are double covering us on both sides and that weakens them for the runs. You can't be everywhere at once, so we take what we are given. Early in the year [defenses] were giving us the short pass and that is what we took. We try not to force anything because when you do the defense sits back and waits on it."[195]

Smith noted the recent rushing success behind these numbers over the past four games: 123 carries, 494 yards, for an average of 4 yards per carry.[196]

The leading ground-gainers included Charles Hopkins and Greg French. And quarterback Perry Nichols knew that this newly established running game would open up future passing opportunities. His targets included Larry Smith (who, at that time, was atop the list among district scorers and a special-teams threat), plus Robbie Irvin and Mickey Reed, a tight end and younger brother of former standout safety Eddie Reed.[197]

Game 7 (October 18): Patrick Henry 15, Andrew Lewis 6

Originally scheduled for Friday, October 17, the game was postponed until the next day due to heavy rain. On Saturday, the Patriots defeated the Wolverines in Salem's Municipal Field.[198]

William Fleming High was still vying to win the Western District and was scheduled to meet winless Pulaski County at Victory Stadium.[199]

The game was tied 6–6 in the third quarter until the Patriots drove 81 yards from their own 18 to the Wolverines' 1 and looked certain to punch it in for the go-ahead points.[13, 200]

But on second and goal, Patrick Henry's George Harris was hit by Bill Britts, who forced a fumble, and teammate Joey Francisco recovered it. The Wolverines took over but soon faced a third and seven from their own 4.[201]

Perry Nichols's pass was intercepted by a diving Lynn Milton, whose momentum carried him into the end zone to give the Patriots the lead they would not relinquish. PH added a 19-yard field goal in the fourth quarter.[202]

Earlier in the game, the Patriots scored during their opening drive behind the running of Harris and Lewis Neal. Harris scored the game's first points on a 12-yard run. Lewis tied the game in the second quarter on a 35-yard pass from Nichols to Larry Smith, but Harry Gaston's kick for the point after was wide. In the second half, two Lewis drives to inside the PH 30 were stalled on interceptions. Nichols was picked off five times in the game.[203]

Up next, the Wolverines battle some fellow Salemites from Glenvar whose band paraded around in Scottish attire befitting of the school's nickname, the Highlanders. Though Glenvar opened in 1966, this game represented just the second of three games that would be played between the two teams before a huge change in the school system occurred.

---

[13] This article and all previous articles dating back to 1974, as well as any subsequent ones, were written by the same person, Brian Hoffman. Hoffman, a native of Telford, Pennsylvania, near Philadelphia, moved to Salem in 1970 when he began attending Roanoke College. After graduation in 1974, he began working at the *Salem Times-Register* the following fall. At first, he worked in both news and sports but later became the only person in the sports department, which remains true to this time, forty-four years later. Hoffman recalled that he seriously considered Roanoke College because of its atmosphere and location. He also liked the idea of nicer weather, and it didn't hurt that the school had a very good basketball team. Hoffman has proven himself a reliable and hardworking journalist in Salem. He also displayed a dry sense of humor when this author asked him, "How do you do it all by yourself?" He immediately replied, "I have a car."

Game 8 (October 24): Andrew Lewis 26, Glenvar 13

The Wolverines doubled-up the Highlanders in the scoring, but the game may best be remembered for a power outage that resulted in lights out on the Lewis side of the field. An entire bank of lights on the Lewis side of the field stopped shining for fully ten minutes. After a brief discussion at midfield, the game went on anyway, and Lewis won the Salem City Championship.[204]

Little Glenvar freshman running back Duane Farris said the lights going on the blink cost the Highlanders the victory. "We had just scored [to make it 20–13 in Lewis's favor], and we were fired up. We had the momentum, but then we had to wait while the coaches and officials talked about the lights. That killed us. We lost the spark."[205]

Indeed, Lewis went on to score, with the lights going on again and off again periodically, and they locked up the victory (with its last) touchdown.[206]

Charles Hopkins scored two touchdowns, and Perry Nichols threw 2 touchdown passes—a 25-yard strike to Greg French and a 4-yard toss to Robbie Irvin—and Harry Gaston kicked 2 extra points to lead the victors.[207]

For Glenvar, Junior Brailey scored on a 3-yard run, and Scott Conner returned an interception 39 yards for the team's other score. Farris had a team best 99 rushing yards after 20 carries.[208]

And that's the way it was—Friday, October 24, 1975, the night the lights went out on Glenvar.[14]

Lewis was now 6–2 on the season with two games remaining against Clifton Forge and then Alleghany.

---

[14] Inspired both by the voice and delivery of former CBS evening news anchor Walter Cronkite in his signature sign-off, as well as the song "That's the Night That the Lights Went Out in Georgia," sung first by Vicki Lawrence and more recently by Reba McIntyre.

Game 9 (October 31): Wolverines Tricked the Mountaineers to the Tune of 41 to 16

Lewis clinched the Blue Ridge District title behind the efforts of Perry Nichols, who threw 3 touchdown passes and ran for another score. His scoring tosses went to Larry Smith, Charles Hopkins, and Robbie Irvin. Greg French also threw a touchdown pass to Smith.[209]

The Mountaineers unveiled a double-wing split-end formation for the first time this season, and it caused some confusion to the Wolverine defenders. Quarterback Lawrence Berry completed 16 of 27 passes, including 2 touchdowns to Clarence Reynolds.[210]

Lewis scored 27 of its points in the first half. Bill Britts had some reps at quarterback late in the game, and Harry Gaston successfully converted all 5 of his point after touchdown kicks.[211]

True to the traditions of October 31, or Halloween night, things had gotten a little scary at some other games, notably in the William-Byrd-versus-Glenvar matchup and the North-Cross-versus-Fishburne-Military-Academy clash.[212]

Let's begin with the former, which was played at Byrd and where Terriers' head coach Don Oakes pulled his Terriers off the field in the second quarter due to his dissatisfaction with the officiating. His decision to pull his team off the field was driven by his concern for the safety of both the players and the fans.[213]

The move resulted in a Byrd 2–0 forfeit loss, and the matter would be reviewed by the VHSL. As for the latter, the Raiders defeated the Caissons 7–0, but the game was marred by a bench-clearing brawl that erupted at the end.[214]

Like his colleagues, Dan Smith's creative style provided a vivid picture for the readers. He began with a dose of irony. "That casual, genteel atmosphere normally associated with North Cross School was rudely dashed yesterday afternoon, turning what should have been a football celebration into a bowery brawl. Immediately following the final whistle, both benches emptied, and a slugging, kicking melee ensued."[215]

Smith had seen it coming.

THE SPARTAN SUCCESSION

There had been pushing and shoving virtually from the time North Cross scored on the fifth play of the game. There were a number of penalties assessed for personal fouls, the teams had been warned about a shoving match, and North Cross's John Parrett was tossed out of the game shortly before the end, just after Fishburne's David D'Addurno was ejected.[216]

Some of the North Cross players told Smith that throughout the game, their opponents had reached into their face masks and had thrown punches in pileups. They believed that Parrett had been thrown out simply for defending himself, and his tussle with D'Addurno resulted from D'Addurno's reported targeting of North Cross center Churchill Robinson throughout the game.[217]

There was the chance that these two teams might meet again this season and some of the North Cross players weren't happy about it, including running back Randy Revercomb, who did not mince words: "I don't want to play them again. This is by far the worst thing I have seen in football. They could wrestle, but they don't have any business playing football."[218]

Revercomb and backfield teammate David Willis both rushed for over 100 yards in the game, and Willis scored the game's only touchdown.[219]

On the defensive side of the ball, Dabo Noftsinger led the defense that stopped the Caissons in their tracks. And he weighed in on what he thought about the fracas: "I want to play football, not fight."[220]

When the Football Stars of the Week were featured, the scholastic defensive honor went to Lewis safety Bill Britts. Described as the team's most consistent defensive player this season, Britts made numerous tackles and assists and had one interception in the big win over Clifton Forge.[221]

The scholastic offensive player of the week was Jimmy Butcher, a running back at Cave Spring. He racked up 232 rushing yards and scored 3 touchdowns in the team's shutout win over Pulaski County.[222]

In the next day's edition, Smith reported that the recent controversies had "revive[d] football interest." He also reported on some upcoming games and playoff possibilities, plus an update on Byrd head coach Don Oakes.[223]

Oakes had been suspended for the team's final game against Blacksburg while a final decision about his case was pending with the sportsmanship committee with the VHSL. In his absence, athletic director and assistant football coach Wallace Thompson would guide the Terriers.[224]

Consider Thompson's humble analysis of his duties and his overall assessment of the team: "It's not my team. It is still Coach Oakes's team. I'm a little too old to get excited about [being head coach for a week]. If we win this week, it could be a tribute to him as an organizer and a head coach. I don't know what to expect from the kids… [They] knew about the change before it hit the papers, but I can't say how all the adverse publicity will affect them." And he was taking over for a man who was, or at least had been, well known in Salem.[225]

As reported in *The Team the Titans Remember*, Oakes played offensive tackle for Andrew Lewis High under head coach Hal Johnston Sr. and was a member of the graduating class of 1956. He then went on to play at Virginia Tech, where he graduated in 1960 and became one of the few local players to ever play in the National Football League.

He played for a few seasons for both the Philadelphia Eagles and the Boston Patriots (of the old American Football League) before retiring from professional football. In 1971, he became an assistant football coach at Lord Botetourt.

Now, back to the Wolverines and their quest for a playoff berth.

Game 10 (November 7): Andrew Lewis 27, Alleghany 15

The Wolverines scored on the first play from scrimmage on a halfback pass from Greg French to Larry Smith of 65 yards. Later, Harry Gaston kicked a 30-yard field goal, Perry Nichols threw 2 touchdown passes to Smith, and French bulled over from 6 yards for

THE SPARTAN SUCCESSION

the last TD. The Lewis offense had balance with 118 yards on the ground and 211 in the air.[226]

Alleghany Coach Bill Jonas was impressed with the Lewis effort and team and made no bones about the playoff picture. "[Lewis] deserves to go to the playoffs… But the Blue Ridge [District] has gotten the shaft in the regionals the last couple of years. Our schedule is as tough as anybody's and we are penalized for it."[227]

And Nichols said this: "We want Martinsville. They have been beating everybody 50–0, but they have been playing a bunch of weak teams. Our schedule is a lot tougher than theirs, and I am sure they haven't played anybody as good as us."[228]

With the playoff picture as clear as mud, the Football Stars of the Week were much easier to select. The scholastic honors went to Lewis's Larry Smith for offense and to Byrd's Chuck Eanes for defense.[229]

Smith hauled in 6 passes for a total of 162 yards and 3 touchdowns of 13, 29, and 65 yards to give him 15 touchdowns on the season. His coach said he had never seen a better wide receiver in high school.[230]

Eanes was credited with 6 solo tackles and 10 assists in the team's win over Blacksburg, which was coached by Wallace Thompson in the absence of Don Oakes.[231]

A week later, the official word on Oakes and William Byrd was announced. The VHSL's final ruling was the issuance of a warning to William Byrd High and these comments: "Inexcusable unsportsmanlike action has occurred, and such action must not be repeated."[232]

Reportedly, Oakes and school principal Robert Patterson testified in Charlottesville before the VHSL's sportsmanship committee, which ruled that game films "did not justify that the physical safety of the Byrd team was endangered by the team's continuing the contest."[233]

Ironically, Oakes had received the Blue Ridge District sportsmanship trophy his first year as the Byrd coach 4 years previously.[234]

* * *

Lewis finished its first season under new head Coach Mike Stevens with an impressive 8–2 overall record and a perfect 6–0 mark in the Blue Ridge District, which it won for the second time in as many seasons.

The Wolverines outscored their opposition 235 to 109. William Byrd finished second at 7–3, 4–2. Glenvar finished even in the district at 3–3 and 4–6 overall.[235]

Despite the successful season, the points system in place at the time did not qualify Lewis for the post season. The Wolverines were denied a playoff spot due to losses to 3-A teams Franklin County and Patrick Henry.[236]

In a recent interview with Stevens, he looked back over that '75 season and said, "We were loaded. It was a senior-laden team that was very talented. It was already experienced. All we [us coaches] had to do was kind of get them to the game. They knew all the stuff and didn't have to relearn anything.[15] We maintained the same type of game that we had when Eddie [Joyce] was there. We had a good quarterback in Perry Nichols, and we remained a passing team. We had two very good receivers: Robbie Irvin and Larry Smith. They were exceptional receivers, and Perry could get the ball to them."

And remember, Nichols would have loved a crack at Martinsville. He and his teammates didn't get it, and we'll never know how that matchup might have played out. But what we do know is that Martinsville won the Group 2A state championship that season when it defeated Southampton in the state finals at 40–18.[237]

Before moving on to the '76 season, let's meet the players selected to the All-Metro Roanoke football teams as selected by the coaches and sportswriters of the *Roanoke World-News* and *Roanoke Times*.

Larry Smith was named the offensive player of the year, linebacker Lewis Neal of Patrick Henry was named defensive player of the year, and Jim Muscaro, who led North Cross to an undefeated season, was named coach of the year.[238]

---

[15] The coaches included Bob Tate, Bill Winter, Rick Guard, and Danny Wheeling.

On the first team squads, Patrick Henry had eight players; Andrew Lewis, five, William Fleming, three; Cave Spring and William Byrd, two each; and Roanoke Catholic, Northside, Lord Botetourt, and Franklin County, one each.[239]

Smith's fellow first-team Wolverines included quarterback, Perry Nichols, and defenders Larry Marrazzo (end), Harry Gaston (lineman), and Bill Britts (secondary). Second-team selections included Lewis's Robbie Irvin (end) and Scott Cole (tackle) and Gaston (kicker).[16] But the Metro player with the name most likely to beered is George George, a linebacker at Roanoke Catholic who was selected to the first team defense.[240]

Bob Teitlebaum recapped the season's biggest plays on offense and special teams.

Smith was singled out for his pass receptions and punt returns for touchdowns, and Perry Nichols threw the most touchdown passes of any Metro quarterback with 16. It was far and away the best performance in this category.[241]

Running back Joe Lambert of North Cross scored the most touchdowns (17) to win the scoring race with 102 points, 12 ahead of runner-up Smith.[242]

---

[16] Sadly, Marrazzo and Irvin were killed in a single-car crash on US Route 11 near Shawsville, Virginia, on July 1, 1978. Marrazzo was driving the car, which ran off the left side of the road near the foot of Christiansburg Mountain. It struck a bridge over a small creek, and Marrazzo died late Saturday morning at Roanoke Memorial Hospital. Irvin, a passenger in the car, was pronounced dead at Lewis-Gale Hospital about one hour after the wreck. Marrazzo was a student at Virginia Tech, where he was returning when the accident occurred. Irvin was a student at East Tennessee State University (source: July 6, 1978, edition of the *Salem Times-Register*, p. 1).

Part 3: The Last Wolverines (1976)

Ned Tarpley on the move

The freshman Brian Stevens would later star at Cave Spring

LEWIS DEFENSIVE ENDS are Mickey Reed (84), Larry Marrazzo (88) and Charles Equi (83).

It was all business as usual, or so it seemed.

The Lewis players—like they had done since 1961—attended the annual 2-week preseason camp in preparation for another season. But no one could have predicted the level of attrition sustained by the Wolverines due to both illness and injury.[243]

Lewis went to camp with a squad of 53 players, who were hit with a massive virus attack and some costly injuries to key personnel. By the time camp was over and the Wolverines prepared for their last preseason scrimmage, the squad had been reduced to 29 players.[244]

Included among the disabled was Kevin Purdue, a cocaptain who injured a shoulder during a drill and was lost for the season. His loss meant that the list of returning lettermen was reduced to 6. Chief among those was Bill Britts—the hard-hitting safety and the team's top college recruit.[245]

The other veterans included Dale Tyree (linebacker and running back), Mark Williams (wingback and defensive halfback), Kelly Crawford (offensive and defensive back), and Jay Alls and Joe Francisco (linemen).[246]

With Perry Nichols lost to graduation, Stevens expected the starting quarterback job would go to Glenn Dutton, a junior, with Britts as a possibility.[247]

The season schedule had a couple of notable changes: Lexington High School replaced Pulaski County and would play Lewis in the season opener, and Northside replaced Patrick Henry and would meet Lewis in the regular-season finale.[17, 248]

Game 1 (September 3): Lexington 40, Andrew Lewis 7

In the first-ever meeting between these teams, Butch Hostetter proved the biggest weather maker among the Scarlet Hurricane. He

---

[17] This latter change officially ended the rivalry between Lewis and PH, which had begun in 1962. The two teams met in fourteen games. Lewis won nine, PH won four, and there was one tie (1974). PH won in 1963 but did not win again until 1972. It added another win in the series in 1973, which was also the year the Patriots won the Group AAA state championship.

scored five touchdowns to lead the Lexington romp, including the return of the opening kickoff for 60 yards.[249]

Lewis managed to keep it close during the first half. Lexington took a 14–7 lead into the intermission, but the Scarlet Hurricane erupted for 20 unanswered fourth-quarter points.[250]

In addition to his kickoff return for a touchdown, Hostetter scored on runs of 29, 79, and 30 yards, plus a 50-yard pass from quarterback Chico Mackey.[251]

For the Wolverines, Ned Tarpley scored on a 2-yard run. Hostetter had a game best 249 rushing yards on 132 carries. Kelly Crawford paced Lewis with 17 carries for 72 yards, and Tarpley contributed 32 yards after 11 carries.[252]

Game 2 (September 10): Cave Spring 7, Andrew Lewis 0

Scoreless through three quarters, the Knights engineered a 75-yard scoring drive capped by a 1-yard touchdown run by quarterback Kelly Moles. Both teams agreed the decisive play during the only scoring drive came on a second down and 9 at its own 26 yard line when Moles connected with end Allen Bostian for 36 yards.[253]

Running back Carl Bates carried the ball 5 times during the drive; that, plus a facemask penalty against Lewis, pushed the ball to the Lewis 1, and Moles then punched it in. Lewis's best chance to score came during the first half when it moved the ball to the Cave Spring before losing possession by a fumble.[254]

Game 3 (September 17): William Byrd 14, Andrew Lewis 3

Lewis led 3–0 at the intermission and appeared to have extended its lead to 10–0 in the third quarter when Mark Williams intercepted a Mike Robertson pass and raced 60 yards for an apparent touchdown, but the play was called back for a roughing-the-passer penalty, which resulted in a Byrd first down.[255]

Four plays later, Robertson—the Terriers' quarterback—connected with Mike Carter, who worked his way across 25 yards and into the end zone, indeed a 14-point swing in the contest. Byrd added its second touchdown in the fourth quarter following an interception.[256]

Lewis's points came via a 35-yard field goal by Zach Towler.[257]

Carter finished the game with 5 receptions for 101 yards and a TD, and linebacker Paul Nester led the Byrd defense that kept Lewis out of the end zone. He had numerous tackles and helped Byrd deny Lewis twice inside the 1-yard line in the first half.[258]

The Terriers improved to 2–1, while Lewis fell to 0–3.

Up next for the Lewis 76ers was a meeting with 3A William Fleming, which was riding high after its upset win over Halifax County at 10–9.[259]

Andrew Lewis and William Fleming had faced off many times in the past.

Fred Smith had coached the Colonels during the 1950s and 1960s and matched wits with Hal Johnston Sr. and later Eddie Joyce. He was succeeded by Don Lee in 1968. And now, in 1976, Lee had turned the reigns over to John McGregor.[260]

Lewis was looking for its first win of the season, while McGregor was looking to show that the win over Halifax "was no fluke."[261]

Lewis had struggled offensively with just one touchdown in three games, and "inexperience and a small group of backs have been two of the factors…the Wolverines' loss last week at Byrd was its first-ever in Blue Ridge District play (which began in 1974) and the team still has hopes for a third title this season."[262]

Two photographs accompanied this story, including one of Coach Stevens conferring with his son Brian wearing jersey number 11.[263]

It was an important number in Lewis lore. Some of the players who had worn that number included Don Russo (class of 1964), Dean East (1967), and David Paxton (1972).[264]

The other photograph was of McGregor looking on intently from the sidelines and wearing an article of clothing popular during the time: a stylish white belt that has yet to make its way back into fashion.

Game 4 (September 24): Lewis 14, Fleming 7

If the question is "How do you get a much-needed win and combine it with exceptional class?" then an excellent answer is, "Read about what Lewis did at Municipal Field on this date."

Leading 14–7 in the final minutes of the game, the Wolverines had the ball at the Colonel 1-yard line, and instead of trying to punch it in during a touchdown-ravaged season, the Wolverines opted to run out the clock.[265]

Lewis amassed 271 yards on the ground, led by Ned Tarpley, who accounted for 115 of those and a touchdown.[266]

The ground game was aided by the blocking of Dale Tyree and Steve Turner, who blocked down the Fleming tackles on trap plays.[267]

Lewis opened the game with an 80-yard scoring drive that included 18 plays, 6 first downs, and capped by a 5-yard touchdown pass from Brian Stevens to Ralph Brooks.[268]

Fleming tied the game in the second quarter when quarterback Butch Crotty connected with William Childress "on a 45-yard bomb."[269]

McGregor said, "They just lined up and beat our tails."[270]

Coach Stevens said, "I knew we were due, and this was a great time to prove we can play football."[271]

Hard-hitting safety Bill Britts was as emotional as anyone else and said, "I knew we had it. These first three losses were tough to accept. But our little guys went toe-to-toe and beat them to death. Give our line the credit."[272]

And this from Tarpley: "I feel like I own the world. That is what we need. We are on our way—just watch us the rest of the way."[273]

Apparently, "good things" were going on for the Byrd and Lewis football teams.

Bob McLelland thought so. He singled out Lewis lineman Steve Turner and Byrd linebacker Paul Nester. He quoted Turner as saying, "I like the line. I have always played there. I wouldn't play in the backfield if I had the chance. It's a lot more fun blocking and playing in the line when the real action comes... Besides, Ned Tarpley and the rest of our runners appreciate us. They're always telling us, 'nice block,' and that's all we want."[274]

Two pictures of head football coaches bookended this article. On the left, was Lord Botetourt's Otis Timberlake, and at the right was Glenvar's Tom Kucer, whose name would soon come to the forefront of developments.[275]

Game 5 (October 1): Covington 14, Andrew Lewis 12

Despite their troubles in the red zone, the Cougars held on for a two-point win at home. One of their touchdowns came on special teams when Neil Huffman recovered a block punt in the end zone.[276]

Lewis's Brian Stevens threw 2 touchdown passes, the first of 23 yards to Mark Williams, which pulled Lewis to within 1 point, 7–6. The extra point failed, and Covington took the 7–6 lead into the intermission.[277]

In the third quarter, the Cougars' Donnell Ross ran 16 yards for a touchdown, and the point after by Dean Martin made it 14–6. Late in the fourth, Stevens connected with John Pace on a seven-yard touchdown reception.[278]

The Wolverines went for the tie, but the 2-point conversion failed when Stevens's pass was batted down at the line of scrimmage. In the first half, the Cougars moved the ball to the Wolverines' 17-, 2-, and 20-yard lines, but all 3 drives stalled without points.[279]

Up next, the Wolverines took on the Cavaliers of Lord Botetourt.

Game 6 (October 7): Andrew Lewis 21, Lord Botetourt 20

Lewis led 15–13, but Lord Botetourt scored the go-ahead touchdown with just over a minute remaining to play in the game.[280]

Up 20–15, the Cavaliers' Donnie Benson kicked off, and the ball was fielded by Glenn Dutton at the Lewis 10. Dutton took advantage of several key blocks, the first of which by Ned Tarpley. Dutton then turned outside and headed up field where he picked up more key blocks from Joey Francisco and Jall Alls. Dutton then had just one man to beat, and he skipped loose at his own 45 for smooth sailing the rest of the way.[281]

Coach Stevens was quoted as saying, "[Benson] kicked the ball to the wrong person. We were expecting a short kick up the middle and were going to wedge it. Actually, the wedge formed nicely up the middle. There was excellent blocking on the play."[282]

Lord Botetourt got the ball back with less than a minute to play, and Dutton sealed the deal for Lewis when he picked off a pass by Cavalier quarterback Benjie Poff.[283]

In the game, Bill Britts opened the scoring with a 29-yard run. The Cavaliers answered with 2 touchdowns. Poff completed a 67-yard pass to Donald Booth, and later Mike Bryant galloped 58 yards for the score. Later, Ned Tarpley scored on a 2-yard run that capped an 80-yard drive, which tied the game at 13–13.[284]

On the ensuing point after try, Dutton replaced Britts as the holder and, after taking the snap, jumped to his feet and looked for a receiving target. He found one in Kelly Crawford in the end zone for the 2-point conversion and a 15–13 lead.[285]

Lord Botetourt put together a 92-yard drive capped by a 3-yard touchdown run by Bryant with 1:15 remaining in the game.[286]

For the Wolverines, it was an exciting, come-from-behind win in the closing minutes of a closely contested game, but their excitement was dulled when they learned that Covington had eliminated Lewis from its district title hopes when it defeated William Byrd.[287]

Covington topped the standings with a perfect 4–0 district record and was 5–1 overall, Alleghany was 2–1 and 4–2, and Lewis was next at 1–2 and 2–4.[288]

Game 7 (October 15): Andrew Lewis 7, Franklin County 0

The Wolverines had plenty of incentive to play well and to win. Thankfully for them, 7 points was enough to accomplish the mission. Those points came in the second quarter when Lewis drove 60 yards on 9 plays and capped the drive with a 4-yard touchdown toss from Brian Stevens to Ned Tarpley.[289]

The scoring drive also included a 25-yard Stevens pass to Bill Britts that moved the ball to the Franklin County 10. As for the incentive, the Eagles had kept the Wolverines out of the playoffs the past 2 seasons, plus this year's game was played in Salem.[290]

Coach Stevens was quoted as saying, "The kids wanted to play them and win. I can't say they were emotionally wild about the game, but they were determined. They knew it would be a struggle."[291]

Sportswriter Tony Stamus saw it this way: "And a struggle it was as neither team could mount much of an offense despite almost perfect conditions for football... Were it not for some fines passes from quarterback Brian Stevens in the first half, the game could have easily ended 0–0."[292]

Instead, Lewis took the victory and pushed its record to 3–4 with a chance to get to the 0.500 mark if it continued its dominance against its fellow Salemites, the Highlanders of Glenvar. It would be the last meeting between the two rivals before merging into the new Salem High School next season. Lewis had a 2–0 advantage in the series.[293]

"Will the Wolverines make it 3 for 3, or will the Highlanders end the series with a win and gain a little more self-esteem before becoming one?" inquiring minds wanted to know.

The answer would come on October 22, 1976.

Game 8 (October 22): Lewis 8, Glenvar 6

Played on the above date, Lewis engineered a come-from-behind victory, which included a moment of fast thinking on a broken play.[294]

Final score was Lewis 8, Glenvar 6.

Erstwhile starting quarterback Brian Stevens came off the bench and led the Wolverines with less than 4 minutes to play. Trailing 6–0 with 3:31 remaining in the game, Stevens connected on 3 passes—the last for a game-tying touchdown to Ralph Brooks.[295]

Placekicker David Light came on for the go-ahead point after touchdown when things seemingly went awry. Following the snap from center, placeholder Bill Britts bobbled the ball and screamed "Red!" which was the signal for his teammates to get open for a pass play.[296]

Brooks, after making his block, ran to the middle of the end zone, and Britts threw a perfectly placed pass to him to connect for the 2-point play.[297]

Knowing that Salem High School was scheduled to open next season and not knowing who would be named the first football coach of the team, Dan Smith asked Stevens about the future of his son, Brian.[298]

Completely consistent with Stevens's recent account during our interview, he told Smith that Brian would go wherever he goes. When Smith likened that scenario to that of having one's own first-round draft choice, Stevens happily agreed.[299]

Prior to the game against Glenvar, Brian Stevens had been the starting quarterback but was nursing a strained back. He and his teammates were fortunate to have trailed by just 6 points as Smith reported that Glenvar dominated the game prior to Stevens's insertion. The Highlanders had taken the lead on a 4-yard run by Steve Mountcastle.[300]

Pictured above the story was a photograph of Brooks (no. 85), seen hauling in a pass with Glenvar's Mike Pickle closing in.

Lewis ended the series with Glenvar at 3–0.

Next season, the two teams will join forces and become one, at least theoretically.

Until then, Lewis still had two games remaining on this year's schedule: first against Alleghany, and then the finale against Northside.

Game 9 (October 29): Andrew Lewis 35, Alleghany 20

Ned Tarpley had a game best 157 rushing yards and scored a touchdown, and Brian Stevens tossed 2 touchdown passes of 56 and 34 yards to Ralph Brooks to pace the Wolverines. In the fourth quarter, Kelly Crawford's touchdown run capped a 15-play drive that consumed over 7 minutes of the clock. David Light connected on all 5 PATs in this one.[301]

Meanwhile, the Vikings had already qualified for the 3A post season and were looking to finish the regular season on a winning note. The Wolverines, classified as 2A, would surely love a win over their bigger opponent.[302]

Who was better suited to write about the rivalry than Bob McLelland, who had been covering football before Northside High School opened in 1960? Answer: no one.

He interviewed players from both teams, including Lewis's Kelly Crawford, who doubled as a running back and the team's monster on defense.[303]

"It will be the last game for Andrew Lewis and this will make us all-the-more up to win," said Crawford. "Northside will be bigger than we are, but we're used to that. They have a darn good team—by far the best we have played. But we like it that way."[304]

Pictured alongside this article was Lewis's Bill Britts (no. 23) running for yardage, with Crawford (41) blocking. Parenthetically, Crawford wore the same number as at least 2 former and prominent Wolverines: Grant "G" Sprinkle (class of 1973) and Larry Lee (1970).

Game 10 (November 5): Northside 37, Andrew Lewis 6

With the win, the Vikings finished the regular season at 9–1 and primed for a run in the regionals, while the Wolverines fell to 5–5 and played for the last time as a high school team. Northside scored on its opening drive on a 4-yard run by Robey Manuel.[305]

Later, Jay Ballentine ran 14 yards for a score, Dickie Woolwine caught a 5-yard halfback pass from Manuel to score, Jack Saunders blocked a Lewis punt out of the end zone for a safety, and Northside led convincingly at the intermission, 23–0.[306]

Lewis kicked off to start the third quarter, and Northside's Mike Deal returned the ball 85 yards for a touchdown. Teammate Mark Wingfield scored the team's last touchdown on a 4-yard run.[307]

The Wolverines avoided a shutout loss when Ned Tarpley ran 15 yards for the score, which was set up by a fumble recovery by Jimmy Fisher.[308]

Offensively, the Vikings operated from the wishbone engineered to perfection by quarterback Eddie Otey, who had a game best 73 rushing yards. He also passed for 42 yards.[309]

Covington won the Blue Ridge District title. The Cougars went 4–0–1 in the district and finished 7–2–1 overall. Alleghany finished next at 3–2, 6–4, and Andrew Lewis finished third at 3–2 and 5–5.[310]

Less than two weeks later, McLelland wrote a season summary about each of the eleven Metro teams. Those included North Cross, Northside, Lord Botetourt, Patrick Henry, Cave Spring, Andrew Lewis, Franklin County, Glenvar, William Byrd, William Fleming, and Roanoke Catholic.[311]

Here is what he wrote about Lewis: "It is unfortunate that the Wolverines didn't enjoy a winning record in its last football season before merging next year with Glenvar. But the break-even year was not bad considering the team's size and inexperience. Freshman Brian Stevens threw seven touchdown passes to give promise to future stardom. But Glenn Dutton provided the top individual thrill for the Wolverines when he returned a kickoff 91 yards in the final moments for the 21–20 win over Botetourt. The star of the team was Bill Britts, a veteran defensive back who, despite his size—5'10", 170 pounds—is a top college prospect."[312]

Glenvar finished the season at 4–6, and McLelland noted that its biggest win came against William Byrd (23–17), that Brian Hooker was the top offensive threat, and that Chris Blomberg paced the defense.[313]

The following week, the 1976 World-News All Roanoke Metro teams were announced.

The awards for Offensive Player of the Year went to Carl Bates of Cave Spring, for Defensive Player of the Year to Bill Britts of Andrew Lewis, and for Coach of the Year to Jim Hickam of Northside.[314]

In fact, Northside had the most first-team selections, with 9 players named, while Patrick Henry had 6, Cave Spring 3, Fleming and Byrd 2 each, and Lewis and Lord Botetourt 1 each. Northside end, Lee Turner was the only player to be honored on both the first offensive and defensive teams.[315]

Two weeks later, the 24-player All Blue Ridge District team was announced.

Andrew Lewis placed 6 players on the team, Alleghany had 5, Lord Botetourt and champion Covington had 4 each, William Byrd 3, and Glenvar 2.[316]

For Lewis, Ralph Brooks (end) and Jay Alls (tackle) were selected to the first-team offense, and Joey Francisco (lineman), Kelly Crawford (linebacker), Bill Britts (defensive back), and Mark Williams (punter) were named to the first-team defense.[317]

For Glenvar, Duane Farris (running back) was named to the first offense and Mike Pickle (defensive back) the first defense.[318]

In further postseason news, Britts reportedly was number one in his class of 272 students with a perfect 4.0 scholastic average, and he signed an athletic grant to Clemson University, where he planned to major in engineering.[319]

Next, 2 Lewis players—Dale Tyree and Mark Williams—signed with Randolph-Macon College, whose coach, Ted Keller, said he planned to play Tyree at defensive end. Tyree played offensive guard and linebacker at Lewis. Williams played punter and defensive back for the Wolverines and would be given the chance to play both positions for the Yellow Jackets.[320]

In a recent interview with Mike Stevens, he remembers very well—forty-two years later—the '76 team and its season: "We had nine lettermen from the 1975 team. One of them was Bill Britts. He was a college prospect. He and Kevin Purdue were two of our captains. Kevin got hurt the first day of practice and was out the whole season. He was one of our linebackers.[321]

"We started off very slow. I had a son, Brian, who was playing on the team. He was a freshman—very talented. I possibly could have installed him earlier. That was my fault. Here he is a freshman, and I've got a junior and senior playing quarterback.[322]

"Brian was a backup quarterback, and that's the way it started out. The first three games were tough. We lost those. We had won one game when we put Brian in. If I had installed him as the starting quarterback earlier, we might have done better. I don't know."[323]

"We ended up with a 5–5 record. My assistants were encouraging me [to play Brian]. I wasn't sure. I'm proud of this group. I probably did a better coaching job with the 5–5 team than the 8–2 team."[324]

"Brian didn't start in the Glenvar game. He came in with 3 minutes to go. Glenvar was ahead 6–0. He took the team down the field and scored a touchdown. It was 6–6. Bill Britts was holding the ball for the kicker. He fumbled the ball. We had this little gimmick where he would holler out a name, which meant that we were in trouble and for the receivers to get out. He got up and scrambled and threw the ball to our tight end for the 2-point conversion, and we won it 8–6. That was how it ended: the confrontation between Glenvar and Andrew Lewis. The last game was against Northside, and they were very physical. They just manhandled us."[325]

* * *

The 1976 team was the last of its kind.

The following spring, Andrew Lewis High School—which had opened in 1933—would graduate its last class and then join Glenvar as intermediate schools that would provide students to the newly created Salem High School, which would open its doors for the 1977–78 school year.

An era had ended, and a new one had officially begun; its completion, however, was many years to come.

Chapter 3

Fire Left

Back row left to right: son-in-law Ben Krell, son Jacob and son-in law Hunter Stultz

Front row: daughter Laura Krell, dogs Delilah, Merida, Buzz and Woody, wife Debbie, granddaughter Lilly Krell, Equi, granddaughters Lorelai Krell and Emma Jane Krell, daughter Sara Stultz and dog Mayo. Photo provided by Equi

Charles Equi, Andrew Lewis class of 1976

Throughout the previous book, *The Team the Titans Remember*, numerous examples are provided to explain why the Andrew Lewis High School football teams were so successful during the Eddie Joyce years (1960–1974).

His innovative concepts—chief among those, the annual two-week preseason football camp—produced the close and lasting bonds that developed between the players. His concepts also yielded a level of confidence and expectation to succeed that players exemplified both on and off the field and well into their lives. One chapter, "Band of Brothers," is fully devoted to these concepts.

In sum, the Lewis football players were well disciplined, well trained, physically and mentally tough, and clearly unified.

Mike Stevens was certainly aware of these team-hallmarks, for he had served under Joyce as an assistant for several years. But what was it like for a player to have played at Lewis under both Joyce and Stevens?

Charles F. Equi (class of '76) is someone who did. As a contributor to this and to the previous narrative (see page 133 of *The Team the Titans Remember*), Equi devoted careful consideration to composing a history of his football-playing days in Salem—from sandlot through high school—and includes his memories of his coaches, his teammates, the practices, the games, and his favorite drill.

What any reader can easily glean from his writing is that the process of becoming tough starts at an early age; that going to the Friday night football games to watch Lewis play was the most exciting event in town; that a young football player's hope was to eventually become one of those Lewis players exiting the cinderblock locker room, running down its steps, and breaking through the paper banner the cheerleaders had made as their names were being announced, as the fans in Salem were on their feet, and as the band was playing; that he and his teammates enjoyed a special camaraderie; and that the constant practice drills—one in particular—made the players tough for a lifetime.

Here then is his story.[326]

Tough Enough

"I grew up in Cherry Hill Park and went to East Salem Elementary School… Cherry Hill Park was made up of lower to middle class income families… It was the sixties with the Vietnam War, drugs, and alcoholism very noticeable throughout the neighborhood. Not too many families escaped the trappings of the time. However, it was a great place to grow up and, at the same time, a very hard place to grow up.

"Most of the kids in the neighborhood played football, basketball, and baseball as pickup games, and not many played organized sports. Most of the basketball games resembled a football game with hard-hitting at each shot.

"We had regular boxing matches, where I was usually pounded on. However, if you missed a match, it usually was a painful experience. The next time you came, you were boxing someone twice your size in middle school or even high school. All of this experience toughened me up, and I learned not to back down no matter what the size of the person challenging me…

"Let me just say being a teenager is hard in any generation. The frustrations of the day could be overwhelming, but the ability to go out after a school day and knock the hell out of someone without getting in trouble was stress reliever to me…"

A Mustang First

"It was during the mid to late sixties, and I was in the fifth or sixth grade, a little skinny kid who got to play for the East Salem Mustangs or mainly watch from the bench. Our family had only one car like most of the families in the neighborhood, so getting to and from practice was hard at times. I rode my bike to practice on some occasions. The seasons were uneventful, but going to Friday night football games to see Andrew Lewis High School play was the most exciting event in town for me. It was like going to see famous superstars… I told myself I was going to play on that field one day. This was my private goal."

The Hiccup

As a seventh grader, Equi attended Salem Intermediate School, where his ability to play football was a little hampered.

"My first year at Salem Intermediate, I was in the seventh grade, and I had heard of the football team there but that you couldn't play until you were in the eighth grade. By the time I could play, the football team—as best as I can remember—was discontinued, and some of the students were trying to play for the Andrew Lewis freshmen team. Again, I missed the cutoff for tryouts. I was starting to see that I was not as well connected to the Salem sports arena as most of my Salem classmates. Some of my classmates were already on the freshmen team, and during my freshmen year, some of them were playing for the junior varsity team… I saw that I needed to be more proactive to have any chance of making the freshman team in my first year at Andrew Lewis.

"The summer before my freshman year, I ran and lifted weights on my own. People in my neighborhood [teenagers] told me I was wasting my time, that not too many from our neighborhood had made it because the coaches didn't like anyone from Cherry Hill Park."

A Freshman

"Coach Helms was my freshmen coach. I was going to have to bring my A game and keep my nose clean, or at least not get caught doing something stupid. I was an undersized kid and wasn't a college prospect by any means. I just wanted to play… I started at left defensive end, and that was the position I would play the most during my four years at Andrew Lewis. Coach Helms was an excellent coach, and he was a player's coach. Every game we played was close. We won some, tied some, and lost some close ones, but the games were downright battles.

"At the end of the season, we had the annual battle of the freshmen team versus the junior varsity which was a dog fight… When I looked up from my stance, [I could see] Coach Joyce watching from a distance. I knew then that the real test started next season."

The Preseason Camps

"The three years I attended camp, it was just a hard grind, which weeded out those players not serious about playing. That said, we were still teenagers and managed to have endless energy while being beaten up from our daily practice. Some of my teammates may say I was out there, on and off the field. After all, you had to be a little wild and crazy to go to a two-week camp and beat up on each other from morning to night.

"A tradition for the junior varsity players was for them to play Shawsville High School's varsity team before camp ended. The upperclassmen on the [Lewis] team told us not to come back to camp if we lost. The Andrew Lewis junior varsity team never lost to them. I prayed on the bus all the way to the scrimmage. It was a big deal for Shawsville to play us. They had the scoreboard on and an announcer. We were losing 7-6 late in the scrimmage on a very hot day. I was playing defensive end, and on the snap, the quarterback's handoff was fumbled, and he and the running back went down… It was like everyone stopped playing, and I was in fast motion and picked up the fumble and ran for a touchdown, the only one I ever scored.

Coach [Danny] Wheeling, the junior varsity coach, yelled at me with 'You are supposed to fall on the ball!' The scrimmage ended about five minutes later, and we won 13–7."

A Sophomore and Coach Stevens

"[During] my sophomore year [1973 season], my biggest honor was being able to dress out two times for a varsity game. Although I did not get to play, just the experience of running onto the field before the game and being on the sideline was amazing. Also, you saw what took place during halftime and how the coaches made adjustments.

"Coach Stevens was my position coach at defensive end, and he was a very good coach and very knowledgeable about football. I had a good understanding of what he wanted out of the players. The only problem was, he always wore dark sunglasses, so you could not see his eyes to see what he was thinking."

On and Off as a Junior

"My junior year, I was on and off the field constantly. I played on about every special team and was substituted in and out on left and right defensive end, but I didn't get to start a single game. It was a lot of fun, and most importantly, I stayed healthy.

"The first game of the season stays in my memory. It was against a newly consolidated Pulaski County High. We lost our starting center, Mike Pace—a leader on the offense—with a broken leg early in the game… We were losing at halftime, 14–7, and we got a butt chewing.

"The beginning of the second half the [Pulaski] kicker came out and wasn't the same one who kicked off earlier. This guy was huge, and he looked like the older beer gut and overweight Sonny Jurgensen of the Washington Redskins. Of course, I was in the middle of the blocking wedge, and when we met, it was an explosion. I didn't see it, but Larry Smith took the kickoff and ran it back. We ended up winning 28–14. Thus, the rivalry of Salem versus Pulaski County started.

"However, the most noticeable difference for my junior season was the loss of Coach Joyce, who resigned from Andrew Lewis football at the end of the season."

That's Just a Nickname, You Know

"I had great teammates during my time at Andrew Lewis. Just about everyone had a nickname. Perry Nichols, our quarterback, was called Ostrich, and he was the prototype of Eddie Joyce Jr. Bobby Williams was our center, and he was called Bucket Head. Charles Hopkins was Hop, and he was our running back and could run like a rabbit. Scott Cole was known as Cole Bear. Once he got low on you, you were blocked, period. Mickey Reed was our tight end. Robbie Irvin and Larry Smith were both excellent receivers. Billy St. Clair, or Big'in, was an excellent defensive tackle and a quality person whom I played beside most of my time at Andrew Lewis.

"On defense, we had Greg French at monster and Ray Byrd at linebacker, but the most talented player on our team, in my opinion, was Harry Gaston, the defensive nose guard. He would tear through the line and was very difficult to block. He also kicked extra points and field goals."

His Senior Season of '75

"We had twenty-plus seniors that year, and they all contributed to the team and to the Andrew Lewis success for three years. The camaraderie of the players from the graduating class of 1976 is something I don't think I will ever experience again in my lifetime. The varsity record during our three-year term was 24–5–1, I believe, with two Blue Ridge titles. The crazy point system hurt us for two years in making the playoffs. In today's scenario, we would have definitely been in the playoffs each year.

"My senior football season was the most rewarding while also being the most disappointing year that I played. My senior year started off with a different feeling. For the first time since I started following Andrew Lewis football, we had a new head coach, and I had a different position coach that I was trying to relate to. The one thing I know for sure was that we had a known leader in Coach Stevens. This was not his first rodeo, and the group of seniors rallied around him to carry on the winning tradition.

"I knew this was my last year to play and to start a game for Andrew Lewis. For the past four years, I had dedicated my whole being to play football for Andrew Lewis. I lifted weights for four years, constantly ran and jogged, and chose to focus only on football instead of playing other sports. Academically, I did enough to stay on the team but did not apply myself for college. I had a good camp and worked my way into the starting lineup."

Equi remembers vividly the games played in '75, from beginning to end.

"We were scrimmaging Cave Spring before our opening game with Pulaski County and I sprained my right ankle and it put me on crutches. I probably sprained my ankles numerous times while playing at Andrew Lewis. In fact, I can't do much today without them hurting once the temperature gets down below forty degrees. Anyway, I returned before the games started but was not 100 percent.

"Our first game against Pulaski County was not as contested as in years past, and we easily won. A lot of people played in this one, and it was a fantastic start.

"Our second game of the season was away at Franklin County. It was a close game until they pulled it out in the end. I remember on the goal line stance, they had tried to come around my end on three plays, and we stopped them each time. I remember specifically that Rick Garst, who had played left defensive end the previous year and had graduated, traveled to the game and was yelling at me that they were not going to score on me on my side and they didn't.

"I kept yelling on fourth and goal that they were going up the middle, and sure enough, their big running back went up a crease in the middle to score. I saw the handoff and wanted to fire on the play, but the call was goal line.

"When a fire left was called, it meant I could shoot into the backfield as fast as possible to cause disruption, chaos, and pain to the quarterback without worrying about containment. It worked most every time to our advantage. It was my favorite call, and if I may say so, it was something I was pretty good at.

"That touchdown still haunts me today because I know on a fire left, I could have hit him. On the bus ride back to Salem, the players were crying, and we were embarrassed—just totally disgusted with our play. We let one get away from us, and the loss was on the players. The coaches had done their part. We just didn't show up…"

After the loss, the team prepared for its next opponent, William Byrd. Equi said: "I got the word I was starting that night at left defensive end, and the defense was being announced at the beginning of the game—a dream come true for me that took a long time to reach but a goal worth obtaining. Hearing my name called and running out of the little cinder block dressing room and running onto the field while tearing the banner in two that the cheerleaders were holding was amazing. I will never forget that moment for as long as I live.

"I had a fire left called that night, and I knocked the ball out of the quarterback's hand and recovered the fumble. When I got off the field, Coach Wheeling asked me why I hadn't picked it up and ran for a touchdown. I didn't know I was that wide open, and I fell on the ball. That's what he coached us to do—to fall on the ball. He just laughed and hit me on the helmet. I wasn't messing that perfect night up."

But something did get messed up, and it happened the following week in practice.

"I had a running back come at me full speed when the rest of us were walking through the play. The running back hit me under my shoulder pad and injured my shoulder. I still have a small knot there today. The coaches sent me to Lewis-Gale Hospital, and the doctor said nothing was broken and that I should be good in a week.

"I sat out the [William] Fleming game… They gave me a little piece of foam rubber to put under my shoulder pad, which didn't help. As a matter of fact, the pain got worse every time I hit someone. I went to see my family doctor, and he told me I had a severely bruised shoulder and I shouldn't play for six to eight weeks. I knew I was just as good as anyone on the team at that position, but the truth is, I was at about 60 percent.

"The next two games against Covington and Lord Botetourt, I played sparingly, if at all… Next up was Patrick Henry, one of the best teams on our schedule. As luck would have it, I twisted my other ankle but was able to tape it up and keep playing. By Thursday, the day before the game, I had a bad cold, and by game time, I was hacking and coughing and had a temperature of 101 or 102 degrees. I told no one.

"Right before game time, the coaches told me I was starting at right defensive end. I was in bad shape. All I can remember from the game was going over to the visitors' sideline and puking several times after each play. Fortunately, the only one who noticed was the sideline referee, and he asked me if I was going to make it. I told him I was just nervous.

"The next three games, I ended my season like I started my football career with the East Salem Mustangs—with a sideline view. It sucked… Today, I still have some of my old teammates ask me what happened to me late in the season. I had to have an attitude adjustment many times to make it through the next three games.

"Before our last game, Coach [Bill] Winter told us this will be the last time we put on our uniforms. For me, mentally that happened in the PH game. Although it was a hard lesson at the time, it helped prepare me for some other challenges that life has thrown my way. No matter what situation you are in, you have to keep competing."

Lessons Learned

"I had aspirations of playing, or walking on, at the college level. A few Salem Sports Foundation members encouraged me to continue to play, but financially and academically, I wasn't ready. After all, playing at Andrew Lewis, I had already experienced what it was like to play 'small college' ball. Football quickly passed me by. In the end, I do appreciate everything our coaches did for us. They had families, jobs, and businesses they were dealing with, but they took the time and pride to help young men like me and my teammates become men and play a game I still love today."

Life Beyond Lewis

"After high school, some of my close teammates went into the service. As the song sung by Charlie Daniels goes, 'A rich man goes to college and a poor man goes to work.'[18] I had to go to work, and I took night classes part-time and earned an associate's in business with a minor in marketing at National Business College [located in Salem]."

He later took classes at Virginia Western Community College of Roanoke and transferred to Virginia Tech, where he earned a bachelor of science degree in business management with a concentration in accounting. He passed the examination to become a certified public accountant (CPA) in 1990 and also passed the certified valuation analysts exam in 1998.

He has been practicing for thirty-two years now and previously owned a firm until it merged with Brown, Edwards & Company of Roanoke. He married his high school sweetheart and Lewis cheerleader, the former Debbie Webster, in 1979.

"She definitely fired left on me!" quipped Equi.

He and Debbie will soon celebrate their fortieth wedding anniversary. They have two daughters—Laura, who is also a CPA, and Sara, who is a fourth-grade math teacher at East Salem Elementary—and a son Jacob, who works in the Math Department at Virginia

---

[18] Equi's inclusion of Charlie Daniels refers to the popular and longtime musician by that name who began his career in the 1960s. Currently 81, Daniels is still touring. The lyrics Equi quoted are taken from a hit song called "Long Haired Country Boy," which was one of many songs on the album *Fire on the Mountain*, which was released in 1974. A native of North Carolina, Daniels has had great success as both a gospel and Southern rock singer. This author is very familiar with Daniels's songs and saw him in concert at the Salem Civic Center on October 24, 1976, and owns several of his albums. For more information about Daniels, please visit his official website at www.charliedaniels.com.

Western. He and Debbie also have two granddaughters, Emma Jane and Lillian Claire.

"My kids and my grandkids are my proudest 'fire left' in my life."

The Edge

During stressful situations, Equi goes back in time and imagines how satisfying it would be if he could put into practice some of what he learned as a Lewis player.

"Sometimes I think that it would be nice to suit up and do it [the old football drills] today. I could think of some people I would love to go through 'sticking drills' with. The problem is, we are probably all too old now, but it would be fun trying.

"On occasion, in my professional life—and in my mind's eye—I still use the 'fire left' when I am in a courtroom or in negotiations with the opposition. I imagine sticking the opposing attorney or representative, and it sure helps give me an edge."

This "edge" is something he has in common with many of the former Wolverine players even to this day.

Chapter 4

ONE TRIBE OF SALEMITES

I'm Salem born and Salem bred
And when I die I'll be Salem dead...[19]

Part 1: The Resistance

The official opening of Salem High School was the culmination of a plan set forth several years before. Exactly when the idea was originally conceived might be difficult to pinpoint, but beginning on October 1, 1974, articles appeared in the local newspapers about a concept that set the proverbial wheels in motion.

The first such article reported on the possible annexation of the western area of Roanoke County.

It would occur west of the "yellow line," which represented a proposed boundary line between Roanoke and Salem—if the county were divided between them. If this occurred, Mr. Wilbur S. Pence, a school consultant, indicated that he would recommend that Glenvar and Andrew Lewis High Schools convert to intermediate schools and that Salem Intermediate School would become an elementary school.[327]

---

[19] Taken from the "Salem Fight Song" found online marked salemfightsong.pdf, which had these popular lyrics known to many a Salemite: "I'm Salem born and Salem bred, and when I die, I'll be Salem dead. So Rah Rah for Salem, Salem. Rah Rah for Salem, Salem. Rah Rah for Salem. Rah, rah, rah."

Obviously, a new high school was already in the planning stage and, if built, would serve the entire city of Salem.

In fact, Pence had testified during the tenth day of a trial that Roanoke was attempting to take over all of Roanoke County; that Salem was attempting to get the western area; and that the town of Vinton (home to William Byrd High School) was attempting to become a city and take control of the eastern area.[328]

The next article of relevance appeared on October 9, which reported that Salem was planning to build a new high school that would replace Andrew Lewis High. The Salem City School Board set forth a plan that included a 42-acre tract, and the architect chosen was Roy Kinsey Sr. of Kinsey, Shane and Associates of Salem.[329]

Quoting from this source, the architectural plan factored in "using the lay of the land and the seasonal shift of the sun to advantage." The school would be designed for 1,800 students and possibly more. As officials scrambled on the political and logistical fronts to make this plan come to fruition, an inevitable controversy developed over the actual naming of the school.[330]

Before providing the contents of some of the editorials that appeared in the local newspapers, it is important to provide some of the history associated with the school system in Salem, Virginia.

In my previous work, *The Team the Titans Remember*, I cited information provided by the Salem Educational Foundation and Alumni Association's website pertaining to the local history that had been compiled by the late Dr. Walter A. Hunt, the association's second president.

Here is what he reported: "Salem High School first came into existence in 1895. From then through 1912, the school was located on Academy Street. Beginning in 1912, the school was located on Broad Street. This remained true until 1933 when Andrew Lewis High School came into existence."

Andrew Lewis High was the only high school in Salem until Glenvar opened in 1966. That means that from 1933 to 1966—thirty-three years—people in and outside Salem thought exclusively of Andrew Lewis when they thought about the high school located in Salem.

THE SPARTAN SUCCESSION

Beginning in 1966, a natural rivalry (school pride) developed between Andrew Lewis and Glenvar. From 1966 to 1977—eleven years—the rivalry continued until the new Salem High School opened its doors for the consolidated students from both Andrew Lewis and Glenvar High Schools.

Perhaps that rivalry continued in some way, but the point of fact is that beginning in 1977, there was but one high school in Salem.

Given the much-longer period of tradition associated with Andrew Lewis High School, it is understandable that the several generations of Lewis students would insist on maintaining their traditions.

Following are some excerpts taken from a letter to the editor which puts forth the importance of those traditions; note, too, the implicit disdain the writer felt about how the new school's name was chosen.

"The Salem City School Board has named its new school Salem High School. Since their decision was a private one, I would like to give a few public reasons why I hope they would reconsider."[331]

"The main objection I have is based on the traditions of Andrew Lewis High School. Andrew Lewis has for years brought recognition to Salem, not only throughout Virginia, but in many cases throughout the southeastern states."[332]

The author put forth many examples of how Lewis had brought such widespread recognition and then continued with this: "I do not understand the reasoning that we must stop these traditions and start new."[333]

Recognizing that students who attended Glenvar might oppose these traditions, the author put forth this assessment: "Roanoke County has carved out three schools [Cave Spring, Northside, and Glenvar] of what was formerly Andrew Lewis. There were emotions involved in each of the splits, but their problems were overcome. The 500 [approximately] Salem residents who will attend the new school instead of Glenvar will simply be returning to the fold. Since they have developed top-notch programs in many areas at Glenvar, they will be able to contribute significantly to continuing what Andrew Lewis has meant to the community. I would hope that they would rather return to and continue a great tradition at Lewis rather than start again from scratch as they have already had to do at Glenvar.[334]

"Finally, I hope the citizens of Salem will let the media, their school board, and their local officials, who are willing to let Andrew Lewis become just a name for a junior high, know that the citizenry think Andrew Lewis's contributions to the community have been significant enough to be continued."[335]

People were listening. In fact, people were acting on this very thing.

Several students and a teacher at Andrew Lewis had formed a group in opposition to the name selected for the new school. The group called itself SALT (Save Andrew Lewis for Tomorrow) and was headed by the president of the Lewis student body, Morgan Griffith, who wanted the new school named Andrew Lewis.[20, 336]

---

[20] These were early days of advocacy for H. Morgan Griffith and, in retrospect, foreshadowing of bigger things to come, including platforms on which he would advocate on a much-larger scale. He is currently a member of the US House of Representatives, and the following information was taken from the website www.morgangriffith.house.gov: Griffith was first elected to represent the Ninth Congressional District of Virginia in the US House of Representatives on November 2, 2010, and is currently serving his fourth term. Morgan is a member of the House Energy and Commerce Committee, which has jurisdiction over some of the most important issues facing Virginia's Ninth District, including public health and federal regulations. For the 115th Congress, Morgan was named vice chairman of the Energy and Commerce Committee's Subcommittee on Oversight and Investigations. In addition, Morgan serves on its Subcommittee on Health and the Subcommittee on Energy. Prior to his election to the US House of representatives, Morgan served as a member of the Virginia House of Delegates from 1994 to 2011, where he represented the Eighth District. In 2000, Morgan was elected house majority leader, the first Republican in Virginia history to hold that position. Morgan is a graduate of Salem's Andrew Lewis High School and an honors graduate of Emory & Henry College. After completing studies at the Washington and Lee University School of Law, Morgan returned to Southwest Virginia, where he practiced law for nearly three decades. He and his wife, Hilary, have three children. Further, in an article that appeared in the *Salem Times-Register* on November 10, 1983, he accepted a position with the law firm of Lutins, Shapiro and Kurtin of Roanoke just prior to the publication of the article.

This same article revealed the exact date that the decision had been made to name the new school Salem. The designation was agreed upon by the Salem School Board on August 12 (1975). Board chairman B. G. King said the decision was based on the numbers: 60 percent of the students in the new school would be from Andrew Lewis and 40 percent from Glenvar.[337]

King conceded that a lot of nostalgia was associated with the name Andrew Lewis, but the board acted to create a favorable climate for the education of the students.[338]

Back to Griffith, he set forth the committee's reasons for wanting the new school named after Andrew Lewis. First, he pointed out that there were already at least thirty schools in the United States named Salem and only one Andrew Lewis. He said that Andrew Lewis would be a better name psychologically and would stress individuality.[21, 339]

Would the Glenvar students be on board? Griffith reasoned that some of the Glenvar students would be unhappy with the Lewis name for two or three years but that the majority would not be upset.[340]

Next, Griffith pointed out that since the new high school would not open until September 1977, the majority of its students would come from Salem Intermediate and Hidden Valley Schools.[341]

King recognized the potential explosion. He said the SALT movement might spark similar action at Glenvar, and "first thing you know, we've got a confrontation between two well-meaning groups." He indicated that the board would be happy to hear from SALT, and it was possible that it could turn the board around.[342]

An unnamed Glenvar student said, "We don't want it [the new school] named Glenvar because we know it's a new school. But we don't want it called Andrew Lewis either."[343]

Members of SALT pointed out the relevance of history. The nation was about to celebrate its bicentennial and that it would

---

[21] What no one knew or could have known was that there would come a time when Virginia would have two schools named Salem. In 1989, Salem High School in Virginia Beach was opened and became the second of its name.

be "contrary to the spirit of the times to ignore a local historical figure."[344]

Next, consider these words and their scathing yet eloquent tone taken from a letter to the editor that appeared in the November 12, 1975, edition: "I would like to add my voice to the growing number of persons who are concerned about the killing of a proud Salem-Roanoke County tradition. For years, Salem's City Council domination of sports fanatics has caused them to forget the hundreds of Salem children at Glenvar.[345]

"Now, with an election a few months away, this faction and its minions on the school board have laid to rest the name Andrew Lewis, as if this hollow gesture could correct years of distorted priorities.[346]

"The name Andrew Lewis has served the Roanoke Valley well for generations. No other place has as much right as Salem to use it. Salem High School is as ugly a name as it is political. This is a Bicentennial year: a particularly poor time to throw dirt in the face of the hero of Point Pleasant.[347]

"I would hope that the dominant faction in charge of Salem government will change its mind and give the forgotten Salemites of Glenvar what the whole city needs: a deemphasis on expensive projects of civic vainglory and a return to the revolutionary virtue, to the prudent moderation which should be called by the name, Andrew Lewis."[348]

Was the writer truly speaking for "the forgotten Salemites of Glenvar" when he advocated that the new school should be named Andrew Lewis?

The next day's edition (November 13, 1975) featured a letter that served as a rebuttal to the one previously featured, which championed the continuation of the Lewis traditions. Here are a few excerpts from it: "I strongly disagree with his first contention that Andrew Lewis traditions will be lost…Regarding his second point, it is only a name and the spirit of the school will not be changed. The student body as a whole would be more unified and the 'esprit de corps' would be much stronger because students of Glenvar would not feel excluded… As a matter of record, there were and are teachers in the valley who are graduates of the pre-Andrew Lewis High School-Salem High School.³⁴⁹

"[The previous writer] also makes the point that tradition would have to 'start from scratch' if it were named Salem High School. To this I reply bunk! This new school should only be a continuation of two fine traditions without hindering either."³⁵⁰

The next letter to the editor provided insight and perspective while warning the readers of the possibility that not all SALT members may be citizens of Salem. This one appeared in the November 15, 1975, edition below the headline "Life didn't begin when Lewis was built," suggesting the flavor to follow and its predictable conclusion and recommendation.³⁵¹

The writer first established her credentials. She was a graduate of Andrew Lewis, was a citizen of Salem, and had two children who graduated from both Lewis and Glenvar. As she pointed out, she was as qualified as anyone to opine on the matter.³⁵²

She wrote that the people in Salem originally attended Salem High School long before Andrew Lewis High was built, and she recommended that members of SALT have their citizenry checked out to make sure they were residents of Salem.³⁵³

"The county students now attending Andrew Lewis have no right to vote on the naming of our new school as they won't be attending it anyway… I might mention that no one gave a second thought to the people who graduated from [G. W.] Carver High School [the school where black students attended prior to integration]. They did away with their name without a second glance.³⁵⁴

"We now have a chance to start over and really unite behind one school the city of Salem can be proud of—so let's don't muff it."³⁵⁵

Alongside this letter was another that supported the preservation of the Lewis name.

Written by an alumnus of Andrew Lewis, the writer was currently residing in Washington, DC, and considered the name of the new school as "unimaginative." He was "appalled at the thought of the name Andrew Lewis disappearing from the annals of Virginia history."³⁵⁶

As a resident of DC, he noted that more people there had heard of Andrew Lewis than they had heard of the city of Salem. He noted that throughout Virginia high schools "predominantly are named for distinguished persons," and he cited several examples.[357]

He concluded with these words: "For the sake of Salem's proud history, for the alumni of Andrew Lewis, and for future graduates, please consider naming Salem's new high school Andrew Lewis. It deserves no less."[358]

Next, in the weekly Forum section of the *Roanoke World-News*, which put forth the question of the week, the November 20, 1975, edition revealed the answer to the most recent question: "Should the new Salem high school be named Andrew Lewis?"

Nearly fifty responses were shown on this one-page section, and the results were thirty-four (34) responders in favor of naming the school Andrew Lewis and sixteen (16) opposed.[359]

In the next day's edition of this same source, a letter to the editor appeared, which revealed the person's very thoughtful and philosophical assessment of the topic. His message: don't let what happened to other schools happen to this one; keep what is important to this one.[360]

He wrote:

> Roanokers, viewing the issue from some small distance, cannot help remembering that to Roanoke schools with proud histories—Jefferson and Addison—have been all but lost in the shuffle of legal concepts and populations…
>
> The arguments for and against naming the new Salem school after Andrew Lewis are laid out in boggling profusion on this page (a reference to the fifty responses reported above). One can take either side and not be considered a fool or a sentimental slob. But if there is a guiding rule, that should in matters of nomenclature, it may well be; in the absence of persuasive objections,

names—particularly ones that honor flesh and blood rather than mere geography—should be retained.

The main argument for naming the school Salem High (and one used by the Salem School Board) is a good one. The new school will be attended by both Glenvar and Andrew Lewis students, and a 'neutral' name will offend neither group. But the arguments—sentimental, historical and common sense, for naming the new school Andrew Lewis weigh heavier.

The issue is not arithmetic: that there will be more former Andrew Lewis students at the new school than former Glenvar students. Arithmetic has no soul. Rather, it is a matter of philosophy: Why not conserve that which is so meaningful for so many people in the valley?[361]

Where There's Salt, There's Pepper

The Salem School Board met on January 13, 1976, and welcomed student delegations from both Andrew Lewis and Glenvar High Schools who presented opposing views as to the name of the new high school.[362]

SALT members insisted that the name of the new school should be Andrew Lewis, but a delegation of students from Glenvar, which used the counter acronym PEPPER (Preventing Erratic Protest: Protecting Everyone's Rights), took the position that the name Salem High School was appropriate because the name was neutral.[363]

School Board Chairman B. G. King told both SALT and PEPPER that the board was sticking with the name Salem High School.[364]

But Dr. Richard H. Fisher, a school board member who had made the motion last August to change the new school to Salem High, reported he had changed his mind. He said the name of the school should be left up to the voters in a referendum next November.[22, 365]

When his motion died for lack of a second, Fisher indicated that he would ask Salem City Council—as a private citizen and not as a board member—to put the question to a vote of the people.[366]

---

[22] Dr. Richard H. "Dick" Fisher was born on November 17, 1923. He was a graduate of both Andrew Lewis High School and the University of Richmond. He excelled in football at both schools. The late Bob McLelland wrote a feature story about Fisher that was published by the *Roanoke World-News* on June 3, 1965. McLelland spoke with Fisher about the increase in injuries to football players. At that time, Fisher was an orthopedic surgeon at Lewis-Gale Hospital in Roanoke, and he served as the team physician for the Andrew Lewis football team. Fisher lived a long life. He died on August 16, 2015, at the age of ninety-one. The following information was taken from an article published on August 23, 2015, by the *Salem Times-Register* and written by Kelsey Bartlett: "According to those who knew him well, Dr. Richard Harding Fisher Sr. gave like no other to the people of the place he loved…he lived his entire lifetime in Salem, and never stopped trying to improve his hometown…Fisher loved the history of Salem, and dug to uncover the obscure. He was especially interested in the life of Gen. Andrew Lewis, and is largely responsible for the bronze statue of Lewis that sits in front of the Salem Civic Center. 'Dick Fisher was the backbone of a lot of organizations, including the historical society,' Salem Museum Director John Long said. 'He started the Educational Foundation, which made a profound difference for a lot of people.' He received the Salem Historical Society James Simpson Award in 2001. 'His dedication to raise awareness for Gen. Andrew Lewis is why he was honored,' Long said. Fisher founded the Salem Education and Alumni Association and served as its president for 18 years. The association has awarded more than $2.8 million to Salem High School graduates. He cared deeply for education and was also the chairman on the City of Salem School Board from 1974–85. It was while he was on the school board that he first met U.S. Rep. Morgan Griffith, who was serving as student body president. The two bonded over discussions about the importance of Andrew Lewis. 'There have been a lot of people who contributed to Salem,' Griffith said. 'I don't know that anyone equals him.' Griffith says Fisher's greatest gift to the community is his example of a life well lived. 'I think his greatest accomplishment is setting an example of how to give back to the community,' he said. Fisher was also a founding member of the Lewis-Gale Medical Foundation, and was instrumental in establishing Life-Guard 10, the hospital-based air ambulance service at Lewis-Gale Hospital. Fisher had a passion for sports and used his medical skills to serve as team physician for multiple teams throughout the valley."

The following month, the Salem City Council declined to overturn the city school board and order a referendum on the school naming. Instead, the council adopted a resolution that the naming of a school is a matter to be decided by the school board.[367]

Dick Fisher and Morgan Griffith were just two examples of people in Salem who were passionate about keeping the tradition of Andrew Lewis in place. And they were not the only people privy to the historical contributions of the man named Andrew Lewis.

In the July 9, 1976, edition of the *Roanoke World-News*, a contributing writer by the name of M. Carl Andrews wrote a historical account of Lewis's Revolutionary War victories as part of the *World-News*'s bicentennial feature.

Here are some key excerpts taken from it:

> Gen. Andrew Lewis, the Roanoke Valley's No. 1 military hero, is remembered chiefly for leading the victorious colonials against Chief Cornstalk at the Battle of Point Pleasant, Oct. 10, 1774 (during Dunmore's War). 51
>
> But as important as that event was in securing the frontier for the coming War of Independence, he deserved equal or greater praise for the role he played from then until his death seven years later.
>
> It was exactly 200 hundred years ago July 9 that Gen. Lewis, commander of the hastily raised Virginia army, ended the rule of John Murray, Earl of Dunmore, as royal governor of the Old Dominion at the Battle of Gwynn's Island, or Cricket Hill.
>
> Lewis…was given command and was assisted by a close associate from the Indian campaigns, Col. Adam Stephen. Their troops composed the core

of the regiments that encamped at Williamsburg by March 3.

Lewis was already a member of the House of Burgesses and had been named to a committee to prepare a plan of defense under Gov. Patrick Henry.

In Philadelphia, the Continental Congress had ignored the recommendation of Gen. George Washington that Lewis be made a major general and he had to settle for brigadier rank... Washington considered Lewis the foremost fighting man in the colonies and would have preferred him in command.

Unfortunately, most of our history has been written in New England with emphasis on what happened there, and so Gwynn's Island got scant or no attention. Yet, in its way, it was fully as important as the battle of Bunker Hill or the skirmishes at Lexington and Concord.

Lewis subsequently served as aide to Washington, as did Stephen, but never was given the command he richly deserved. Once, in 1777, he resigned more- or-less in disgust. It was a cruel fate that he was to die (on Sept. 26, 1781) less than a month before victory at Yorktown (Oct. 19, 1781).

Suffering from fever he contracted in the Tidewater climate, he was on his way home, accompanied by his two youngest sons and Col. William Fleming, when he died at the home of a close friend, Capt. Talbot, near Montvale in Bedford County, Sept. 23, 1781.[368]

The colonial hero was one of four sons of John Lewis, a man of French Huguenot descent who married a Scot, Margaret Lynn. Andrew was born at Donegal, North Ireland, Oct. 9, 1720 and came with the family to America in 1732 and settled near present Staunton (Virginia).

He is described as 6-feet-4, blond with brown eyes and heavy eyebrows, of extraordinary strength and iron constitution. Known as a stern disciplinarian, he frequently drew complaints from his soldiers, but they trusted him and never doubted. He kept his volunteers together.

Lewis had a commanding presence and perhaps the colonial governor of New York, after they negotiated a treaty with the Indians at Ft. Stanwix, said. "The earth seemed to tremble under him as he walked along."

If any man personified the rugged, courageous frontiersman of Virginia it was Andrew Lewis. After 200 years, his fame endures.

Mr. Andrews apparently presented these historical facts to an audience gathered at the grave of Andrew Lewis, located in Salem's East Hill Cemetery.[369]

One person in attendance wrote a letter to the editor that appeared in the July 14, 1976, edition of the *Roanoke World-News*. This writer not only made the plea to keep the name Andrew Lewis for the new high school but envisioned a time when Glenvar would once again become a high school.

She wrote:

> As I stood at the grave of Gen. Andrew Lewis and listened to M. Carl Andrews relate the history

of this brave Virginian, many thoughts passed through my mind.

First, I realized the fine school board of more than three people who had chosen to honor this valley's great general. Now a mere three-member school board (vote of two) tosses aside the name.

I recalled, too, that a letter from the Salem Historical Society that had been delivered in person with the assurance that it would be in the hands of City Council that night was never read. That letter requested that the citizens of Salem be permitted to vote on the choice of the school's name in the spring election.

It is our tax money going into the building. Yet two people decide for 22,000 taxpayers. I call the council to increase this school board to five members.

I challenge the City of Salem, the fine citizens (including students) of our neighbors, and close friends of Glenvar to preserve the name Andrew Lewis.

This will open the way when Glenvar grows to the capacity to populate their own high school to name their own high school Glenvar.[370]

Part 2: We Shall Be One

Salem High School opened for the 1977-78 school year. Salem High School and its list of achievements. (photo taken at the Salem Museum and permission granted to print copies).

In time, the "furor" among Lewis and Glenvar graduates and their fellow partisans about what name would be chosen for the new high school would surely subside. By October 20, 1976, there arose evidence of healthy reconciliation—at least on the football field.

In an article published by the *Roanoke Times* on this date, Dan Smith reported on the last meeting between Wolverines and Highlanders and showcased running backs Ned Tarpley of Lewis and Duane Farris of Glenvar. They were about to meet for the last time as opponents because the following year they would be teammates at the new Salem High School.[371]

Smith wrote that an "air of intensity ha[d] developed for the last 'Championship of the City of Salem.' It ha[d] taken some bazaar forms. Locals [were] claiming that the coach whose team wins the game should be the Salem High coach… There are the usual bets, the boasts, but perhaps surprisingly, little bitterness. There seems to be an acceptance of the concept of the new school. The name 'Salem High School' which caused such a furor among graduates is a dead issue."[372]

In the June 8, 1977, edition of the *Roanoke Times & World-News*, cowriters Jeff Hopper and Melinda Jordan combined to produce an article that appeared under the headline "Bitterness no longer marks phasing out Glenvar, Lewis."

Here are some of its contents:

> Only the insiders feel the impending loss as both schools prepare to close their doors for the last time as high schools. Beginning next fall, students from Glenvar and Andrew Lewis will attend the new Salem High School, a product of redistricting and economizing by the Roanoke County School Board… Students at both schools regret the way things turned out.[373]

At least two students and one teacher weighed in on the subject.

"It's sad to see the new high school come if Glenvar has to end," said Glenvar sophomore John Leftwich.[374]

"We were bitter [at the school board] for a long time," said Bobby Brugh, the senior class president at Andrew Lewis. "But not anymore. We just hate to see a great school come to an end."[375]

The writers then opined: "Bitterness was a problem in late 1975 and early 1976 when faculty, students and parents from both schools fought the county board to save their schools."[376]

Melinda Sayres, an English teacher at Andrew Lewis and who was involved with SALT, was quoted as saying, "If bitterness is still here, it isn't spoken of anymore. This year we've had the double job of finishing up and getting ready for next year at the new high school. There isn't much time for bitterness, and we don't talk about it anymore."[377]

That was good news, but a different issue came to light. This one pertained to the Salem Sports Foundation (SSF) and its all-male membership policy.

In the June 24, 1977, edition of the same publication, the reporter Fran Coombs wrote that Salem might lose its annual football camp if the Salem Sports Foundation insisted on its all-male membership.

Leading the legal charge was the attorney for the Roanoke-County-Salem school system, Edward A. Natt, who reportedly was about to tell school and foundation officials that dealings with a discriminatory organization could cost the schools their federal financing. His ruling would be based on federal Title IX regulations prohibiting discrimination on the basis of one's sex.[378]

Wisely, school and foundation members declined to comment for the most part while the matter was pending, but one foundation member raised an important question: "When you give a gift [a reference to businesses sponsors who supported the foundation], why do you have to go through all this grief and agony?"[379]

Coombs continued to track the developments and authored an article that appeared in the June 28, 1977, edition under the headline "Football camp ruled OK."

Natt met with school and foundation officials and, upon further review, changed his opinion about the interpretation of Title IX and how it applied in this case.[380]

"The key is that the Salem Sports Foundation does not receive the benefits of the funding from the school board. I don't think it's a violation."[381]

Foundation members refrained from commenting about the ruling and, as Natt reported, had not attempted to put any pressure on him for a ruling in their favor.[382]

He realized his earlier interpretation of the law was wrong. Since the federal funds do not benefit the foundation, the organization is not required to meet the Title IX guidelines.[383]

How did this feeling of exclusion come about?

This same article indicated that controversy arose about the exclusion of women when the Salem group invited male members of the Glenvar High School boosters club to join. This club had women members, a number of whom were upset over being left out of the foundation. The foundation had recently voted against allowing women to join.[384]

* * *

Meanwhile, the plan to open the new high school remained right on schedule.

Salem High School principal Bayes Wilson reported that the new school would benefit the entire Salem community by having only one school. Students living in Salem and in the county near Salem were soon to become united as Spartans. Incidentally, the student committees came up with that nickname and the school colors the previous year.[385]

Already, there were indications that the combination of Wolverines and Highlanders into Spartans would prove successful. Wilson said the Salem cheerleaders, the best of Lewis and Glenvar, already had won first place in a cheerleaders' workshop this summer. Further, parents had formed the Salem Band Guild, a booster club.[386]

The new high school was scheduled to open on August 29, 1977. And it did just that.[387]

By ten thirty that morning, 1,418 students had enrolled with 12 more waiting in the guidance office to go through the necessary placement process and paperwork. The school expected to have as many as 1,550 students, with many expected to enroll after Labor Day.[388]

Earlier in the morning, shortly before nine, the last school bus pulled on to the school grounds, followed by a dump truck full of gravel. It was the beginning of school as usual, with a few last-minute touches necessary for the building itself.[389]

Pending any future divisive moments, it seemed safe to assert that former Highlanders and Wolverines were now one tribe of Salemites, sporting the maroon and silver and rallying under the nickname Spartans.

Together, they will be able to relate to the "Salem Fight Song" (whether they sang it or not) and take pride in the "Salem born and Salem bred" concept, which helped define the deep civic pride among Salemites.

* * *

Author's note: I began seeing the Wolverines play when I was seven years old, or in 1964. I remember quite well the Salem Fight Song, and several of my family members were alumni of Andrew Lewis, including a paternal uncle who had been a star running back during the early 1950s.

I attended Glenvar for two years before transferring to Fork Union Military Academy, where I graduated in 1976.

Twelve years later, in 1988, I relocated to central Virginia, where I have lived ever since.

As of the typing of this manuscript, I had literally lived half my life outside Salem, yet I still feel the civic pride associated with being from Salem, and I try to see the Spartans play each year during the playoffs.

Understandably, some people outside Salem simply don't get that Salem pride and mind-set.

In fact, Steve Peacock—a personal friend and the person who has partnered with me broadcasting Culpeper football games since 1998 and Eastern View High since 2008—was perplexed enough about the whole Salem thing that he said a few years ago, "I don't know why you like Salem [High School's football team]. You didn't go to school there."

Steve, the below information will help explain.

In the September 1, 1978, edition of the *Roanoke Times & World-News*, columnist Mike Ives reported on this very subject. He interviewed Lyle DeWilde, a lifelong Salem resident who had recently vacated a "palatial Salem mansion in which he [had] existed the past two years." But no matter the change in residence, DeWilde was not about to change his personal habits or his city of residence.

Ives wrote: "Lyle's problem is that he is 'Salem born and Salem bred'…and he cannot bear the thought of living anywhere else. All the DeWildes are that way. They would go to the poor house before they would move across the line into Roanoke."[390]

Ives asked him, "What's the difference between Salem and its Roanoke neighbor?"[391]

DeWilde said, "The difference is that Salem is more than a city, more than a geographic area. Salem is a state of mind."[392]

Ives wrote:

> Indeed, despite its proximity to the rest of the world, Salem has always existed as a separate state, a sort of no man's land where strangers did not venture without a passport.
>
> Salem's society and politics have always been a source of wonderment to those who did not belong…the seat of Salem's government is in the back of an appliance store. There is a cafeteria in that back room, but there is no sign on the street to tell passersby it is there. If you're not from Salem, you simply don't go there.

Later in this article, Ives quoted DeWilde with saying this: "Sports are the backbone of the city. The presidential election pales in significance next to Salem High School football."

Ives, who included his customary sardonic wit, wrote:

> Lyle describes Salem as a wellspring of democracy because you can see judges and town drunks drinking elbow to elbow at certain watering holes.
>
> "Salem people are much like the Irish," said DeWilde. "They have a fine appreciated for John Barleycorn."[393]

He apparently told Ives that the democracy extends only to Salem residents and said, "When you talk to outsiders, you automatically assume an air of condescension. If you've ever noticed, you seldom see Salem people by themselves. You see clumps of people all over town, but few loners."[394]

Then Ives continued:

> Most people who are born in Salem die in Salem. That is the nature of the place. Generation after generation has grown up and passed on within the confines of Salem.
>
> Occasionally, a native Salemite will venture out into the cold world beyond the city limits, but that matters not, because they remain Salemites until the end. They are proud to be from Salem, and they will not fight unless someone wrongly accuses them of being from ROANOKE, for God's sake.[395]

Steve, any questions?

Chapter 5

KUCER NAMED KING OF THE SPARTANS

Tom Kucer, Salem's first head coach

History teaches us that the famous Spartan army was normally led in battle by two kings, but in later times just by one.[23]

---

[23] As reported by Wikipedia.

With the Spartans of Salem now assembling as former Wolverines and Highlanders, who would be chosen "king" to lead them on the gridiron?

The answer appeared in the January 20, 1977, edition of the *Roanoke World-News*.

Longtime sportswriter and later Metro sports editor Bob McLelland informed the readers that the honor had been bestowed to Tom Kucer, the head coach at Glenvar.[396]

The decision was announced by Mr. Arnold R. Burton, superintendent of Roanoke County Schools, who told McLelland that the decision-making process had been "very difficult" and "one to which I had given much thought and time for the past few months. We had many outstanding candidates from the outside and from within our own system."[397]

Kucer, who came to Glenvar in 1970, had just completed his fifth year as the head coach of the Highlanders and previously had served on the staff as an assistant coach for two years.[398]

A native of Wintersville, Ohio, and a graduate of West Virginia University, Kucer was also a three-year varsity starter for the Mountaineers as an offensive lineman.[399]

He described this new opportunity as one that "you would expect only once in a lifetime."[400]

When thinking about how former Wolverines and Highlanders might gel as one, Kucer said: "I think we will have great cooperation and friendship among the two squads. Most of them know each other already, and I really feel they are looking forward to playing together."[401]

McLelland reported that Salem will compete as a member of the 3A Roanoke Valley District.[402]

Kucer and other school coaches would soon be working with the school's first principal, Mr. Bayes Wilson, who was named last year.[24, 403]

---

[24] Burton previously served as assistant superintendent for business and finance for Roanoke County schools. He was a native of Russell County and had taught at William Byrd High School. He was a graduate of both Virginia Tech and the University of Virginia. He served as president of the Salem Kiwanis Club and

As for Kucer's coaching record at Glenvar, Brian Hoffman, sportswriter with the *Salem Times-Register*, reported in the January 20, 1977, edition of that publication that Kucer was 30–17–3 over those five seasons.

McLelland also reported that Mike Stevens was among the finalists in consideration for the head football job.[404]

What was Stevens's reaction to not getting the job?

In a recent interview for this book, Stevens looked back on the conversation he had had with Dan Smith following the Glenvar game in 1976 about his son, Brian, and the comparison to having a "first-round draft pick."[405]

"I don't know if that had anything to do it with [the decision] at all, but maybe they didn't want a coach whose son was playing quarterback at that time. I don't know why I didn't get it. For me, it was just move on."[406]

"Were you disappointed?"

"Maybe somewhat, but I wasn't interested in coaching as an assistant at Salem. I felt like I was more capable of things than that. Brian would go wherever I was."[407]

For Stevens and son, that meant going to Cave Spring, where the older Stevens served under head coach Charles Hammes, and the younger Stevens soon became the starting quarterback.[408]

"[Hammes] was a very basic coach," said Stevens, "but he was very open-minded. He gave me the responsibility for the offense—no questions asked. I installed the passing game. Brian went over there with us and he was quite successful."[409]

In retrospect, not getting the job at Salem and moving on to Cave Spring paid dividends for both coach and son.

"By the time we went through the first season, we could see that [Brian] was going to be really good. He started as a sophomore ahead of two seniors. He had talent to run and pass.[410]

"The next year, we were 11–0 and reached the regional finals against GW-Danville. Brian had a partial separation to his shoulder

---

had been the chief witness in the annexation trial of 1974. (Source; May 20, 1976, edition of the Salem Times Register, Vol. 123, No. 21, Page 1.)

against Heritage [the week before], so we were kind of limited with his throwing skills.[411]

"Under Coach Hammes, after my first year, his defensive coordinator decided he didn't want to do it anymore, and he turned it over to me. I installed the monster defense. We were back running the program I learned under Eddie Joyce. And we had a good time with it.[412]

"I was over there for about seven years. My last coaching season was 1983. It was all positive over there also. It was like being at Andrew Lewis, so to speak. You'd be surprised what winning does for a response."[413]

And Stevens's recollection of the events brings to mind the meaning behind the expression "When one door closes, another one opens."

Simply put, things worked out quite well for Stevens and his family.

"I last coached at Cave Spring but continued to teach there. I took an early retirement in 1996 at the age of 55."[25, 414]

Now, let's introduce some of the other individuals named to prominent positions at Salem High School whom Kucer would get to know as fellow Spartans, the news of which appeared in this same edition:

> Dale LeRoy Foster, 39, who was the head guidance counselor at Salem Intermediate School, was

---

[25] Stevens is married to Sharon Littreal Stevens, also a graduate of William Fleming. They began dating as freshmen in high school and married in 1960. They both have degrees in biology. They have two sons. Brian was born on July 23, 1961, and Todd on June 4, 1964. Brian is married, has two daughters, and lives outside Miami after retiring as an ATC for the federal government. He graduated from Virginia with a degree in biology. He attended on a full scholarship where he played some under Coach Dick Bestwick. Todd also attended Cave Spring, where he played quarterback and was an All-Region selection. He attended Virginia Tech, where he earned a degree in civil engineering. He is currently employed as a construction engineer for VDOT in the Staunton District. Stevens and his wife currently reside at Smith Mountain Lake. They enjoy traveling and the outdoors. They have hiked in several countries, including Brazil, Ecuador, Australia, New Zealand, China, and Japan and over the continent of Africa. They are both birdwatchers and have seen 2,300 different species.

named as an assistant principal; Dennis Reaser, 36, the band director at Andrew Lewis High School, was named band director; and Robert D. Lipscomb, an assistant principal at Andrew Lewis, and J. Steve Hyer, an assistant principal at Glenvar, were named assistant principals.[415]

And should Coach Kucer have any concerns about the choir, William G. Snyder, 33, who had been the choir director at Andrew Lewis, was named choir director at Salem.[416]

Let's next check Foster's recollections about this juncture in time.

"Tom Kucer became the first head football coach at Salem High School. We were a member of the Roanoke Valley District. The first meeting we had was at a restaurant on Williamson Road in Roanoke. All the principals and athletic directors were there for the seven schools in the District: Cave Spring, Northside, Patrick Henry, William Fleming, Franklin County, Pulaski, and Salem.[417]

"We had to get a schedule for all sports, and we [Salem] had a hard time scheduling football because we were in a middle of a contract year. You contract football for two years, home and away games. We were in the middle of the contract, so we had a hard time getting four other schools to play. We finally got Blacksburg, Covington, Lexington, and Phoebus. We checked all over the state and those were the only ones we could get. All the Roanoke Valley District schools had good facilities. We had the best but all of them were good. All of them had good football stadiums."[418]

* * *

Change had come to Salem.

Not only was there a new high school in town and that the two previous high schools were now junior highs, but the football culture was changing too.

One of the best authorities on the subject was Bob McLelland. Not only had the longtime sportswriter been following football since the 1940s, but he had also been a successful sandlot football coach through the years. Many of the kids he coached later went on to play at Patrick Henry High School in Roanoke. He had firsthand experience coaching the sport, writing about it, and witnessing changes as they came about.

On March 1, 1977, he reported on the latest trend, which he would later find out was here to stay. His article, which appeared under the headline "Winning football—a 'weighty' problem," reported on the rising popularity of having a weight program in the schools to make the athletic programs, especially football, better.[419]

Head coach Otis Timberlake of Lord Botetourt told McLelland, "We would like to have a more complete program. But the majority of our kids play two or more sports. We encourage them to play any sport where they can help."[420]

William Fleming head coach John McGregor was busy improving the school's program and reported that the school had purchased an Olympic weight system.[421]

Several other local coaches weighed in on the progress of their programs, including Salem's Tom Kucer, who had organized a weight program for the athletes at Andrew Lewis and Glenvar. The combined group would work at two locations. Kucer was in charge of one group at the Baptist Home, and Dale Foster was in charge of the other group at Salem Intermediate.[422]

McLelland concluded the article with his assessment of the times.

> There was a time when football players reported for practice in the fall, did the best they could to get in condition, and then played their games. Once the season was over, they would forget about football until next fall.
>
> Those days are gone—at least for the top athletes and teams. Now the winners can be seen keeping busy during the offseason in the various weight rooms.[423]

Chapter 6

THE FIRST TWO BATTLE WAVES

Part 1: 1977

Dale Foster, a guiding force then and now

THE SPARTAN SUCCESSION

Not Oakland's Marv Hubbard, but Salem's Duane Farris.

Salem's Charlie Gunter aptly wore jersey no. 1

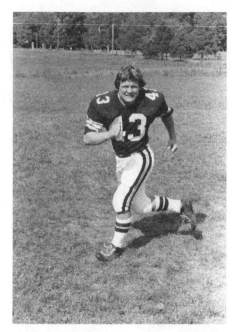

Salem's tough and talented Chris Blomberg

Early indications of a Spartan rising appeared in the August 9, 1977, edition of the *Roanoke Times & World-News* when McLelland reported that 650 Roanoke Metro scholastic football players would soon be reporting to the official opening of practice.[424]

Among those eleven Metro teams, the Spartans were expected to have the largest turnout with 87 varsity and junior varsity candidates. Kucer reported that the newly formed Spartans had 36 lettermen from the combined teams of Andrew Lewis and Glenvar.[425]

Four of the eleven teams were scheduled to leave this week for special camps. Those 4 included Salem, Northside, William Byrd, and Lord Botetourt. The Spartans would train at Camp Alta Mons on August 14–26.[426]

And truly the times had changed.

McLelland reported that the coaches expressed their concerns with the hot weather, and many were planning their afternoon practices day by day according to the weather reports.[427]

As for fluids, which had been withheld in the past, recent reports by pediatricians warned of the dangers of withholding those and that water and salt should always be available to the players. By withholding water and salt, a player can become dehydrated, and that can bring on heat prostration or, even worse, heat stroke.[428]

Two weeks later, McLelland reported on the progress of the camps.

Each of the four coaches responded with "togetherness" when asked what was the advantage of a preseason camp. McLelland included these quotes from Kucer: "This is my first experience with a pre-season camp around here. But it's been great. The kids get to know each other much better from both a football and personal standpoint. I know it's made us into one unit. There's no more Glenvar High or Andrew Lewis. We are all looking forward to entering our new school."[429]

His biggest concern was developing the offensive line. "We just aren't coming around like we had hoped. Our defense has been impressive. We looked good in our first scrimmage."[430]

Among the most impressive players were end Chris Graham, linebacker Price Mutter, and back Mike Pickle. On offense, Brian Hooker and Glenn Dutton were battling for the job at quarterback, and Duane Farris had been the most impressive runner.[431]

The injury report listed only James Alexander, a halfback who had suffered a broken leg as out for the season.[432]

Six days following this report, Salem High School officially opened on August 29, 1977. Soon, the Spartans—who were now the combination of former Wolverines and Highlanders—would debut on the football field in this inaugural season.

Where would the Spartans play their home games?

Like the Wolverines before them, the Spartans would play at Municipal Field, which was also a baseball field where the local minor league team played. During football season, the lines were drawn for the gridiron.

Because it was a baseball field, a portion of the playing field was dirt.

In *The Team the Titans Remember*, former Wolverines explained in great detail the nuances of the field and how its geometrics were used to their advantage. Opposing teams disliked playing there, especially E. C. Glass. The Lewis players often referred to their home field as the Snake Pit, where it was difficult for opponents to win.

Beginning in 1977, the Snake Pit became the friendly environs to the Spartans and would remain so for nearly a decade. After that, the Spartans would play in one of the most impressive stadiums in all of Virginia.

* * *

Less than a month before the start of the 1977 football season, an ever-faithful Brian Hoffman reported that Bill Britts of Andrew Lewis and Chris Blomberg of Glenvar were named Athletes of the Year in Salem.[433]

And the day before this season officially kicked off, Hoffman reported on Kucer's assistants.

They included Bill Winter (a graduate of Marshall University), Danny Wheeling (Andrew Lewis High and Guilford College), John Finnerty (West Virginia University), Tom Roth (Catawba College) and last but not least, Dale Foster (Bridgewater College).[434]

Game 1 (September 2): Salem 35, Lexington 0

The game was as lopsided as the score indicates, and every Spartan played in the debut of the Spartan football team in its romp over the Scarlet Hurricane.[435]

The Salem defense limited Lexington to 1 first down and just 25 yards of total offense.[436]

Salem had no problem showcasing its offensive power, even with running back Duane Farris sidelined with an ankle sprain. He watched his teammates grind out 339 rushing yards behind the combined efforts of running backs Ned Tarpley, Kevin Collie, and Barry Rhodes and quarterback Brian Hooker.[437]

Tarpley became the answer to a trivia question. Who was the first Salem Spartan to score a touchdown? He did so on a 2-yard run.[438]

Hooker ran for a 4-yard TD and threw a 27-yard touchdown pass to Tarpley. Rhodes scored 2 touchdowns in the second half, and Tommy Mountcastle and Zach Towler took turns kicking the extra points. Defensively, Brian Horne recorded 2 interceptions for the Spartans.[439]

Following Salem's easy romp over Lexington and just before the Spartans' next battle against the Knights of Cave Spring in the first Roanoke Valley District game of the season, McLelland wrote of the early Spartan success in the September 8, 1977, edition of the *Roanoke Times & World-News*.

He interviewed Salem player Mike Pickle and Salem head Coach Tom Kucer.

Pickle, a senior safety and slot back, had started for two seasons at Glenvar and spoke proudly of the new unity. "I know we at Glenvar were uncertain as to how it would go. I know they felt the same way at Lewis. But things couldn't be better."[440]

"I guess it started last spring when we began our weight program together. It grew over the summer, and then our two-week camp put it all together. We are all real close. Heck, you can't tell a Glenvar player from a Lewis player. We are all Salem now."[441]

Pickle was one of three tri-captains on this inaugural Spartan team. The other two were Brian Hooker and Jon Pace.[442]

Of Pickle, Kucer said, "He loves to hit and is one of the best defensive backs around. He is experienced and is proving a good leader just as are our other two captains."[443]

Pace plays the monster on defense, and Hooker is the quarterback. Pickle spoke highly of his fellow captains and further noted the contributions of Steve Turner, Duane Farris, and Ralph Peck.[444]

Game 2 (September 9): Cave Spring 17, Salem 14

Knights' quarterback Brian Stevens guided the home team to victory. He completed 10 of 15 passes for 120-plus yards, mainly to Allan Woodrum and Bob Garrett, and he tossed 2 touchdown passes.[445]

Stevens opened the scoring with a 39-yard pass to Jay Peery and soon added a 73-yard punt return for a score. During the return, Stevens shed several tacklers and left Salem coach Tom Kucer witnessing history.[446]

Kucer reported that this was the first return for touchdown against any team he had ever coached.[447]

His Spartans punted 5 times and fumbled twice during their first 7 possessions.[448]

During the first half, Hooker scored on a 5-yard run, which was sparked by Kevin Collier's 23-yard gallop during the drive. Mountcastle kicked the point after, and Salem trailed 14–7.[449]

In the third quarter, Salem engineered an 80-yard scoring drive capped by a 36-yard halfback pass from Farris to a wide-open Charlie Gunter.[450]

Cave Spring responded with a drive to the Salem 9, where the Spartan defense stiffened, and the Knights went for a field goal. Greg Caldwell booted the game winning kick from 26 yards.[451]

Said Kucer, "We had eight third-down situations and didn't convert a single one…and the other [key] was an excessive number of penalties and fumbles."[452]

With the loss, Salem (at 1–1) next faced another 1–1 team, the Colonels of William Fleming. The two were scheduled to meet in Roanoke's historic Victory Stadium. Often referred to simply as Fleming, the Roanoke City school had been one of Andrew Lewis's longest and toughest rivals. The games between Fleming and Lewis were always tough.

During what Dale Foster referred to as "the best years of Joyce" (1962 through 1971), the Colonels handed the Wolverines their worst defeat during that time period, a 28–0 shutout in 1970. And who better to weigh in on the rivalry and what to expect next than Foster?

No one.

"Dale Foster has been around. He was a top assistant and defensive leader during the heydays of Andrew Lewis football. He knows the Roanoke Metro area, and when he says a tough game is ahead, a tough game is ahead," wrote Brian Hoffman of the Salem Times-Register.[453]

Foster was now an assistant and defensive coordinator at Salem and was concerned that the Spartans might not be taking Fleming too seriously.[454]

"Even when we had those championship teams at Lewis, Fleming gave us trouble. There is just something about football that makes one team especially tough for another. Fleming is that way. Besides, this year they are much improved and can do more things. They will be sky high. They may never land at the stadium. I know it's going to be a long night, and we will have to be at our best. I just hope our kids realize it."[455]

Game 3 (September 16): Salem 17, William Fleming 14

Salem's Chris Graham stopped William Fleming running back Archie Mayo to save the victory.[456]

"We were in our blitz defense on that play, and it worked," said Kucer.[457]

Mayo had a good night in tallying 148 rushing yards. He and his fellow Colonels trailed 17–14 late in the game and put together their final drive beginning at their own 22.[458]

Behind Mayo, the Colonels moved to the Spartans 22 and eventually faced third and one.[459]

To no one's surprise, Mayo got the call.

"He'd been carrying the ball all night, so there wasn't any reason why he wouldn't carry it again," said Kucer.[460]

But this time, Graham shot through the line and hit Mayo in the backfield for a 5-yard loss.[461]

On fourth and six, Mayo got one more try and, with second effort, bulled his way just short of a first down. The Spartans then took over on downs and promptly killed the clock.[462]

"We didn't play well at all," said Kucer. "The defense had poor technique, poor tackling, and poor execution. You can bet we'll be working on fundamentals this week in practice."[463]

The Colonels opened the scoring with an 8-yard run by Charles Cheatwoodssss, who then followed with the kick for the point after.[464]

The Spartans responded with an 80-yard scoring drive capped by a Farris 5-yard run. The kick by Mountcastle was no good, and the Spartans trailed 7–6. Cheatwood returned the ensuing kickoff 80 yards and stopped short of the goal line by Barry Rhodes. On third and goal, Mayo scored, the point after was good, and Fleming led 14–6 at the half.[465]

In the third quarter, Hooker connected with Farris for a 20-yard touchdown, and then Farris completed the 2-point conversion to tie the game at 14–14.[466]

Mountcastle found true redemption. His 24-yard field goal later in the game proved the game winner.[467]

When the "Stars of Week" were announced, Salem's Duane Farris was named the Offensive Player of the Week. The junior tailback scored 2 touchdowns, ran for a 2-point conversion, and provided clutch yardage in the big win over Fleming.[468]

The Defensive Player of the Week honor went to Patrick Henry linebacker Darryl Jones, who had become a tackling machine. In the team's win over Franklin County, Jones had 11 individual tackles, and the previous week against GW-Danville, he recorded 14.[469]

As fate would have it, Jones and Farris were about to meet; Salem was preparing to welcome Patrick Henry to Municipal Field.

Game 4 (September 23): Salem 3, Patrick Henry 3

Before an estimated crowd of 7,500, the Spartans and Patriots settled for a 3–3 tie.[470]

"We finally played about the way we should play," said Kucer. "We had our opportunities to win, and we played well enough to win. It was a good game."[471]

Salem drove deep into PH territory in the fourth quarter but came up empty after both a third down pass and a long field goal attempt failed.[472]

Another critical moment came earlier in the game.

During the first quarter, the Spartans faced a fourth and nine at the Patriots 21. Kucer recognized it was a crucial situation, so he called a timeout. Should he go for the first down or ask Mountcastle to try a 38-yard field goal? He opted for the former.[473]

"They [PH] were overshifting to our strong side, and no one was in the flat to cover the back out of the backfield."[474]

So the Spartans went for it and looked to Tarpley as the backed out of the backfield. Hooker got the pass to him, but Tarpley couldn't hang on.[475]

Ugh.

Salem turned the ball over on downs, and PH put together a drive but stalled when Chris Blomberg intercepted a Patriot pass. The Spartans took over and drove to the Patriots 20, and on fourth down, Mountcastle attempted a go-ahead and 37-yard field goal, but the ball sailed wide to the right.[476]

The limited scoring came during the teams' opening possessions. Mountcastle delivered first when his 28-yard kick was good. Patrick Henry's Buddy Mitchell booted a 33-yard field goal for his team.[477]

The statistics were as close as the scoring. Salem had 185 yards in total offense, and PH had 187. Both teams punted 5 times for an identical average of 37.2 yards per punt.[478]

Salem's James "Bobo" Dame had a game best 70 receiving yards.[479]

* * *

At this point in the research phase for this manuscript, this author drifted back in time reminded of what the movie *Remember the Titans* was chiefly about: overcoming an obvious racial divide to perform as one team.

The setting was Alexandria, Virginia, and the movie portrayed the coming together of black and white students after the three public schools in that city were combined into one massive school known as T. C. Williams.

In contrast, growing up in Salem meant very few instances of racial turmoil. In nearby Roanoke City, that was not the case. Many of us had heard of the racial problems, especially at William Fleming High School, where its problems among the races had been made public.

In October of 1977, fighting between black and white students had forced school officials to close the school. At least 1 student had been arrested, and police anticipated that more arrests would follow.[480]

School Principal James Wood decided to call in the buses early to send students home. Fighting broke out again between students after the buses arrived to take them home.[481]

An unidentified reporter asked Wood if the fighting had been racially motivated. Without hesitation, he replied, "Of course, it is racial." Here's your sign.*, [482]

Four days later, the news reported that classes at the school had resumed. The school had just reopened after "a three-day cooling off period." Nine students had been suspended for their parts in the fighting, and 3 persons, including 2 girls, had been arrested and charged. Seven persons had been treated at a local hospital for their injuries.[483]

The scheduled football game between Fleming and Pulaski County had been postponed from Friday night to Saturday morning. Only a few hundred people showed up for the game at Victory Stadium, where Fleming lost, 14–7. The homecoming activities, including a dance Saturday night, had been postponed indefinitely.[484]

Now, back to Salem's gridiron news.

Game 5 (September 30): Covington 23, Salem 0

This one was originally scheduled to be played at Glenvar High, but due to space limitations, the venue was switched to Salem's Municipal Field after school principal Bayes Wilson reported that he expected as many as 6,000 spectators. True to expectation, over 6,000 in attendance watched the Cougars steal the show.[485]

In the end, Kucer summed it up succinctly: "We were out-blocked, out-tackled, out-hustled, out-hit, and out-coached."[486]

Ouch.

Covington's Ronnie Shue and Chipper Mack did most of the damage, and their teammates enjoyed balanced scoring. Donnell Ross scored on a 5-yard run that not only capped a 63-yard drive but also consumed 7 minutes of the game clock.[487]

Gary White hauled in a 13-yard touchdown pass from Ross in his halfback position, and Shue exploded for a 47-yard TD run. Place kicker Wayne Payton kicked a 24-yard field goal.[488]

The Salem offense was "dormant" in this one, and Kucer said, "If we're not ready to play this week, it will be more of the same."[489]

Evidently, the Cougars stayed ready this season. After this win, Covington remained unbeaten at 5–0.

Game 6 (October 7): Salem 23, Blacksburg 6

Consider this takeaway: lessons learned. And the 17-point margin of victory left Kucer elated. "I'm pretty happy about the whole game. The kids did a great job."[490]

Rumor had it that Brian Hooker might be replaced before the game with Glenn Dutton. Instead, Hooker "turned the beat around." The Spartans worked a first-quarter drive capped by a 15-yard run by Hooker, and Mountcastle booted the point after.[491]

The biggest play of the drive came on fourth down when Hooker connected with Bobo Dame, who bulled his for a first down.[492]

Two plays later, it was Hooker's turn, and he scored off the option.[493]

"[Hooker] did a good job throwing the ball, and he ran well at times," said Kucer. "I think everybody had something to prove."[494]

Indeed, Hooker had his best game of the season and dismissed the rumor as Dutton took just one snap from center. Dutton, however, shined from his defensive back position and anchored a secondary that held Blacksburg quarterback Joe White to just 12 completions in 26 attempts and 131 yards and 5 interceptions, of which

Dutton had 3. Teammates Mike Pickle and Jimmy Fisher had 1 theft apiece.[495]

Fisher played the monster position in place of Jon Pace, who was out with an illness. Another pivotal change involved Blomberg. Kucer moved the hard-hitting linebacker to nose guard.[496]

"Blomberg did a real good job. He does good when he's down like that [in the nose guard position] because he's quick," said Kucer.[497]

And Blomberg's switch in position wasn't the only chess move for Kucer. Dale Weeks played at linebacker to earn Kucer's praise, as did Price Mutter, who Kucer said was hurt after Wednesday's practice. He did not practice on Thursday "but sucked it up and did a great job."[498]

In addition to Hooker and Dame, the Spartan offense had lifts from Kevin Collier, who ran for 2 touchdowns on 7- and 17-yard runs, and Zach Towler kicked a 26-yard field goal.[499]

The Indians averted a shutout when Joe White connected with Phil Carr for a 14-yard scoring strike.[500]

Salem needed a much-improved performance, and the team delivered.

Kucer said, "There was a big difference in the way they played. We moved the ball well all game and had opportunities to punch it across once or twice more. I hope they learned a lesson. We worked hard in practice all week and the kids responded."[501]

At this point in the season, Cave Spring topped the Roanoke Valley District with a district record of 4–0 and an overall mark of 4–2. Pulaski County was next at 2–1, 4–1–1, followed by Northside (2–2, 4–2), Salem (1–1–1, 3–2–1), William Fleming (1–2, 2–4), Patrick Henry (1–2–1, 1–4–1), and Franklin County, winless at 0–4 and 0–6.[502]

Up next, the Spartans traveled to Rocky Mount to take on Franklin County for the Eagles' homecoming game.

Game 7 (October 14): Salem 21, Franklin County 6

After a scoreless first half, the Spartans spoiled the Eagles' homecoming when they scored 3 second-half touchdowns.[503]

The first score came during Salem's opening drive in the third quarter. The 62-yard drive was capped by Brian Hooker's 22-yard run for TD. He finished the game with 2 touchdowns and 113 rushing yards, most of which came off the option play.[504]

The second scoring drive also spanned 62 yards. This time, Duane Farris took the honors on a 5-yard TD run. He finished with 110 yards on 21 carries.[505]

The Eagles scored their only touchdown when, during the fourth quarter, Cecil Edwards ran 19 yards into the end zone. The Eagles went for 2, but the try failed.[506]

Moments later, Salem drove 74 yards with Hooker and Farris doing most of the work. Hooker capped this final scoring drive with a 26-yard run. Tommy Mountcastle booted 3 extra points.[507]

The Spartans improved to 2–1–1 in the district and to 4–2–1 on the season, while the Eagles remained winless at 0–7.

Up next for Salem was the homecoming game against the Phoebus Phantoms of Hampton, Virginia.

Brian Hoffman previewed the game, which included an interview with Dale Foster, athletic director and assistant football coach at Salem.

"Our schedule will get tougher every year," said Foster. "We'll go outside the area if we have to, but, win or lose, I want to do it against a good school. I think that's what people want."[508]

Recall that Foster was quite familiar with the concept of travel. As an assistant under Coach Eddie Joyce, the Wolverines did not hesitate to travel, which was necessary to play some top-caliber teams. This concept is well documented in *The Team the Titans Remember*.

Before revealing the results of the Salem homecoming, the "Stars of Week" went to Salem's Chris Blomberg for defense and to Northside's Mike Webb for offense.[509]

Blomberg, a senior, had recently switched playing positions. Coach Kucer had moved him from linebacker to middle guard. The moved helped the Spartan cause and resulted in wins over Blacksburg and Franklin County. Against the latter team, Blomberg had two tackles for losses, plus six individual tackles and four assists, and he deflected a pass.[510]

Kucer said, "Chris did a good job at linebacker, but he is doing even better at middle guard. He is quick and strong which comes from his wrestling.[26] His play gives us a much-improved defense."[511]

As for Webb, he, too, had made a recent switch in position. Projected as one of the team's linebackers, he impressed his coaches with his offensive skills at the team's preseason camp, and head Coach Jim Hickam decided to move Webb to running back. Webb helped his fellow Vikings get a big win over the Terriers of William Byrd.[512]

Game 8 (October 21): Salem 18, Phoebus 14

"This was an important win," said Kucer. "Even though it wasn't in the district, it gave us points we might need for the playoffs."[513]

The Spartan defense withstood the challenge from a Phantom team reportedly bigger and faster. And Salem punter Ralph Stevenson played a major role. He punted 5 times for an average of 42.0 and pinned the Phantoms deep in their own territory several times.[514]

Indeed, field position belonged to the Spartans.[515]

Salem opened the scoring with a one-yard run by Barry Rhodes. The PAT failed, and a scoreless second quarter sent the two teams to the intermission with the Spartans up 6–0.[516]

Phoebus took the lead in the third when its quarterback, Dwayne Jenkins, jolted the Salem defense on a 69-yard run; then teammate Scott Parker kicked the point after, and the Phantoms led 7–6.[517]

After Salem failed to move the ball on its next possession, Stevenson helped the cause with another punt that pinned the Phantoms back deep.[518]

Unbale to mount an offense on this possession, Phoebus punter Fred Armstrong kicked from his own end zone, and Rhodes fielded the ball at the Salem 36. He broke a couple of tackles, picked up

---

[26] People in the sports community were fully aware of Blomberg's prowess on the wrestling mat. During his sophomore season at Glenvar, he won the 2A state championship in the 138-pound weight class in 1976. Source: personal knowledge and the VHSL record book, Page 165.

some key blocks, and scored his second touchdown of the game to put Salem back in front.[519]

The PAT failed, and Phoebus took over, trailing 12–7.[520]

The Phantoms responded with a 61-yard drive finished off by a 1-yard touchdown run by Bryan Roberts. Parker then kicked the point after, and Phoebus was back on top 14–12.[521]

But Salem dominated the fourth quarter highlighted by a 67-yard scoring drive, which resulted in a 5-yard toss from Hooker to Randy Hodson for what proved the game winner.[522]

Though Phoebus outgained Salem in total yardage, 228–183, Salem had five more first downs and Stevenson's punting proved pivotal.[523]

The Spartans improved to 5–2–1 with two games remaining on their schedule: Pulaski County and Northside.

Game 9 (October 28): Salem 34, Pulaski County 6

This win tightened up matters in the Roanoke Valley District.

Salem improved to 3–1–1 in the district and 6–2–1 overall, but Northside—which defeated Cave Spring—topped the list at 4–1 and 7–2.[524]

Salem's win over Pulaski was particularly impressive considering that the Cougars had only allowed an average of 8.3 points per game coming in. Apparently, this statistic did not impress the Spartans, who scored 5 times and gave up just 1 touchdown.[525]

"The fact is," said Kucer, "we had the ball so much that the defense was hardly ever out there. A good offense is the best defense. That helped us a lot. The defense was always fresh when they went out there."[526]

How good was the offense?

Salem amassed 354 total yards, and Hooker had the bulk of those. He rushed for 153 yards and threw for 63 after completing 4 of 8 passes. He also scored 3 touchdowns (7-, 1-, and 38-yard runs).[527]

Farris scored twice on runs of 1- and 15-yards. Pulaski's lone score came when quarterback Timmy Venable threw a 5-yard pass to Anthony Young.[528]

Salem's dominant win put it in good position to take on the defending district champions the following week with the title on the line.

When the Stars of Week were announced, Salem's Brian Hooker was named the Offensive Player of the Week, and Northside's Greg Neese earned Defensive Player of the Week.[529]

Under Hooker's leadership, the Spartans had won 4 straight games and had improved to 6–2–1 on the season with 1 game remaining and the Roanoke Valley District title on the line against Neese and his fellow Vikings.[530]

Of Hooker, Kucer said, "He has done everything I could ask of a quarterback. He has developed, and the team has developed with him."[531]

Hooker was no longer just the surname of a famous Civil War general.[27] In the future, his name could be the answer to a trivia question, if the question was "Who was the first quarterback for the Salem Spartans?"

Yes, but Not the Hair of my Chinny-Chin, Chin

Incentives come in many forms, and players and coaches sometimes go to great lengths to get the most out of their teams. Bob McLelland reported on this topic in his feature story under the curious headline of "Kucer creates 'hairy' situation for Salem."[532]

Here was the deal: If Salem defeated Northside and won the Roanoke Valley District title, then Kucer would let his players cut the locks from his thick head of black hair. It seemed like a small price

---

[27] For fellow history buffs, this is an obvious reference to General Joseph Hooker of Civil War fame. He rose to the rank of major general and succeeded General Ambrose Burnside as commander of the Union Army of the Potomac. Despite a successful military career, he may be best remembered for his stunning defeat at the Battle of Chancellorsville in May of 1863. Source:www.history.com.

to pay; after all, a district title was coveted, and hair tended to grow back.[533]

This "hairy situation" all started back during football camp when some of the Spartan players shaved their heads, hoping to develop unity and team spirit. They tried to talk their coach into doing the same, but he declined. He did, however, tell them that he would let them shave his head if they won the district title.[534]

Quietly, it seemed like a safe bet for Kucer. Even though he knew the Spartans would be solid, winning the district title was somewhat of a stretch. His locks were safe then. But now, one win away from the championship, he had to imagine himself with a different hairstyle.[535]

The only question was, where the cutting would take place: on the field, in the dressing room, or before a large student assembly?[536]

Tri-captain and wide receiver Jon Pace put it all in perspective: "Cutting his hair will be great, but game is the thing. If we don't win, nothing happens."[537]

Pace pinpointed the loss to Covington as a pivotal turning point in the season. "Losing to them was probably the best thing that could have happened to us. If we had beaten them, we would probably have lost another game and to a district opponent. But after we lost like we did, the players made up their minds to get together. And you can see what we have done."[538]

The Spartans were about to take on a band of Vikings led by ace quarterback Eddie Otey.

"That Otey, he's something else," said Pace. "He's been a star for three years and seems to get better every game. But we have a damn good quarterback ourselves. Brian Hooker won't take a back seat to anyone."[539]

Game 10 (November 5): Northside 14, Salem 13

Due to heavy rain, the district showdown was postponed from Friday to Saturday with rain still in the forecast. Salem gave it a gallant effort but fell just short to Northside, which claimed its second straight Roanoke Valley District title. The Spartans trailed 14–7 in the fourth quarter and had a realistic chance of winning in the end.[540]

How so?

With 5:14 remaining in the game, Hooker led the Spartans and scored on a 1-yard run that made the score 14–13. There was no reason to kick the extra point and force a tie because Salem needed a win to surge past Northside. Everyone on hand knew it and waited for the 2-point try.[541]

The Spartans did their best to fool the Vikings. Place kicker Zack Towler went through his usual steps to kick the extra point, but it was a ruse. Salem tried the "muddle huddle," and it almost worked.[542]

Almost.

Chris Blomberg lined up over the ball, while the rest of the team hustled to the right side of the field, with only Kevin Collie behind Blomberg. Blomberg pitched the ball back to Collie, but it got behind him, and Northside's defenders had time to react.[543]

Brian Hoffman saw it this way: "Had the play been executed properly, Salem would have scored. The Spartans had eight blockers on three Vikings and the right sideline was as open as a Kansas field."[544]

Said Kucer, "We worked on that play all week. If we would have gotten the snap, he would have scored."[545]

Early in the game, Salem scored on a 6-yard run by Hooker and Towler kicked the extra point to make it 7–0. But Northside quarterback Eddie Otey guided the Vikings back. He scored on a 16-yard run to tie the game momentarily before teammate Mike Hudgins tacked on the go-ahead extra point.[546]

After a scoreless second quarter, Northside took the lead in the third when Mike Webb scored on a 1-yard run. Hudgins made it 2 for 2, and the Vikings led 14–7. While Northside repeated as district champions and would move on to the post season, Salem had to call it a season.[547]

"I can sum up the season in just one word," said Kucer. "Fast."[548]

In his first "fast" season, the Kucer-led Spartans finished at 6–3–1.

THE SPARTAN SUCCESSION

Hoffman included the list of Spartan seniors who had just played their last game in a Salem football uniform. He listed them numerically: Jon Pace, Brian Hooker, Glenn Dutton, Mike Pickle, Tim Beckner, Randy Hodson, Jimmy Kirchner, Enos Glaspie, Ned Tarpley, Chris Blomberg, Melvin Nowlin, Keith Campbell, Steve Turner, Price Mutter, Jim Gresham, Ralph Stevenson, Mike Lynch, Sonny Talley, Jim Carroll, Dale Davis, David Duffy, Reid Acree, Ralph Peck, Steve Burton, David Layne, and Vic Brancati.[549]

* * *

Jon Pace was right. That Eddie Otey really was "something else." But so was Pace.

When the 1977 Roanoke Metro football team was announced, Pace and Otey had been chosen as members of the first team offense, and Otey was also named Offensive Player of the Year. Coach of the Year honors went to Salem's Tom Kucer.[550]

Northside won six places on the twenty-four-member first teams. William Byrd and William Fleming won five positions each, while Patrick Henry and Salem each had three and Cave Spring two. In addition to Pace, the Spartans had two first-team defensive players named in Chris Blomberg and Kelly Gladden, both linemen.[551]

Pace and Blomberg were both seniors and Gladden a junior.

Byrd had the only players to win places on both the offensive and defensive first teams. Further, Jan McMillan was a triple winner. He was named in the defensive line, the offensive line, and the kicker on the honor squads.[552]

Teammate Paul Nester was a linebacker and an offensive running back.[553]

Kucer received eight votes from his fellow coaches and members of the *Roanoke Times & World-News* sports staff. Northside's Jim Hickam, who won the honor last year, finished second with two votes. This same article attributed Kucer's hard work and faith in his players as the reasons he was honored. His task was to blend former Wolverines and Highlanders into unified Spartans.[554]

He succeeded. The team rattled off four straight wins after the midpoint in the season to face Northside with the district title on the line.

* * *

Northside next faced Gar-Field in the first round of the playoffs and came up short. The Indians won 7–3 to end the Vikings' run in the post season. In December, the Salem Sports Foundation sponsored the first annual Salem High football banquet at the Salem-Roanoke County Civic Center.

Awards were aplenty.

Brian Hooker received the Most Valuable Player award. Steve Turner was named Top Offensive Lineman. The Offensive Back Award was given to Duane Farris. The Coaches Award was a tie with co-recipients Melvin Nowlin and David Layne. The Defensive Back Award also resulted in a tie with Mike Pickle and Price Mutter named. The Top Defensive Lineman went to Chris Blomberg, and the Most Deserving Substitute went to Brian Horne.[555]

Part 2: 1978

A menace on the field, Salem's hard-hitting
Dale Weeks sporting a mohawk

Salem's Chance Crawford would suffer a huge physical
blow, but would later excel in a life of public service

Might as well cut to the chase. For the Spartans, '78 won't be great.

As a result, Salem would receive little coverage in the *Roanoke Times & World-News*, which focused on the newsworthy events taking place at other schools. For example, Willis White debuted as the new head football coach at Patrick Henry to replace Merrill Gainer who had retired. White reported that this '78 PH squad had more quickness than any Patriot team in years and that it "can score from anywhere on the field."[556]

PH was scheduled to open the season against Fauquier. Salem would open against Blacksburg, last year's Group AA state champions. The Spartans were the only team to beat the Indians last year.[28][557]

As for these '78 Spartans, Brian Hoffman wrote a comprehensive preview of the team and featured some of its players. He began with Charlie Gunter, who had recently been selected by his teammates as this year's captain.[558]

Gunter recognized the responsibilities that come with the honor and how important it is to set a good example for his teammates. He was a projected two-way starter: a flanker on offense and the safety on defense. He would be making the switch this season from corner back to safety. Thankful to be a two-way player, he hinted at his preference for defense.[559]

"I like to hit people," he said. "I think defense is the best part of my game."[560]

Hoffman included a colorful commentary on special team's phenomenon Dale Weeks, who had established himself as a ferocious hitter. The newspaper awarded him the title Spartan Bell last year, which was given to the player the coaches thought as the hardest hitter on the team or, in other words, the team's chief bell ringer.[561]

---

[28] Growing up in Salem, I always remembered Blacksburg High School as the Indians and only in recent years learned that the school had changed its nickname. In an article written by Preston Williams, a staff writer for the *Washington Post*, about the NCAA's decision in 2005 to ban the display of American Indian images during its postseason tournaments, he noted that several high schools in Virginia had Native American-themed names and that Blacksburg reportedly opted three years ago to switch its nickname from the Indians to the Bruins.

Coach Kucer said, "From the first day of camp, Dale hit everything that moved."[562]

His hitting eventually earned him a starting spot on the defense, and by game ten, "he was a walking terror."[563] He made several vicious hits against Northside and forced a key fumble. As Hoffman wrote, he iced the "Bell" by taking the head off (not literally, of course) of a Viking ballcarrier at the 10-yard line late in the game.[564]

Going into this '78 season, Weeks remained intent upon keeping the trophy. Hoffman noted that Weeks will hit anything that moves—and some things that don't. To enhance his menacing presence, Weeks had just shaved his head into a Mohawk haircut. Hoffman essentially provided Weeks with a Native American name: Chief Ringing Bell.[565]

Author's note: reading the article about Weeks conjured up memories of the playing days of Chicago Bears' free safety Doug Plank, whose career this author followed closely. His ferocious hits became the talk of the NFL, including his hit of Houston Oilers' running back Earl Campbell in 1981. At one time, Plank (Ohio State graduate) was considered the biggest head hunter in the game. He teamed up with strong safety Gary Fencik (Yale), and the duo became known as Chicago's Hit Men. Plank worse jersey no. 46, and the famed "46 defense" the Bears implemented after his career was named in his honor. Fencik wore no. 45 and remained on the team when it won its first, and to date, only Super Bowl in January of 1986 in a lopsided win over New England, 46–10.

Hoffman's season preview and attention to the team and individual players continued. From Gunter to Weeks, he then focused his attention on the Spartan defense, which last season had allowed only 10.3 points per game. Only Patrick Henry had given up fewer points.[566]

This season, the Spartans would have to replace four all-district selections, but many defenders returned, including the team's leading tackler, Kelly Gladden.[567]

Hoffman described Gladden as a "a soft-spoken, hard-hitting tackle who was first team all-Roanoke Valley District as a junior."[568]

Kucer described Gladden as "the key man in the line."[569]

Kirk Hoback would join Gladden at tackle, while Chris Graham would move to linebacker. The ends included David Light or Brian Horne and David Duffy. Bruce Allen was the projected starter at nose guard.[570]

Other players competing for time on the line included Jeff Lawrence, Allen Harrison, and Darryl Ward. Graham will team up with Weeks as the linebackers.[571]

Jimmy Fisher will be the team's "monster" in the monster defensive set and the unit's signal caller. Smaller in stature than his teammates, Fisher, at 5'6", was up for the position. He enjoyed this type of defensive set and attributed its effectiveness to this: "I think it's because it changes with other team's formations. Other defenses don't do that."[572]

Fisher got his first start at the position in last year's game against Blacksburg in place of Jon Pace, who was out of the lineup due to an illness. Fisher made a diving interception in the game won by Salem, 23–6. He had two more interceptions during the season. When not playing the monster, Fisher will see some time in the slot on offense.[573]

Game 1 (September 1): Blacksburg 27, Salem 8

In a game plagued by Spartan mistakes and turnovers, coupled with the Indians' ability to control the tempo, Blacksburg defeated Salem at Municipal Field.[574]

Salem trailed 20–0 before Charlie Gunter hauled in a pass from Rusty Garst and ran 57 yards to the Blacksburg 1-yard line. Kevin Collie punched it over from there and next converted the 2-point play to account for the Spartan points.[575]

Kucer said, "Blacksburg has a fine team and they played a good football game. They made fewer mistakes than we did and that was the difference."[576]

Up next, Salem hosted Cave Spring, which opened its season with a win over Robert E. Lee-Staunton, 27–6, but first, a look at the Metro Players of the Week.

Cave Spring quarterback Brian Stevens was named the Offensive Player of the Week. In last week's opening game against R. E. Lee-Staunton, Stevens guided the Knights to a 27–6 win after completing 7 of 14 passes for 92 yards and 2 touchdowns.[577]

The defensive honor went to Randy Rowland of Staunton River High. Even though his team lost to Natural Bridge, 6–0, Rowland had 9 individual tackles, 16 assists, 2 tackles on punts, 2 quarterback sacks, and knocked the ball loose from the runner once.[578]

Game 2 (September 8): Knights 18, Spartans 10

Unable to connect on the long pass, Cave Spring quarterback Brian Stevens went to the dump pass, or short tosses to the tight end, to lead the team to a come-from-behind victory.[579]

Salem built a 10–0 lead, but late in the second, Stevens engineered a 70-yard scoring drive highlighted by a 20-yard touchdown pass to Alan Wright. The missed extra point made it 10–6, which was the score at intermission.[580]

In the third quarter, Stevens went to work running the ball and throwing the dump pass. The Knights soon took the lead, 12–10. Cave Spring added an insurance score when it marched 74 yards, and Stevens connected with Gary Phelps for a 49-yard touchdown to lead 18–10.[581]

Salem had one more opportunity, but Cave Spring's Kirk Martin made an interception—his second of the game. The Knights improved to 2–0, while the Spartans fell to 0–2 but would next face another 0–2 team, the Colonels of William Fleming, in Roanoke's Victory Stadium.[582]

Game 3 (September 15): Spartans 15, Colonels 13

Despite five fumbles, including three lost, Salem edged Fleming to get its first win of the season.[583]

Chance Crawford went the distance as the Spartan quarterback. Rusty Garst, who played the position against Cave Spring, did not suit up for this one due to an illness.[584]

Crawford completed just two of nine passes, but teammate Barry Rhodes rushed for two touchdowns.[585]

Fleming, trailing 15–7, scored late in the game on a nine-yard run by Benjie Collier. The two-point conversion was a must, but it failed, and Salem held on to victory.[586]

Colonel quarterback Roger Ferguson went to the air often, but Spartan defenders, Dave Redding and Jimmy Fisher, both picked him off once each.[587]

Dale Weeks made his presence known all over the field. He led the team in tackles, caused a fumble, and knocked down a pass.[588]

Game 4 (September 22): Patrick Henry 31, Salem 21

Here's how Hoffman saw it: "Salem seemed poised to win until it continued to suffer from a case of dropsies and dropped another game."[589]

Kucer told him, "We've had seventeen turnovers in four games… It's discouraging."[590]

In this one, Salem had four turnovers and PH just one; plus, the Spartans had forty more penalty yards than the Patriots.[591]

Barry Rhodes scored all three Spartan touchdowns and led the team with 95 rushing yards after 19 carries and 2 TDS. His third touchdown came on a 17-yard pass from Chance Crawford.[592]

Next, the Spartans traveled to South Boston to take on the Comets of Halifax County. In an old Wendy's Restaurant commercial that used to ask "Where's the beef?" it could have been found on the Comet line that boasted 2 tackles weighing at least 255 pounds.[593]

Before taking on their beefy opponents, the Metro Players of the Week were once again announced.

Salem's Barry Rhodes earned Offensive Player of the Week even though the Spartans lost to the Patriots. In addition to his rushing yards, Rhodes caught 2 passes for 32 yards. The defensive honor was awarded to Tony Kelly of Roanoke Catholic, which faced a 19-game losing streak when it took on rival North Cross. Kelly helped the Celtics win, 13–10. He made 20 tackles, several of which were touchdown saving when he caught leading Raider rusher John Douthat numerous times after he had broken into the open field.[594]

Game 5 (September 29): Halifax County 6, Salem 0

It could be said that Salem opted out of this one.

"I was very disappointed in our play against the option," said Kucer. "They were tough to stop, but we kept breaking our assignments."[595]

And the Spartans felt the pinch from operating in bad field position throughout the game. Still, they had a golden opportunity in the fourth quarter to score the game's first points when they drove to the Comet one and ultimately faced a fourth down from that spot.[596]

David Light came on to try a field goal, but his kick went wide.[597]

The Comets took over at their own 20 and engineered the game-winning drive that included 15 plays—all but 1 by the run. Elmer Banks and Kenny Word combined on the rushing attack, with Banks scoring the only points of the game on a 1-yard push.[598]

Halifax improved to 4–1 on the season, its only loss to Franklin County, while Salem fell to 1–4.[599]

While the Spartans were having trouble with their battle lines, the Knights of Cave Spring continued to joust their opponents. At the midway mark in the season, the unbeaten Knights (5–0) were off to their best start since 1970 when they were 4–0–1 at the midway point.[600]

Charlie Hammes was the head coach, and he had been around a while, 36 years to be exact.[601]

Around the Metro, Franklin County had the next best record. The Eagles were 4–1 and scheduled to take on the Knights in game 6 of the regular season. Salem (1–4) was set to host Woodbridge (4–1), whose Vikings had lost only to GW-Danville, 10–0, which was Timesland's top-rated team.[602]

Game 6 (October 6): Woodbridge 36, Salem 7

This band of Vikings led 14–7 at the half and scored on its opening drive in the third quarter to seal the deal.[603]

"We were in position. We just didn't make the tackles," said Kucer.[604]

Tony Lilly had a pick six of a Rusty Garst pass, and Steve Hougasion scored on a 5-yard run.[605]

For Salem, Kevin Collie ran it in from three yards out for the team's only touchdown.[606]

Woodbridge's Warren Steede had a game best 100 rushing yards on seven carries, including two TDs.[607]

These Vikings, clad in green and gold, added a safety when a Spartan snap from center went over the head of punter Brian Horne and out of the end zone.[608]

Now at 1–5, the Spartans will look to regroup when they take on the Eagles of Franklin County for the Salem homecoming game.

The Roanoke Valley District standings had Cave Spring atop the heap at 4–0 in the district and 6–0 overall after its defeat of Franklin County, which was second in the standings (3–1, 4–2).[609]

* * *

He did it again—*he* meaning Brian Stevens.

The junior quarterback for Cave Spring turned in another impressive performance in the team's come-from-behind win over Franklin County, 20–17. For his efforts, he was named the Metro's Offensive Player of the Week for the second time this season.[610]

The announcement included this glowing report:

> Brian Stevens is the most celebrated quarterback to play football in the Roanoke Metro area since Eddie Joyce, Jr. was throwing spirals for Andrew Lewis's championship teams of the 1970s.

Franklin County led Cave Spring 17–14 with 1:18 remaining in the game. Stevens engineered a 65-yard, game-winning, drive capped by a three-yard pass to Alan Wright as time expired.[611]

The article indicated that the biggest play of the drive came on a fourth and nine at the Eagle 29 when Stevens dropped back to pass, eluded a strong rush, and then ran 26 yards to the Eagle three. One play later, the game was over.[612]

Defensive honors of the week went to corecipients and teammates Darryl Jones and Jim Bishop of Patrick Henry, which beat Northside 7–0. The two linebackers helped PH keep Northside out of the end zone. Jones had 14 tackles, including 9 solos, and Bishop was in on 3 or 4 key sacks among his 11 tackles.[613]

Game 7 (October 13): Franklin County 24, Salem 0

As the score indicated, the Eagles found their opponent's end zone; the Spartans did not. And the Franklin County defense impressed the chief Spartan.

"Looking back on the game, that has to be one of the best if not *the* best defensive teams we've played all year," said Kucer. "It didn't help that our offense didn't execute well."[614]

On offense, Salem had 3 fumbles, and on defense, the Spartans were burned by David Turner, who caught a 41-yard TD pass from Arthur Tolliver.[615]

Tolliver hurt Salem on special teams when he returned a punt 73 yards for a score.[616]

Robert Edwards scored on a 5-yard run, and Dennis Laury kicked a 43-yard field goal.[617]

With the loss to a district opponent, the Spartans (1–3, 1–6) would next play outside the district when they made the long trek to Hampton to take on the Phantoms of Phoebus.

For the third time this season, Brian Stevens was named the Metro Offensive Player of the Week. He guided Cave Spring (7–0) to a 42–6 romp over E. C. Glass by completing 15 of 23 passes for 240 yards and 5 touchdowns.[618]

Defensive honors for the week were once again co-shared by teammates. This time, Franklin County's Billy Overton and Dennis Laury were named. They helped the Eagles shut out the Spartans, 24–0, and limited the Spartan offensive output to just 96 yards.[619]

Overton was credited with 10 solo tackles and 4 assists; plus he recovered a fumble and forced another. Laury tallied a total of 14 tackles, 8 of which were solo.[620]

Game 8 (October 20): Salem 21, Phoebus 2

It's not just true that the Spartans recorded a much-needed win; they did so over a team whose only loss this season was to the number one rated team in the state, the Crabbers of Hampton, 14–7.[621]

Coming in, the scouting report on the Phantoms listed them as powerful, speedy, and beefy up front. But in this one, Phoebus committed seven turnovers, including two interceptions by Charlie Gunter.[622]

One of Gunter's picks stopped an early Phantom drive, and his other was key as well. Teammates Bobo Dame and Jimmy Fisher also had picks. On offense, the Spartans got touchdowns from the Collies—Kevin on a two-yard run and David on a three. Abraham Awad kicked the points after.[623]

Gunter also scored when he hauled in a 12-yard pass from Rusty Garst.[624]

The Phantoms avoided a shutout thanks only to another bad snap to Spartan punter Brian Horne. The ball went past him and out of the end zone for a safety.[625]

Salem traveled to Hampton under some duress.

Hoffman noted that Kucer had been "assaulted by a letter in [the] paper a few weeks back and that half the backfield [was] sick…"[626]

Meanwhile, here's an update on the district standings: Cave Spring led the pack unbeaten at 6–0 and 8–0, followed by Franklin

County (4–1, 6–2), and Northside (2–2, 4–4) rounded out the top three.[627]

The league-leading Knights also led in points scored with 201.[628]

Defensively, the Eagles had given up the fewest with 46, and the Knights were second in this department, having yielded 52 points.[629]

In fact, Cave Spring was in position to claim its first Roanoke Valley District football championship if it defeated Northside.[630]

The Knights likely factored into postseason play even if they lost to the Vikings.

There was one caveat; a Cave Spring loss to Northside, coupled with a Franklin County win over William Fleming, would mean that Cave Spring and Franklin County would become co-champions.[631]

To date this season, Brian Stevens had completed 75 of 128 passes for 1,125 yards and 16 touchdowns. He also had rushed for 165 yards.[632]

Teammate and tailback Alan Wright led the league in both rushing and scoring.[633]

Northside head coach Jim Hickam was asked to compare his previous 2 title-winning squads to this year's Cave Spring team.

Hickam said, "They live by the pass, we lived by the run. Both teams have played outstanding defense."[634]

And both teams played 7 or 8 players both ways.[635]

For Salem, only 2 games remained to be played, the first away to Pulaski County.

Game 9 (October 27): Cougars 15, Spartans 6

They may have seemed like domesticated wildcats prior to this one; the Cougars had the dubious distinction of giving up the most points (181) of any Roanoke Valley District team this season.

But in this one, they found their claws and held the Spartans to just 6 points.

They did so by applying regular pressure to Salem quarterbacks Chance Crawford and Rusty Garst. The statistics were proof positive; the 2 combined for just 3 of 14 passes and 3 interceptions.[636]

Salem also had 4 fumbles.[637]

Pulaski's offense proved adequate enough. In the game, quarterback Randy Olverson rushed for forty yards, mainly off the option and which included 1 touchdown. Running backs Jeff Harvey tallied 79 yards, and Joe Hodge ran for a 1-yard score.[638]

Olverson also used his foot in this one. He kicked a 30-yard field goal.[639]

But the game certainly wasn't out of reach; the Cougars led at the half by only 9–0.[640]

How did Kucer see it?

"We just wasted a whole half of football. We couldn't put it together. We've had several games where we've only played one half and we haven't won any of them yet."[641]

Salem's lone score came on its first possession of the third quarter behind the running of Kevin Collie, who had a team best 97 rushing yards.[642]

Up next for Salem was the regular-season finale against Northside, which had just lost to Cave Spring.

Game 10 (November 3): Vikings Clad in Green and White 33, Spartans 0

The onslaught started early, and by halftime, the marauders from north Roanoke led 26–0.[643]

Rick Beard and Mike Turner each scored two touchdowns in the first half, and Mark Wingfield added one in the second.[644]

Do you think Kucer felt disappointed with this loss and the season in general?

That would be a resounding yes.

"It's been a disappointing year… We've worked just as hard this year as in the past. It's frustrating to yourself and to the kids when you don't win. But I assure you it wasn't from lack of effort."[645]

Twenty seniors had just played their last game as Spartans.

Meanwhile, the Knights who hailed from southwest Roanoke had just wrapped up a perfect regular season when they defeated the Bulldogs of Martinsville, 26–0.[646]

The Eagles of Franklin County crashed in their finale when they lost to William Fleming and finished at 6–2 and in second place behind the Knights.[647]

Northside and Patrick Henry tied for third with 5–5 records, followed by Pulaski County, Fleming, and Salem.[648]

Cave Spring would move on to the 3A playoffs and face first-round opponent Heritage.[649]

The All-Metro Football Team was announced in the November, 21, 1978, edition of the *Roanoke Times & World-News*.

Of the 24 players selected, only two Spartans were named to a first team.[650]

Lineman Kelly Gladden and kicker Charlie Gunter made the first team defense.[651]

In a later edition of this same publication, Gunter was listed as All-Northwest Region and honorable mention Group AAA all-state.[652]

Back to the All-Metro selections, Cave Spring had the most first-team selections with eight, including the Offensive Player of the Year, Brian Stevens.[653]

Franklin County was next with five, followed by Patrick Henry with four, William Fleming with three, and Northside and William Byrd with one each.[654]

The Defensive Player of the Year was co-shared by Greg Neese of Northside and Dwayne Drew of William Fleming.[655]

The top Metro coach recognition went to Red Stickney of Franklin County.[29, 656]

---

[29] Ravis "Red" Stickney died on November 1, 2004, at his home in Virginia Beach at age 68 of a heart attack. He spent 43 years as a coach and totaled over 200 victories in his career that included stints at 10 different high schools. His best team was the 1974 Woodbridge team. He began his coaching career in 1960 after graduating from the University of Alabama. Besides Woodbridge, he coached at Maury, Kempsville, and Franklin County. His final coaching stop was at Greenbrier Christian (Academy of Chesapeake), which he led to the state private school playoffs or three seasons before stepping down in 2002. Last season, in 2003, he served as an assistant at Bishop Sullivan in Virginia Beach (source: www.virginiapreps.com, article written by David Fawcett and published on November 3, 2004).

Stickney was just in his first year as the head coach of the Eagles.

Here are some of the notables about Stickney as reported in this same edition: Stickney, 41, is a native of Miami, Florida, and a graduate of the University of Alabama, where he was an outstanding lineman under Coach Paul "Bear" Bryant.[657]

Stickney took over at Franklin County last winter after the Eagles had plummeted to a 1–9 season the previous fall. He had served for three years as an assistant coach under Jimmy Sharpe at Virginia Tech for three years.[658]

He built a strong kicking game and sound defense to enable Franklin County to improve to 6–4 this season.[659] Of those six wins, five were by shutouts against Patrick Henry, Pulaski County, Salem, Northside, and Martinsville.[660]

This article also reported that this was Stickney's fourteenth season of coaching. His resume also included jobs in Tampa, Florida, Oxen Hill and Potomac, Maryland, and Langley and Woodbridge in Virginia.[661]

His last Woodbridge team was the district, region, and Group AAA state runner-up in 1974.[662]

For this year's recognition, he received eight of the thirteen ballots in a vote of the Metro coaches and six members of the *Roanoke Times & World-News* sports staff.[663]

The only other coaches to receive votes were Charlie Hammes of Cave Spring and Willis White of Patrick Henry. Hammes received three votes, and White earned two. Cave Spring finished the season unbeaten and the champions of the Roanoke Valley District.[664]

Patrick Henry, which finished 3–5–1 a year ago during legendary Merrill Gainer's last season, improved to 0.500 this season (5–5) under White in his debut season.[665]

In addition to the All-Metro selections, the All-Roanoke Valley District picks appeared in the November 23, 1978, of the *Salem Times-Register* with the ever-vigilant Brian Hoffman reporting. He also wrote separate tributes to both Charlie Gunter and Brian Stevens.

Let's begin with Gunter. He is an excellent example of how individual players can still shine for a team that struggled throughout the season. His efforts this season did not go unnoticed by opposing coaches who had recently selected him as the defensive back of the year.⁶⁶⁶

The Spartan safety also donned several other hats. He returned kicks and held for conversions following touchdowns and once this season executed a two-point play. He also played wide receiver when the offense was on the field.⁶⁶⁷

Gunter was the only Spartan selected to the All-Roanoke Valley District first teams. And he was one of three Spartans named to the second teams.⁶⁶⁸

On the offensive second team, Gunter and tackle Ted Viars were selected, and on the defensive second team, tackle Kelly Gladden was named.⁶⁶⁹

The Players of the Year awards went to Brian Stevens as the offensive back and to Mike Barber, offensive lineman, both from Cave Spring.⁶⁷⁰

In addition to Gunter being named the defensive back of the year, the other award on defense went to Northside's Greg Neese as the lineman of the year.⁶⁷¹

Team-wise, Cave Spring garnered the most first-team selections with ten, Franklin County was next with five, followed by William Fleming with three, Patrick Henry and Northside with two each, and Pulaski County with one.⁶⁷²

Now, let's turn to Brian Stevens.

Under the headline "Knight to Remember," Hoffman reported that Cave Spring had just come up short in round two of the playoffs against George Washington of Danville, but Stevens had played well, and people had been watching, including scouts.⁶⁷³

Stevens had just completed his junior season and had impressed many people, including Hoffman. Hoffman decided to ask others what they thought of Stevens, and he turned to local authoritarian Dale Foster for expert analysis.⁶⁷⁴

"I think he could play anywhere, especially if he puts on a little weight," said Foster. "He could go to a really good school."⁶⁷⁵

Hoffman was no stranger to talent himself. After all, a lifelong sports fan, he began watching local athletes in action during his college days at Roanoke College in Salem. Recall, too, that he began working in the sports department of this newspaper in 1974 and has remained there through the present time, some forty-four years later.

Here is Hoffman's skinny on Stevens:

> He can roll left and throw right like no other righthander you'll see in the prep ranks. He's also a deceptive runner who can pick up tough yardage when needed... When the time comes (for Stevens to play in college), it will make things a lot easier for six other coaches in the (seven-team) Roanoke Valley District.[676]

Now that the individual selections had been made, let's consider what happened this season for the Salem football team.

In keeping with the military jargon periodically used in this text, the second Spartan battle wave had officially receded. The Spartans finished the '78 campaign with a record of 2–8.

Could they regroup and form tougher battle lines next season?

If so, it would happen under a different "king."

In the April 3, 1979, edition of the *Roanoke Times & World-News*, Bob McLelland provided the news of Coach Kucer's resignation.

Kucer told him, "It was a tough decision to make, but there comes a time in every man's life when he has to make a decision on what he plans to do for the rest of his life. I have reached that time. I just had to think about what would be the best thing for me and my family.[677]

"I know I will miss coaching, especially the kids. This has been a wonderful part of my life. It was a great experience, and I know I have made many good friends. I wouldn't have taken anything for the experience of teaching and coaching in the Salem area."[678]

Salem High principal Bob Lipscomb told McLelland that he had no successor in mind, "but I know that replacing Coach Kucer will be difficult. He was a great asset not only to our football team but to the entire school and student body. He was a great influence on everyone who came in contact with him. His players loved him, and we think he did a terrific job in everything in which he took part.

We will miss him greatly, but he carries with him our best wishes for success and happiness."[679]

Author's note: Kucer opted—politely and respectfully—to decline an interview with this author. Noting that forty years have passed since he last coached in Salem, much has changed for him personally. While he enjoyed his time coaching and the good times he had, his decision to walk away from coaching was a permanent, no-look-back one.

Chapter 7

CAN THOMPSON RALLY THE SPARTANS?

With Kucer no longer the "king" of the Spartan "army," who would lead them into their next "battles"?

The job was first offered to Dale Foster, and he immediately declined.

He recalled the event during one of our several personal interviews.

"The school superintendent, Mr. [Arnold] Burton, had a deadline that spring for 1979 applications. Ruth Wade called me up again. I was working with 'Weenie' [Barnett, the principal] at Salem Intermediate School. She said, 'Come on over. He wants to talk to you again.' So I went in there. Ruth came in and laid an application on Burton's desk. She looked at him and said, 'Eddie Joyce came by and brought in his application.'

"Mr. Burton's exact words to me were these: 'I would like to hire Coach Joyce, but my Roanoke County School Board will not approve it.' I guessed he had already asked in the past that if Eddie applied would they approve it. He repeated, 'They will not approve it. I would hire him if they would.'"

Make no mistake about it: Foster would have welcomed the reunion with Joyce.

He told this author, "I was thinking it would be nice to work with Coach Joyce again. I was hoping [Burton] would hire him, but he couldn't do it."

During our numerous conversations, Foster has asserted on more than one occasion that the county had plenty of folks who didn't like Andrew Lewis High School, the town (and later the city of) Salem, and Coach Joyce.

Burton, however, was never one of them.

"He liked Salem," said Foster. "He lived in Salem, not far from the Civic Center, in a big brick house. He loved to play cards. He played poker with Jim Taliaferro and B. G. King. He would have hired Coach Joyce. He knew that people in Salem wanted him."

He also knew that plenty of people in Roanoke County did not.

News of Joyce's application and intentions appeared in the April 6, 1979, edition of the *Roanoke Times & World-News*.

Sportswriter Bob Teitlebaum reported that Joyce had applied for the job at Salem and that he planned to apply for other high school coaching jobs as they became open. He quoted Joyce as saying, "When I get my [teaching] certificate back, I'll find a job coaching even if it's not in Salem."

Joyce had quite an entourage of supporters.

In the April 20, 1979, edition of this same source, Steve Haner reported that a campaign to have Joyce named as Salem's coach was growing and that some of Joyce's supporters indicated that more than just sports was at stake.

Petitions were circulating around town, and already three thousand people had signed them in support of Joyce.[680]

Further, two dozen "Hire Eddie Joyce" T-shirts, printed by Howard "Mooch" Semones of Spartan Silk Screen & Sign, sold out immediately. Semones, a member of the 1962 state champion Wolverines, said more would probably be printed.[681]

But one prominent former Lewis player had not signed the petition, nor did he have a T-shirt. Likely he would have signed the petition and donned a T-shirt had he been in the local area.[682]

Instead, Carey Casey (Andrew Lewis class of 1974) expressed his support of hiring Joyce during a telephone interview with Brian Hoffman.

Here's how Hoffman reported the interview: After seeing a copy of the *Salem Times-Register* that reported on the number of petitions and the other displays of support for Joyce, Casey telephoned Hoffman to endorse Joyce for the job. At the time, Casey was a recent graduate of the University of North Carolina (UNC), where he had first played running back and was later switched to wide receiver following a severe knee injury. He told Hoffman that having played football in high school under Joyce was an asset in preparation for college.[683]

He said, "I didn't come across anything in college that I hadn't already seen from Joyce. He put enough into our hearts and into our minds that we could take anything. There was nothing in college I couldn't go through."[684]

Casey compared Joyce to Bill Dooley, who had recruited Casey to UNC.[685]

"He [Joyce] never treated me differently than any other player, but he helped me as a man. He'd sit down and talk to me when I needed help. I remember I almost quit my freshman year. He didn't have to do it, but he did. Not only that, but his record speaks for itself."[686]

When asked if he thought Joyce's time in jail worked against him, Casey indicated that even that experience could be used to help people.[687]

"As much as he helped me out, it just eats my heart out to read some of the things people say. We've all done wrong ourselves."[688]

Casey was about to attend Gordon-Conwell Theological Seminary in Boston, Massachusetts.[689]

Today, Casey is well known throughout the country.

Consider the following biographical information taken from www.amazon.com: Casey is chief executive officer of the Kansas City-based National Center for Fathering, joining the Center in March 2006. Through his work across the country, Casey has earned a reputation as a dynamic communicator, especially on the topic of men being good fathers, and as a compassionate ambassador, especially within the American sports community.

He is also author of the book *Championship Fathering*. On the topic of books, Casey wrote the foreword for the book *The Team the Titans Remember*.

Returning to what he is doing today and to the aforementioned website, in 2009, Carey was asked to serve on the White House Task Force on Fatherhood and Healthy Families. He also serves as a member of the National Fatherhood Leaders Group, which promotes responsible fatherhood policy, research, advocacy, and practice. Casey joined the center after eighteen years in various roles with the Fellowship of Christian Athletes, where most recently he was president of the FCA Foundation, gaining significant leadership experience with a large successful national nonprofit organization.[30]

But it wasn't just about getting Joyce restored as the head coach in Salem.

Haner reported that one city leader, who asked not to be named, warned that if the school board did not hire Joyce, it could "win a battle and lose the war." Haner said the implication was that Salem would pull out of the county school system when the current contract was up in four years.[690]

---

[30] His career has also included serving as chaplain at the 1988 Summer Olympic Games in Seoul, South Korea; chaplain for the Dallas Cowboys under Hall of Fame Coach Tom Landry; and chaplain for the Kansas City Chiefs. He continues to speak on life issues for numerous professional and college sports teams across America. Carey also served for five years as pastor of Lawndale Community Church—the inner-city church in Chicago's west side recognized by the George H. W. Bush Points of Light Foundation. At Lawndale, Carey helped the church empower the community with health care, housing, education, and economic growth. He has also served as a lecturer at the World Congress on Sports, the college football Senior Bowl, the National Association of Basketball Coaches Convention at the Final Four, and the Super Bowl. He has been featured in many local and national publications and broadcasts, including *The New York Times, Atlanta Journal-Constitution, Los Angeles Times, Kansas City Star, Chicago Tribune, Focus on the Family*'s radio broadcast and webcast, *Ebony, Christianity Today, Sharing the Victory, Fox and Friends,* ESPN. com and ESPN's *Quite Frankly with Stephen A. Smith, The Hour of Power* with Dr. Robert Schuller, and *Leadership Magazine* (source: www.amazon.com).

"We've invested $8 million in that high school and the people of Salem really should have a say in who becomes the coach. The majority of people in this city will support his return to the job."[691]

But the prospect of hiring Joyce appeared unlikely, and this was exactly what Jack Chamberlain, education writer with the *Roanoke Times & World-News*, reported in the May 4, 1979, edition.

Even if Burton recommended Joyce for the job, Joyce would not have support of the Roanoke County School Board.[692]

The Salem School Board, which had nothing do with running county schools, endorsed Joyce for the Salem High School job, and so did some prominent citizens of Salem.[693]

They included retired judge James Moyer and Salem mayor James Taliaferro.[694]

And true to Foster's assertion that Salem was behind Joyce and that Roanoke County was not, Chamberlain wrote that Joyce's support was largely confined to Salem and that there was heavy sentiment against hiring him in the county, particularly among teachers, because he was convicted of misusing school money.[695]

Though Burton was not available for comment pertaining to this article, Chamberlain stayed on the trail and, on May 24, reported that Burton had backed Joyce's plea for reinstatement of his teaching certificate.[696]

Burton did so by submitting a letter to the state Department of Education, and sources indicated that Burton had made this promise to Joyce at the time of Joyce's conviction.[697]

In contrast to Foster's assertion that Burton would have agreed to hire Joyce, this same article indicated that Burton did not want to recommend Joyce for the job even though he had been under pressure from Salemites to recommend him.[698]

State Superintendent W. E. Campbell told sources that state regulations require a recommendation from the employing school superintendent when teachers seek to have expiring or expired certificates renewed, but those regulations did not cover restoration of teaching certificates that had been revoked because of a felony conviction.[699]

In the next day's edition, May 25, 1979, Chamberlain next reported that Joyce had appeared before a closed meeting with members of the State Board of Education.

Rorbrecht, who appeared as counsel with Joyce at the meeting, told Chamberlain that the board members had been "very cordial" but noncommittal during the 45-minute meeting.[700]

Chamberlain reported that, regardless of the outcome, Joyce's case will set a precedent for the State Department of Education because, as far as anyone knew, no person convicted of a felony had ever applied to the department to teach, and no former teacher convicted of a felony who had lost certification had ever applied for a new certificate.[701]

Campbell told Chamberlain that Joyce's case represented "a new policy decision."[702]

Conceivably, what Joyce had in his favor was that Campbell indicated that there were no rules for the Joyce situation.

The department had discretionary powers to either reinstate the certificate or to deny it. The decisive language in the rules was likely this: "Such application will not be granted…unless the board is satisfied that reinstatement would be in the best interest of the former certificate holder and the public schools of the commonwealth of Virginia."[703]

Campbell acknowledged receiving Burton's letter on behalf of Joyce, but Chamberlain wrote that Burton had made it clear that the county was not offering Joyce a job. Burton did not want to recommend Joyce for any county teaching job, and even if he did, the county school board would not support the recommendation.[704]

In retrospect, Burton kept his promise to Joyce—that he would support Joyce's application for a new certificate; however, if Chamberlain and his sources were accurate, Burton simply took the path of least resistance to use a popular idiom. In this way, Burton could keep his promise to Joyce and, at the same time, not go against the prevailing opinion of the county school board, which ran the schools.

In Burton's defense, he was well aware of the board's sentiments and his—or anyone else's—endorsement of Joyce would have proven futile. He would have simply been outvoted by those who were not the least interested in Joyce coaching in the public school system within the county.[705]

The following month, specifically on June 28, 1979, the *Roanoke Times & World-News* published an article written by Margie Fisher, who reported that a committee for the State Board of Education recommended that Joyce's request for reinstatement be turned down but that the state board should reconsider the request next spring if Joyce still wanted his coaching certificate.

The recommendation came from the three-member Personnel and Professional Relations Committee after a closed session that lasted nearly two hours. The full board was expected to vote on the matter in a few days.[706]

While Joyce awaited the state board's decision, Burton was still in the hunt for a replacement of Kucer. He once again approached Foster.

"He and a school board member came by my house," recalled Foster. "Mr. Burton said, 'We want you to coach football again.'"

Foster, who served one year as an assistant under Kucer, agreed to coach (as an assistant) for another year but told them that his wife had been out of a job because she had been home with their youngest, Dale Jr., since he was born. However, Dale Jr. was back in school, and Foster told Burton, 'I'll do it if you get her a job.'"[707]

With a small chuckle, Foster said, "The next day, she had a job teaching the fifth grade."[708]

His recollections continued: "Mr. Burton told me that they were going to hire Coach [Wallace] Thompson, who used to coach with us at Andrew Lewis. At that time, he was over at [William] Byrd [High School]. They said he's going to be the head coach and for me to help him."[709]

On May 31, 1979, the official word—almost—was out.

Under the headline "Ex-Joyce aide may get Salem job," Bob McLelland reported on this date that Thompson was expected to be named at today's meeting of the Roanoke County School Board.

Thompson declined to comment when contacted by members of the media but indicated that he first applied for this position two years ago when the school first opened.[710]

Among the candidates were Eddie Joyce, Red Stickney, and Norman Lineburg, who coached at Radford High School. Lineburg reportedly withdrew his name from consideration earlier in the week.[711]

Brian Hoffman also reported on this topic.

Consistent with the reports in the Roanoke newspaper, Hoffman reported that the Roanoke County School Board was expected to name the new Salem High football coach on May 31.[712]

The leading candidates included those already mentioned, but also C. A. Burton and John Chmara. Burton was at Covington High School and Chmara at Bluefield High in West Virginia. Lineburg was not only the head football coach at Radford, but also the track coach and athletic director.[713]

Hoffman reported that Lineburg had previously turned down the job at Salem two years ago. There were hints that the job at Salem was his if he wanted it. And on June 1, 1979, it was official. Thompson had been named the new Spartan king. Both McLelland and Chamberlain wrote articles publishing this news.[714]

As did Hoffman, who even wrote that Lineburg had decided that he wanted to stay in Radford, a decision that clearly opened the pathway for Thompson.[715]

Foster could accept the appointment of Thompson.

The two of them traced their original ties to Bridgewater College. In a telephone interview with Thompson, he said he and Foster met at Bridgewater, where they were roommates for a while and teammates on the football and track teams.[716]

"I was a second- or third-string defensive back and quarterback on the football team, and I was the captain on the track team and competed in the 400 and 200 races," said Thompson, who majored in physical education and biology and graduated in 1960.[717]

He soon joined the army with a three-year enlistment during which time he served as a military policeman. He was honorably discharged in 1963 and immediately began his coaching career.[718]

Buffalo Gap High School, located in Augusta County and which opened in 1962, afforded him his first coaching job.[719]

Previously, his only connection to that area was that his younger sister, Dorothy, and her husband—who worked as a farmer—lived in the county.[720]

In fact, Dorothy was the youngest of four children born to the marital union of John Wallace Thompson and Blanche Boyd Thompson.[721]

Older brother Wallace Lee Thompson was born on January 24, 1937, in Stuarts Draft, Virginia, and third in the birth order. He and Dorothy, who is commonly called Dottie, have two older sisters, Edna and Sarah.[722]

Their father died in a vehicular accident when Thompson was five years old. Their mother had limited formal education and lacked the financial ability to provide for them as a single parent. Thompson and his three sisters went to live with a paternal uncle and his wife—Ernest and Harriett (Powell) Thompson in the Washington, DC, area.[723]

Thompson attended schools in Arlington, Virginia, until high school when he decided to attend Carlisle Military School in Bamberg, South Carolina, where he played football, basketball, and baseball.[31] After graduating from Carlisle, Thompson attended Fork Union Military Academy as a postgraduate where he ran track.[724]

---

[31] "While the Camden Military Academy tradition dates back to 1892, operations on the current campus began with the 1958–59 school year. The Academy combines the traditions of three institutions—Carlisle Military School, which operated in Bamberg, South Carolina, from 1892 to 1977; Camden Academy, which was located on the campus from 1949 to 1957; and Camden Military Academy. Camden Military Academy has operated as a non-profit, tax-exempt institution since 1974 and is governed by a self-perpetuating board of trustees. Carlisle Military School was established in 1892 as the Carlisle Fitting School of Wofford College. This military school was named in honor of Dr. James H. Carlisle, who was for many years the president of Wofford College in Spartanburg, South Carolina. In 1932, Carlisle was leased by Colonel and Mrs. James F. Risher and in 1938 was purchased by them. They, and later their son, Colonel William Risher, operated it as a military preparatory boarding school until it closed in May 1977." Source: www.camdenmilitary.com.

Following his graduation from Bridgewater and his service in the military, he later attended Radford University, where he earned a master's degree in education.[725]

Even later, he worked toward the completion of a doctorate and completed all the necessary requirements except for the written dissertation, which he shelved after he decided not to enter the administrative realm of education.[726]

As for coaching, which he always loved, his first season at Buffalo Gap was in 1963. He coached the junior varsity football team for two seasons.[727]

When the head coach was "let go," Thompson became the head coach beginning the 1965 season.[728]

He installed the "monster" defensive set he learned from Foster.[729]

And the two former Bridgewater students and athletes conversed regularly.

In fact, Foster informed Thompson of a vacant teaching and coaching position at Andrew Lewis High School.

No need to twist Thompson's arm. He had been interested in coaching at Andrew Lewis for some time.[730]

"I wanted to coach with Foster and Joyce," he said. "I wanted to go to Andrew Lewis, but I was not interested in going to any of the other Roanoke County Schools."[731]

At least, not at that time.

Thompson was hired as a physical education teacher and joined Coach Joyce's staff as an assistant beginning in 1966.[732]

That season, he coached the defensive ends and helped with the offensive line. The next season, he coached both the offensive and defensive lines, which remained true for the rest of his time at Lewis.[733]

Because Thompson had run the monster defense at Buffalo Gap, his transition as an assistant at Lewis came easy. His last season at Lewis was 1970. About four years later, he returned to coaching.[734]

He became an assistant coach under Don Oakes at William Byrd High School located in the town of Vinton, which is in Roanoke

County. Oakes was a former Andrew Lewis and Virginia Tech graduate who played professional football for the Philadelphia Eagles.[735]

Oakes also had on his staff Dean East, a former head-knocker of a defensive player and backup running back at Andrew Lewis and then a starting defensive back at Hampden-Sydney College. Thompson served as an assistant until he became the head coach at Salem in 1979.[736]

How did he land the Spartan job?

"I just applied," he said. "I think a lot of people turned it down."[737]

And what did he find when he took control?

"We had good kids, but I don't think [the combination of players from] Andrew Lewis and Glenvar ever felt like a team to them. When Kucer took over [in 1977] he did a good job. He had a good group of seniors. [When I started] we had kids who didn't come out and who had played before."[738]

Alluding to the annual preseason football camp, which was first begun in 1961, Thompson said: "There may have been some hazing going on there between the Lewis and Glenvar players. I don't think the situation got right until the two separated again."[739]

Regardless of what may or may not have happened at camp, Thompson was now the new Salem head coach.

What was his initial strategy to rally the Spartans?

Once again, McLelland and Chamberlain combined for answers.

In the June 1, 1979, edition, McLelland quoted Thompson as saying, "The first thing I have to do is meet with the squad and introduce myself. I know a few of the players, but I don't know them like I should... This summer I hope to meet with each player in his home with his family. You know you have to have support at home if you are to have a successful sports program."

McLelland also reported that Thompson would soon have to decide on four assistants but noted part of that problem had been solved when Foster agreed to serve.[740]

Among the players included Thompson's sons, Jimmy (a junior) and Dale (a sophomore).[741]

As for Thompson's assistants, Foster was the first named to the staff.[742]

When he thought about their mutual approach to a new season, Thompson said, "We're going at it low key. There's a lot of work to be done. Too much publicity has hurt us already. You won't see us [the coaches] do a lot of hollering. We'll let the team speak for itself… We'll be undermanned most every game. There's a lot of teaching that has to be done. You can't build a program overnight. It's not going to be easy."[743]

And publicity was certain to continue.

Let's look to Chamberlain, who served the newspaper as an education writer. He noted that the Roanoke County School Board had voted unanimously for Thompson.[744]

But the board's action was not without fallout.

Joe Thomas, a county school board member for four years and a former board chairman, told a reporter that he would not seek reappointment to the board because of the personal grief that the Joyce controversy caused him.[745]

"This Eddie Joyce thing has been a very emotional thing locally," Thomas said. "This thing has divided friends—my friends—on one side or the other. And I'll be perfectly frank with you, this thing has hurt me considerably."[746]

Thomas said the Joyce controversy had affected him more than the other five board members because his contracting firm does a lot of business in Salem, and he has many friends there. Further, his refusal to support Joyce may have affected his business, "but the main point is my friends. Many of my friends are feeling hard toward me because of my stand. And I had to stand up and be counted on the Eddie Joyce issue. This is the hottest spot I've ever been in."[747]

Chamberlain spoke to Joyce by telephone and quoted Joyce as saying this about the board's decision. "It's just one of those things. I didn't have a chance at it. They never did consider me."[748]

Did the decision not to hire Joyce fan the flames of secession talk?

James Moyer, the reader will recall, was a retired Salem judge who supported Joyce. He was quoted as saying, "There isn't anything to feel about it. It's done and that's it."[749]

But he also indicated that it was too early to discuss Salem's forming its own school system because the educational contract with the county did not expire until 1983.[750]

"We should never have had a contract in the first place," said Moyer.[751]

Other board members opted not to comment on the decision, but later in this article, Thomas explained why he voted the way he did.[752]

"The decision not to hire [Joyce] at this time is based on logic and sound principles as to what is in the best interest of the children and the school system itself. I feel it would not be in the best interest of Salem High School and the students…to be brought into the middle of a political controversy. Unfortunately, the Eddie Joyce application, to me, is a political issue and not just a school or educational issue."[753]

Thomas also said Joyce had as many detractors as supporters.[754]

"I hope these friends and supporters will understand the considerations I have mentioned and will not bring political pressure that will interfere with our educational system."[755]

It was too late. The Salem School Board had expressed its support of Joyce, as did some other prominent Salem officials, and there were a reported 3,000 citizens who had signed petitions wanting the county to hire him. And let's not forget that there had already been much talk of Salem having its own school system.[756]

But perhaps the biggest issue to Salemites wasn't so much that Joyce wasn't hired as much as it was the principal in all this.

Salem city councilman Robert L. "Bob" Barnett summed it up succinctly.

"I don't think Salem has enough say in what is going on."[757]

And more than anything else, Salem wanted its say. Until then, Wallace Thompson was the new head coach. He had kept his distance from the political issues, and he was ready to start coaching the Spartans.

"I'm just real happy this whole thing is over," he told McLelland. "Now it's time to quit talking and get down to work."[758]

Author's note: Thompson was interviewed by telephone on March 14, 2018, at his home in Grand Junction, Colorado.

Chapter 8

HIS TRIO

Part 1: The Beleaguered (1979)

Spartan head coach Wallace Thompson would serve three years at the helm of the Spartans

THE SPARTAN SUCCESSION

The transfer from Culpeper County to Salem, Jay Brock

To the average sports fan in the Roanoke Valley, Wallace Thompson wasn't exactly a household name. But to insiders like Bob McLelland, Thompson was a well-known entity with an impressive-enough resume.[759]

The savvy sportswriter wrote about him in an article below this headline: "Only his record will solve Thompson's identity crisis."[760]

When Thompson was announced as the new head football coach at Salem, there were some sports fans in the valley who asked, "Who is he?"

But sportswriters and coaches knew of Thompson's credentials and his character.

They described him as a solid citizen, sound in fundamentals, willing to work hard, and willing to listen to advice.[761]

He was low key and let his coaching record speak for himself. His teams were well coached and ready to play. Thompson had worked his way up the coaching ladder after rubbing elbows with many an influential coach.[762]

The list included Eddie Joyce, Dale Foster, Mike Stevens, Don Oakes and Paul Barnard—a co-assistant with Thompson under Oakes at William Byrd.[763]

Thompson would take what he learned from each of these individuals and combine it with his own approach to the Spartan players.

"I don't want to come on too strong with the kids too quickly," he told McLelland. "I want to feel my way around just like they will want to do. I want to develop a warm, sincere relationship. I want each player and his parents to know that I am interested in him as a person and not just as an athlete. I want them to feel free to come to me anytime with their problems, personal or football."[764]

Bob Patterson, an assistant principal at William Byrd, told McLelland that Thompson was "a winner" and "an outstanding member of our faculty… His athletes liked him and had great respect for him. He is just the type of person any school is looking for in a head coach."[765]

Thompson wasn't looking to shake things up when it came to the Spartans' defensive and offensive sets.

"We will probably use some variation of the 5–2 monster defense, and our offense will be broad enough to cover all situations. We want to do anything to move the football, but we will have to play within our limitations… Running a successful offense is really a combination of many things."[766]

On a personal level, McLelland described Thompson as a quiet, religious man.[767]

"Many of the qualities that are needed to be a good athlete are the same qualities that are needed to be a good Christian," said Thompson.[768]

McLelland concluded the story with his own question and answers.

Just how successful will Thompson prove as the head coach at Salem?

Only time and his record will tell.

That is how Thompson wants it.[769]

* * *

About four weeks later, McLelland reported on the difficulties that area high school football teams were having assembling full coaching staffs.

The biggest problem was the lack of teaching positions required of assistant coaches.[770]

One disgruntled head coach said, "Nobody really seems to care but me. There ought to be some way we can get around that. There are too many teaching positions usually taken by coaches that are now filled by people who do no coaching at all. There ought to be a combination job for coaches. If he quits coaching, he also loses his job on the faculty."[771]

Thankfully for Salem, Thompson's staff had come along nicely. It was headed by assistant principal Dale Foster plus Danny Wheeling and Bob Tate, all members of the old Salem staff.[772]

As for the players, about 70 showed up for practice, among those were twenty-seven seniors.[773]

The number 70 represented about half of what the turnout was when Salem made its debut in 1977.[774]

That season, there were 120 Spartans.[775]

Dale Foster was an assistant coach at Andrew Lewis beginning in 1962. He was on the staff in 1971 when Lewis played T. C. Williams High in the Group AAA state championship game on December 4, 1971, in Roanoke's Victory Stadium.

Recall that T. C. Williams, in 1971, had become the combination of all three public high schools in Alexandria, Virginia. The other two had been George Washington and Hammond. Those 2 schools became intermediate schools, and Williams was nothing short of massive.

That said, Foster was an expert witness on what tends to happen when 2 or more schools combine.

"When two schools come together [in this case, Andrew Lewis and Glenvar], it eventually levels out," he said. "Look at how big a team T. C. Williams had their first year. What have you heard from them since?"[32, 776]

Going into his first season, Thompson agreed that depth was nonexistent.

"We have none," he said. "We don't have a lot of big kids and no depth at all."[777]

Thompson, Foster, Wheeling, and Tate were about to oversee camp life. The team was scheduled to conduct its annual 2-week preseason camp at Camp Alta Mons.[778]

After that, the Spartans—under first-year coach Wallace Thompson—would begin the regular season during the first week of September.

Their opening opponent? The Indians of Blacksburg.

* * *

Game 1 (September 7): Blacksburg 19, Salem 0

It was an inauspicious start for the Spartans.

In summary, the Salem offense was plagued by mistakes, and the team was penalized to the tune of 60 yards. The Indians went on the warpath and tallied 233 total yards on offense compared to just 77 for the Spartans.[779]

It helped Blacksburg's cause that 8 of its defenders were returning as starters from a year ago, but Coach Thompson said his team was just as tough. It simply made too many mistakes.[780]

The Indians led at the intermission, 10–0, after Mark Hill scored on a 2-yard run, and Mike Coleman booted a 32-yard field goal. Coleman kicked a second field goal in the third, and Greg Keys ran for a score to complete the scoring.[781]

---

[32] Very little would have been the answer to Foster's question. After the Titans won the 1971 state title, they had not won it again at the time Foster spoke in 1979. They did, however, advance to the state semifinals in 1973, only to lose by shutout, 13–0, to Patrick Henry-Roanoke, which next defeated Lafayette (23–0) for the state crown. The Titans would not win the state championship again until 1984 (source: VHSL record book, page 28).

Game 2 (September 14): Cave Spring 28, Salem 0

Knights' quarterback Brian Stevens passed for 156 yards and 1 TD, and he ran for another as Cave Spring handed Salem its second shutout loss in as many games.[782]

Stevens's totals would have been even more impressive had several of his passes not been dropped. He consistently eluded Spartan defenders when he ran the ball, and a strong offensive line gave him all the time he needed when he decided to pass.[783]

Thompson said Salem's secondary actually did a good job.

The problem?

Stevens had too much time to throw the ball. His counterparts, Chance Crawford and Rusty Garst, alternated at the position for the Spartans. Cave Spring, now unbeaten in its first 2 games, had outscored its opponents 60–2. Salem, still scoreless after 2 games, hoped to fare better against William Fleming next week.[784]

Game 3 (September 21): Salem 8, William Fleming 6

The Spartans and Colonels played this one in the mud at Municipal Field. In fact, Brian Hoffman described the field as a riceless rice paddy.[785]

For Salem, Jay Brock threw a halfback pass to Todd Hall for a touchdown, and Ted Viars tackled Fleming quarterback Roger Ferguson in the end zone for a safety.[786]

Punter Rusty Garst consistently pinned the Colonels deep in their own territory.[787]

Thompson singled out long snapper Geoff Davidson, who snapped the ball on eleven punts and all were accurate.[788]

"That kid must have some kind of good nerves," said Thompson.[789]

For Fleming, Jeff Barrett ran 37 yards for the team's only score.[790]

Brock's situation had some uniqueness to it.

He lived at the Salem Baptist Home and was a senior transfer to Salem from Culpeper via Richmond. He came to Salem last spring and was an All-Metro intermediate hurdler on the track team.[791]

He was elected president of this year's senior class.[792]

As for Hall, he was also a trackman and had not played football for two years. His catch for touchdown was just inside the out-of-bounds marker.[793]

Game 4 (September 28): Patrick Henry 27, Salem 0

The Patriots turned in a consistent performance and handed the Spartans their third shutout loss of the season. The PH defense was stifling. Salem had but 13 rushing yards in the game.[794]

Chance Crawford and Rusty Garsty alternated at quarterback and combined for just 7 completions out of 21 passes for 84 yards. The Patriot secondary got much of the credit because Coach Thompson singled out the play of the Spartan offensive line that enabled that many passes.[795]

Individually, he credited Allen Harrison, John Dickerson, and Ted Viars.[796]

Game 5 (October 5): Salem 7, Halifax County 0

Salem was hardly spectacular, but the Spartans didn't need to be Friday night as they made a first-quarter touchdown by David Collie stand up for a 7–0 non-district football win over Halifax County.[797]

Salem, 2–3, earned its win by intercepting 2 passes and recovering 2 fumbles, both by Halifax County running back Barry Word[33].[798]

The game's lone score was set up when Randy Smith intercepted a pass from Halifax quarterback Mark James and returned the ball some 20 yards to the Comet 33.[799]

Three runs by Jay Brock and an offsides penalty gave Salem 2 first downs before Collie bolted up the middle for a 7-yard touch-

---

[33] Barry Word went on to play at the University of Virginia and was later drafted in 1986 by the New Orleans Saints who chose him in round 3. After one season in New Orleans, he played for the Kansas City Chiefs for three years and closed out his career with the Arizona Cardinals for one season. He currently lives in Haymarket, Virginia, and owns Speed Pro Imaging of Centreville (source: Wikipedia).

down. Ted Viars' extra point gave Salem a 7–0 lead with 3:25 left in the first period.[800]

Brock led Salem with 90 rushing yards on 24 carries, and the Spartans needed him most after Collie left the game early in the second half with a sprained ankle.[801]

Salem limited Halifax to less than 100 yards in total offense and junior linebacker Carlton Ertel led the team in tackles.[802]

Word's first fumble came as the fourth period opened. Todd Holliday's recovery gave Salem a good chance to pad its margin from the Comet 23, but Salem got nowhere in four tries.[803]

Word's second fumble proved more damaging. After moving into Salem territory, James completed a screen pass to Word for 18 yards to the Salem 22, but on the next play Word sliced off tackle and fell forward to the 15 before the ball popped loose. Brock was there for the recovery.[804]

Salem ran out the remaining 2:27 with the aid of a personal foul penalty against the Comets.[805]

Salem's defensive stars included Viars, Ertel, Dale Weeks, and Alan Cole.[806]

Notably, Salem had zero turnovers.[807]

As for the Roanoke Valley District standings, Patrick Henry was now the leader after its 19–14 win over Cave Spring. After PH, Northside was next, followed by Cave Spring, Pulaski County, Salem, William Fleming and Franklin County.[808]

Game 6 (October 12): Woodbridge 21, Salem 0

Salem blew a scoring opportunity in the first quarter and lost to Woodbridge 21–0.[809]

The Spartans, who fell to 2–4, had a chance to score in the first quarter but Tony Lilly intercepted a pass in the end zone for Woodbridge[34]. The Vikings went on for touchdowns in the first, second, and fourth quarters for their fifth win against one loss.[810]

---

[34] Tony Lilly went on to play at the University of Florida and was drafted in 1984 by the Denver Broncos in round 3. He played for four seasons with the team

Quarterback Jerry Roadcap scored 2 touchdowns, and Richard Houston scored one.[811]

Salem QB Chance Crawford connected on 8 of 16 passes.[812]

In the standings, PH remained at the top after defeating Northside, 7–0. Cave Spring moved up to second place, while Pulaski County was in third and Northside in fourth.[813]

Game 7 (October 19): Salem 21, Franklin County 7

Jay Brock threw for 1 touchdown and ran for another, and Salem downed Franklin County to spoil both the Eagles' homecoming and the birthday of Coach Stickney.[814]

The Spartans took a 14–0 halftime lead thanks to an 11-yard run by Brock and a 3-yard run by Blair Thompson. Salem added its third TD in the fourth quarter when Brock threw an option pass to Todd Hall for a 9-yard score.[815]

According to Coach Thompson, the Eagles tried to catch them off guard when they switched from an I formation to the wing T offense.[816]

"I don't know if they think we're stupid or what," he said. "It didn't matter to us."[817]

The switch must not have helped much. The Eagles had 3 fumbles and 1 interception.[818]

Thompson credited Dale Weeks with having played his best game of the season.[819]

With the win, the Spartans improved their district record to 2–2 and looked to even their overall record next week at home against the Phoebus Phantoms.

---

before retiring. Since then, he has coached two different public high schools in Virginia. He was the head coach at Potomac from 2005 to 2009, and he became the head coach at C. D. Hylton in 2010 to the present (source: Wikipedia).

THE SPARTAN SUCCESSION

Game 8 (October 26): Phoebus 21, Salem 6

This loss was unprecedented; no, not the loss that showed up on the scoreboard, but rather the enormous loss of key players in one game.[820]

The Spartans lost their No. 1 and 2 quarterbacks, a running back had to play quarterback, a running back who was supposed to fill in at running back was injured, and a defensive back who had never carried the ball had to fill in in the offensive backfield.[821]

"I've never seen anything like it," said Coach Thompson. "I've never seen that many injuries in a game in my life. We had people playing where we never thought of putting them before."[822]

Chance Crawford was the starting Salem quarterback. After Phoebus took a 7–0 lead, Crawford engineered an 86-yard scoring drive that was capped by a halfback pass from Jay Brock to Todd Hall for a 15-yard TD. The extra point failed, and the Phantoms led 7–6.[823]

Backup quarterback Rusty Garst was injured during Phoebus's opening drive while playing defense. Garst spent the rest of the evening trying to remember his own name.[824]

And Crawford, on Brock's touchdown pass, was injured while blocking. He suffered a broken collarbone.[825]

In the second quarter, Brock moved to quarterback. His backup, David Collie, moved to halfback, but Collie sprained an ankle. Defensive back John Walker was thrown into the breach, and things did not go well for him. He ran the ball 2 times for minus 3 yards.[826]

It was a microcosm of the game. The Spartans had just 23 yards rushing and 63 passing while the Phantoms piled up 222 yards on the ground.[827]

Derek Jenkins paced Phoebus with 147 rushing yards on 17 carries and 2 touchdowns.[828]

His running impressed Dale Foster.

"I can't remember seeing a better one around here," he said. "I've seen 'em that big and that fast, but not at the same time. He runs a 9.7 hundred on the track team."[829]

The Spartans spent most of the fourth quarter just trying to keep the Phantoms from scoring again. In the final minutes of play, Salem's Randy Smith intercepted a Phoebus pass in the end zone.[830]

Salem fell to 3–5 on the season with 2 games remaining.

It seemed a safe bet that Thompson would be busy switching players around in practice this week.

Salem next faced Pulaski County at home.

Game 9 (November 3): Pulaski County 46, Salem 7

The huge win pushed Pulaski to 8–1 overall and 4–1 in the district, just behind Patrick Henry, which was also 8–1 overall but unbeaten in the district at 5–0. The two teams would meet next week in the regular season finale.[831]

The Cougars crushed the Spartans in Salem.

"It didn't seem like we were the home team," said Thompson, "but I wasn't too surprised. When you're losing, they [the fans] don't come to see you. When you win, they'll come."[832]

After the game, tempers flared, and players shouted at each other.[833]

Salem's shining spots included Viars, David Swain, Weeks, and Harrison.[834]

Pulaski County's Gary Clark and Curtis Bland sparked the Cougars to their eighth victory overall against one setback. Clark took the opening kickoff and returned it 80 yards for a touchdown and later grabbed a 34-yard scoring pass from Bland, who also had a 3-yard TD pass to Blake Farlow[35].[835]

---

[35] Gary Clark went on to play for James Madison University. He was chosen in the USFL (United States Football League) by the Jacksonville Bulls in 1984 and played for one season. He was selected by the Washington Redskins in the second round of the 1984 NFL Supplemental Draft of USFL and CFL (Canadian Football League) players. He played for the Redskins from 1985–1992, then for the Phoenix/Arizona Cardinals and Miami Dolphins. His career highlights include: two-time Super Bowl Champions, four-time Pro Bowl selection, three-time All-Pro, 70 Greatest Redskins, and Washington Redskins Ring of Fame (source: Wikipedia).

Pulaski's other scores came on touchdown runs of 22 yards by King Harvey, 29 by Curtis Trail, and 19 by Ron Bevins, plus 1 score in the air when Jeff McClelland tossed 11 yards to Joe Blankenship.[836]

The Pulaski defense limited Salem to 1 first down in the first half.[837]

The Spartans fell to 3–6 with 1 game remaining during the regular season.

Game 10 (November 9): Northside 18, Salem 0

Arguably, no one enjoyed the Vikings' victory more than senior lineman Greg Neese, who grew up in Salem, still lived there, but transferred to Northside after his eighth-grade year.[838]

Neese likened the personal rivalry between Salem and Northside to that of Virginia and Virginia Tech.[839]

Things went so well against the Spartans in Friday night's win that Neese even had an opportunity to play at linebacker.[840]

Head coach Jim Hickam moved him there with 1:02 remaining in the game, and Neese responded with an interception of a Rick Garst pass.[841]

"Greg has always wanted to play linebacker," said Hickam, "and we worked him there a little bit in practice this week. When I saw Greg and one of our linebackers, Mark Bessell, huddled together late in the game, I knew what they were talking about. So, I told Greg, 'OK' go ahead and do it."[842]

The Vikings scored on 3 touchdown runs, including 1 by Tony Lawrence, who tallied a game best 113 yards on 13 carries, which included 1 for 60 yards.[843]

The Northside defense was stingy and held Salem to 49 yards of total offense, which doomed the Spartans to their fifth shutout loss of the season. Salem, 3–7 under first-year head coach Wallace Thompson, scored more than 8 points in just 1 game this season.[844]

"I think we could have held [Northside] to a touchdown if we had any offense," said Thompson. "But we've really been crippled the last half of the year... We're small, but we don't have any speed and when that's the case, you're in bad shape. We have some good kids, but not enough of them."[845]

Neese could have been one of them, and the Salem kids knew it. Neese went to bed Friday night, fully expecting to have his house rolled with toilet paper.[846]

"I know the Salem kids will try to roll my house tonight, but they better be quick. I caught 'em last year."[847]

As Neese waited in anticipation of such shenanigans, he felt some disappointment with his team finishing the season at 6–3–1.

"We expected to win the district championship, then the region and go on to the state playoffs. I really feel like PH and Pulaski were lucky to beat us and, as for Cave Spring, they were just up. Everybody seems to be up when they play Northside."[848]

"I can't say who our natural rival is," said Hickam. "For some of our kids, it's [William] Fleming. For others, it's Cave Spring. But for Greg, there's no question, Salem's the biggest. And I think you could tell out there tonight."[849]

From the Salem perspective, Rusty Garst completed four of 18 passes and spent much of his time scrambling for his life.[850]

Looking ahead, Thompson said, "Next year could be a turning point for the program as a whole. We kept improving up to the point we were hit by injuries."[851]

Who was the toughest team that Salem played this season?

Thompson gave the nod to PH.[852]

Patrick Henry won the Roanoke Valley District championship with an overall record of 9–1 and an unbeaten league record of 6–0. Pulaski County finished second at 8–2 and 4–2, followed by Cave Spring (6–3, 4–2), Northside (6–3, 3–3), William Fleming (5–5, 2–4), Salem (3–7, 2–4), and Franklin County (0–10, 0–6).[853]

* * *

When the All-Roanoke Valley Football team was announced, the Spartans had 3 players selected to the second teams.[854]

THE SPARTAN SUCCESSION

Ted Viars was named to the offensive squad, and Darrell Ward (nose guard) and Dale Weeks (linebacker) were named to the defensive unit.[855]

A little over a month later, the All-Timesland teams were announced.

Let's begin with mentioning the Coach of the Year honor, which was bestowed to Joel Hicks of Pulaski County.[856]

Hicks led the Cougars to an overall record of 9–3. He came to the team after serving as an offensive coordinator for West Virginia University. Pulaski County had finished a season with a winning record only once since Dublin and Pulaski were consolidated five years ago.[857]

Hicks came in and began a new slate.

"I just tried to erase everything that had been done in the past," he said. "We started a weight program and a running program. Then I tried to get as many people as I could out for the squad."[858]

Hicks had to start this season by booting 30 players off the team before practice got underway. But that may have been key to Pulaski's success.[859]

"It wasn't that hard to do, since the players did it to themselves," said Hicks. "We had rules and laid down what needed to be done. Those players didn't abide by those rules. But it united the team. The only players we had left were those that wanted to play."[860]

After finishing this regular season at 8–2, Pulaski qualified for the playoffs and defeated George Washington of Danville in the first round but lost in the next to Patrick Henry[36].[861]

The Offensive Players of the Year were Larry Fourqurean of Alleghany and Timmy Jones of Parry McCluer, and the Defensive Player of the Year was Keith Allen of Patrick Henry.[862]

Allen was a mainstay on a unit that only gave up 99 points this season on its way to the Group AAA runner-up spot.[863]

---

[36] Patrick Henry won the Roanoke Valley District and Northwest Region crown and after winning a state semifinal game, advanced to the state finals where it lost to Petersburg, 14–6. Source: VHSL record book, page 28.

As for Salem, reflective of its losing record and combined with an injury-riddled and small roster, it had no first- or second-team selections.

Will 1980 be any better for the beleaguered Spartans?

Part 2: The Nearly Crushing Blow (1980)

Salem's Rodney Varney shows some passing form

During the spring of this year, Eddie Joyce was back in the news.

Joyce was expected to have his teaching certificate restored this date after the state Board of Education's personnel and professional relations committee had voted to reinstate his certificate for the 1980–81 school year.[864]

Joyce attended the hearing in Richmond and told reporters that he hoped to continue coaching football at Roanoke Catholic—a private school accredited by the state board—and to begin teaching there soon. He said officials at the school had promised him a teacher's position next fall if one became available.[865]

Apparently, Joyce soon had a change in heart.

He not only quit the job at Roanoke Catholic but also planned to leave the Roanoke Valley for a job with a sporting goods firm in Tennessee.[866]

Joyce's explanation was simple and basic enough.

"I just had to find a job," he said after he reportedly had sold his home in Salem and was living in North Myrtle Beach, South Carolina, where he usually spent his summers.[867]

"I'm still negotiating with a company in Tennessee, but I'll probably leave Salem. It depends on where I have to go."[868]

Joyce's teaching certificate was restored in April and likely set a precedent in the Commonwealth of Virginia. This was the first time anyone in the state Department of Education could recall a person convicted of a felony applying for a certificate to teach in Virginia.[869]

"I just wanted to see if they would give it back to me or if [Arnold] Burton [the retiring superintendent of Roanoke County schools] still had enough influence on them," said Joyce. "But I wanted it back. I really wanted a job."[870]

Though he had planned to stay at Roanoke Catholic, he was only coaching there, not teaching. He simply needed a job.[871]

"I couldn't find any other work." said Joyce. "They didn't have any teaching jobs. I think they [Roanoke Catholic] would have given me a job if they had one. They were trying to help me find something, so I could work and coach."[872]

Joyce also said, "Jobs are pretty hard to find. I hate to leave Salem. There's nothing I can do. I would have preferred not to."[873]

Then, in July 1980, he was hired by Natural Bridge High School near Lexington, Virginia. He was appointed to the position at a special meeting of the Rockbridge County school board. Further, an unspecified newspaper in South Carolina reported that Joyce had signed a contract to coach football at Wallace High School outside Bennettsville.[874]

But Joyce had not reneged. He told a reporter, "We had come to an agreement except for a couple of things, but we hadn't finalized anything."[875]

Natural Bridge was the only school in Virginia to contact Joyce about a coaching job.[876]

"I think it'll be a good situation," remarked Joyce. "They were very straightforward with me. They're good people, and they wanted me to come to Natural Bridge."[877]

Meanwhile, Wallace Thompson was about to embark on his second season as the head coach of the Spartans, whose schedule had them opening the season at home against the Indians of Blacksburg High.

* * *

Game 1 (September 5, 1980): Blacksburg 6, Salem 0

Sportswriter Bob Teitlebaum of the *Roanoke Times & World-News* covered this one, and his article was a succinct account. It painted the only picture needed for readers to envision just how this one unfolded.

Here is what he wrote:

> Although it seemed officials at the Salem-Blacksburg high school football game called everything, the visiting Indians scored the game's only touchdown in the third quarter on a play where the official's whistle was obviously missing.
>
> Blacksburg's Daniel Frederick picked up a loose ball ruled a fumble by Salem's quarterback Chance Crawford and stumbled 36 yards to the end zone, giving the Indians a 6–0 win. All this came as Salem coaches shouted that Crawford had tried to throw a forward pass that should have been ruled incomplete.
>
> The play started on the Blacksburg 46. Crawford dropped back to pass, was rushed and lost control

of the ball as his arm appeared to come forward. The ball slipped away and Blacksburg's Greg Wesley kicked the ball as he tried to pick it up.

Frederick finally got control at the Salem 36 and made his way into the end zone. A bad snap stopped Blacksburg's extra-point try, but it didn't matter.

Silence, usually golden, was quite noticeable on that play. That's because the officiating crew had been dealing out penalties by the dozens. Eighteen were assessed on the two teams for 187 yards, and there were others refused.

"It was a backward pass that slipped out of his hand and was a fumble," said the referee, who refused to give his name as he explained the call on the fumble return. "You can read it (my name) in the paper."[878]

Salem, 0–1, next faced Cave Spring, which opened the season last week with a 0–0 tie against Martinsville.

Game 2 (September 12): Cave Spring 34, Salem 7

Teitlebaum's colleague—Bill Eichenberger—covered the Cave Spring romp.
He wrote that both teams, after last week's performances, were looking for their lost offenses. The Knights found theirs, but the Spartans did not.[879]
Cave Spring quarterback Mike Sampson threw 2 touchdown passes of 54 and 51 yards to flanker Tim Wiseman, 1 of 57 yards to split end Jay Simmons, and ran 63 yards for yet another score as the Knights rode high in the saddle.[880]

Salem scored its lone touchdown in the second quarter while trailing 14–7.[881]

Quarterback Chance Crawford completed several passes during the scoring drive to both James Jackson and Jimmy Thompson to move the football to the Cave Spring 2-yard line.[882]

Blair Thompson, listed as a 137-pound senior fullback, punched it in on his second try.[883]

Cave Spring's offense came alive behind a revamped offensive line. The new insertions were tackles Jay Smith and Bill Orr, tight end Travis Morgan, and junior guard Jerry Weinbarger.[884]

Salem, which was limited to minus-31 yards against Blacksburg, sputtered again against Cave Spring, especially during the second half when it mustered only 2 first downs and 39 yards of total offense.[885]

Up next, the Spartans took on the Colonels of William Fleming in Roanoke's Victory Stadium.

Game 3 (September 19): William Fleming 48, Salem 0

In the annals of matchups between Fleming and any team from Salem, this one goes down as one of the most lopsided defeats ever inflicted by the Colonels.

From a review of the records dating back to 1949, which was the year that William Fleming became part of the Roanoke City school system, it is evident that prior to 1980 the previous best Fleming trouncing of a Salem-based team came in 1959 when the Colonels waxed the Wolverines of Andrew Lewis, 34–0.[886]

Thereafter, the next best Fleming performance came in 1970 when the Colonels shut out the Wolverines 28–0, which represented the most points scored against Lewis by any opponent during what Dale Foster referred to as "the best years of [Eddie] Joyce," or 1962–1971.[887]

In 1959, it wasn't just the Colonels that cruised past the Wolverines. The records also indicate that Lewis suffered lopsided defeats to Jefferson (43–6), E. C. Glass (54–0), and Halifax County (31–6).[888]

THE SPARTAN SUCCESSION

As for 1970, Fleming running back Mike Dowe scored 3 of his team's 4 touchdowns and his defensive teammates simply smothered the Lewis offense and took away its most dangerous tandem: quarterback Eddie Joyce Jr. to receiver Roger Surber.

And Coach Joyce conceded as much when he said, "They just completely swarmed us. Their line controlled ours. We never had a chance."[889]

But there was something different about Fleming's big win in 1980.

Did the Colonels score *too many* points in this one?

Salem head coach Wallace Thompson hinted that Fleming ran up the score against Salem.[890]

Sportswriter Doug Doughty covered the game and quoted Thompson as saying, "I think they would have scored one hundred points if they could have."[891]

Fleming skipper John McGregor disagreed: "We didn't try to run it up," he replied.[892]

Thompson countered with, "Yeah, but I don't think they tried to hold it down."[893]

What the Spartans couldn't hold down was tailback Darryl Robinson, who rushed for a game best 115 yards on 18 carries and 2 touchdowns.[894]

The Colonels led 33–0 at halftime. Before that, the Spartans had just 1 first down.[895]

After a scoreless third quarter, Fleming added 2 fourth-quarter touchdowns to push their lead to 48–0 while Salem responded with its best drive of the night and pushed to within inches of the Fleming goal line.[896]

Sophomore quarterback Rodney Varney led the drive that began on the Salem 29-yard line. On the last play of the game, he was tackled at the Fleming one.[897]

As Doughty wrote, a starter at safety, Varney played running back briefly during the first half before replacing regular Salem quarterback Chance Crawford in the third quarter.[898]

"He [Varney] is going to be a good quarterback," said Thompson. "But we really haven't had a chance to work him there. Of course, he's also been working out at running back and safety."⁸⁹⁹

Salem fell to 0–3 on the season while William Fleming pushed its unbeaten record to 3–0.

Up next, Salem took on last year's Group AAA state runner-up, Patrick Henry.

Game 4 (September 26): Patrick Henry 14, Salem 0

The Patriots scored a touchdown in both the first and fourth quarters, and their defense limited Salem to just 3 first downs in the game.⁹⁰⁰

Robert Harley scored on a 30-yard run for the first touchdown and David Talley on a 12-yard quarterback keeper for the second.⁹⁰¹

Salem quarterback Chance Crawford completed just 4 of 21 passes and was picked off 3 times, twice by John McGillamy.⁹⁰²

And the cavalry wasn't available to Crawford: backup quarterback Rusty Garst injured his throwing hand in practice, and his playing time was limited to his role as the team's safety.⁹⁰³

Salem tried to open up the long ball but with little effect.

"We opened up our offense as wide as it can get," said Coach Thompson. "We came close to connecting a couple of times tonight, and if we had, I know we would have put some points on the board."⁹⁰⁴

But the hallmark of PH's football program since the days of Merrill Gainer and its continuance under Willis White was a stingy defense.

White was delighted to see the Spartans throw.

"I like to see any team throw," he said. "I've always felt if you can stop a team on the ground, you can beat 'em."⁹⁰⁵

Game 5 (October 3): Salem 14, Bassett 6

Yes, the Spartans picked up their first win of the season, and yes, it happened at home. But the win was hugely offset by the shock that game with it.

Salem's starting quarterback Chance Crawford suffered a broken neck and was immediately treated at the University of Virginia Hospital in Charlottesville.[906]

In a recent interview with Dale Foster, he recalled vividly what happened to Crawford.

"We had a home game with Bassett. I was the athletic director, and I was there at the stadium. During the game, Crawford—who was the quarterback—ran a bootleg and was kind of going through the line off tackle and the linebacker, who was the son of the superintendent of Henry County, made the tackle. Chance was running low and looked like he may have stumbled. The linebacker was a pretty-tall guy, and he kind of got over top of Crawford, and he grabbed him and took him down to the ground. The way his [Crawford's] head hit the ground fractured his vertebrae.[907]

"The rescue squad had to come get him; he was paralyzed, and they took him to Lewis-Gale Hospital. I went over there right after it happened. I was walking down the hallway there and a physician came out and said, 'It doesn't look good.'"[908]

Subsequent narrative provides much more attention to Crawford's status and the community's reaction and huge outreach, but for now let's briefly return to the game itself and to how Salem got its first taste of victory this season.

As for the game details, two touchdowns by Rodney Varney, playing halfback instead of quarterback because of a broken thumb, and the running of Blair Thompson carried Salem to a 14–6 victory at Municipal Field.[909]

It was the first victory in 5 starts for the Spartans of the Roanoke Valley District, while Group AA Bassett dropped to 2–3.

A fumble recovery by Billy Price spoiled a Bassett reverse in the second period, and Salem marched 40 yards in 8 plays for the first TD. Thompson, who rushed for 125 yards in 23 carries, ran 5 times on the drive before Varney, a sophomore, scored from the 14. Bryon Eubank kicked the extra point, and it was 7–0 with 6:43 left in the half.[910]

The Spartans struck again just 1:14 before halftime on a 65-yard pass play from quarterback Chance Crawford to Varney, who was all alone. Salem had tried the play on its first series, and Varney was free, but Crawford overthrew him.[911]

"There's no way a linebacker can cover a back, especially one with Rodney's speed," said Crawford, who was injured in the first half. "We had that first TD, but I missed him. The next time I just layed [sic] it up."[912]

Bassett got its only score with 2:20 remaining in the game on a desperation screen pass on fourth down and 17. R. J. Scott made a nifty 18-yard run on the pass from Lee Forbes.[913]

For the Spartans, the regular season continued the following week with their scheduled trip to Fauquier to take on the Falcons.

But first, let's follow up on the plight of Crawford.

His injury was among the most serious.

He reportedly had suffered a broken neck and spinal cord injury and was being treated at UVA's spinal cord center.[914]

Doctors indicated that they would have a better idea about the extent of his injuries early this same week.[915]

Two days later, Crawford reportedly "still ha[d] no movement from his chest down" as his father, Gary E. Crawford, told the newspaper staff.[916]

Further, the elder Crawford said, "The doctors have told us it looks pretty bad but there is always hope for a miracle."[917]

On a positive note, he added: "He [Chance] has always been in good spirits since the accident. He keeps trying to cheer everyone else up. I don't know where he gets that from. It must be his faith in God. I think everything is in God's hands. I think Chance is prepared to face whatever God wills."[918]

* * *

People in the community were working like beavers in support of the injured player.

School officials, student leaders, and interested community representatives were scheduled to meet in the morning at Salem High to set up the organization for a fund drive for Crawford.[919]

"There is so much interest and emotion at school," said Steve Hyer, assistant principal. "We wanted to channel it into one consolidated effort."[920]

Salem High students had raised more than $2,000 for Crawford over the weekend before any organized drive had been set up. The upcoming meeting was an effort to coordinate students, school personnel, and representatives of the Salem Sports Foundation and Salem Recreation Department and any other interested people in a fund-raising effort to help with the medical costs that might not be covered by insurance.[921]

"There's been a lot of concern here," said Foster. "We've had coaches and people from other schools calling to see how he is."[922]

At Bassett, principal Oliver McBride told students there of the injury during morning announcements and asked them to keep Crawford and his family in their thoughts.[923]

Bassett linebacker Sidney Jones, who made the tackle of Crawford on the play that resulted in the injury, went to Charlottesville to visit Crawford. Coaches from both schools agreed that the tackle was a clean hit.[924]

"It was just a freak thing," said Foster. "He [Crawford] faded back, saw an opening, ran eight yards, then ducked his head and tried to run over the defensive player."[925]

"There wasn't anything dirty about it," said Wallace Thompson. "He didn't even look like he got hit that hard."

Crawford, a 5–11, 185-pounder, was also a baseball star for the Spartans. He was named to the *Roanoke Times & World-News* All-Metro team last spring.

Would Crawford recover enough to return to either sport?[926]

His status was subject to changing from day to day.

In fact, the next day, Crawford's father reported that his son could feel a physical therapist touch various parts of his body.[927]

"His enthusiasm today was really nice," reported Hyer. "His spirits are much better."[928]

Hyer was coordinating fund-raising efforts to help pay for Crawford's treatment. A committee met earlier and established three locations where donations were being accepted.[929]

"Everyone is hoping for a miracle that he will recover," said Hyer, who coached Crawford in American Legion baseball. "We're just hoping to plan for the possibility that he won't."[930]

The Salem Sports Foundation pledged a sizeable contribution, and the Salem Parks and Recreation Department planned to donate money from its concessions and planned to ask for contributions at the sandlot football and cheerleading championship games.[931]

Next, Virginia school officials—who were meeting in Roanoke—had donated money for the cause after Henry County superintendent Paul Jones, also president of the school administrators' association, rose and said, "My son was the young man who tackled that fellow."[932]

At the time, the Virginia Association of School Administrators and the Virginia School Boards Association were holding their annual convention at Hotel Roanoke. The spontaneous donations began after Dot Childress, a board member from Hampton, said she had read about Crawford in the newspaper, and she suggested a collection to help with his medical bills.[933]

With Crawford hospitalized and his recovery not yet known, let's return to the gridiron for news of Salem's next game. The Spartans were scheduled to travel to Warrenton to take on the Falcons of Fauquier County.

Game 6 (October 10): Salem 13, Fauquier 7

Rusty Garst's 8-yard touchdown pass to Jimmy Thompson late in the third quarter lifted the Spartans to victory.[934]

The Falcons scored first when quarterback Jeff Sisson connected with Tony Janoskie for a 5-yard TD pass.[935]

Salem soon countered when Rodney Varney went around end for 14 yards. The 2-point conversion failed, and the Spartans trailed 7–6 at the half.[936]

Getting the win was great news, but worse news about Crawford dashed any feelings of euphoria over the victory in Warrenton.

News reporter John Witt delivered a gloomy message; he opened with these words: "Doctors say Salem High School quarterback Chance Crawford will never walk again."[937]

His father told the news source that doctors at UVA had concluded that damage to the fifth, sixth, and seventh vertebrae is irreparable.[938]

Witt also provided more detail about the play that resulted in Crawford's injury, which everyone agreed was a clean tackle.

He wrote:

> Crawford tried to run through Sidney Jones. Game films show the quarterback's head was about waist level to the linebacker, who hunched over to make the tackle. Jones gripped Crawford in a bear-hug and both fell to the ground.
>
> Noting that the improper handling of a broken neck can be fatal, Witt reminded readers that Crawford was well attended to from the onset.
>
> Salem team doctor Dr. Richard Fisher, an orthopedic surgeon, was the first person on the field and immediately took charge of moving Crawford, first to Lewis-Gale Hospital, and then to UVA.[939]

Despite what doctors told him, the Spartan athlete hoped to prove them wrong.

"Miracles happen every day," said an ever-optimistic Crawford. "I really do think I'll walk again… I pray every day and I have faith."[940]

It would be at least a month before Crawford could be moved from the spinal care unit, and then he would have to undergo weeks of arduous physical therapy to increase the strength and movement of the muscles he still controlled.[941]

Crawford refused to become bitter.

"I've wondered why a couple of times, but God has a reason for everything. This has already brought my family close together."[942]

His parents, Gary and Janice Crawford, agreed and said his enthusiasm had cheered them up.

"He won't let you feel sorry for him," said his father.[943]

His mother said, "I've always loved him dearly, but I never realized before what a special person he really is."[944]

Crawford may have been out of the Spartan lineup, but football occupied a lot of space in his head.[945]

According to news sources, Crawford lay in his room, watching one game on television and listening to another on the radio.[946]

Located above his head on a shelf were two footballs—one autographed by the Pittsburgh Steelers, and another by his Salem High teammates—who were preparing for their next game, at home against the Eagles of Franklin County.[947]

Game 7 (October 17): Franklin County 10, Salem 7

"Penalties and mistakes will kill you every time."[37]

Two major penalties against Salem after the Spartans had taken a 7–3 fourth-quarter lead set up Franklin County's winning TD as the Eagles beat Salem 10–7 in a Roanoke Valley District game Friday night at Salem Municipal Field.[948]

Trailing 3–0, the luckless Spartans went ahead with 7:31 to play following Rusty Garst's 2-yard, fourth-down pass to tight end Bennie Edwards. The TD was set up following Tony Dillon's recovery of a fumbled punt at the Franklin County 26. It took the Spartans (0–4 district, 2–5 overall) 7 plays to take the lead.[949]

But the Spartans were hit with an unsportsmanlike penalty on the TD and had to kick off from their 25. Then, on the kick, Salem was assessed another 15-yard penalty for a late hit that set the Eagles up on the Spartans' 36.[950]

---

[37] This is a favorite line by Steve Peacock in his ongoing analyses of high school football games. He likely would have uttered this line after this game.

THE SPARTAN SUCCESSION

Franklin County moved to a first down inside the 10, but a holding penalty left the Eagles (1–4, 3–4), with a third down and goal at the 19. Quarterback Tim Harris rolled out, reversed his field, and sprinted for the winning score with 4:25 left.[951]

"I wanted to pass," Harris said, "but Salem had everyone covered. I waited too long to throw, so I ran the other way and got a good block from Jeff Robertson."[952]

Two vital statistics in this one: Salem punted the ball seven times for 37 yards a kick and was hit with 10 penalties for 100 yards.[953]

Up next for the Spartans was a home battle against the Hilltoppers of Lynchburg's E. C. Glass High School.

Game 8 (October 24): E. C. Glass 42, Salem 0

Salemites and Lynchburgers would have to go back to 1964 to recall such a lopsided game between them. That's when Andrew Lewis defeated Glass by a 41-point margin, 53–12.

In 1961, Glass walloped Lewis 33–0, which prompted Wolverines' center Roy Kinsey Jr. to later say, "We learned that Glass will kick your butt."[954]

Two years before that, Glass kicked butt in larger fashion when it pulverized the Wolverines, 54–0. Some people thought the Hilltoppers had run up the score. In fact, in the November 7, 1959, edition of the *Roanoke World-News*, Bob McLelland wrote the game story that appeared under the headline "Glass runs up score on Lewis."

Unofficially, this may have been the beginning of bad blood between the 2 teams. Their fierce rivalry is well chronicled and more than worth reading about.

Now back to the business at hand in 1980.

On a cold and rainy night in Salem, Glass rolled to a 42–0 victory.[955]

Before the start of the game, Salem High School honored Chance Crawford and donated the proceeds from a special commemorative $1 game program to the family of the paralyzed senior quarterback.[956]

217

Crawford was remembered in an emotional moment of silent prayer before the playing of the national anthem, but the game's momentum shifted quickly in favor of the visitors from Lynchburg.[957]

Glass head coach Bo Henson said his players had something to prove after 2 previously frustrating losses to William Fleming (19–7) and Cave Spring (12–7).[958]

In the latter, the Hilltoppers lost three fumbles inside the Knights' 10-yard line, but the Hilltoppers didn't squander many scoring opportunities against a Spartan defense that had been decimated by injuries.[959]

Glass scored on its third play from scrimmage. Senior tailback Kim Deane turned the corner on a sweep left and sprinted 45 yards into the end zone.[960]

Deane scored again on Glass's next possession racing 44 yards through the middle of the Salem defense. But this one was called back because of a holding penalty on the Hilltoppers.[961]

After that, there was no stopping the Hilltoppers, whose win over the Spartans marked their fourth straight victory of the season.[962]

Junior quarterback Matt Mumper threw a 62-yard scoring strike to tight end Greg Brooks. Fullback David Jones carried 4 Salem tacklers into the end zone on a 9-yard run. Deane scored again from 4 yards out to cap a 6-play, 45-yard drive and give the Hilltoppers a 8–0 advantage at the half.[963]

In addition to the lopsided score, consider this lopsided statistic: in yards rushing, Glass tallied 270, while Salem was minus 13.[964]

Up next, the Spartans traveled to Dublin to take on the Cougars of Pulaski County.

Game 9 (October 31): Cougars 27, Spartans 0

Another shutout loss, and this time, a fellow by the name of King Harvey did most of the damage.[965]

Harvey scored three touchdowns and Pulaski County's defense stopped Salem in the second half, carrying the Cougars to a 27–0 Roanoke Valley District football win Friday night.[966]

Salem took the opening kickoff and drove to the Pulaski 5-yard line but lost a fumble to end its most serious threat of the evening. Still, the Spartans controlled the ball most of the first two periods.[967]

The Cougars, now 5–4 overall and 2–3 in the league, finally scored with 3:27 left in the half on fullback Ron Bevins's 10-yard run. And with just 14 seconds left in the half, Harvey caught a 39-yard Curtis Bland TD pass, a toss that was tipped by a Salem defender but grabbed by the Pulaski star.[968]

Harvey, who rushed for 4- and 11-yard touchdown runs after intermission, finished with 55 yards in 15 carries as Coach Joel Hicks substituted freely after 3 quarters.

Salem quarterback Rusty Garst gave the Cougars first-half problems, completing 5 of 8 passes for 52 yards. But in the final 2 periods, Garst was 0-for-12 with an interception.[969]

Salem was now winless in 5 district games and 2–7 overall.

The Spartans will play the 1980 regular-season finale against the Vikings, whose pillagers and plunderers pile up goods in north Roanoke at Northside High.

Game 10 (November 7): Northside 55, Salem 0

The Vikings struck in nearly every imaginable way. Five of their touchdowns were from 39 yards out or more, including a punt and an interception for scores.[970]

Northside quarterback Bill Catron rushed 7 times for 104 yards, a game best, while Salem QB Rusty Garst completed 21 of 49 passes, 10 of those to Steve Hall but none for paydirt.[971]

Ironically, Northside's offense ran just 30 plays compared to Salem's 76, and the Spartans had twice as many first downs as the Vikings, 15–7.[972]

"First downs don't win ball games," said Thompson. "Touchdowns do."[973]

And against Northside, Salem had none.

* * *

On the season, the Spartans finished with an overall record of 2–8, their only wins against Bassett and Fauquier.

The 1980 campaign surely left many in Salem feeling sad.

But the saddest news did not show up in wins or losses but instead in what happened to Chance Crawford.

Thankfully, his multifaceted story contains positive lessons for all of us.

Let's begin with the community's outpouring of support as recalled by Coach Foster.

"There was a 'Chance Crawford fund,' and I was in-charge of it. Schools sent money for his therapy. We gathered $50,000. Today, that would be the equivalent of $100,000. Chance used that money for his therapy. Bob Barnett went with him."[974]

"Charlie Hammersley, Price Richards, Malcolm Tingler, and I were on a committee. We started a 'Chance Crawford Benefit Softball Tournament' and over a hundred teams would play in that tournament every year. The entry fee that teams paid went to the 'Chance Crawford Fund.'"[975]

"It was *unbelievable* the amount of money they made."[976]

* * *

And "unbelievable" may be the best word to describe Crawford's personal story.

Born on February 18, 1963, and named Gary Chance Crawford, he grew up in Salem and recently looked back at his shocking moment in time.[977]

"It was my senior year. I was about 5'11" tall and weighed 185 pounds. I had been the team's starting quarterback predominantly, but Rusty Garst competed for the spot. Before we both went to Salem, I went to Glenvar and he went to Andrew Lewis [middle schools] I think Rusty was a carbon copy of Eddie Joyce Jr. He could really throw the football 70 yards on a rope, and he was very talented."[978]

"My attitude was 'Do what the coaches tell you to do.' I loved football, but I was a better baseball player."[979]

"Football brings out the best in people. It builds character and intestinal fortitude. It gives you the attitude, 'I'm not going to let this (or anything else) beat me.'"[980]

And he certainly proved his doctors wrong.

Crawford said that the doctors, who treated him in Charlottesville, told him he would remain paralyzed from the neck down.[981]

WRONG!

Though confined to a wheelchair, he has feeling from head to toe.[982]

How could medical authorities have been so wrong?

Let's begin with Crawford's personal resolve to improve.

"I was determined I was going to get better. I felt very blessed and very fortunate to have family there for me. And I had extended family and the Salem community. I had such wonderful support, and some of my friends from Salem came to see me daily when I was in the hospital."[983]

He concedes that things would have been different had his spinal cord been severed. It was not; it was bruised.[984]

After his release from UVA hospital, Crawford began therapy at Woodrow Wilson Rehabilitation Center in Fishersville, Virginia.[985]

Crawford diplomatically said that his treatment at this location did not produce the desired results.[986]

But thanks to the efforts of the Salem Sports Foundation, he would have the opportunity to undergo therapy with one of the best in the business.[987]

"Gene Trammell, Price Richardson, and Malcolm Tingler of the Salem Sports Foundation worked together to raise money," said Crawford. "They came up with the idea for the 'Chance Crawford Benefit Softball Tournament.' It was a huge success. They not only wanted me to go to Florida for rehab, but they also managed to purchase a car for me."[38, 988]

---

[38] The website www.chancecrawford.org reports that the Chance Crawford Benefit Softball Tournament began 36 years ago to help Crawford. For the first ten years of the event, proceeds helped Chance through school and college and provided for his medical needs. Chance is now serving as Clerk of Circuit Court

Why Florida?

"There was a therapist there known for his work with patients who had spinal cord injuries. He was a godsend. He worked the living daylights out of me. His name was Ray Cralle.[39] He was a monster of a man—6'6" tall. I worked with him for three years. At first I could hardly do one sit-up. When I left I could do 45 to 50 sit-ups. He had me in tremendous shape. He pushed me to the limits. I reached a point where I plateaued and I had a choice: continue (in therapy) or finish my education and get on with my career."[989]

"I had a strong interest in the insurance business. I never wanted to be a burden to my parents or to society."[990]

After leaving Florida, Crawford completed his education at Radford University and was soon hired by Allstate.[991]

"I got a job as an underwriter at Allstate in 1990. I was proud to have that job. I had been interested in insurance for a long time, and I wanted to someday have my own insurance company."[992]

But a life of public service was soon in the offing.

"I wasn't there very long when a [Salem] city councilman told me that this job [Clerk of the Salem Circuit Court] would be the best for me. Also, I had come to know Terry Murphy [Andrew Lewis alumnus, class of 1971]. He was an older guy who gave me some confidence."[993]

"I took their advice and ran for the office. I was elected in November of 1990. The job began in December and I have been here ever since."[994]

---

for Salem and no longer needs the help, but he continues to make contributions to the community by allowing the tournament to be played in his name to help others. All proceeds are now used to help many different worthy causes and give several college scholarships. Crawford recently said that the most recent tournament included 161 teams.

[39] A Google search yielded these findings: Ray Cralle is an internationally known physical therapist who has designed a program to treat stroke, cerebral palsy, traumatic brain injury, and other neurological conditions, such as multiple sclerosis and near drowning. The business is located in Delray Beach, Florida. (Source: www.raycralle.com).

Nearly twenty-eight years later, Crawford can say with confidence, "I've met a lot of wonderful people, including a lot of great lawyers and judges, and I've made a lot of friends."[995]

He is well aware of what it means to be a public servant.

"We go above and beyond to try to take care of people. We've been fortunate to have great leadership in our schools and community."[996]

And as a perfect example of that whole "Salem born and Salem bred" mind-set, Crawford said, "I'm just a Salemite. And Salem is a great place to grow up and raise a family. In Salem, we put a lot of emphasis on taking care of kids and giving young people a chance to succeed. I feel blessed that the community gave *me* an opportunity. I've enjoyed being the clerk. I love people. Hopefully, when my time is done, people will remember me for caring about people in general, and taking care of them when they came in."[997]

Doctors could not have possibly imagined what the future held for Crawford.

Though it's true he is confined to a wheelchair, he drives a motor vehicle and has committed his life to serving others.[998]

His wife of nearly nine years, Danielle C. Crawford, recently became a public servant when she was elected as city treasurer in 2017.[999]

When not helping others, Crawford has a couple of hobbies.

"I'm a sports fan. I go to the Salem and Virginia Tech (football) games. I've also traveled the United States."[1000]

What does he say is his biggest accomplishment in life?

"Being able to contribute to society. The foundation has been a way of giving back."[1001]

And when asked what message he would like to convey to people for all time, he said, "No matter how bad the situation seems, with enough faith and determination you can succeed—provided you don't allow yourself to give up. You have-to dig deep and realize you can overcome [your circumstances]. Of course, I had family and community support; it wasn't just Salem, it was the Roanoke Valley. When it gets right down to it, we're all family. We need to look out for each other."[1002]

Crawford has obviously overcome, but Foster noted that Crawford's frightful injury had a shocking effect on the community.

"Nothing like that had ever happened around here," said Foster. "I think some kids didn't come out for sandlot football for that reason. It took a while to get over it."[1003]

In time, the kids came back, and Salem's football team is a true success story.

And Crawford's personal story of resolve, gratitude, and public service should serve as an enduring inspiration to us all.

Part 3: Little Fun in Eighty-One

Jody Sease signs letter of intent to Clemson University with his parents looking on.

A preview of the season appeared in the August 30 edition of the *Roanoke Times & World-News*.

It listed Northside as the top team in the Roanoke Valley District with William Fleming a close second.[1004]

Northside's team included Kent Thomas, an all-state defensive tackle who was likely the district's most promising college prospect.

THE SPARTAN SUCCESSION

But the team's greatest strength was likely its offensive line that averaged about 215 pounds.[1005]

Quarterback Billy Catron was expected to throw more passes out of the wishbone attack.[1006]

Where were the Spartans in this preview?

At the bottom of the list, but Salem was at least expected to have an improved team that offered a deeper offensive backfield led by Rodney Varney.[1007]

These words were used to describe the Spartan defensive unit: "Linebacker Larry Love is the leader of a mediocre defense."[1008]

The 1981 Spartan football schedule:

- September 4: at Blacksburg
- September 11: at Cave Spring
- September 18: William Fleming
- September 25: Patrick Henry
- October 2: at Bassett
- October 9: Fauquier
- October 16: at Franklin County
- October 23: at E. C. Glass
- October 30: Pulaski County
- November 6: Northside[1009]

* * *

Thanks to Brian Hoffman, his comprehensive preview of the Spartan football team provided readers with a clear picture of the strengths, weakness, and intangibles of the '81 Salem team.[1010]

What particularly stood out was the strength of this year's offensive line.

Hoffman reported that this unit was bigger and quicker and had benefited from the teaching of assistants Billy Miles Jr. and Danny Wheeling.[1011]

The starters averaged 200 pounds, and the biggest was tackle Jody Sease, who weighed in at 230.[1012]

The other tackle spot belonged to Henry Taylor, while Mike Scott and Reid Garst were the guards and Scott Baker the center.[1013]

This year's team captains were Sease and Bobby Pickle.[1014]

Other players to watch included Curtis Taliaferro, Rodney Varney, and Eddie Riley.[1015]

Larry Light provided a solid kicking game.[1016]

Game 1 (September 4): Blacksburg 18, Salem 7

Tied 7–7 late in the third quarter, Blacksburg's Ricky Graham tossed an 11-yard scoring pass to Chuck Young to give the Indians the only lead they would need.[1017]

Late in the fourth, Salem had a chance to score a tying touchdown, but Blacksburg linebacker Mike Tait intercepted a Spartan pass and returned it 30 yards for a touchdown.[1018]

The Spartans scored on their first possession of the game when Rodney Varney threw 39 yards to Curtis Taliaferro, which capped an 11-play, 72-yard drive.[1019]

Salem committed 4 turnovers—3 fumbles and an interception—and was also assessed 92 yards in penalties; 2 of those turnovers resulted in Blacksburg touchdowns.[1020]

Game 2 (September 11): Cave Spring 20, Salem 12

The Spartans surprised the Knights—and likely the spectators as well—when they jumped out to a 12–0 lead.[1021]

But they couldn't hold the line, thanks to Cave Spring quarterback Todd Stevens.[1022]

Trailing 12–7 at the half, the Knights took the lead in the third when Stevens threw to a wide open Robert Stratton on a second and goal from the 8 to make it 13–12.[1023]

The Knights added an insurance score just 3 minutes later. Salem quarterback Rodney Varney fumbled at the Salem 10, and on fourth and goal, Stevens connected with Mark Overfelt on a 7-yard touchdown pass.[1024]

"We just ran out of gas in the end," said Varney. "When you go both ways like that, it makes it awfully tough."[1025]

Varney was 1 of 6 Salem regulars who went both ways.[1026]

Salem's first score came on a 4-yard run by James Jackson and its second from that distance by Eddie Riley.[1027]

Varney had a team best 96 yards rushing on 17 carries.[1028]

Salem coach Wallace Thompson said, "We are going to get better each week. We're still making mistakes. Mistakes in key situations have hurt us."[1029]

Game 3 (September 18): William Fleming 14, Salem 7

Brian Ferguson rushed for 156 yards, 76 of those on a touchdown, in Fleming's narrow win.[1030]

Salem came razor-close to scoring the game-tying touchdown, but with 29 seconds to play, the 94-yard drive stalled on the Fleming 1-yard line.[1031]

Game 4 (September 25): Patrick Henry 21, Salem 14

Patriots fullback Robert Harley pounded his way for 110 rushing yards, and all three of his team's touchdowns, including the game winner.[1032]

Tied 14–14 with 1:13 to play in the game, PH had moved the ball to the Salem 17, and on a third and 13, a pass may have seemed the preferred play call, but the Patriots went to Harley, who ran it up the middle and all the way for the score.[1033]

On his game-winning touchdown run, Harley broke at least 3 tackles and carried 2 Spartan defenders across the goal line.[1034]

For Salem, Curtis Taliaferro ran 55 yards for a touchdown in the first quarter, and Eddie Riley scored from 2 yards out in the fourth, which tied the game.[1035]

Taliaferro posted some good numbers. He carried the ball 5 times for 61 yards and caught 3 passes for 39.[1036]

Teammate James Jackson tallied 67 rushing yards on 8 carries.[1037]

* * *

Just shy of the midway point in this '81 season, the Spartans were winless at 0–4.

But it wasn't just losing that bothered at least one Salem fan.

In a letter to the editor, the disgruntled writer alluded to the battle between the Roanoke County and Salem school systems and more.

> As a resident of Salem, I have observed with awe the saga of the Salem football team and the Roanoke County-Salem school system battle. My congratulations go to Richard Phlegar who led the Spartans to a near win (against Fleming)...
>
> After comparing the game program with programs from other schools, Salem's is the pits. There were no names under the pictures, not even a football schedule or any mention of the other athletic teams at Salem.
>
> Of all the cheering outfits the Salem cheerleading have, why did they wear the tacky ones last Friday? And when did the band go into mourning with the black uniforms? Thank goodness for the Spartans. I hope the people of Salem will make changes for the better.[1038]

Of this, you can be sure...

* * *

Meanwhile, the '81 season continued, and up next for the Spartans was a tangle with the Bengals.

THE SPARTAN SUCCESSION

Game 5 (October 2): Bassett 13, Salem 9

Trailing 9–6, Bengals' quarterback Daryl Mayes connected with R. J. Scott for a 70-yard touchdown play in the last 2 minutes to give Bassett the victory.[1039]

Salem (0–5) went ahead 9–7 on a 29-yard field goal by David Light with 1:40 left. When Bassett (3–2) took over, it took only 2 plays from scrimmage to score the game winner.[1040]

Salem's other points came on a 1-yard run by Eddie Riley in the fourth quarter. He led the team with 100 yards rushing.[1041]

Game 6 (October 9): Salem 12, Fauquier 7

"Rah, rah for Salem..."

The Spartans claimed their first win of the season when they grounded the Falcons.

Salem scored 2 first-half touchdowns, and its defense played well enough to lift the team to victory.[1042]

Spartans' quarterback Rodney Varney ran for a 3-yard score and passed for a 9-yard TD to Curtis Taliaferro.[1043]

Salem had the opportunity to tack on more points, but field goal attempts of 25, 29, and 37 yards in the fourth quarter by David Light missed the mark.[1044]

"We were sluggish on offense and we missed three field goals, but the defense played well," said Coach Thompson.[1045]

The Falcons (2–4) had a couple of golden opportunities in the fourth, but the Spartans' Robert Houchens intercepted a pass, and later, on a fourth and 4 deep in Salem territory, Houchens came up big again when he jammed a sweep with 1:23 remaining the game.[1046]

"I just broke to the ball," said Houchens. "Our defense is doing great. There was no way they were going to score on us again."[1047]

Game 7 (October 16): Franklin County 10, Salem 0

Bobby Taylor ran for a 27-yard touchdown, and Jeff Turner kicked a 38-yard field goal to lift the homestanding Eagles to their third win of the season against 4 losses.[1048]

Taylor finished with 78 yards in rushing, and teammate Tommy Holland had 80.[1049]

Scoreless at the half, Turner's field goal made it 3–0. In the fourth, Taylor ran for a score, and Turner tacked on the point after.[1050]

Salem had its best opportunity to score late in the first half. The Spartans had moved the ball to the Eagles' 6 with 16 seconds left before intermission, but Tommy Riddle picked off a pass and ended the threat.[1051]

Game 8 (October 24): E. C. Glass 24, Salem 6

This one was played on Saturday after Friday's scheduled contest was postponed due to inclement weather.[1052]

The Hilltoppers nearly pitched a shutout, but with 45 seconds remaining in the game, Rodney Varney connected with Larry Light for a 7-yard touchdown pass.[1053]

Glass scored points in each of the 4 quarters: 3 in the first and 7 in the rest.[1054]

Bo Withers scored 2 touchdowns, a 2-yard run, and a 27-yard pass reception from Gus Miller.[1055]

Glass's defense held Salem to 126 total yards. Varney was 6 of 22 passing with 3 interceptions and 76 yards, including a 43-yarder to Curtis Taliaferro on the Spartans' first possession of the game.[1056]

Withers led Glass with 77 yards rushing and defensive teammate Cap Putt sacked Varney 3 times.[1057]

Salem fell to 1–7, and Glass improved to 2–6.

Game 9 (October 30): Pulaski County 10, Salem 7

Pulaski's win created a 3-way tie with William Fleming and Patrick Henry in the race for the Roanoke Valley District title.[1058]

After a scoreless first quarter, Pulaski's Billy Myers returned a Salem punt 40 yards and, with the addition of a personal foul penalty, placed the ball at the Salem 12.[1059]

Three plays later, Cougars' quarterback Terry Finley ran the bootleg and into the end zone from 5 yards out. Chris Kinzer kicked the point after, and the Cougars led 7–0.[1060]

In the third quarter, Kinzer booted a 34-yard field goal to make it 10–0.[1061]

In the final segment, Salem got on the scoreboard when it capped a 66-yard drive with a 5-yard touchdown run by James Jackson. David Light's point after made it 10–7.[1062]

Salem (1–8) had possession just one more time, but its drive stalled, and Pulaski methodically drove 64 yards and, more importantly, consumed the final 7 minutes of the clock.[1063]

The loss left Salem skipper Wallace Thompson feeling the frustration.

"We just can't seem to win one," he said. "We had our chances but couldn't hit a big pass when we needed it."[1064]

For his part, Jackson had a game best 63 yards in rushing on 15 carries.[1065]

Varney was 6 of 15 passing with 1 pick and 68 yards.[1066]

For Salem, the season finale would be played against the Norsemen from north Roanoke, more commonly referred to as the Vikings of Northside.

Game 10 (November 6): Northside 35, Salem 7

The wind is an invisible factor.

And the Vikings had it in mind when, up 14–7 at the intermission, they opted to kick off to start the second half so that they would have wind advantage in the fourth quarter.[1067]

But things unexpectedly went better than they planned.

Salem's David Adams fumbled the kickoff, and Northside's Jerry Richmond recovered the ball on the Salem 28. Six plays later, Tony Lawrence scored from the 3 to give the Vikings some cushion.[1068]

Northside coach Jim Hickam noted just how crucial the turnover was. "We were agonizing as to what to do, and we finally decided to take the wind in the fourth quarter. And we got the ball anyway."[1069]

Billy Catron scored 2 touchdowns, and teammate Randy Plunkett tallied a game best 145 yards on 15 carries and a TD.[1070]

Salem's lone score came in the second quarter when Rodney Varney ran for the longest touchdown of the night—79 yards.[1071]

"We were still in the game at the half," said Salem coach Wallace Thompson. "We are a much better team than that. We just didn't come to play tonight."[1072]

Statistically, Northside had 22 first downs to just 7 for Salem and 394 rushing yards to Salem's 124.[1073]

Neither team had much success in the air. Catron was 1 of 9 for 25 yards and an interception, and Varney was 5 of 13 for 33 yards.[1074]

The loss left Salem at 1–9 on the season, while Northside finished 7–3, including a fourth-place finish in the district.[1075]

William Fleming won the district with a 9–1 record and defeated Gar-Field in the first round of the playoffs.[1076]

The following week, Fleming fell to GW-Danville, which ended the Colonels' season.[40, 1077]

The All-Roanoke Valley team was announced on November 19.

Fleming placed 7 starters on the first teams, and its coach, John McGregor, was named coach of the year.

The 7 Colonels named were quarterback Mike Reed, tight end Sheldon Johnson, linebacker Ronnie Lewis, running back Roger Fracker, defensive end Tony Taborn, linebackers Ronnie Lewis and Tim Overstreet, and defensive back Steve Brammer.[1078]

Were there any Spartans named?

Yes, flanker Curtis Taliaferro.[1079]

Taliaferro sparked the Spartans with 35 catches on the season for 358 yards.[1080]

---

[40] GW-Danville went on to play Hampton in the state finals and lost, 15–9 (source: VHSL record book, page 28).

THE SPARTAN SUCCESSION

Four of his teammates earned second team honors. Jody Sease was named to both the offense and defense as a tackle, David Taliaferro to the offense as a tight end, and Rodney Varney and Eddie Riley to the defense as a safety and end, respectively.[1081]

The Spartans held their team awards banquet at the Salem-Roanoke County Civic Center; it was hosted by the Salem Sports Foundation. Sease and Curtis Taliaferro were named the team's MVPs.[1082]

The guest speaker at the event? None other than Carey Casey.[1083]

Taliaferro's selection provided some positive news about a Spartan team that had little to celebrate this season.

Would next season bring more of the same, or would the Spartans turn things around?

Either way, they would do so under the leadership of a different coach.

A little over a month after this season concluded, Wallace Thompson announced his resignation.[1084]

"I think it was the best thing for all concerned," he said. "The kids at Salem were wonderful to work with, and I appreciate their interest in the sport. But I think it would be best to get some new blood on the scene. It might be best for the football program to have some new direction."[1085]

Thompson also cited a lack of community support.

"I felt like the kids needed a change. I don't feel like they have enough support outside the school and they deserve it. With a change, maybe everyone will get behind them and that's what they need."[1086]

Bayes Wilson, superintendent of Roanoke County schools, said he will begin to advertise for the position, as well as the coaching position at Glenvar High.[1087]

"Coach Thompson is a fine individual and dedicated school person," said Wilson. "His interest and decision [are] based on doing whatever is best for the players and students at Salem High."[1088]

Thompson indicated that he planned to remain in the county school system and continue as a driving instructor.[1089]

Wilson noted that since the city of Salem will assume operation of Salem High in 1983, he will consult with Frank Cosby, superintendent of Salem schools, to decide on a replacement for Thompson.[1090] Cosby would look eastwardly for such a replacement.

Chapter 9

A Secession of Sorts

Salem mayor Jim Taliaferro
(Photo provided courtesy of Mike Stevens, Communications Director for the City of Salem)

MARK A. O'CONNELL

Virginia's Championship City is also a city of champions. Photo taken by author with permission of the Salem Museum

THE SPARTAN SUCCESSION

The welcome to Salem sign includes the city's official seal of a dove carrying an olive branch.

Most breakups don't happen overnight; they are typically the culmination of a series of events, or acts, that undermine and gradually dissolve the foundation of a relationship or union.

Relevant here is that the ongoing news in the local community—including the stated opinions of top officials—must have served as advanced notice that a breakup was in the works.

What breakup?

Salem's school system under the control of Roanoke County

Even without the benefit of hindsight, it is reasonable to assert that the people in Salem would not be content as long as they remained beholden to the county.

But while it may be difficult—if not impossible—to pinpoint exactly when such feelings surfaced, our review of the history took us back to at least the spring of 1979 for early signs of evident dissension.

In conjunction with Salem High School looking for a football coach to replace Tom Kucer and the campaign to reinstall Eddie Joyce, the move toward independence had taken hold.[1091]

Salem officials had proposed a $1.64 million plan for establishing an independent Salem school system after the 1982–83 school year, though the city council was not ready to commit itself to the idea just yet.

The proposal was prepared by Salem County school superintendent Arnold Burton at the request of Salem City manager William Paxton and the Salem School Board.[1092]

It was apparently unrelated to the controversy over hiring Joyce, and Salem School Board Chairman B. G. King was emphatic about the subject. "It would be a mistake to interpret the capital proposal as a decision to go into the school business."[1093]

But some city council members thought otherwise.

Carl E. "Sonny" Tarpley Jr., who played under Joyce at Andrew Lewis, said county superintendent Burton's apparent unwillingness to name Joyce to the Salem job was indicative of the city's problems with the school contract.[1094]

Vice Mayor W. Mac Green said he did not like the arrangement where the county school board "tells us what we'll give them."[1095]

And Councilman Robert E. "Bob" Barnett directly tied the Joyce issue to the school situation.

"I don't think Salem has enough say in what's going on. Most of the people in Salem want Joyce to be the coach. We're paying for the school, so why shouldn't we get it?"[1096]

The path toward independence continued, with or without intentionality.

In June of 1979, the Salem City Council directed city attorney R. S. Cline to prepare an amendment to the city's charter expanding the Salem School Board from 3 members to 5.[1097]

The expanded board was expected to study the possibility of the city forming its own system.[1098]

Speculation about a separate school system heightened when the county board chose Wallace Thompson as Salem High School's football coach instead of Eddie Joyce, who had strong support in the city and the endorsement of the Salem School Board.[1099]

By mid-August 1979, the Salem Planning Commission had approved a revised $9 million capital improvements plan with a watered-down section on the needs of a possible independent school system.[1100]

This commission voted to recommend to city council that the revised plan be approved.[1101]

The city had been buying the school buildings with its boundaries from the county in annual installments that would be completed in the fiscal year 1982–83.[1102]

"I Can Help"[41]*

Salem set December 10, 1979, as the date for a public hearing on a proposed charter change that would increase membership on Salem's school board from 3 to 5 members. An alternate plan would be for Salem to have voting representation on the county school board.[1103]

If the alternate was pursued, Salem would get help from state senator Dudley J. "Buzz" Emick. He told a city county legislature meeting that he would submit legislation to the general assembly to have Salem represented on the county board if city officials asked him to, and he would intercede on the state level if urged by Salem's elected leaders.[1104]

And by early August of the following year (1980), Salem had just hired someone to aid in contract talks.[1105]

That someone was a man by the name of Frank A. Cosby.[1106]

He had served as the school superintendent in Covington for the past 2 years and in neighboring Craig County before that.[1107]

Considering that Salem had no independent school system yet, Cosby's job for the next 3 years would be helping Salem officials negotiate with Roanoke County officials on a new education contract.[1108]

---

[41] News of this assistance prompted this author to think of a former no. 1 hit song, "I Can Help" by Billy Swan, whose recording was released in 1974. The opening lyrics are "If you've got a problem, I don't care what it is. If you need a hand, I can assure you of this, I can help. I've got two strong arms, I can help. It would sure do me good to do you good, let me help" (source: Wikipedia).

Here's some important history: Salem was part of the county until becoming an independent city on January 1, 1968. Since then, Salem children had continued attending county schools under a contract between the city and county. The said contract was due to expire in 1983.[1109]

As for naming Cosby, the Salem School Board made the appointment at an informal meeting that lasted less than two minutes.[1110]

Chairman Richard "Dick" Fisher asked for a vote to hire Cosby, and all 5 board members said yes.[1111]

Fisher said Cosby, who attended the meeting, was selected from among 6 qualified applicants (names not mentioned) and after the vote, Bayes Wilson, the county's new superintendent, congratulated Cosby.[42, 1112]

Fisher indicated that Cosby's main job would be advising the board on a new contract.[1113]

"We look forward to him [Cosby] representing us in educated fashion, so we can arrive at a contract that is beneficial to Salem and the county," said Fisher.[1114]

In case Salemites were asking "Frank who?" or "Who's Cosby?" Wilson reported that he had known him for several years and expected to have a very good working relationship.[1115]

The move toward independence had truly gained momentum.

In the past, Salem officials had expressed discontent over the education contract. The city provided about 20 percent of the school budget but had no vote on the county school board and no say in school and education policy and administration.[1116]

---

[42] On the subject of Bayes Wilson, Dale Foster told this author that Wilson became the superintendent of Roanoke County Schools, effective July 1, 1980. Foster thought well of him: "He was one of the finest gentlemen I ever worked with. He was the one most responsible for getting that school (Salem High) started. I still talk to him about once a week. Before he left for the job to become the superintendent of Roanoke County, he came by my office and laid a $15,000 dollar check on my desk and said, 'Now go down on 4th Street and buy that blue van. We need the van for cross country and track, golf and all that stuff.' I did so the next day. To this day, when I call him, I'll ask him, 'Do you have any more of those $15,000 dollar checks?!'"

THE SPARTAN SUCCESSION

As for his academic credentials, Cosby was a graduate of Randolph-Macon College and the University of Richmond. He had taught in elementary and high schools and had also served as an elementary school principal in Southampton County.[1117]

His wife, Mary Page, was an elementary teacher in Alleghany County and taught reading at Mason's Cove and Catawba elementary schools in Roanoke County, while her husband was superintendent in Craig.[1118]

Cosby, 40 years of age at the time, indicated that his wife would quit her job and that the family would move to Salem as soon as their house in Covington had been sold.[1119]

Three days after the news of Cosby's hiring, an article appeared in the August 8, 1980, edition of the *Roanoke Times & World-News* written by an unnamed author whose writing was indicative of someone well versed in history, politics, and the law.

Consider the following.

> Frank A. Cosby, named this week as Salem's first school superintendent, will head a nonexistent system. Under a 10-year contract to expire in 1983, the city's youngsters are educated in schools run by Roanoke County.[1120]
>
> Until now, legal requirements have been met by designating the county superintendent as the superintendent for Salem also. But with the expiration of the contract approaching, Cosby has been hired to explore possible new arrangements from the city's point of view and to advise Salem officials during the negotiations.[1121]
>
> In that light, having 2 superintendents for 1 system is not necessarily a farcical extravagance. But hiring a full-time educator for the negotiations, rather than simply securing legal or accounting consultation, suggests that more could be at

stake than relatively minor adjustments to the contract. The creation of a separate Salem school system appears to be a live possibility.[1122]

Already, the city owns the recently constructed Salem High School, though it is run by the county, and by 1983, the city will have completed the purchase of county school buildings within municipal boundaries. About 4,500 Salem youngsters are of school age, enough to lend plausibility to the idea of a separate system.[1123]

Negotiations between localities over joint services sometimes have a way of accentuating differences rather than common interests, of turning friends into adversaries. Already, the structure of local government in the Roanoke Valley—with two cities, one town, and an urbanized county—fails to reflect the truth that the area is an economic and social unit. Unless there is very good reason, the valley shouldn't be balkanized further.[43, 1124]

The Opening Salvo

When it comes to seeking one's independence, someone—somewhere and somehow—must "fire the opening shot."

---

[43] The writer used the word *balkanized* as a likely reference to what happened in the Balkans or the Balkan Peninsula, a geographic area in southeastern Europe. In recent history, the First Balkan War broke out in 1912. The First World War was sparked in the Balkans in 1914. During World War II, all the Balkan countries, except Greece, were allies of Nazi Germany. Despite the alliance, German troops eventually occupied the region, and the people suffered considerable hardship due to repression and starvation, to which the population reacted by creating a mass resistant movement. At the end of 1944, the Soviets entered two of these countries, Bulgaria and Romania, which forced the Germans out but also left a region largely ruined as a result of wartime exploitation (source: Wikipedia).

THE SPARTAN SUCCESSION

By November of 1980, one could be "heard."

Analogous to the firing on Fort Sumter in 1861, the first shots had to be fired for Salem's independence too.

But when and by whom?

During the time mentioned above, an article hinted at this very thing.

These are some of its excerpts:

> This winter Cosby will earn his $33,000 salary by continuing to gather information to help the Salem School Board and City Council decide whether the city will remain with Roanoke County schools or make the final break from the county.[1125]

> "They have not indicated to me, 'Hey, we're going independent,'" said Cosby of the Salem board members. "They have indicated to me that we're going to try to get something better than they have now... They want a little bit more local control."[1126]

> County officials had made it clear that they wanted Salem to continue with county schools after the current contract expires in 2 ½ years. They fired the first shot earlier in this month, offering Salem essentially the same terms that are on the current contract—total county control.[1127]

> It landed with a thud, bouncing off Salem officials like a cannonball off Old Ironsides.[1128]

> Cosby indicated that he and the School Board would consider the extremes of going independent versus another contract with the county, then "negotiate something in between."[1129]

Cosby said he knew he was taking a chance when he left Covington, a city with a school system, for Salem, a city without a school system. He expected to get a full four-year contract next year…and said he'll have plenty to do regardless of Salem's relationship with the county.[1130]

The writer put forth a key question to Cosby: "Isn't it an advantage to your future if you recommend separate schools for Salem?"[1131]

Cosby replied, "Golly, it is. But I don't operate that way. I think I can be objective."[1132]

Either way, he said there is plenty to do, either building a school system from scratch or protecting the city's interests under a new contract.[1133]

Further, Salem officials had grumbled about the city's lack of a vote on the county board, but they had no leverage when the contract was negotiated in the early 1970s.[1134]

But the leverage was no longer lacking.

Why?

Because when negotiations for a new contract begin next year, Salem would have leverage because Salem High, which it built and owned, is one of ten county schools and former schools that had become Salem property under the current terms of the contract.[1135]

The next key development occurred during the first week of December in this same year.

Roanoke County school officials had extended an open palm to Salem in hopes of a handshake commitment to continue their joint school system.[1136]

At a special county school board meeting, Chairman William Ergle read an open letter to Salem officials, reiterating the county's support for a combined system.[1137]

"Everyone on the Roanoke County School Board and the Roanoke County Board of Supervisors feels that the quality of education will suffer it separate school systems are established," said Ergle.[1138]

The letter also explained why Roanoke County asked Salem officials to decide by January 20 whether they will negotiate a new contract when the current pact expires.[1139]

Salem officials indicated that they could not meet the deadline but that they were committed to negotiating a new contract but only if the city can obtain equitable terms. City council members had openly criticized terms of the current contract, which led some city officials to suspect the city planned to establish an independent school system.[1140]

But what loomed as the dark cloud to the prospect was this caveat: The county's new proposal would not give Salem a vote on the governing board, but it would provide for separate maintenance of schools by each locality. It would also give Salem an interest in buses purchased by the school system.[1141]

Salem officials didn't feel hurried and apparently weren't going to be rushed.[1142]

It remained committed to negotiating with Roanoke County an extension of their joint school services contract.[1143]

Salem Mayor Jim Taliaferro reiterated the view of other city officials that Salem probably would not meet the county-imposed deadline for setting up negotiations.[1144]

"Regardless of what has transpired, it will not deter us from our commitment to negotiate an equitable school contract," said Taliaferro after a city council meeting.[1145]

Negotiations on a new contract were expected to be complicated and to take several months. If Salem chose to establish an independent school system, the county would need time to reassign students, teachers, and other school personnel.[1146]

One can easily infer—based on the aforementioned information—that Salem was not going to meet the county's deadline of January 20, 1981.

On January 13 of that year, at least one news source indicated that negotiations between Salem and Roanoke County on a new school service contract would begin within the next few weeks.[1147]

Dr. Fisher told news sources that a report by Cosby would be ready later in the week. He was quoted as saying, "We will then set up some special school board meetings to discuss the report and name a negotiating committee to meet with the county."[1148]

He added, "We will respond to the county's request and ask that negotiations be delayed until a more appropriate time."[1149]

Cosby reminded readers that his role was to provide statistical and financial information and information about programs.[1150]

Salem reportedly remained committed to negotiating a new contract, but only if the city can get equitable terms.[1151]

Salem Mayor James Taliaferro said, "The present contract contains clauses that do not represent good government on the part of Salem. We won't sign another one like it."[1152]

He also indicated that Roanoke County's new contract proposal was unacceptable.[1153]

In a nutshell, Roanoke County's new ten-year contract proposal would not give Salem a vote on the governing school board, but it would provide for separate maintenance of schools by each locality—a position favored by some council members.[1154]

The county's proposal would also give Salem interest in buses purchased by the school system.[1155]

Those offers, and about 0.75 cents, would buy Salemites a 0.75 cent cup of coffee.

And Then There Were Three

The following month, the Salem School Board met and named three individuals to negotiate a new school services contract with Roanoke County with hopes that talks could begin within a month.[1156]

The three were Dr. Fisher, June Long, and John Moore.[1157]

The school board members had just discussed, in closed session, a preliminary report by Cosby, whose report would serve as the basis for negotiations. Cosby would not make a final recommendation on contract negotiations until spring.[1158]

Fisher indicated that he expected negotiations to take four to six weeks.[1159]

Roanoke County officials felt encouraged by Salem's willingness to negotiate but wanted the talks to begin soon.[1160]

If Salem opted for a separate school system, then Roanoke County officials wanted sufficient time to work out personnel changes.[1161]

Three days later, news sources reported that school officials for both Salem and Roanoke County planned to meet on February 26, 1981, to begin negotiations for a new contract.[1162]

"I am looking forward to the opportunity to sit down with Salem and discus the points of agreement and disagreement," said William Ergle, chairman of the county school board.[1163]

It appeared the ball was in Salem's court, as the expression goes. Why?

Because this same source indicated that the county school board had already proposed a new contract, while Salem officials said they planned to seek additions to it. They had not yet revealed what those additions were.[1164]

The contract proposed by the county would run for ten years, but each locality would have the option of terminating it earlier with two and a half years notice.[1165]

Based on what we have explored about Salem and its residents, is there any question that some degree of resentment existed in the minds of Salemites about being under the county's control?

It's a safe bet that the short answer to that question is yes.

This same news source reminded the readers of some important historical facts.

Indeed, 1968 was a very pivotal year.

When Salem was a town, it was part of the county, so there was no question about school operation. But in 1968 Salem became an independent city, and it was then that it entered into a contract, allowing the county to operate city schools.[1166]

But could Salemites have been truly happy with that situation?

Likely not, but the complete breakaway from this union—like so many others before or after it—could not happen overnight.

Clearly, the steps toward independence continued to fall into place.

* * *

In February of 1981, Salem officials postponed opening talks on extending the city county school services contract.[1167]

Salem's school board indicated that it was deeply concerned by the supervisors' decision to act as contract negotiators. Two weeks prior, supervisors named themselves negotiators and relegated the county school board and school administrators to advisory roles in the talks.[1168]

Salem officials made the decision to postpone talks until March 5 to give the county time to reevaluate its position. And Cosby called the supervisors' decision to act as negotiators as "political in nature."[1169]

* * *

One can easily predict that tensions would soon rise, and at least one news source reported on this very topic.

Consider these excerpts:

> Rising tension between Salem and Roanoke County threaten to subvert the localities' school contract negotiations before any meetings take place.
>
> For the past three days, local leaders have traded barbs over the issue of whether county supervisors should participate in contract talks.[1170]
>
> Lawrence Terry, vice chairman of the county Board of Supervisors, issue a prepared statement intended to halt conflicts, but that statement did not meet the concerns of city officials.[1171]

Terry said Salem officials had misinterpreted the board's intent in joining the talks. Supervisors were interested only in legal and financial matters in the contract and would leave educational issues to school administrators and School Board members.[1172]

He also said that recent moves by Salem City Council and its School Board casted "grave doubts on the sincerity of those parties in entering into fruitful school contract talks."[1173]

That statement, predictably, angered Salem officials.[1174]

Here's how Salem Mayor Jim Taliaferro responded: "In a nutshell, I believe [Terry's prepared statement] absolutely proves our position that negotiations should be left to educators and the school boards… If egos are involved, they should be cast aside."[1175]

Terry clarified his position with this: "We do not want to get involved in operating the school system. Anything Bayes Wilson [county school board superintendent] and the School Board say on those things, we'll accept, if it's in reason."[1176]

And Taliaferro's closing statement in this article?

"The supervisors simply do not, and cannot, understand the necessity that educational issues be in writing. If they're in the contract, there is no problem having everyone understand them."[1177]

And Ergle?

"It would be a grave tragedy perpetuated on the children of Roanoke County and Salem if two groups, one representing each other, don't sit down and talk to each other."[1178]

And future communications would likely remain private.[1179]

The news report of March 16 indicated that negotiators had decided that this would be the forum. And even that decision was made in private.[1180]

During their private meeting, officials broke down into little private meetings as well.[1181]

And for the public?

Public information would be limited to joint press releases and news conferences by the county and city school superintendents after each session.[1182]

Dr. Fisher expressed several Salem concerns in a prepared statement. They included city participation in decisions on school personnel, curriculum, pupil assignments to schools, finance, building maintenance, school facilities, pupil transportation, and the duration of a new contract.[1183]

And Cosby was certainly looking ahead to a what-if scenario.

He told a news source that he will have to double his staff if contract negotiations with Roanoke County do not work out.[1184]

And now this important reminder: the contract between Salem and Roanoke County was due to expire on June 30, 1983.[1185]

Tick tock…

Yes, but Only If…

It was no April's Fools when the Roanoke newspaper reported that the county made a conditional offer to Salem.[1186]

Here's the deal: Salem would have a voting member on the Roanoke County School Board if the city and county continue their education contract beyond 1983.[1187]

The reporter wrote:

> The lack of a voting member on the county board has been an irritant to Salem officials for many years, often mentioned when talk of an independent school system for the city comes up.[1188]

Cosby's Comprehensive Report

Cosby presented his findings.

The gist of those were: Salem could run its own comprehensive, quality school system for about the same money it paid Roanoke County for education services.[1189]

Cosby had just completed a "feasibility study," which included 110 pages. He indicated that, regardless of the outcome of the negotiations, "I think there will be opportunities to work together."[1190]

Let's consider some very important numbers.

Salem had about 4,000 pupils, which represented about 31 percent of the county schools' 19,500 pupils. If Salem opted to create its own school system, it would be in the top half of Virginia School divisions in size and among the top 20 percent in the nation.[1191]

Having a vote on the board was not the only thing Salem wanted. Its officials wanted to discuss personnel and pupil assignments and financial arrangements for a new contract. Both Salem and county officials agreed that contract negotiations should be completed by June 1.[1192]

* * *

Remember those closed sessions between Salem and county officials?

They remained in place, but in mid-April members of the Salem School Board indicated that they would hold a public information meeting on May 12 to give citizens a closer look at a study that says the city could have a separate school study.[1193]

Dr. Fisher described Cosby's report as "very comprehensive" and "gratifying" to him that the report showed that Salem could function adequately with its own school system.[1194]

Of course, it takes money to make most things happen, and negotiations were clouded by the prospect of massive cuts being pushed by supervisors who were concerned about the county's rest estate tax rate.[1195]

From Salem's perspective, Cosby's report indicated that Salem could operate a quality school system of its own at about the same cost or less than it was paying the county for education.[1196]

The report clearly indicated that Salem could pull off having a separate school system with success, but it stopped short of any outright recommendation for an independent system.[1197]

Cosby did, however, intimate that Salem had a unique opportunity.

"It is an unusual opportunity for a community to be able to structure its educational commitment on the desires and needs of the community. An opportunity to build a total school system from the bottom based on actual needs during present economic times is unprecedented in the commonwealth of Virginia, and perhaps nationally as well."[1198]

* * *

What happened at the public information meeting scheduled for May 12?

About 75 Salem residents filled into the city council chambers to hear Cosby explain how Salem could have its own school system for about the same or slightly less money than it cost the city to contract with the county.[1199]

This crowd was the largest for a city school board meeting. One board member, Glenn Thornhill, remarked, "Nobody ever shows up."[1200]

But not everyone supported the prospect of Salem having its own school system, and Cosby fielded questions with considerable confidence about Salem's ability to pay the costs. Under the contract at the time, Salem paid 21 percent of all school operating costs, based on the city's percentage of total enrollment, and it cost more per pupil to run school buses in rural areas of the county than in Salem.[1201]

Cosby said Salem was paying about $6.6 million this school year on education, with most of it going to the county. This amount represented 48 percent of Salem's revenue.[1202]

Two days later, Roanoke County and Salem officials ended school contract talks still miles apart on major issues.[1203]

It appeared, however, that Salem would form its own school system, but neither side indicated that all hope for an agreed-upon resolution was lost.[1204]

Cosby said that in mid-June officials would return to the public forum for more input. He also said that he expected the school board to decide by July 1 whether to continue a school contract with the county or create its own school system.[1205]

What was the county's position on this matter?

Its officials made it clear that they wanted Salem to stay with the county schools, but they were not willing to relinquish any control of the schools to the city or renegotiate the present contract as Salem had proposed.[1206]

A Report on Salem's Mayor

By 1981, Jim Taliaferro was in his eighth year as the mayor of Salem.[1207]

In June of that year, his health was a topic of conversation.[1208]

He had open-heart surgery due to a blockage and would likely need about six weeks to recuperate.[1209]

One of his fellow council members was asked if Taliaferro had considered resigning, and the unnamed member candidly replied, "Of course not. I wouldn't let him even if he wanted to."[1210]

And while Taliaferro underwent surgery and looked to recuperate, the political tug-of-war between county and Salem officials continued.

In fact, county officials gave Salem a deadline to decide what it was going to do.[1211]

A "showdown" was nearing when the county school board said it wanted to know by June 30 if Salem intended to continue with the county school's system or create one of its own.[1212]

Not only that, but the county may opt to cut the city loose.[1213]

Apparently, county officials were none too happy about Salem's intentions.[1214]

Here is some of what Jack Chamberlain wrote on the subject:

> And in a scathing report repudiating some of Salem's claims, County
>
> Superintendent Bayes Wilson said he doubts the city can create and maintain a school system as good as the county's as cheaply as Salem School officials have told the public. Board members seemed especially angered at Salem's delay because of the uncertain future of 115 Glenvar junior high students starting 10th grade at Salem High School this fall.[1215]
>
> If Salem breaks from county schools, those students will spend their senior year back at Glenvar…without Salem as part of the county system, Glenvar would become a high school again.[1216]

Some board members accused Salem of purposely dragging their feet. Board chairman Bill Ergle said Salem's decision was long overdue.[1217]

And Wilson disagreed with Cosby's report on several points. Further, he indicated that he had met with about 100 parents of the 115 Glenvar students starting at Salem High School this fall. The parents voted 99–6 to send their children to Salem for the next 2 years, even if they had to return to Glenvar in 1983–84.[1218]

Wilson opined, "Salem and county children attending other schools in or near the city (of Salem) would also have to change schools if the current school system is disrupted by Salem going on its own."[1219]

Salem officials said they would make their decision soon, but first, they wanted to hear from the public again, which was set to take place at the Salem-Roanoke County Civic Center.[1220]

* * *

Likely, it mattered little what county officials thought when it came time for Salem to make its ultimate decision. The move toward independence had gained traction. It would have taken a major turn of events to stem the momentum in this direction. Nevertheless, people made their opinions known, including the *Roanoke Times & World-News*.

In an editorial published by that news source on June 15, 1981, this was its conclusions:

> It would be a shame if the harsh words of county officials evolve into the kind of ultimatum that forces Salem into a corner from which there is no graceful exit, thereby assuring that the city will decide to go it alone. Local government in the Roanoke Valley is already too balkanized; separate schools for the county and Salem would make this worse.[1221]
>
> County Superintendent Bayes Wilson is skeptical of Cosby's conclusions, and so are we…apart from dollars-and-cents considerations, there are also intangible costs—the disruption of pupil assignments and teacher relocations, probable cuts in the scope and quality of programs—that would be felt on both sides.
>
> Salem's threat to withdraw from the county system and the county's threat to expel Salem from that system may be nothing more than negotiation tactics to obtain concessions from the other localities. If so, it's a dangerous game. The situation cries out for imaginativeness and good faith directed not toward separation but toward cooperation.[1222]

The public hearing was held on June 17, and nearly 300 persons showed up. The majority said they wanted the city to stay with Roanoke County schools.[1223]

Most of the 300 lived in Salem, while 25 to 50 were county residents.[1224]

The Roanoke County Council of PTAs offered to mediate if Salem and county officials agreed to resume talks.[1225]

Dr. Fisher opened the meeting and said there appeared to be "no way" to negotiate a contract that Salem could accept.[1226]

As for the huge crowd in attendance, Fisher told a reporter that people who oppose change usually turn out, while those who favor change stay home.[1227]

And those who opposed Salem leaving county schools don't know all the facts.[1228]

One such resident was particularly outspoken.

Clarence P. Caldwell Jr. was his name. He reported that he had been a resident of Salem for 30 years and a business vice president of Roanoke College. He disagreed with Cosby's report.[1229]

"Many of the citizens with whom I have talked are highly suspicious that this public hearing is only an exercise in futility because the decision in this very important matter has already been made, at least in the minds of the majority, if not all, of both the Salem School Board and Salem City Council. I hope this is not so."[1230]

Further, he believed that the current contract, civic pride and emotion [were] major influences on Salem officials' feelings about the city's relationship with county schools, none of which [were] objective or valid."[1231]

Caldwell even mentioned "the Eddie Joyce debacle a couple of years ago" as the last straw for Salem officials who wanted Joyce hired as Salem High School's football coach, but the county school board and administration refused to hire him.[1232]

The audience applauded Caldwell several times, and some stood to applaud at the conclusion of his speech.[1233]

Jim Cromer, a self-described "Salem boy all [his] life," attributed athleticism rather than education as the reason Salem officials wanted their own system.[1234]

"To be honest with you," said Cromer, "I feel the whole movement lies in athletics. God help us."[1235]

Individuals also expressed their concerns by submitting letters to the editor.

Consider the contents of this one: "I have yet to talk with anyone who is for a separate system. It is so unrealistic… Since this decision will affect our children and the entire community, I believe it should be voted on by the community, not by a chosen few who at times appear to be out of touch with the real needs of the community."[1236]

* * *

The sheer turnout and the opinions expressed at the public information hearing encouraged Roanoke County's supervisors and School Board members. Supervisors' chairman Bob Myers was open to any reasonable suggestions from Salem, including reopening negotiations.[1237]

Dr. Fisher said the Salem School Board wanted to talk to county school superintendent Bayes Wilson next.[1238]

Fisher said he did not want a separate school system just so Salem could have its own, but neither did he want another contract with the county that was unfair to Salem.[1239]

The deadline for Salem's decision was extended from June 30 to July 7 when the city's school board was next scheduled to meet.[1240]

* * *

Though originally assigned as a fact finder, Cosby soon became the messenger of good news. He told reporters that Roanoke County negotiators appeared willing to make concessions to Salem on a new school contract.[1241]

Wilson said he talked to Cosby about reconsidering a contract. Cosby used the word *concessions*, while Wilson used the words *discuss* and *consider*.

Cosby had met in closed session with the Salem School Board and provided more information on forming a separate school system or continuing with the county schools under a new contract.[1242]

When asked if he expected the county to make enough concessions to satisfy Salem, he said, "No. That's my opinion."[1243]

* * *

At least county and city officials had agreed to resume school pact talks.

This time Wilson used the word *concessions*. "We requested another meeting with the Salem School Board to discuss some reconsiderations or concession we are willing to consider."[1244]

Cosby, however, said he thought the Salem School Board was near a decision before it received the county's new invitation to meet, but he declined to say what that decision was.[1245]

The Salem School Board was next scheduled to meet for its annual reorganization as required by state law and planned to announce then whether to form its own school system or continue with the county.[1246]

County negotiators had already agreed to give Salem a voting member on the county school board under the new contract by increasing the school board size from five to six members.[1247]

Salem demanded more.[1248]

And its official decision would come on July 9, 1981.[1249]

"The Union Is Dissolved"[44]*

Jack Chamberlain had followed this story from the beginning, and it seemed only fitting that he would follow it to its fateful conclusion.

---

[44] the use of this phrase was inspired by this author's love for history, especially the War Between the States. The declaration is chiefly attributed to The Charleston Mercury's "The Union is Dissolved." It was the first Confederate publication as South Carolina was the first state to secede. It went to press 15 minutes after the secession ordinance was passed. Source: amhistory.si.edu/militaryhistory.

He did so in his article that appeared under a three-word headline that told the story then and for all time: "Salem declares independence."[1250]

The vote was unanimous.[1251]

Predictably, county and city officials responded differently.[1252]

County officials reacted with expressions of disappointment, while photographs of Dr. Fisher revealed a sequence of facial expressions that depicted his satisfaction with the decision.[1253]

William Ergle, county school board chairman, said, "I've always had serious doubts about the sincerity of the negotiations on their [Salem's] part."[1254]

A smiling Fisher said, "We need to have control in the areas we discussed."[1255]

His fellow board members were seen smiling, too.[1256]

And Cosby?

"I think it was a proper decision," he said.[1257]

And Wilson?

"I'm surprised by the suddenness of it after we met [previously] and made what we consider[ed] some major concessions."[1258]

The county school board said it would not contract with Salem for any school services if the city broke away from the county system.[1259]

"That's their loss, then," said Cosby.[1260]

Approximately three weeks after the decision, Salem City Council met on July 27 and supported the school board's decision to form a separate school system. Council unanimously acknowledged the decision as final and called upon "all citizens to work together in order that Salem may have one of the best school-system in the commonwealth."[1261]

Salem's decision represented a secession of sorts.

Was it a good one?

As is true with any other decision, the passage of time is the best indicator.

People who had lived in Salem during the 1960s had witnessed Salem go from being a town to a city (1968), and the decision to create a separate school system and establish its independence must have seemed inevitable to them.

Both county and Salem officials were well aware of the civic pride that existed in Salem: call it the "Salem born and Salem bred" state of mind.

But that hardly trumped Salem's official concerns; city officials wanted a fair shake for Salem, and they remained determined to get it.

While many Salem residents had expressed their concerns and fears about a separate system, Salem School Board members voted otherwise.

In time, those same people may have found themselves grateful that Dr. Fisher and his fellow board members had not caved to public opinion.

* * *

Salem's break from the Roanoke County school system can also be likened to a divorce. A final decree sets forth the terms of the divorce, which often include custody and support.

In fact, *divorce* was the word the editorial section of the *Roanoke Times & World-News* used in that source's edition of November 11, 1981.

And like many divorces, the breakup wasn't exactly "amicable."

But it might also be fair to say that the differences were irreconcilable.

Though the spilt would not be effective until 1983, here—in 1981—there was sufficient evidence to conclude that the two systems did not plan to have much to do with each other once the final decree was entered.[1262]

Which party asked for the divorce?

Salem.

What was part of the fallout?

Students in the western part of the county would go to school in Glenvar instead of continuing to attend Salem High, while Salem students would not have access to a vocational-technical school.[1263]

What's the worry?

The signs pointed to rising costs and a decline of quality education.[1264]

As for Cosby's proposal that programs in business and industries could serve in lieu of a vocational-education technical school, the editorial took the position that if it's a better way to provide a vocational connection, why was the vocational-technical school built in the first place?[1265]

This is a reference to the Arnold R. Burton Vocational-Technical Center located in Roanoke County.

The writer opined:

> The Salem plan sounds suspiciously like a make-do answer mandated by the inadequacy of the city's educational resources. Nobody can be certain of the impact of the divorce on the cost and quality of public education in Roanoke County and Salem. But one thing is for sure: If the proposed solutions don't work out very well, neither the county nor Salem as separate systems will have as much flexibility in trying to make improvements.[1266]

In keeping with the analogy of a divorce, Glenvar gets the role as the helpless child that witnesses the unamicable breakup of the parents but can do nothing to influence the outcome and who gets the final say.

To help put this analogy in perspective, let's consider some important historical facts pertaining to both Salem and Glenvar.

For thirty-three years, Andrew Lewis High—which opened in 1933—was the only high school in Salem.

In 1966, Glenvar was opened and the students in the western part of Roanoke County attended the school. Most of the student body would have attended Andrew Lewis had the school not been established.

In 1977, Salem High School opened, and the former high schools—Andrew Lewis and Glenvar—became junior high schools.

Here, in 1981, Glenvar area residents were told they were getting their high school back.

The cause of it all?

Salem.

County officials said they wanted to make Glenvar a high school again because Salem was leaving the county school system in two years.[1267]

About 300 Glenvar residents were present at the public forum when this decision was announced.[1268]

Their reaction?

"Thank God you are," said Herbert Hopkins, a Glenvar grocery store owner.[1269]

Next, consider the reaction from Roanoke County school superintendent Bayes Wilson after Salem School Board chairman Dr. Richard Fisher suggested that Salem would allow county residents to continue at Salem High if the county would allow Salem students to continue at the vocational-technical center.[1270]

"In the absence of a contract, we do not feel we can rely on Salem taking our children and [us] taking their children," he said.[1271]

Salem School Superintendent Frank Cosby said Salem didn't need the county to have a vocational program. His program would be based on job training with the facilities of area businesses and industries.[1272]

The breakup meant that some county students in the Salem High School attendance zone would graduate from Glenvar High.[1273]

Cosby fielded 15 to 20 calls from county residents who wanted to know where their children would finish high school, particularly those who would be transferred for their senior years.[1274]

* * *

With Salem High School the primary subject of this treatise, much more will follow in the narrative about the school and its football program.

But first, let's consider what it was like for the students at Glenvar when they assembled for the school's official opening once more as a high school.

That happened on August 25, 1982, and the consensus among the students was that it was good to be back and be a part of Glenvar High School. Students liked the idea, and no one interviewed expressed any regret about no longer attending Salem High.[1275]

Glenvar principal James Earp addressed the study body, which assembled in the school gymnasium.[1276]

After his initial and welcoming comments, Earp (with a name aptly suited for his position) announced some of the rules that would ensure law and order. Those included a no-smoking block, no display of affection beyond holding hands, and no inappropriate attire, i.e. no shorts.[1277]

Of those, the no-smoking rule aroused the loudest gasps.[1278]

Guess with a "new sheriff in town," the Highlanders would have to "mind their Ps and Qs."

* * *

For the record, what was the official date of Salem's separation from Roanoke County?

July 1, 1983.[1279]

Next: when did Salem's independent school system officially open its doors to students and teachers?

August 31, 1983.[1280]

And Superintendent Walter Hunt made stops at all six Salem schools beginning at South Salem Elementary.[1281]

There, he met with school principal Martha Smith who said, "I don't think the children know it's a new system."[1282]

But the teachers did.

There was the sense of a new beginning for many who were working in a new system without changing schools. And the change provided a "lift" for many.[1283]

To the west, William Brubeck, the principal at West Salem Elementary for the past 15 years, said little was different, but his attendance line was different, and about half of the children and nine of the 15 teachers were new to the school.[1284]

Over at Salem High, about half the students were new this year. Previously, Salem had grades 10–12 under county administration, but this year added the ninth grade, which meant that its ninth and tenth graders were new to the school. Salem's students also included about 20 who lived in the county and would be allowed to graduate without paying tuition.[1285]

All total, the "independent" Spartans mustered 1,300 students.[1286]

* * *

With the passage of time came opportunities to analyze whether Salem's decision to declare independence had been a good one or not.

For example, in March 1984, Salem High School principal Robert "Bob" Lipscomb shared his thoughts in an interview with Alex Smith, news editor of the *Salem Times-Register*.

Lipscomb had been involved with Salem schools for nearly ten years—four as an assistant principal at Andrew Lewis and six at Salem High.[1287]

Lipscomb had grown up in Mullins, West Virginia, and attended Concord College and Virginia Tech, where he earned a masters.[1288]

In the interview, Smith asked Lipscomb several questions, including this one: It seems that all eyes in the valley are on the Salem School System to see if it will flounder or flourish. Have you felt the pressure?[1289]

Lipsomb's answer: "I think all of us in the system have to be conscious that everybody is looking and has been looking at Salem. I had some friends that sometime ago asked, 'Why on earth did you stay with Salem?' There is, I think a little bit even, perhaps a little paranoid thinking about Salem…Certainly people seem to be perhaps super sensitive to what Salem does… People often accuse Salem of being different, provincial. If you just stop and look, they are the ones who are acting in a paranoid fashion… [There were those] who thought Salem wouldn't do this and when they made the decision to go their own way, they said it would fail...we knew that this was not going to happen. There is too much pride here in the city and in what we can do, and this is what we are going to do. We are in our first year, but I think we will make believers out of them. They are just wrong to think it is not going to function."[1290]

Five months later, Robert Downey, the photo editor for the *Salem Times-Register*, interviewed Bayes Wilson, the superintendent of the Roanoke County School System, about his feelings toward the Roanoke County-Salem split.[1291]

Wilson, who had been with the county since 1956, was asked several questions by Downey, including this one.

How do you feel about Salem forming its own school system?[1292]

Wilson's answer: "At the time, I thought that it would be better for Roanoke County and Salem to stay together. My opinion has not changed on that. But that decision has already been made, and it is behind us now."[1293]

Yes, it sure was.

There would be no turning back for Salem.

Independence had come, and it was here to stay.

Chapter 10

1982: WE SHALL NOT KICK

Carl Richards in a Varina High jacket will
wear the Salem jacket in 1982

A good man and a good coach—that's the consensus among those who knew Wallace Thompson.

THE SPARTAN SUCCESSION

And before moving on to his successor, let's consider some of Thompson's memories from his three seasons as the chief Spartan, plus a summary of his life after Salem.

During our telephone interview for this book, he noted that at the forefront of his memories from his trio of years at Salem is the tragedy that unfolded in 1980 when Salem quarterback Chance Crawford was hit during a playoff game against Bassett High and went down with a paralyzing injury.

Even today, one can hear the anguish in Thompson's voice when he recalls what happened.

"I never got over it. I never will. That was tough. It kind of killed my desire to be a head coach."[1294]

Like any good leader, Thompson assumed his share of the responsibility associated with Crawford's crushing blow.

"I felt some responsibility. We always told him to keep his head up. He put his head down and tried to run over this guy and that was it. The guy that tackled him later went to medical school where he met my son. While there, he expressed some responsibility for what had happened to Crawford."[1295]

As has been shown, Crawford's story—while sad that he was seriously injured—is one of personal triumph, and neither Thompson nor Sidney Jones (the Bassett defender who tackled Crawford) had any personal responsibility for the injury.

So let's switch gears. What was the best thing about ever coaching in Salem, either at Andrew Lewis or at Salem High?

"The best thing was at Andrew Lewis," said Thompson. "All the coaches worked together. Eddie Joyce was a fantastic coach. He let [his assistants] coach. He would never dress you down in front of the kids. I learned a lot from him and from Dale Foster. Foster was my main reason for going to Andrew Lewis."[1296]

But after his three years as Salem's head coach, Thompson knew it was time to step aside.

"In 1982, Salem broke away from Roanoke County and established its own school system," he recalled. "The new superintendent at Salem, Mr. Cosby, wanted to offer the head coaching job of the football team to someone [Carl Richards] in Richmond. Cosby had a brother who was a football coach and who recommended Richards to him."[1297]

When Richards got the job at Salem in 1982, Thompson returned to William Byrd High. The Terriers were under second-year head coach Jeff Highfill, a former Lewis player and 1970 graduate who debuted at Byrd in 1981.[45]

Thompson stayed on for twelve seasons, from 1982 through 1993, where he coached the offensive and defensive lines. While at Byrd, he also coached the boys' outdoor track team, which won a Group AA state championship in 1988.[1298]

After 1993, he started a commercial driving school which he operated for two years. When his father-in-law became ill, Thompson closed the business and devoted his time to taking care of him.[1299]

Now fast forward to 2006. J. R. Edwards, a former William Byrd quarterback and later assistant coach there, took the head coaching job at Hidden Valley High School (located in southwest Roanoke County) in 2005 and contacted Thompson in 2006 about joining him there as an assistant. Thompson agreed, and that year, Hidden Valley won a region title in Division 3 but lost in the state semifinals.[1300]

Thompson returned in 2007, which was officially his last year in coaching.[1301]

Today, Thompson and his family live in Grand Junction, Colorado.[1302]

Thompson is married to Elaine Estella Garber. The couple has two boys. James "Jimmy" Thompson, 56, and Dale Thompson, 55, who was named in honor of Dale Foster.[1303]

More than a decade has passed since Thompson last coached. How does he like to spend his time?

"My wife and I try to go to the gym about three days a week. I also started playing pickleball which is a lot of fun."[1304]

Special note: Thompson said his father-in-law was a preacher in Champaign, Illinois. Former Olympian Bob Richards was a youth at

---

[45] In 2018, Highfill announced that this would be his last after thirty-eight years at the helm (source: *The Roanoke Times*, 09/07/18, Ray Cox).

the time and, along with some of his rowdy friends, used to throw rocks at the church. The preacher encouraged Richards to come to church and soon became a mentor to him. After high school, Richards attended Bridgewater College, where he excelled in track, and later at the University of Illinois. He became an Olympic pole vaulting champion and was the first athlete pictured on the front box of Wheaties breakfast cereal.[46, 1305]

After a telephone conversation with Thompson, it is easy to understand why people thought so highly of him.

* * *

---

[46] "Bob Richards, byname of Robert Eugene Richards (born Feb. 20, 1926, Champaign, Ill., U.S.), American athlete, the first pole-vaulter to win two Olympic gold medals. Sportswriters called him "the Vaulting Vicar" because he was an ordained minister.

"Richards was interested in athletics from boyhood, participating in diving and tumbling before taking up the pole vault in junior high school. He was also a football quarterback in high school. After a difficult adolescence and the breakup of his home by divorce, he was reared by a minister in the Church of the Brethren. He began his higher education in 1944 at Bridgewater College (Virginia), where he played basketball and continued pole vaulting, and then transferred to the University of Illinois, where he received his A.B. degree in 1947. He had become a Brethren minister in 1946 and in 1948 received his M.A. from Illinois

"Richards won or tied in the pole vault at Amateur Athletic Union (AAU) meets nine times (1948–57). In the same period, he also won eight indoor championships. He was the second person ever to pole vault over 15 feet (4.6 m), a feat he accomplished in 1947. At the 1948 Olympic Games in London, he won a bronze medal, and he won his first gold medal at the 1952 Olympic Games in Helsinki, repeating this accomplishment at the 1956 Olympic Games in Melbourne. He also won decathlon championships in the 1951 and 1954–55 AAU meets. He received the James E. Sullivan award in 1951 for outstanding amateur athlete.

"Richards retired from athletics in 1957 and became a spokesman for Wheaties cereal. He taught sociology at the University of Illinois in the late 1940s and later was a member of the faculty of La Verne College (California; now University of La Verne) as well as holding pulpits in the Church of the Brethren. His autobiography, *Heart of a Champion*, was published in 1959" (source: www.britannica.com. At the time this author imported this information, Richards was 92 years old).

Obviously, the hiring of Coach Richards meant that Salem had gone outside the local area to find a new coach.

How did it come about?

Blair Kerkhoff, the high school sports editor at the *Roanoke Times & World-News*, informed local readers of the decision in his article published by that source on February 12, 1982.

Roanoke County superintendent Bayes Wilson announced the appointment of Carl Richards Jr. to the Salem job and of Roger Martin to the position at Glenvar, which was about to reopen as a high school.[1306]

Richards, 39 years of age at the time, had been the head coach at Varina High, a Group AAA school near Richmond for several years and, in 1981, had led the Blue Devils to their first Dominion District championship since 1964.[1307]

He had five losing seasons at Varina before producing his first winner in 1980.[1308]

When he was asked about what he did to improve a "down" program, Richards exclaimed, "Down? That's the understatement of the year. It was at a low ebb for a lot of reasons, so motivation was a major job. We did everything to motivate those kids. I even put up a Christmas tree in the locker room."[1309]

"At Varina, we had to learn not to lose, first. Then we had to learn how to win. When we started to win, we had to learn how to overcome adversity. We made progress each year and became a winner."[1310]

Richards was about to embark on a similar situation at Salem, but he hesitated to equate the two.

"The Salem team has a community to back them. We didn't have that here... We're going to start from square one. To say I can come in here and win a district championship would be asinine."[1311]

Richards would be coming in after being chosen among the other 23 applicants.[1312]

* * *

Kerkhoff stayed on the prep football trail and provided readers with a preview of the 1982 season as it pertained to the Roanoke Valley District.

He predicted that Pulaski County would win the district championship, which it co-shared with William Fleming last season, but based on the points system, Fleming advanced to the playoffs and Pulaski did not.[1313]

Fleming would be a formidable opponent this season, but so would Patrick Henry, which arguably had the most potent offensive backfield in the district.[1314]

And Northside could not be discounted. Its weight-training program had helped develop the Viking linemen as the strongest in the district.[1315]

As for Salem, new head coach Carl Richards inherited a team that finished 1–9 a year before, but he indicated that he had ample reason to believe that this year's Spartans could reach the 0.500 mark.[1316]

Salem, under its third head coach, would open the '82 season against Blacksburg.

Game 1 (September 3): Spartans 26, Indians 14

There were a few firsts in this one.

Besides Richards coaching his first game for Salem, the Spartans also scored on their first play from scrimmage by a gifted athlete making his debut as a varsity football player.[1317]

It all started when Salem quarterback Cam Young connected with Richard Morgan for a 58-yard passing score on a play designed just for Morgan, a basketball and track star at Salem who made his first touch of the football one to remember.[1318]

And the point after touchdown or 2-point try? Neither was mentioned in the article, but either failed because the Spartans led 6–0.[1319]

The Indians retaliated when quarterback Ricky Graham passed to tight end Gavin Haycocks for a 10-yard scoring strike. The point after was good, and the Indians led 7–6.[1320]

Late in the first half, Young hooked up with James Jackson for a go-ahead touchdown and the ensuing 2-point conversion to give Salem a 14–7 lead, which was the score at the intermission.[1321]

The biggest stumbling block for the Spartans came in the punting department. They fumbled 3 punts, and the Indians capitalized on the third when they capped a short-scoring drive with a 9-yard run by Will Nuckolls. The kick after tied the game.[1322]

Salem regained the lead in the fourth quarter when it engineered a 70-yard drive highlighted by a 3-yard run for touchdown by Robert Cooper, which gave the Spartans a 20–14 lead with 4:52 remaining.[1323]

Blacksburg, which had ample time to respond, saw its ensuing drive stall when it turned the ball over on downs, and Salem took over at the Blacksburg 30.[1324]

The Spartans worked the clock and added a touchdown when Cooper ran 13 yards to the end zone.[1325]

Cooper, a senior and transfer from Patrick Henry, finished with a game best 103 yards rushing.[1326]

"We [Salem] had a bad season last year and I don't want to be a loser as a senior," he said. "If the line keeps blocking, I'll keep running."[1327]

"We showed we could overcome adversity," said Richards, alluding to the three fumbles. "We made some bad mistakes, but we came from behind and still won."[1328]

Would this initial success on the gridiron serve as an omen for things to come?

After last year's 1–9 season, the Spartans and their partisans surely hoped so.

Game 2 (September 10): Cave Spring 42, Salem 6

On the ground and in the air, the Knights lanced the Spartans.

Cave Spring running back Tim Fulton scored 4 touchdowns—3 in the first half—and quarterback Todd Stevens completed 6 of 9 passes for 123 yards and 2 touchdowns.[1329]

The statistics were as one-sided as the score. The Knights tallied 363 yards of offense, while the Spartans mustered just 74 and committed 6 turnovers.[1330]

Despite the trampling, the Spartans would get no respite in their schedule, which included next week's game in Roanoke's Victory Stadium against the Colonels of William Fleming.

Before the Spartans and Colonels clashed, Kerkhoff featured a story about the matchup.

He wrote that Fleming head coach John McGregor had reason to feel anxious.

He remembered what happened last year when Fleming narrowly beat Salem at Municipal Field.

"Salem has always gotten after us," he said, "even when they didn't have great teams. But our youngsters will remember last year's game."[1331]

The Spartans were coming into this one on the heels of last week's drubbing by Cave Spring.

"I don't believe we were emotionally ready to play that game," said Coach Richards. "Our players were wondering how to react to the fact that we've never beaten Cave Spring... We've worked on the premise that the biggest enemy we have this year is ourselves. I don't know if we've overcome that yet. Did Cave Spring beat us that bad? Yes, but they didn't do anything we didn't expect them to do. We gave them their first 21 points."[1332]

Game 3 (September 17): Salem 8, William Fleming, 6

The biggest win in Salem's history?

Spartan assistant coach Billy Miles thought so.

"You better believe it," he said. "As long as we've been down, you better believe it."[1333]

Miles would know as well as anyone.

A 1966 graduate of Andrew Lewis High, he played football under Eddie Joyce and was a member of both the 1962 and 1964 state championship teams. Plus he later served as an assistant under Joyce.

This, and much more, was written about Miles in *The Team the Titans Remember*, and he wrote the foreword for this book.

Now let's return to the biggest win in Spartan history.

Not only did Miles put things in perspective, but so did head Coach Richards.

"Me and Sputnik are flying together right now," he said.[47, 1334]

How did the Spartans fly so high?

After a scoreless first half, Salem drove for its only touchdown during its opening drive in the third quarter. It covered 54 yards and was capped by Robert Cooper's four-yard run.[1335]

Salem went for 2, and quarterback Cam Young hit Richard Morgan on a slant route in the end zone.[1336]

In the fourth, Fleming quarterback Chris Sheppard scored from 2 yards out. The Colonels went for the tie, but Salem's Hugh Dooley and E. B. Obenchain pressured Sheppard into throwing an incompletion.[1337]

Fleming eventually got the ball back with less than a minute to play, but its hopes of winning were dashed when a pass from Brian Ferguson was batted up in the end zone and Morgan was there for the interception.[1338]

The win over Fleming was huge, arguably the biggest in Salem's history.

But the Spartans would have little time to savor the sweet taste of that victory because they were soon returning to Roanoke's Victory Stadium to take on another familiar rival—the Patriots of Patrick Henry, unbeaten after 3 games.[1339]

---

[47] Richards' use of the word Sputnik was a reference to the first artificial Earth satellite. The Soviet Union launched it into an elliptical low Earth orbit on October 4, 1957, orbiting for three weeks before its batteries died, then silently for two more months before falling back into the atmosphere (source: Wikipedia).

Game 4 (September 24): PH 27, Salem 0

A "stifling" Patriot defense limited Salem to 44 total yards on 28 plays compared to PH's 63.[1340]

"They're the best team we've seen all year… We couldn't get any offensive punch going at all," said Spartan head Coach Carl Richards.[1341]

In fact, Salem lost 3 of 4 fumbles, while PH had no trouble hanging on to the football.[1342]

The Patriots had 2 touchdown runs by Robert Harley and 1 by Brian Jones. Plus Jimmy Mallis kicked 3 PATs and 2 field goals of 32 and 35 yards.[1343]

How good was this year's PH team?

By the numbers, the Patriots had outscored their opponents 112–17 and appeared destined to play the Cougars from Pulaski County with the Roanoke Valley District title on the line.[1344]

Salem, meanwhile, had dropped to 2–2 overall and would next battle Bassett.

Game 5 (October 1): Bassett 21, Salem 18

The Bengals capitalized on a couple of Spartan miscues to get the 3-point win at Municipal Field.[1345]

Late in the game, the Spartans drove the ball to the Bengals' 2-yard line, but as the Spartans lined up for the next play, a penalty was called against Salem running back Rodney Varney for "improper equipment," i.e., not having his mouthpiece in place. The ball was moved back to the Bassett 7, and on the next play, Bassett's Alan Foley intercepted a Cam Young pass to seal the deal.[1346]

Bassett's D. D. Manns was the game's biggest playmaker. He returned a punt 39 yards to set up Alan Lawson's first-quarter score, and his 85-yard kickoff return in the third gave the Bengals a 13–12 lead.[1347]

Bassett made it 21–12 when Alan Stone ran 24 yards for a touchdown with 9 seconds left in the third.[1348]

Salem got 2 touchdowns from Robert Cooper, who gained 100 yards on 14 carries.[1349]

The Spartans (2–3) scored their first points when Young connected with Eddie Riley for a 7-yard score.[1350]

Game 6 (October 8): Heritage (Lynchburg) 38, Salem 12[48*]

Quarterback Kevin Markham threw 2 touchdown passes and kicked a pair of extra points to pace the Pioneers to a big win over the Spartans in Salem.[1351]

Markham finished on 10 of 12 passes for 158 yards, and teammates Dennis Jefferson and Lorenzo Hawkins scored rushing touchdowns of 27 and 2 yards, respectively.[1352]

Salem starting quarterback Cam Young suffered a sprained ankle, and Rodney Varney replaced him, but his first 2 passes were intercepted.[1353]

Heritage led at the intermission 25–0.[1354]

In the second half, Varney ran for a touchdown and passed for another to Eddie Riley.[1355]

Freshman JoJo Harris led Salem in rushing with 77 yards in seven carries, all in the fourth quarter.[1356]

Timeout for a New Emphasis

Salem and its opponents were at the midway point in this '82 season, and it was at this point that a previously underemphasized component of the game had now taken on more acclaim; high school coaches had begun to recognize the value of a good kicking game.

---

[48] The designation of Heritage's location is provided because, as of the preparation of this manuscript, there were three high schools in Virginia named Heritage with locations in Lynchburg, Newport News, and Leesburg. The schools' mascots are Pioneers, Hurricanes, and Pride, respectively (source: www.maxpreps.com).

Veteran sportswriter Bob Teitlebaum wrote a feature story on the topic and reported that area high school coaches could attest that a field goal could be the difference between winning and losing.[1357]

Pulaski County head Coach Joel Hicks said the Cougars won 5 district games last year—all by 3 points. He had a dependable kicker in Chris Kinzer, who had booted at least 3 game-winning field goals to date.[1358]

Other head coaches around the area weighed in on the subject, including Willis White at Patrick Henry. He told Teitlebaum that place-kicking might be characteristic of certain leagues. PH did not yet have that tradition, and neither did many of its fellow Roanoke Valley District opponents.[1359]

"The Roanoke Valley is dominated by defense," said White, "so three points can be very important."[1360]

Which area team was ahead of the grading curve at this point? Cave Spring.

Its kicking tradition started with Bernie Sanders (class of 1967), then Paul Page, and later Greg Caldwell.[1361]

Farther south, Martinsville's longtime head coach Dick Hensley did not believe in place-kicking, unless he had an outstanding kicker.[1362]

He figured his teams were successful in more than 50 percent of their 2-point conversions.[1363]

And Salem?

Hard to say, because neither Coach Richards's name nor his philosophy on the kicking game appeared in this article.

After the "timeout," the Spartans returned to the gridiron—this time for the homecoming game against the Eagles of Franklin County.

Game 7 (October 15): Salem 20, Franklin County 12

Teitlebaum summed this one up nicely in about three paragraphs:

> It was Richard Morgan through the air and Robert Cooper on the ground for Salem… The two-man

attack on offense and a punishing defense was enough to give the Spartans a 20–12 homecoming football victory over Franklin County.

Cooper had a career-high 156 yards rushing and Morgan made an alley-oop grab of a second-quarter pass for a touchdown that proved to be Salem's winning points.

And the pass rush? Jimmy Bean, Reid Garst and Tim Sutphin were Salem's stampeders.[1364]

Coach Richards used the abbreviation BYOB when he reflected on what happened, but he was not referring to the popular use of the abbreviation, as in "Bring your own booze." Instead, those letters stood for "bring your own blocker," which he said that Cooper did.[1365]

Cooper scored 2 of the Spartans' 4 touchdowns. Quarterback Cam Young ran 3 yards for a score and threw 38 yards to Morgan for another.[1366]

As an interesting anecdote, Salem's Chad Krupft kicked 2 extra points but couldn't attempt a third due to an injury.[1367]

Salem improved to 2–2 in the district and 3–4 overall, while Franklin County fell to 0–5 and 1–6.

Up next was continuing an old rivalry with the older school in Lynchburg, E. C. Glass.

Game 8 (October 22): Hilltoppers 40, Spartans 6

Obviously from the score, Glass dominated this one.

But losing by a wide margin is not what bothered Coach Richards as much as something else.

What bothered him most is that Glass attempted seven passes on the last 9 plays of the game with the final falling incomplete in the end zone as time ran out.[1368]

When the coaches and players met to shake hands after the game, Richards refused to talk to Glass' head coach Bo Henson.[1369]

"I didn't even talk to him," said Richards. "I shook the hands of the other [Glass assistant] coaches… It's one of those things, the less said the better."[1370]

Henson denied trying to run up the score.

"That's [passing] our game. Our [second-string] quarterback's a junior. I wanted him to get as much experience as he can get."[1371]

The outcome of this one was decided after the first 10 minutes, during which Salem committed 3 turnovers and Glass capitalized on all 3 for scores.[1372]

In the first half, Glass ran 32 plays for 292 yards compared to Salem's 16 plays for minus-1 yard.[1373]

The Spartans dropped to 3–5 and faced the Cougars of Pulaski County next.

Game 9 (October 29): Cougars 40, Spartans 0

Quarterback Terry Finley rushed for 2 touchdowns and 111 yards and passed to Billy Myers for another touchdown, Finley's ninth of the season to lead Pulaski County over Salem.[1374]

The Cougars amassed 347 yards total offense and recorded their fifth shutout of the season.[1375]

Now about the kicking game that had recently garnered some attention, Pulaski's Chris Kinzer booted 2 field goals and went 4 of 5 in PAT kicks; plus he doubled as a passer and completed 3 tosses for 23 yards, including a touchdown throw to Brian Turpin.[1376]

Now at 3–6, Salem prepared for the regular-season finale against Northside, while unbeaten Pulaski County and Patrick Henry would finally meet with the district championship on the line.[1377]

Salem was a common opponent of both teams, and Richards provided this assessment: "Pulaski County executes better, but I think PH is a little more physical. I would rate them pretty-even. [The Patriots'] physical play will be balanced here in front of Pulaski County's fans."[1378]

Game 10 (November 5): Northside 24, Salem 12

The Vikings doubled up the Spartans in the scoring department and tripled their advantage in total yards—241 to 79.[1379]

Randy (not Jim) Plunkett spearheaded a balanced running attack to lead the Norsemen to victory with 77 yards after 17 carries, while teammates Darrell Porter (not the former Major League Baseball catcher for the St. Louis Cardinals) provided 59 yards on just two carries, and Danny Price carried the ball 13 times for 51 yards.[1380]

Quarterback Brent Mitchell completed just 2 passes, but both were for touchdowns.[1381]

For the Spartans, JoJo Harris scored on a 1-yard run, and James Jackson returned a kickoff for touchdown from 75 yards.[1382]

Before recapping this not-so-impressive Spartan season, let's look at how the big matchup between Pulaski County and Patrick Henry played out.

The Cougars scored first and last to slip past the Patriots, 10–7, claimed the Roanoke Valley District championship, and had home-field advantage for the first round of the Northwestern Region playoffs.[1383]

Mathematically, a field goal by Chris Kinzer was the difference.[1384]

Though PH lost, it still qualified for the playoffs. PH (9–1) would play at GW-Danville (10–0), while Pulaski County (10–0) would host Fauquier County (9–1).[1385]

Those 4 teams were among the mix of 16 in search of the Group AAA crown.

In other first-round action, Mount Vernon would take on Chantilly, T. C. Williams would tangle with Vienna's James Madison, Highland Springs would host Hopewell, Dinwiddie matched up against Lee-Davis, Lake Taylor lined up against defending state champion Hampton, and First Colonial faced Norcom.[1386]

The winners were Pulaski County (by the score of 13–7), GW-Danville (20–7), plus Mount Vernon, T. C. Williams, Hopewell, Lee-Davis, Lake Taylor, and First Colonial.[1387]

THE SPARTAN SUCCESSION

In the quarterfinal rounds, GW-Danville ended Pulaski County's run with an impressive 37–7 win.[1388]

The Eagles, who finished as a runner-up to the Crabbers of Hampton last year, would go on to claim the school's second state championship under head coach Alger Pugh.[49, 1389]

Back to local football, when the selections for the All-Roanoke Valley District football team were announced, the Cougars and Patriots claimed 15 of the 24 places on the first teams. The Spartans had 2 selections in Reid Garst (guard) and Eddie Riley (defensive end).[1390]

An even higher honor was announced when the state's All-Group AAA football team hit the news.

But only two Timesland's players made the cut, and both were members of Pulaski County's fine squad, defensive tackle Robert Cody and place-kicker Chris Kinzer.[50, 1391]

Kinzer's kicks helped the Cougars throughout the season. He finished with having connected on 29 of 35 extra-point attempts and 7 of 12 field goal tries for a total of 50 points.[1392]

* * *

Back to our valiant, but unsuccessful, Spartans, the '82 campaign was over, and it had yielded little highlights.

Arguably, the biggest of those was the win over William Fleming. Coaches Richards and Miles clearly thought so.

And the 1982–1983 Salem High School yearbook reported that the win over the Colonels was *the* "highlight of the season."

---

[49] Pugh began his head-coaching job at GW-Danville in 1964. The Cardinals, as they were known then, claimed the Group AAA state championship in 1968 (source: *The Team the Titans Remember*, p. 312). Also see chapter 14, part 3: "Red Birds Take Flight," beginning on page 538 for a synopsis of the '68 season. In 1982, the Eagles—as they had come to have been known—went 14–0, tallied 485 points, and allowed just 113. They defeated the Titans of Lake Taylor in the finals by a whopping 53–15. That would be Pugh's last championship. He died from a stroke in 1984 at the age of forty-seven (source: www.gwfootball.com).

[50] Timesland's refers to the wide catchment area of the *Roanoke Times* newspaper.

But limited "highlights" spelled doom for Richards's aspirations of returning for another season.

In fact, some prominent Salemites saw the proverbial writing on the wall before the season began.

Charlie Hammersley recently recalled this event: "The Salem Sports Foundation was going to be introduced to the new coach, Carl Richards. This event was at Billy's Barn.[51] Richards talked about the upcoming season and what he wanted to do. Everything was fine until he mentioned the kicking game. He said, 'I don't kick—I go for two; I figure I can make 50 percent [of 2-point conversions] so why not just go for two?' I remember that some of us looked at each other and said, 'I hope he doesn't sell his home in Varina.'"[1393]

Hammersley's point of reference is extremely important. He played under Eddie Joyce and Dale Foster, 2 innovators among high school football coaches.[1394]

"With Eddie and Dale, they put so much emphasis on the special teams, the kicking team," said Hammersley. "We had an edge on people because we spent time working on that, and to come in and say you're not going to kick extra points? It's alright if you're winning by four touchdowns, but if it's 7–6 and you're going for two to win the game? I think that would be [a huge gamble]. You're not going to win in the district [with this strategy]. It was a pretty-strong district."[1395]

Foster, who authored the book *The Slanting Monster Defense in Football*, added this: "One year we had three kickers. One would kick short, one would kick long, and one would kick medium. Eddie would call the kick after the receiving team lined up. All three would approach the ball at the same time."[1396]

One of those three was Hammersley, who said, "You all had me on the left side because I was left footed. [Our opponents] didn't know what was going on."[1397]

---

[51] Billy's Barn is a long-standing and popular restaurant and lounge in Salem. It specializes in American fare and hosts events and concerts. Like many Salemites, this author has patronized the business many times in the past. It is owned and operated by Billy Miles.

As for his introduction to Coach Richards, Hammersley looked back and said, "We had a big laugh about it. We didn't know him, but as much emphasis as Eddie and Dale put on special teams, we didn't think it was going to be the right fit. It's hard to follow a legacy and winning six or seven games in a season wasn't an option."[1398]

Six or seven? Salem had not won that many games since its debut in 1977 when the Spartans finished at 6–3–1.

After that, the team had gone 2–8, 3–7, 2–8, 1–9 and 3–7.

Those numbers simply would not do in Salem, Virginia where football had been crowned king of all sports long ago and had led to much acclaim.

For Salemites old enough to remember the glory days of Andrew Lewis football under Eddie Joyce Sr., they wanted—and tacitly demanded—that Salem get good again.

What only a few knew was that good news was on its way.

The "power brokers," if you will, were about to make a decision that would prove to be the turning point in the history of the Spartan succession.

Note: Richards is no longer with us to opine on the season or anything else. He died more than 10 years ago. In 1984, Brian Hoffman of the *Salem Times-Register* mentioned Richards in a story about Salem football. He noted that after leaving Salem following the 1982 season, Richards' next job was at Petersburg High School, as the head coach of the school's football team. Date of article was October 25, 1984.

The following was taken from his obituary:

> Carl Edward Richards, Jr. was born in West Virginia on December 17, 1942. He died on April 4, 2008 at the age of 65. He was a retired employee of the Wise County school system, a graduate of East Tennessee State University, and he received his master's degree in mathematics in Oklahoma. He began his coaching career at Lebanon High School and went on to the Richmond, Virginia area until moving to

Coeburn, Virginia. He was head football coach for the Coeburn Blue Knights from 1985 to 2001, Daniel Boone High School in Tennessee from 2002 to 2004, and then was an assistant coach for the University of Virginia at Wise from 2004 to 2006. He was an avid golfer and fisherman. Surviving are his wife Rose Hughes Richards and their three sons, Warren, Theron and Brett.

Note: Coeburn High School is no longer in existence.

In August of 2011, Eastside High School opened as a consolidation of both Coeburn and St. Paul High Schools. Eastside is in Coeburn and serves 350 students annually.

Chapter 11

1983

Part 1: An Effective Trap Block

Early in the year, some of Salem's teachers and parents of students had a sneaking suspicion that something big was in the works.

And their suspicion only heightened on February 8 when the Salem School Board met but did so without school superintendent Frank Cosby present. What's more—his name was never even mentioned.[1399]

What, in tarnation, was going on?

Answer: Cosby had recently resigned under pressure from the school board after its chairman, John Moore, had requested it.[1400]

In exchange for his resignation, the board agreed to pay Cosby $43,725.00, which was equal to one year's salary, plus his unused vacation time.[1401]

Cosby's assistant, John Montgomery, was appointed as acting superintendent.[1402]

Though Cosby declined to comment to reporters, his retained attorney—Charles Phillips—indicated that his client had made the decision based on a "basic difference in educational philosophy" between Cosby and the school board.[1403]

Okay, but was the board's decision legal?

Phillips said that under state law a superintendent can be fired for "sufficient cause," which Phillips said was rather vague. Further,

Cosby had never been given any specific reasons why the board had sought his resignation, and state law allows a superintendent to appeal a dismissal to circuit court.[1404]

Cosby, who had been the chief architect of Salem's first independent school system, was under contract until July 1985, but he doubted that he would appeal the decision; instead, he would work on a doctoral degree.[1405]

People were talking.

Jerry Adams, president of the Andrew Lewis Junior High PTA, said, "I'm sure that many people in Salem are wondering what in the world is going on," because Cosby had certainly worked well with that PTA and had hired a good staff. "There seems to be a lot of undercurrent, a lot of rumors, a lot of unknown."[1406]

And it wasn't his job performance that doomed Cosby. His most recent evaluation indicated that he had "performed in an extremely satisfactory manner, in all areas, during a difficult period of time."[1407]

But it was also true that the relationship between Cosby and the school board had visibly deteriorated over the past year. The board had rejected several of Cosby's recommendations.[1408]

In the editorial section of the February 10 edition of the *Roanoke Times & World-News*, the writer opined that the Salem School Board may have set a record; it had fired a superintendent before the soon-to-be independent system's first class met.

It had been a mistake for Salem to withdraw from the Roanoke County school system and, with the dismissal of Cosby, things weren't looking any better.[1409]

Though Cosby technically had resigned, in actuality, he had been dismissed and without adequate explanation. His dismissal had come at a critical juncture since it preceded Salem's first year of independent operation.[1410]

Maybe there's more that hasn't come to light. But it's hard to shake the disturbing impression that Salem School Board members think they can set school policy without regard for public opinion. The board is also sadly mistaken if it thinks it has no responsibility to tell the public its reasons for asking Cosby to resign. And teachers and parents were none too happy about it. Few were surprised by the decision, but all were puzzled.[1411]

One parent believed that Cosby had been made a scapegoat but didn't know exactly what he was being blamed for.[1412]

In a city where high school sports are followed very closely, high school coaching appointments for the following year had not been made.[1413]

Naturally, then, Carl Richards pondered his future.

"I'm really trying to find out where I stand in that regard," he said. "Somebody's got to tell me pretty quick."[1414]

Though Moore said that coaching appointments were not a factor in the board's decision, one parent—who asked not to be identified—said, "If Salem High had had a winning [football] team, all this wouldn't be happening. And I'm not the only parent who feels that."[1415]

All things considered, how could people not think the board's actions were clandestine in nature or that board members had not acted surreptitiously?

Walter Hunt, the assistant superintendent for Roanoke County and a runner-up to the elected Frank Tota, expressed his interest early on in filling Cosby's position.[1416]

There was sufficient reason to believe that Hunt, also a former principal at Andrew Lewis (when Lewis was a high school), had been contacted before Cosby was asked to resign.[1417]

And Moore, aware of the inappropriateness of making a firm commitment to a candidate, admitted that the board had considered the availability of a suitable replacement before it sought Cosby's resignation.[1418]

Next up, the Salem School Board announced it would hold a closed meeting with Dr. Hunt, who applied to replace the "fired" school superintendent Frank Cosby.[1419]

Applications would be taken up to February 22, the date of the next regularly scheduled school board meeting.[1420]

Steve Haner, staff writer with the *Roanoke Times & World-News*, concluded that Cosby had resigned under pressure from the school board on February 8, effective immediately.[1421]

On February 22, the board met, and the results were all too predictable: Dr. Hunt was appointed as Salem's new superintendent of schools.[1422]

At the meeting, parents questioned and criticized the board for its decision to fire Cosby.[1423]

Hunt had been 1 of 9 applicants for the position, but Hunt was clearly the frontrunner; he had been approached about applying before the board asked Cosby to resign. And Hunt was the only applicant interviewed.[1424]

Parents and PTA officials praised the choice of Hunt, which ended the meeting on a positive note considering it had begun with criticism of Cosby's forced resignation.[1425]

Edwina Riley, president of the Salem Council of PTAs, described Cosby's ousting as one that "created anxiety, mistrust, and discontent in the community."[1426]

She requested that the school board immediately adopt a 1983–84 teacher salary scale so that teachers would know what they would earn, and "the retention of the current Salem High football coaching staff," which caused the crowd of about one hundred people to erupt in applause.[1427]

Other speakers directly asked the board whether Cosby was fired because he refused to replace Salem High head football coach Carl Richards. Rumor control in Salem believed that was the case.[1428]

Many people were convinced that the board wanted to bring back Eddie Joyce.[1429]

Van Gresham remarked, "Where there is smoke there has to be fire."[1430]

And this from W. Perry Bailey Jr: "Perhaps my strongest emotion is one of sadness—sadness that your [Salem School Board's] basic concerns appear to be cost-efficiency, politics and a winning football team."[1431]

Howard Packett, whose son played on Salem's football team, said, "You need to listen to the students and the parents in Salem and not to those living in the past." It was an obvious reference to the glory days of Andrew Lewis football under Eddie Joyce.[1432]

THE SPARTAN SUCCESSION

Members of the Spartan football team had signed a petition that requested that the current coaching staff be retained, but school board members denied there had been any discussion about changing the coaching staff.

During an impromptu news conference after the meeting, Hunt said, "I have not followed Salem football that closely. I don't intend to make any rash judgments about anybody."[1433]

Despite the board members' denials, several people still suspected that football was a factor in Cosby's firing.[1434]

"I don't see how a rumor can be that widespread without somebody on the school board knowing something about it," said Packett.[1435]

Then Riley said this about Hunt, whose credentials were impressive enough: "I think he's going to be the one to bring us closer together."[1436]

Good thing: Hunt was taking over at a time when Salem was about to embark on its first try as an independent school system.

The next day, Hunt was interviewed again and said that during his discussions with the school board and prior to his hiring that "nobody suggested that a single person be hired in any position, and the board did not suggest replacing anybody." If people were still convinced some secret deal had been struck, "you probably can't change their minds until they see how things happen."[1437]

In the editorial section of the next day's edition of the *Roanoke Times & World-News*, the writer opined that the selection of Dr. Hunt was a good one, a doctor in more ways than one. But note, too, the apparent innuendo:

> After the surgery comes the need for healing. The city of Salem amputated its schools from the Roanoke County system. It called for the resignation of Frank Cosby as first superintendent of its newly independent system. Now it has called upon a healer to replace Cosby. Walter Hunt is a good choice…[He] seems to be a man the citizens and the school staff can trust. He has been

confronted with a couple of questions that he cannot immediately answer: how much to pay the school teachers and what do to about the football coach at Salem High School. The latter question may be a manufactured issue, created by those who would like to see the return of a winning coach who happened to be convicted of using school funds for personal purchases. The present coach had a losing season, but remains unsullied by scandal (though there are those in Salem who consider a losing season to be a scandal.) Hunt's hands appear to be free on this question, and he quite properly refused to discuss the situation until he has had a chance to inform himself fully....The unexplained ouster of Cosby as Salem superintendent leaves legitimate questions in the minds of Salem citizens. But if we set that issue aside, the School Board made a wise choice in his replacement.[1438]

Less than a month later, one Salemite put into written perspective what likely had happened:

> It's not easy to keep abreast of politics in Salem these days. I'm beginning to believe that the hiring of Dr. Walter Hunt had been on the minds of some of our school board members for quite some time. I attended the Salem School Board meeting of March 8 and was...favorably impressed. [Dr. Hunt] had done his homework before that meeting and he answered questions comprehensively and generally inspired confidence. He will, I am certain, be an effective superintendent for Salem schools. What concerns me is the way we have tossed Mr. Cosby aside. He did a commendable job of getting Salem ready to operate its own

school system. I hope our board members will have the maturity to give Mr. Cosby the positive job evaluation that he deserves. He performed well for us.[1439]

* * *

Okay. Cosby was out, and Hunt was in.

That settled, was Richards in or out? If out, then who would replace him?

Readers of the *Roanoke Times & World-News* got the answer on April 7, 1983.

Written by Steve Haner, the story appeared under the headline "Willis White to be named Salem coach."

White would be recommended for the job by Dr. Hunt at the Salem School Board's next scheduled meeting of April 12.[1440]

Salem High School principal Bob Lipscomb explained that it was "a change that we had to make for the good of the school."[1441]

And White's reaction?

"I have mixed emotions. I hate to leave Patrick Henry, but Salem is a challenge in a new direction."[1442]

Steve Haner, who wrote the story, miscalculated when he reported that White would be the fifth Salem head football coach in nine years. In actuality, White would be the fourth in seven years following, Tom Kucer, Wallace Thompson, and Carl Richards.[1443]

White added: "I don't think anybody would go into a program like Salem has been without a promise of cooperation and time to get the job done. Salem wants to excel, and I think that's a big plan."[1444]

Patrick Henry High principal Jack Graybill was not surprised. "I had heard rumors for several weeks. I understood [White] wanted a different challenge. That's the main thing he indicated to us. This is a great loss for us. He is a great coach and teacher. He's thought well of by administrators and is a positive influence on the young."[1445]

And how did this all make Richards feel?

Disappointed. "Who wouldn't be?" he asked rhetorically. "There's not a whole lot a person can say."[1446]

Had Lipscomb felt pressure to replace Richards?

"Not as much as people think," he said, but asked to specify the reason for the change, he said, "I really would rather not get into the details."[1447]

This author sensed that the tenor and tone of the article defended Richards. Maybe it did; maybe it did not. But five days after its publication, Blair Kerkhoff, the high school sports editor for this same news source, made a compelling case for Richards that would have earned the affirmation from any attorney.

His article appeared under this headline: "Salem didn't give Richards a fair chance."

Consider its contents:[1448]

> Seldom is a first-year coach released after improving on the final record of his predecessor. This is especially true in high school, where a fundamental of athletics is to provide educational experiences not offered in the classroom that contribute to the individual's development as a better person.
>
> If that's the idea, why did first-year football coach Carl Richards lose his job at Salem High this week to Patrick Henry coach Willis White? Salem principal Bob Lipscomb's only comment was: "The change was made for the good of the school."
>
> That means Richards was not good for the school or, at least, not as good as the school would have liked. How so? Richards was released as the football coach but received fine grades as a math teacher and was popular with the students. As a reaction to rumors of his firing two months ago, the football players even circulated a petition in Richards' favor.

THE SPARTAN SUCCESSION

Upon accepting the job last February, Richards billed himself as a motivator and could support that assertion. At Varina High near Richmond, he transformed a perennial loser into a district champion in 1981...

At Salem, he inherited a team that finished 1–9 in 1981 and improved that record to 3–7 last fall...the season could not be considered disastrous or even a failure by recent Salem standards. But the season obviously fell short of Salem's expectations.

Apparently, Salem wasn't willing to engage in the same uphill battle Richards fought in Varina.

That's a school's prerogative, but Richards deserved more than one season to prove himself. His hasty departure leaves one wondering how long Richards' job had been in jeopardy. Some believe Richards' days were numbered when former Salem Superintendent Frank Cosby was fired in February...

And White, a Salem resident who will be the school's fifth coach in nine years, wasn't hired after an extensive search. He was in the same day that Richards was out. The transition must have been in the works for some time.[52]

---

[52] Both Haner and Kerkhoff wrote that White represented the fifth Salem head coach in nine years. Technically, this was not the case. Salem High opened in 1977, and Tom Kucer was the school's first head football coach. He coached for two seasons, 1977 and 1978. Wallace Thompson succeeded him and coached the Spartans for three seasons, '79, '80, and '81. Richards replaced Thompson in '82, and White took over the reins in '83. Likely, Haner and Kerhoff included Mike Stevens in the mix. Recall that Stevens replaced Eddie Joyce beginning in

> While Salem may be faulted for Richards' premature dismissal, it gained some redemption in hiring a person of White's quality. He is a most respected and admired teacher and coach. White's five Patrick Henry teams compiled a 37–16–1 record. Last season the Patriots won their first nine games. The chairman of Patrick Henry's math department, White spent much time tutoring his players before practice sessions…
>
> Salem is looking for stability in the first year in is independent school system.
>
> Whether Richards could have provided it will never be known. And should the Spartans finish 3–7 or worse in 1983, don't expect another coaching change.[1449]

And with that, Kerkhoff may have rested his "case" and let the court of public opinion decide whether Richards had been treated fairly.

Regardless of its "verdict," it mattered not. Salem had just brokered a change that would one day yield huge dividends and zero regret.

* * *

Thanks to Haner, Kerkhoff & Co., who wrote of the events when they happened, we know about the process that forced Richards out and invited White in.

Today, we still have Dale Foster's recollections, which he shared with this author thirty-five years post-1983.

'74. Stevens coached at Andrew Lewis during its last two years as a high school and while Glenvar was also in operation as a high school. The two high schools came together as one with the opening of Salem in 1977, and this should be the starting point of the calculation.

THE SPARTAN SUCCESSION

"[In 1982, the Salem] football coach was Carl Richards; the results were negative. The [Salem] School Board told [school superintendent Frank] Cosby that he needed to replace Richards. Cosby had promised Richards more than one year and he wouldn't replace him, so the School Board replaced Cosby![1450]

"They replaced Cosby with Dr. Walter Hunt, who was the [Assistant] Superintendent of Roanoke City Schools at that time. He had been the principal at Andrew Lewis High. He came there in about 1963 or '64.[1451]

"Dr. Hunt's first day on the job was July 1, 1983. He called me and wanted to meet me that day. He knew that his first task was to get a football coach. As soon as I saw him his first words were, 'What do we need to do?' I said, 'Dr. Hunt, we need a new football coach.' He said, 'Do you have any idea of anybody who we can get?' I said 'Yes,' and I told him about a conversation I had had back in February [1983] at the Roanoke Valley District Basketball Tournament at the Salem Civic Center with Willis White. I talked with [White] for about three hours. We talked football. I coached against him when I was with Coach Thompson and was athletic director watching his teams play Salem. When we finished talking, I said, 'Coach White would you come to Salem if you are offered the job?' He said 'yes.'[1452]

"That's what I told Dr. Hunt. He said, 'Where does he live?' I said he lives here in Salem. I wasn't there 15 minutes and he asked me to leave. He knew what he had to do. He called Coach White's home and Sharon, his wife, answered and said he was still at the field house at Patrick Henry in the weight room. I went home and called [Sharon] at 7:00 and asked if Willis was home and she said no, that he was still at the weight room. I waited until 9:00 and I called again. Willis answered, and this is exactly what he said: 'Dr. Hunt just called me and offered me the job and I took it.' That was it; in just four hours, Dr. Hunt had just done what he was hired to do: get a football coach. Dr. Hunt was a character! He knew what he had to do. He would have hired him sooner than that if he had found White at home!"[53, 1453]

What Hunt, Foster, and prominent Salemites knew was an important truism.

"Salem is a *football town*," said Foster.[1454]

In 1983, Hunt must have recognized that it was time for Salem to bring back the winning tradition that Andrew Lewis had enjoyed.

Using some football imagery, to bring the necessary change about, the Salem School Board had utilized an effective "trap block," which created a wide-opened running lane for its newest "running back."

The new "ball carrier" would be Willis White.

"Fumbling" was not an option.

But before we meet the man that would score "touchdowns" for the Spartans, consider the interesting twist of events that occurred in the life of his predecessor.

In May of 1983, Richards was named head football coach at Petersburg High School following the resignation of Norman Jenkins.[1455]

Richards had not only applied at Petersburg but also at Patrick Henry, where the position had been vacated by White.[1456]

Petersburg, did you say?

Yes, just four years previously, White had coached the Patriots against the Crimson Wave in the 1979 Group AAA state football finals.[1457]

Conceivably, White and Richards could match wits in the postseason.

And coaching was something Richards was not about to give up.

---

[53] According to www.virginia-24e-lions.org, Dr. Walter Akers Hunt was born on December 15, 1929, in Franklin County, Virginia. He earned a doctorate in educational administration from Virginia Tech. He served the community in numerous of capacities, including as principal at Andrew Lewis High School from 1964 through 1970, president of the Salem Educational Foundation and Alumni Association and superintendent of Salem schools until he retired in 1989. He died on May 25, 2007, at the age of seventy-eight.

Reportedly, Salem High School principal Bob Lipscomb had previously indicated to Richards in 1983 that, even though he would not return as the school's football coach, he could—if he wished—remain on staff as a mathematics teacher.[1458]

Do you think Richards ever contemplated such a decision?

"Are you kidding?" he said.[1459]

Part 2: A Country Boy Named Willie

We come from West Virginia coal mines
And the Rocky Mountains and the western skies
And we can skin a buck, we can run a trot line
And a county boy can survive[54]

Many people are familiar with him as both a teacher and coach.

Some of his former students still return to him to thank him for the influence he had in their lives.

In fact, one former student recently told him that he chose engineering as a profession simply because he had made mathematics so interesting.

That, the retired teacher and coach agreed, is as good as it gets.[1460]

Despite his influence on his students and players, he has always kept himself at a safe distance; he has allowed very few people—if any—to get too close.[1461]

That's the way it's always been for this son of a coal miner from Jeffrey, West Virginia, born to the marital union of Willis Howard White Sr. and Macel Jordan White on November 26, 1941, and named Willis Howard White Jr., whose nickname is Willie, and the tenth of their eleven children.[1462]

Despite coming from such a large family, White described himself as always "a loner" and said, "I never got close to people. I had

---

[54] These are some of the lyrics from the song "A County Boy Can Survive," written and recorded by county music artist Hank Williams Jr. and taken from www.lyricsmode.com.

no confidence. They only place I had confidence was playing sports. I knew what I could do out there. I mean, I did great in the classroom—almost straight A's all the way through—and I had confidence in the classroom."[1463]

His parents were hardworking, honest folks. His father earned meager wages working in the coal mines, and his mother was a devoted homemaker,[1464]

"My family beat in my head from the time I was a little kid that I had to get out of the coalfields," said White, who grew up working on the family farm and playing sports.[1465]

"When I was born my two older brothers were in World War II. My dad and my oldest brother, Henry, bought the farm. I think it was thirty-eight acres. They both built houses on it and we all worked the farm. If you didn't raise it, you didn't eat. We raised hogs, chickens—oodles of chickens—and cows and horses."[1466]

When he wasn't doing his chores on the farm, he was in school and playing sports.[1467]

He has always loved football, basketball, and baseball.[1468]

In time, he went to college, earned his degrees in mathematics and physical education, and became a coach and teacher.[1469]

Considering his influence on his students, it is almost surprising that he never really aspired to teach; instead, he always wanted to coach.[1470]

In time, he did both—and he did both quite well.

But among the roles in which he has served and among the names he has known, survivor might top the list as the biggest surprise of them all.[1471]

That's because White dealt with a myriad of health concerns and among those the unknown.[1472]

In a recent interview, White told this author that he suffers from "familial tremors," which he said is hereditary. The condition is characterized by having too many brain cells. He had surgery at the University of Virginia Hospital, where he had a brain implant. He also has a pacemaker, which shoots impulses to the implant.[1473]

He traced the origin of his condition.

"I started out playing football and baseball. When I was a junior in high school, I was running pass routes. I had a nephew about four or five years younger than me, and he could throw a football like Johnny Unitas.[55] He led me, and I ran face first into a steel door. From that time on, my life was changed. At times, I would have double vision."[1474]

"During my senior year, I started having short term memory loss: I couldn't remember locker combinations, where I put my books, and I was almost a straight-A student. I didn't want to go to college. I wanted to play baseball. I tried out with the San Francisco Giants, and they were going to sign me to one of their farm teams. I went to their camp and had a great camp. They said that tomorrow they're going to make offers, 'And we're going to offer you, so go talk to your parents.'"[1475]

"So I go home and talked to my parents. My dad and I took a walk, and he said, 'You may or may not make the major leagues. Odds are you won't.' It's always been my dream… And he started to cry. It was the first time I had ever seen him cry. He said, 'My dream is for you to go to college.' So I went to college. I didn't even go back to the camp. I went into college half-hearted. I had a pretty-good [football] camp. We were doing three-a-days, and I started noticing things. I'd get hit in the head, and I couldn't see. Of course, you got hit in the head a lot those days. The helmets weren't nearly as good as they are now."[1476]

"I went to a doctor, and he said we would describe your condition as 'a glass jaw.'"[1477]

---

[55] The comparison to Unitas represents the ultimate compliment. This author remembers the legendary quarterback quite well. The following information was taken from the website www.profootballhof.com: Unitas was born on May 7, 1933, in Pittsburgh, Pennsylvania. His full name was John Constantine Unitas. He played college football at Louisville. Cut by the Pittsburgh Steelers in 1955, he was soon signed by the Baltimore Colts and became legendary. He led the Colts to NFL titles in 1958 and 1959 and to victory in Super Bowl V. He played 18 seasons, appeared in 10 Pro Bowls, was named All-NFL 6 times and Player of the Year 3 times. He amassed 40,239 passing yards and threw 290 touchdown passes. He was enshrined into football's Hall of Fame in 1979. He died on September 11, 2002, at the age of 69.

In boxing, that is not a favored condition.

"I had boxed," recalled White. "I was in training for the Golden Gloves, and I got knocked out a couple of times. And I never put two and two together. But when I hit that metal door, they had a concrete stoop out front. I tripped over the stoop and hit that door, and I thought I was dead. Years later, when my son was young, he was helping move some rocks. I told him not to throw them up the hill because they'll roll back. He threw one up the hill, I bent over to pick it up, and it knocked me out cold as a fish."[1478]

Earlier, that run-in with the steel door almost did in his football career, but he never gave up on baseball.[1479]

"The only physical I ever passed was my college physical. When I was in high school, I would go for a physical, and they would keep me over night. I didn't know why. My freshman year, they kept me. My sophomore year, they kept me. My junior year, they kept me. And then I asked, 'Why are you keeping me?' They said, 'You have a bad heart valve.' Nobody had ever told me. My senior year, they made me lay out a week."[1480]

Today, White is happy to report that his cardiologist can no longer find any problems with his heart: not one.[1481]

White credits this phenomenon to God, with whom he has a personal and saving relationship.[1482]

How did this son of a coal miner from such a large family in Jeffrey, West Virginia, find his way to Salem, where football was crowned king so long ago?

Looking back, he said, "My parents had a fourth-grade education. That's the key to poverty, isn't it? Uneducated people having children. My younger brother has a PhD in mathematics and is retired now. I had a sister that became a nurse and worked at Johns Hopkins. But no one ever pushed me to go to school. In Jeffrey, we had an elementary school, grades 1 through 8. I went to Scott High School in Madison, West Virginia." There he played his three favorite sports.[1483]

Following his father's advice, he decided to go to college.

He attended and graduated from Concorde College in West Virginia, where he majored in mathematics and physical education.

"We had to have two teaching fields," he explained. "One thing about Concorde, their degree was accepted anywhere in the United States. It was thorough. It was a good education. I always took 8:00 [am] classes. At our house, we all got up at 5:00. We had chores to do. I did my chores, ate breakfast, took a shower, and went to school."[1484]

And he never forgot his roots or the lessons learned from his parents and other mentors.

"My father taught me to be honest and be straight at you. His favorite thing was to say, 'Pay your bills. Pay them first. Live on what you've got left.' This was a man with a fourth-grade education. He wouldn't shop at the company store because he said the prices were too high, and they take all your money. A lot of people bought everything at the company store, and I watched them. They had a type of money they called 'script,' and you could only spend it at the company store. You could get paid in 'script' or get paid in cash. They enslaved you is what they did.[1485]

"My mother was like this: 'You had better believe in God and you had better behave. Always wear clean underwear when you go out.' We didn't have much, but we ate well. We had a five-acre garden and other plots that raised specialized stuff. Around the house, we grew tomatoes and peppers and onions and potatoes. Down in the field, it was corn and beans and self-sufficient. We had an orchard, and we picked wild berries and made jams and jellies.[1486]

"I would say that my other mentor was my high school coach, Robert Scholl. He was a better baseball coach than he was football. He was the first guy who ever told me that I do some things that other people can't do. And I didn't know how to act. I played so much ball. When I was fourteen years old, fast pitch softball was the big thing. Every coal camp just about had a team. And some had some real talent. We would go to Charleston, and they had ex-baseball players who played. I was the third baseman. This team needed a shortstop, and they told me to play it. Twice a week, they would pick me up and make the fifty-mile one-way trip, and I would play at home for three nights a week. All I wanted to do was play."[1487]

But he couldn't "play" forever.

He took his first coaching job two years after graduating from Concorde. He was hired at Fort Chiswell High School in Wythe County, Virginia, beginning in 1964. He coached there for five seasons and was the head football coach during those last three.[1488]

"Early in my career, I was thought of as an offensive genius," said White. "The trouble was, we weren't winning any games. We scored points. My, we scored points. We ran pro-set and full house. I had one kid catch fifty-five passes in five games. We'd get beat like 50–40.[1489]

"I left Fort Chiswell in the middle of the year. I recognized that it was going nowhere fast. My philosophy has always been 'If I don't succeed, you don't have to fire me.' I wasn't ready to be a head coach. I told the principal I wasn't ready. I had been the head baseball coach and JV basketball coach and assistant in football. They just dumped [the head football coaching job on me] after talking to two or three guys when they couldn't get any of them.[1490]

"Fort Chiswell was a brand-new school.[56] The first year that I was there, in 1964, was the first year they played a varsity schedule. We were in the New River District with Radford, Blacksburg, Christiansburg, and Dublin, which later became Pulaski. We weren't going to compete. We had a bunch of farm boys, and the first time they saw a football was when they came to the eighth grade. I started a sandlot program. It was a great thing for Fort Chiswell and probably the reason they had any success. I went to the civic organizations, and at that time, I got them to put up $500 apiece. There were four of them. I bought equipment to outfit four teams, and we used Fort Chiswell Stadium, which I lined. I ran the concessions and taught the cheerleaders how to run concessions and gave them a cut. We charged twenty-five cents for admission so the program could fund

---

[56] The school's website, www.fchs.wythe.k12.va.us, indicates that the name comes from a frontier fort built in 1758 as an outpost during the French and Indian War. It was one in a chain of forts built by Colonel William Byrd and named in honor of John Chiswell who discovered lead at Austinville in 1756. The school is located at #1 Pioneer Trail, Max Meadows (Wythe County), Virginia. The school opened on August 28, 1960, with an enrollment of 584. The 1966 Pioneers opened their football season with a new stadium.

itself. People turned out like you wouldn't believe. They wanted success. And they got to see those kids play and that was rewarding. I just worked myself to a frazzle. It was either leave Fort Chiswell or get out of coaching because I was burning the candle at both ends and it was killing me."[1491]

White then made his first career change.

"I went with Allstate Insurance in the management program. Well before that, I had been diagnosed with cancer, melanoma. They gave me six months to live. I had the surgery, and I'm still here today. They just give you the worst scenario. I had a knot come up under my arm. I woke up one morning, and the knot was so hot that I put ice cubes on it and they melted. I played golf with a doctor and told him. He said, 'Stop by on your way to school. That's it, probably a sweat gland, and I'll take it out.' He took it out and sent it to UVA for a biopsy, and it was cancer. You talk about a blow. I had been married for two years, and I was twenty-four years old. And they tell you that you're going to die in six months—that's a shocker. I had dropped a lot of weight. They gave me no hope. I went to UVA. They're a teaching school. They have a roundtable of doctors. They sit around and ask you questions. The head doctor said they had to operate or I would be dead in six months. I said, 'What if you don't operate?' He said, 'You'll probably die, but you might have a chance.'"[1492]

White had a family to think about. He married the former Sharon Gale Belcher of Princeton, West Virginia, on May 27, 1964, a week before he graduated from Concorde.[1493]

"The first time I saw her, I fell in love."[57, 1494]

"I took the head coaching job at Fort Chiswell under those conditions," said White. "I worked myself into a frazzle and thought, 'You're probably not going to live that long anyway.' So I might as well make some money to leave Sharon, the girl I love. I got a job with Allstate Insurance, and my pay raise was almost $3K as a trainee, and the pay just kept going up. But there were things about the insurance business that I didn't like. One, I don't like to be cooped up, and

---

[57] They have two children. Suzanne "Suzi" Hiner was born on September 20, 1973, and Vincent Kyle White was born on November 29, 1970.

two, you heard the same complaints from the same people all the time."[1495]

And then, his coaching career was reignited.

Talk about getting "the call."

The one and only Merrill Gainer called White, in need of an assistant.[58]

"He had just taken the job at Patrick Henry, and he had come out of retirement," said White. "I told Sharon I was going to come back to coaching, and that was the nearest she ever came to leaving me. [Her concerns were about the] time [coaching required], and she wanted to have kids. You're never home [when you're a coach], and with Coach Gainer, his typical day was, you got there at six thirty even on a school day, and you did some football work. Then you went and taught five classes. Then you came back and coached the boys on the field. And you went home and got a bite to eat, and then you came back and stayed till about two in the morning.[1496]

"He was single-minded. He was focused. And he went through assistants. I mean, they quit all the time."[1497]

"Tough schedule?"

"It was. To give you an example, when I left Allstate Insurance, I weighed 240 pounds. After my first year at Patrick Henry, I weighed 195. I lost the baby fat!"[1498]

How did White know Gainer?

---

[58] In an article written by Aaron McFarling of the Roanoke Times, posted online on August 29, 2007. McFarling's article covered the dedication of the turf field at the new, $4.1 million Patriot Stadium and bronze sculpture of Gainer. According to McFarling, former Patriot football player Bill Wallace "was part of a group that lobbied school officials to honor the coach, who died in 2000 at the age of 87." Gainer reportedly had retired from coaching over 30 years preceding the date of this article. Gainer led the Patriots to the Group AAA state championship in 1973. McFarling reported that the Patriots went 13–0 that season, outscored their opponents 400–28, and posted 10 shutouts including all three playoff games. Gainer previously coached in his native West Virginia at Big Creek and Bluefield High Schools and tallied four state championships. He came to Patrick Henry in 1969. According to McFarling, Gainer retired after having won 92 percent of his games.

"One of my assistants at Fort Chiswell was Bud Chinault. I had gone to college with him. In fact, he was a roommate. Bud had gone to Beaver High School in Bluefield, where Gainer was the head football coach. He introduced me to Gainer when I was at Fort Chiswell. I remember a time when I said to Gainer, 'Look, I'd like to take some of your films and look at them.' Coach Gainer didn't give out *anything*. He wouldn't even tell you the truth. If you asked him if it was day or night, he would hedge around and not answer. That's the way he was. He coached back in the era before you had all the openness and everything was a secret."[1499]

Gainer called White about joining him at Patrick Henry when Gainer took that job in 1969.[1500]

White soon agreed and made the move.

"What was it like?"

"Even when you coached with him, he didn't tell you a whole lot. He would tell you what he wanted done, and you would do it your way. And if he didn't like it, he'd tell you how he wanted it. My last two or three years there [as an assistant], he finally trusted me.[1501]

"He was a defensive coach. He just wanted his offense to be efficient. Don't give it away. Don't fumble. Don't throw interceptions. I learned so much that I tell people that anything that I accomplished I credit Coach Gainer. Fundamentals I got in high school. They were very, very solid. I never found that anything I was taught in high school was wrong.[1502]

"Coach Gainer was a great personnel man. He could take a 140-pounder and play defensive tackle, and I always thought you had to be big. He said, 'When it comes down to big or quick and smart, give me the quick and smart one.' And at PH, we played little kids, a 160-pound defensive end. He taught me about personnel. It's not their body—it's their will. I found that to be true.[1503]

"He also taught me an interesting technique. He said, 'If you're going to chew a kid out, don't chew them out in front of everybody there.' During the game, he would put his arm around the player, look across the field, and just chew them out good. The only people who knew he was chewing a player out was Gainer and the person being chewed out. And they would say, 'Gainer's a teacher!'"[1504]

"He was hot tempered. Boy, he'd fire you up. It was the same way with officials. Don't chew an official out. Look across the field when he's beside you, and tell him what he's doing wrong. Surprisingly enough, they respect that."[1505]

Five years into his tenure, Gainer and the Patriots won the 1973 Group AAA state championship.[59, 1506]

"We had a bunch of kids that were football players," recalled White. "We had two kids that signed with major colleges. One of those was Shannon Delaney, a punter and linebacker. Before he got banged up, he was the best doggone kicker, and he ran a 4.8. We didn't have a kid that could break 4.8. We shut out three playoff teams: E. C. Glass, T. C. Williams, and Lafayette. I said to myself, 'If you want to win championships, you'd better play some defense.' If you had watched our offense, Gainer didn't run but about five plays [including] one or two passes. We would go out and just punch them in the mouth until they would quit fighting. And then we would score."[1507]

Gainer's last year was 1977.

Would White automatically succeed him?

"I decided I wasn't going to apply for the job," he said. "People asked me why I hadn't applied. I said, 'If I have to apply, then they really don't want me.' The principal came to me during the hiring process and said, 'You haven't applied.' I told him that I wasn't going to. He sat me down and said, 'Why not?' I said, 'As long as I have been in this system, as many people who know who I am, if you don't want me, I'm not your man.' So they ended up giving me the job.[1508]

"Now they have all these committees that talk to coaches, and they don't know anything. We were out of school the day I was scheduled to meet the committee. We had a big snow. I get there, and they start. At first, I'm very polite, and then my West Virginia came out. I said, 'Look, half of you people don't know what you're talking about. You know what type of teacher I am, you can pull

---

[59] In fact, Patrick Henry was not only Virginia's top team that season but was also ranked the number 12 team in the nation by the National Sports Service (source: January 2, 1974, edition of the *Roanoke World-News*).

my records, you should know what type of coach I am, and I've got better things to do.' I got up and left. I went home and told Sharon. She said, 'Well, you can write that one off. You got mad, didn't you?' 'No, I got honest.'"[1509]

But White was selected as the new head coach at PH, and in 1978, he made his debut. He would go on to coach for four more seasons.[1510]

During those five years, PH beat Salem all five times. In 1979, PH played Petersburg in the 1979 state final. "We should have won that game," said White. "We had some kids get the flu [and they exhibited the symptoms] on the bus on the way. We were better than Petersburg, but they were big and physical."[1511]

Another notable pertains to the 1982 team.

"We gave up just 30 points for the season. I played a lot of kids, too. If I couldn't play a lot of kids I felt like a failure."[1512]

White interjected this personal anecdote.

"As an athlete, I played football, basketball, and baseball, and my best sport was probably baseball, but I loved football. It intrigued me. You had all these different personalities you had to meld together. As football coaches, we got the egos and the expectations of the parents, the expectations that you have, that the school has, and you have to meet all these things. I always said that anyone who becomes a high school head [football] coach is a half bubble off center. It's not worth it, monetarily. They can't pay you for the hours you work."[1513]

Yet he did become a head coach.

What changed?

"At PH, I became [Coach Gainer's] top assistant, and people were offering me jobs all the time. He said, 'If you do take a [head-coaching] job, take one in a town where you have one [high] school and one newspaper.'"[1514]

And the "seed" that had been planted a few years back was about to become a healthy "plant."

* * *

For years, the White family resided in Salem on Butt Hollow Road near the Beverly Heights subdivision. It was a great place to raise a family.[1515]

Willis White's daily travels to Roanoke, where he coached at PH, routinely took him down Salem's Main Street and through the traffic lights, including the one at Spartan Drive, where Salem High School is located.[1516]

When Sharon was with him, she had a habit of saying, "One day, you'll be coaching there."[1517]

Her husband always shook off the remark and dismissed it as craziness.[1518]

"Every time we drove across the stop light here [at Spartan Drive], she would say, 'One day you'll be coaching here.' I would say, 'Dream on, woman.' She would say it over and over, and I would finally say, 'Would you give it a rest?'"[1519]

But the love of his life could trust her intuition. Indeed, her remarks proved prophetic.

How did it all come about?

White had a long written list of conditions he didn't believe would ever get checked off. His recollection of how the process unfolded differs sharply with Dale Foster's report.[1520]

But the universal truth is this: regardless of the sequence of events and the words exchanged or not exchanged, Foster was instrumental in Salem's hiring of White who, despite any initial hesitation, did eventually acquiesce and take the job.

Here's how White remembers it all happening.

"Dr. [Walter] Hunt had the supervisor of physical education of Roanoke City [Howard Light] come to see me. He told me that Dr. Hunt wanted to speak to me. I was running the weight program. And it was in the spring of '83, and he just showed up one day and told me that Dr. Hunt wanted to talk to me about Salem.[1521]

"I called Dale Foster and just chatted with him two or three times. Of course, Dale was all for it. I knew I could work with Dale. That's one of the requirements. You have to be able to work with your AD. [Foster was the AD at Salem at the time.] I said no. I was judging a science fair in Roanoke City, and Dr. Hunt called me and said the story is breaking.[1522]

"Carl Richards was the coach at Salem. The principal was Bob Lipscomb, and he was supposed to tell Carl Richards, but no one had told him. Dr. Hunt got in touch with me at the science fair over at Breckinridge Junior High. Here I am judging the science fair with so little knowledge about science. I kept saying no, but it kept coming out yes. I didn't want to do Carl Richards that way. Dr. Hunt said that Carl would be told today.[1523]

"I must have told him no three times, and it came out yes every time. I was saying yes, but my brain was saying no. My mouth wasn't cooperating. He must have thought I was crazy. That was the strangest thing. Next, Dr. Hunt set up a meeting with him and said to 'make out a list of what you need.' This was over the phone. Then to come meet with him, and he gave me a week. All I did was write down the things I had at PH. I had to have control of the weight room and [the football program] at Andrew Lewis Middle School. I would hire all coaches. I think I was halfway hoping he would say no."[1524]

Instead Dr. Hunt met every demand.

It soon became official. Willis White was now the head coach of Salem's football team.

To paraphrase Billy Miles, Andrew Lewis High School class of 1966 and a former standout football player and longtime high school football coach, "White's tenure" officially ushered in the front end of a new winning tradition of Salem football.[1525]

Looking back, White was asked what he thought he brought to the table at Salem.

"One thing is that I was determined for us to be better organized. I looked at the Salem program and thought it was a diamond in the rough. There weren't that many kids playing football. You know the expression, 'If you build it, they'll come'? That was the philosophy I used. Treat the kids right because we're in the kid business."[1526]

He soon discovered that Salem's feeder program of middle school and sandlot was totally separate.

"I put my coaches in place and met resistance at every turn because they had done it this way for so long. I would just call Dr. Hunt, and he would back me down the line. I made a few enemies—until it started working—and then they were all on board."[1527]

"The equipment was in terrible shape. I got there so late and couldn't do everything I wanted to do before the season started. I couldn't order jerseys because the jersey [orders] had a six-month turnaround. We got some old jerseys from Virginia Tech that had no names on them, but they were maroon. We were a rag-tag outfit the first year."[1528]

How did he choose his coaches?

"Coaches have to realize that they are not on a clock and they have to get along as a staff. I brought one coach over from PH, Steve Oliver. He had been my offensive line coach. I had all kinds of guys apply. I brought in John Hinkle from Carroll County, and Marty Yuhas. I talked to Billy Miles, who played for and coached for Coach Joyce. I felt like I needed community ties. And Danny Wheeling [another former Lewis standout]. That gave me two Salem people and then Larry Bradley, who was the head coach at Lexington who had set out to come to PH, but when I took the Salem job, I called him and asked him if he'd go to Salem instead of PH, and he said, 'Sure.' Bradley said he liked to work with the younger kids, so I put him at Andrew Lewis."[1529]

That shored up the middle school, but the sandlot program was a different story.

"Thankfully," recalled White, "the sandlot program had backing from Charlie Hammersley [Andrew Lewis class of 1969 and retired director of Salem Parks and Recreation]. He is a great guy—A1 in every aspect. If he told you something, it got done. I know how sandlot coaches are, so I didn't ask for much help from them. I just brought them in and gave them clinics every year and took them on the field and showed them techniques that we were running and defenses we were running. I was there any time they needed me. And they started trusting me. Once they started trusting me, they started putting [our techniques] into their system."[1530]

And it was a Gainer-type system.

THE SPARTAN SUCCESSION

"Over at PH, Gainer liked to run what he called the rover. We didn't stick with the principles of the monster. We ran the 52 with a rover linebacker, which Shannon Delaney had played really great in '73. I ran it. That's what I coached for Gainer. He left a really good sophomore class. I worked as many of them in as I could. I've always been loyal. If you have played for me for two years, it's hard for me to replace you because I think you've earned something, and I'll give you every chance to succeed. But if you show me that you don't want to succeed or can't succeed, that's different. [In 1978] we won our last two games. We beat E. C. Glass and Pulaski and ended the season on a high note. The next year, we went to the state finals in '79, and I think the flu got us that day."[1531]

Then White felt compelled to make a change.

"What happened was, I started looking at my stats one day and my rover wasn't making any plays. They were running away from him. I'll have to change this, so I started running a one-linebacker defense. And I played two strong safeties, one on each side. Everybody called them linebackers and said, 'You run a 53,' but I never ran a 53. The safeties could play up near the line, or they could play back and against the pass. There again Gainer comes into play. He knew how to choose personnel."[1532]

As White put his coaching staff in place in Salem, he had one basic philosophy.

"If I gave you a job to do, I let you do it. And when you weren't doing it to suit me, I told you. I'm an organizer. I never really considered myself a coach. I was a teacher who enjoyed coaching. I had been at Patrick Henry and had played Andrew Lewis and Salem all that time. I saw Salem as having gone downhill after the [Eddie] Joyce era, and there was some controversy over Mike Stevens [the man who succeeded Joyce], but I thought Mike had done a good job. He had kids that were great athletes. He took an assistant's job at Cave Spring High School and took his boys with him. They beat Salem like a drum![1533]

"When I came to Salem, I just sat about to do what I do, and the organization was not what I wanted. I came to Salem at a unique time. Dr. Hunt was the superintendent. He had been the superintendent over in Roanoke City, and he and I got along real well. He asked me what it would take to come to Salem. I hadn't considered leaving PH but had been offered several jobs, including small colleges, but I loved those kids over at PH.[1534]

"They got a superintendent from Syracuse, New York, named Frank Tota, and he decided middle school would not have football. His logic was they could play football in sandlot. But sandlot had a 120-pound limit: your big kids couldn't play. And I said, 'This is disaster.' We had three junior highs feeding us. And I was going to have none. And I looked around—and this was in the 80s—and I think that was the zenith of football in the Roanoke Valley. The talent was really good. Kids had size and were beginning to get that big size that they have now. Everybody was just so even. We just pounded each other every week. That was during that 3A system, and [PH] was the smallest school in it.[1535]

"The numbers were down at PH. People were fleeing Roanoke City. I didn't really want to leave PH. I didn't want to stay just teaching, and they offered me the head of the Roanoke City Math Department. That got me out of the classroom, but I didn't think I would be happy shuffling papers. Then Salem formed its own school system, and Dr. Hunt got in contact with me and asked me to make a list of all my requirements to come to Salem.[1536]

"At PH, I had authority over the football program. I gave the AD a list of what I needed, and he got them for me. And the last two years that I was there, I was also the AD for football, so I had free run with the football program. I wasn't going to leave that to come to Salem."[1537]

But he did.

And it didn't take long to draw the ire of some Salemites.

It happened when White decided to end the annual tradition (which had begun in 1961) of sending the Salem boys to the secluded two-week preseason football camp.

He had his reasons.

"I had heard the stories of what happened at camp. A lot of the old timers got mad at me. They used that as a time to go up there and drink and play poker. My philosophy was this: a teenager is going through a trying time. Football is rough enough. Let him sleep in his own bed. He'll do better. He'll be at ease with his surroundings. The philosophy of the camp was to get them away from everything."[1538]

What about the argument that the camp served to bond the players in such a way that they wouldn't get elsewhere?

"That's good," replied White. "I can't argue with that, but you have to weigh your options there. You get a kid that's scared to death and has never been out for football, and he can't go home?"[1539]

When this author quoted a former Andrew Lewis football player who said that, as a result of the trials of camp, the Lewis players were "ready to eat nails," White said, "Well, let's put it this way: we came out of our summer camp at the school and played Blacksburg every year, and I think our record against them was something like 20–3."[1540]

He then reflected on what football was like then and now.

"When I came along, all we did was block and tackle. If you can block, you can block. If you can tackle, you can tackle. Why not teach them how to play football in between? With Coach Gainer, we did a little bit [of blocking and tackling] early in the year, and every now and then we had a refresher course, but we played football. We scrimmaged without hitting the backs, which I kept up until I quit. Our backs didn't get hit in practice after the two-a-days. You could hit backs in the upper body, but you couldn't hit their legs. They've got to run. They've got to have their legs if they're going to run. They get hit early in the year, for two weeks and two scrimmages. After that, in practice, we're going to bang you up there in the chest."[1541]

1983

As we welcome Coach White as the newest leader of the Spartans, let's look back in the world of sports in 1983.

As an avid sports fan, this author remembers quite well how, in professional football, the Washington Redskins defeated the Miami Dolphins in Super Bowl XVII, 27–17. In professional basketball, the Philadelphia 76ers, thanks to the off-season acquisition of Moses

Malone, finally beat the Lakers in the NBA Finals, and did so with a sweep, 4–0.

In men's college basketball, NC State—under head Coach Jim Valvano—defeated Houston to win the NCAA championship.

Later in the year, the Baltimore Orioles defeated the Philadelphia Phillies in five games to win the World Series.

And in Salem, Virginia, 1983 was the year that Willis Howard White Jr. debuted as the head coach of Salem High's football team.

The people who remembered the glory days of Andrew Lewis football under Eddie Joyce longed for Salem's return to gridiron glory.

They had watched as Mike Stevens at Andrew Lewis and Tom Kucer, Wallace Thompson, and Carl Richards at Salem all courageously stepped up to the task, only to come short of the glory.

Perhaps they had stood hindered in the long shadow of Joyce.

And Willis White was the next man up with the shadow still looming.

But White's case was different for several reasons.

He had served as an assistant under Merrill Gainer, who led Patrick Henry to its only state football championship in 1973, and White had taken over the reins in 1978 and coached the Patriots to a state runner-up finish in 1979.

He had also coached against Salem and seemed like the perfect candidate for the job.

In fact, his wife had predicted for some time that one day the job would be his.

And now it was.

How long would the folks in Salem have to wait before the Spartans claimed their first football state championship?

Longer than they wanted, but in time, they could count their blessings that a country boy nicknamed Willie knew a thing or two about survival.

And success.[60]

---

[60] Note: White provided his detailed and personal account during an interview with this author on January 12, 2018.

THE SPARTAN SUCCESSION

Part 3: Now That Was the Right Call!

Cam Young signs letter of intent to N.C. State while his parents and Coach White look on

Coach White emphasizes key points to the Spartan players

Salem assistant coach Marty Yuhas points players in the right direction.

On the topic of success, who wouldn't agree that behind every successful head coach is a capable group of assistants? (Need examples? Please see pages 104 and 105 of *The Team the Titans Remember*.)

And here, in his debut season as the chief of the Spartans, when it came to the hiring of his assistant coaches, an intangible concept topped Willis White's list of qualifications required.

"I chose assistants based on compatibility," he said.[1542]

His first choice was Larry Bradley, who would head up the junior varsity squad. Bradley had been the head coach at Lexington High and, in the previous season, led the team to a 9–2 overall record. Of course, Bradley was a well-known surname among high school football coaches. His father, Lawrence Bradley, had been the head coach at Graham.[1543]

Next on the list was John Hinkle, who crossed over to Salem from Carroll County. A native of New Jersey, Hinkle would work with the defensive backs.[1544]

The list continued with Steve Oliver, who had served for three years as an assistant under White at Patrick Henry. Oliver, along with Billy Miles Jr., would work with both the offensive and defensive lines.[1545]

THE SPARTAN SUCCESSION

Miles, a 1966 alumnus of Andrew Lewis High, represented the lone holdover from last year's Spartans under former head coach Carl Richards.[1546]

Another Lewis grad and former football standout, Danny Wheeling, made White's list too. Wheeling (Lewis class of '65) was assigned to work with the offensive backs.[61, 1547]

Marty Yuhas, a graduate of Patrick Henry-Roanoke; and Brian Hooker, a Salem alumnus and the football program's first-ever quarterback and who more recently served as an assistant at Northside, would assist Bradley.[1548]

This year's roster included the names of forty-four players. White hinted at the notion that his first hoplites were certainly smart enough to be successful. And that was important to him, for he believed that good or bad decisions make or break a team.[1549]

"Dumb will kill you," he said. "When you get beat you get beat by dumb. Most games aren't won. They're lost."[1550]

High intelligent quotients could be found on this year's offensive line. Both tackles, Pete Fox and John Packett, were honor students. What's more, that pair and their three teammates up front were all seniors. The guards were Bill Warren and David Murphy,

---

[61] Danny Wheeling was a very popular player, coach, and friend to many who knew him. Unfortunately, he is no longer living to share his memories of football in Salem. On November 18, 2018, Daniel Francis "Scooter" Wheeling died after battling primary progressive aphasia and Parkinson's disease. Born on July 17, 1946, he was a graduate of Andrew Lewis High and Guilford College. He soon returned to Salem and taught at Salem Intermediate School and West Salem Elementary School. He coached football and track at Salem Intermediate and Andrew Lewis and Salem High Schools. He was described as an avid reader, a painter of Santas, a teller of jokes, a beach music lover, and an extraordinary dancer. He is survived by many family members, including his devoted wife, Jean (source: www.memorials.johnoakey.com). Wheeling was a tri-captain on the 1964 Andrew Lewis High state championship team along with Steve Cromer and Dan Brugh. And consider this testimonial: Billy Miles considers Wheeling, along with Russell Harris and Dan Brugh, as one of the top three players on Andrew Lewis's state championship football team of 1964. "[He] was a great running back," said Miles. "He and I coached together for twenty-eight years with Andrew Lewis and Salem" (source: *The Team the Titans Remember*, p. 353).

and the center was Drew Thompson. Though listed at just 177 pounds, Thompson made up in lack of stature with experience and a high football IQ.[1551]

Rob Vaughan was designated as the long snapper, and the reserve linemen included Tim Sutphin, Doug Moore and Brian Ellis.[1552]

Behind this intelligent and experienced set of linemen was southpaw quarterback Cam Young, a junior who a year ago completed 56 of 153 passes for 706 yards and 6 touchdowns, but he also gave up 16 interceptions.[1553]

James O'Quinn was listed as the backup quarterback, and David Thomas would likely serve as an emergency quarterback.[1554]

Lynwood Hutchinson and Dickie Arnold were expected to compete for the tight end spot, while Kevin Phipps was a sure bet at flanker. The receiving corps also included Richard Heller, Doug Cole, David Harrison, Grady Spradlin, Charles Joyce, and Lee Joyner.[1555]

The rushing attack featured fullback James Riley and tailback JoJo Harris. If Harris needed a breather, Frank "Tiny" Morris would get some reps, while Riley had backups in Don Jones, Trey Gregory, and Mike Gray.[1556]

On the defensive side of the football, the one area of concern coming into this season was the secondary, but Hinkle had been working overtime to get it ready for the season opener.[1557]

Joyner and Heller won the two spots at corner, and O'Quinn was the safety. In the event those players needed replacing, their backups included Tillow Dishon, Spradlin, and Phipps.[1558]

The linebacking corps consisted of hard-hitting William Kimbrough and Dickie Arnold and Morris. Kimbrough was second on the team last year in tackles. He recorded 45 solos and 29 assists.[1559]

The five-man front featured Fox at nose guard and Sutphin and Packett as the tackles. Pat Keister, who previously played linebacker, was moved to end to take advantage of his quickness. On the opposite end of the line stood Todd Smith.[1560]

Drew Thompson, Paul Ferguson, Vaughan, Doug Moore, Brian Ellis, and Gary Nowlin were named as reserve linemen.[1561]

THE SPARTAN SUCCESSION

As White and his able assistants readied the Spartans for a new campaign, which Roanoke Valley District team was considered this year's frontrunner? It had to be the Cougars of Pulaski County, which had won two straight district titles and seemed poised for more.[1562]

In Joel Hicks, they had one of the best head coaches in Virginia.

Born in Richmond, West Virginia, Hicks attended Richmond High, where he played running back. He then attended West Virginia University, where he played running back, and soon took his first coaching job at Big Creek High in War, West Virginia.[1563]

After Big Creek, Hicks became the head coach at Woodrow Wilson High in Beckley and then returned to West Virginia University, where he coached the backfield.[1564]

He took over the program at Pulaski County in 1978.[1565]

Now, in 1983, he welcomed the return of eight starters, including quarterback Terry Finley, who was considered a triple threat: run, pass, and hand off with dexterity. Tackle Todd Grantham—a 6'4", 241-pound tackle—was considered the best college prospect in the area. The speedy Ron Kimbrough would switch from tailback to flanker, while Dickie Johnson would convert from tight end to fullback and Jack Turner from fullback to tailback.[1566]

Hicks reported that the offense would use more power-I than option. His son, T. J. Hicks, would play at one of the ends, and Ricky Finley, the quarterback's brother, would be at the other end.[1567]

Who would fill the shoes vacated by Chris Kinzer, one of the best kickers in district history?

An able fellow by the name of Charlie Bryant.[1568]

And the defense?

Solid: it returned six defenders.[1569]

Pulaski County would open the season in Charlotte, North Carolina, against West Charlotte High. Meanwhile, the Salem Spartans under their newest chief would battle Blacksburg.

Game 1 (September 1): Spartans 9, Indians 7

Trailing 7-3 with just under 7 minutes remaining in the game, Salem's Kevin Phipps hauled in a pass from quarterback Cam Young and turned a routine over-the-middle reception into a 59-yard score.[1570]

Blacksburg had 2 more possessions, but the Spartan defense—which held the Indians to 148 total yards in the game—did its part to preserve the victory.[1571]

Salem's JoJo White rushed for a game best 128 yards on 20 carries, and Blacksburg's Waymon Martin paced his team with 17 carries for 94 yards.[1572]

After a scoreless first half, Salem scored the game's first points when Allan Wiley booted a 42-yard field goal in the third quarter.[1573]

In the fourth, Martin gave Blacksburg the lead when he ran for an 11-yard touchdown. Tim Jones kicked the extra point.[1574]

Young provided his analysis of the game-winning score. "It was a bootleg pass left. All we were trying to do was get a first down… But Kevin Phipps just got open in the middle, caught the football, and outran everybody else."[1575]

Blacksburg, which entered the game smarting from the previous week's drubbing, 36–0, to Northside, made Coach White dread the trip to Blacksburg and its newly christened Bill Brown Field.[1576]

"We were awfully inconsistent on both offense and defense," said White "We threw the [2] interceptions, but we didn't fumble. It was a typical opening night. We've got a long season ahead of us. So far, I've enjoyed working with these young people, and I think they've responded well."[1577]

That night, or the following morning, White would have learned that defending district champion and Virginia's fifth-ranked team, Pulaski County, had lost to West Charlotte, 12–3.[1578]

Salem and Pulaski County would meet late in the season.

Up next, the Spartans were slated to clash with the Knights of Cave Spring, who finished last season with a record of 8–2 and third in the district. One of their two losses was to Patrick Henry, 17–3.[1579]

Cave Spring head coach Charlie Hammes gathered his thoughts on the matter. "It's been hard to think of Willis being at Salem. I've caught myself saying 'Patrick Henry' at coaches' meetings a couple of times when I meant 'Salem.' I look at their team and style. It's just like PH on offense and defense. This game isn't like preparing for a new coach."1580

While Salem edged Blacksburg in week 1, Cave Spring blasted Martinsville, 35–12.

Game 2 (September 8): Knights 21, Spartans 14

Tied 14–14 with 2:15 remaining in the game, Cave Spring running back Tim Fulton scored his third touchdown of the game to lift the Knights to victory.[1581]

All 3 of his touchdowns came on 1-yard runs, but his biggest play of the game was his long kickoff return after Salem had tied the game with 4:50 left. His return to the Salem 36 kept Cave Spring in business.[1582]

For the Spartans, Cam Young threw 2 touchdown passes, 1 to Eddie Riley and the other to Kevin Phipps. Allan Wiley kicked both crucial extra points.[1583]

Young completed just 9 of 23 passes for 104 yards and 1 pick. His passes, however, were distributed to 5 different receivers. His counterpart, Nathan O'Dell, proficiently completed 11 of 15 passes for 141 yards, but he too gave up an interception.[1584]

Fulton led all rushers with 82 yards after 19 carries, while Riley led Salem with 15 carries for 63 yards.[1585]

Salem was now 1–1 on the season and had the tough task of taking on William Fleming next. Several of their fellow Roanoke Valley District rivals had already played 3 games.[1586]

Northside, Franklin County, and Cave Spring were all unbeaten with 3–0 records. Among this trio, Northside had the distinction of having recorded 3 shutouts. The Vikings hoped to continue their pillaging and plundering this week when they faced the Bulldogs of Martinsville High.[1587]

Game 3 (September 16): Colonels 34, Spartans 12

Running backs Darryl Rosborough and Kurt Jennings each scored 2 touchdowns and rushed for over 100 yards apiece to lead Fleming to victory at Salem Municipal Field.[1588]

The Colonels amassed 470 yards on offense but didn't pull away from the Spartans until the third quarter. Leading 14–6 at the intermission, Fleming outscored Salem 13–0 in the decisive third.[1589]

For the Spartans, quarterback Cam Young threw 2 touchdown passes to Kevin Phipps, but both 2-point tries following those touchdowns failed.[1590]

Phipps finished with 3 catches for 117 yards and now had 4 touchdown catches in 3 games.[1591]

Now 1–2 on the season, Salem will look to even its record at home next week against Patrick Henry. This game will represent Willis White's first coaching job against his former team.

Around the league, Northside stayed unbeaten—but not unscored upon—after it doubled up Martinsville, 28–14, and Franklin County remained among the unbeaten by outpointing Patrick Henry, 14–9.[1592]

Game 4 (September 23): Salem 7, PH 6

Think about a popular cheer that goes, "Block that kick! Block that kick!"

The Spartans did just that, and it enabled them to slip past the Patriots and pull to 2–2 on the season.[1593]

Frank Morris blocked a PH field goal attempt with just 34 seconds remaining in the game to seal the deal for Salem.[1594]

Morris had a plan.

"I told William Kimbrough to go inside the end and I would go outside," said Morris. "I told him to go for it, but I got it instead."[1595]

For the record, this was Salem's first win over PH since Andrew Lewis won in 1971.

And yes, it was particularly sweet for Coach White, who had previously patrolled the Patriot sidelines for 14 years as either an assistant or head coach.

"It was weird," said White. "It didn't hit me until I saw Patrick Henry warm up and I realized I wouldn't be on their sideline."[1596]

Salem got its lone touchdown on its first possession. The scoring drive began with a little trickery. Halfback James O'Quinn tossed a 44-yard option pass to Kevin Phipps and then 2 plays later, JoJo Harris ran from 7 yards to the end zone. Allan Wiley kicked what would turn out to be the decisive point after.[1597]

White said that the trick play was suggested to him by assistant coach Billy Miles.[1598]

"Anybody who knows me, knows that I don't just do that sort of thing," said White.[1599]

PH's touchdown came via workhorse running back Tim Dudley, who rushed for a game best 142 yards. His score came with 3:34 remaining in the game, during which he broke 2 tackles and ran 25 yards. The PAT was blocked by a wave of Spartans.[1600]

Up next, the Spartans (2–2) travel to Bassett to take on the Bengals.

Game 5 (October 1): Salem 14, Bassett 7

Down 7–6 in the third quarter, James O'Quinn punted for Salem, the ball bounced off a Bassett player's leg, and Rob Vaughn recovered on the Bassett 17.[1601]

After 2 carries by James Riley, JoJo Harris scored from the 4 to win it for the Spartans.[1602]

Salem improved to 3–2 at the midseason point for the first time since 1977.

"We really needed a break," said Coach White. "If you noticed, we didn't have any until that point. We played dead in the first half and got ourselves in a hole. The biggest factor is we were ready to play Friday, and they called it off at 5:00 [because of the rain]."[1603]

So the two teams played on Saturday, and Bassett capitalized on a turnover and scored on its first possession when quarterback Allen

Lawson tossed a 45-yard scoring strike to Rodney Robinson. Before the play, Bassett's Aaron Staples picked off Cam Young's first pass of the game to turn the ball over to Bassett.[1604]

Salem answered with a touchdown in the first quarter when Young connected with Eric Pellant for a 22-yard strike.[1605]

The Spartans fumbled 3 times in the first half. They recovered 2, but the 1 that they lost came at the Bengals' 1 with 6 minutes remaining in the first half.[1606]

Riley led Salem with 101 rushing yards, and Young's passing numbers were better than in previous games. He completed 8 of 13 passes for 102 yards.[1607]

Around the league, Northside topped the district with an unbeaten 6–0 mark, while all other district foes—Pulaski County, William Fleming, Franklin County, Patrick Henry, and Salem—were all 3–2.[1608]

For the Spartans, they were scheduled to play at home to the Pioneers of Heritage High of Lynchburg next.

Game 6 (October 8): Heritage 10, Salem 7

A late field goal helped Heritage defeat Salem, but the more important news pertained to the health of Willis White.[1609]

The Spartan skipper was taken to the emergency room at Lewis-Gale Hospital earlier that day after complaining of chest pains. He was admitted into the coronary unit.[1610]

Stay tuned for a status report on White.

As for the game, Heritage scored its touchdown on its first possession. Robert Ford ran 38 yards to set up an option toss from Ralph Hayes to Lanksford Hankins for a 10-yard touchdown run.[1611]

Salem (3–3) tied the score with 8:10 remaining in the game when JoJo Harris scored from 12 yards out. Kevin Phipps kicked the extra point, and the score was 7–7.[1612]

The scoring drive was highlighted by 2 key Cam Young passes, both to Eric Pellant, plus a key interference call against the Pioneers.[1613]

Heritage came right back. The Pioneers began on their own 28 and drove to within field goal range. Glenn Shelton had to kick the field goal twice. After the first, a penalty moved the ball back 5 yards, and on his second, he connected from 22 yards for the game winner.[1614]

What was it like along the Spartan sidelines without White?

The assistants coached with none acting as the head coach.

"All of us worked together [as far as running the team]," said Billy Miles. "We knew the game plan. It was a matter of executing it. It was an emotional game, and an emotionally draining day."[1615]

Less than a week later, a status report of White's condition revealed that he had an abnormality in his heart. The plan was for him to undergo further tests to determine which course of action to take.[1616]

Game 7 (October 15): Salem 21, Franklin County 14

Coach White remained hospitalized, but his able assistants helped coach the Spartans to victory against the Eagles in the game played at Ferrum College Field.[1617]

Billy Miles coached the offense and Steve Oliver the defense. Miles must have been pleased to witness quarterback Cam Young run for a touchdown, pass for another, and finish the game with 12 of 18 passing for 172 yards.[1618]

No doubt, Young felt happy.

"We wanted to open up since we had a good week passing last week [145 yards in 10–7 loss to Heritage]," said Young. "And the line did a good job of blocking."[1619]

Young's touchdown run in the first period capped an impressive drive that included passes to Eric Pellant and Pat Keister.[1620]

Salem's second touchdown came courtesy of James Riley from 3 yards out in the second quarter. The Spartan defense set up the team's next score in the third quarter when Franklin County's Eddie Smith bobbled a James O'Quinn punt and Tim Sutphin recovered for Salem at the Franklin County 36.[1621]

Young went back to the air and connected with Kevin Phipps on a 24-yarder and then to Riley on a 4-yard screen pass for the score.[1622]

When would White return to the sidelines?

Possibly for next week.

"Willis is getting out of the hospital today [Saturday], and there is nothing permanently wrong with his heart," said Oliver. "We are going to carry the game ball over to him. And we expect to see him… to view the [game] film."[1623]

And if White soon returns to duty, he will help prepare the Spartans for their upcoming clash in Lynchburg against the Hilltoppers of E. C. Glass.

Game 8 (October 22): Salem 0, Glass 0

Sometimes, a tie can feel like a win.

It certainly felt that way to Willis White, who was all too happy to return to action.

"It felt so good to be back," he said. "I've never been so happy to tie."[1624]

The Spartan defense held the Hilltoppers to 113 yards on offense, and Pat Keister killed Glass's only serious scoring threat, which came late in the game. The Hilltoppers had driven to the Spartans' 26, but Keister picked off Tom Garnett's pass at the 12 to end the threat with only 3 minutes remaining.[1625]

Salem (4–3–1) had 1 last possession, and running back James Riley helped push the ball eventually to midfield. On the drive, Cam Young threw deep to intended receivers, David Harrison and Eric Pellant, but both throws eluded their grasps, and the Spartans failed to get in field goal range.[1626]

Still, getting a tie against Glass—especially at Lynchburg's City Stadium—had to inject some confidence into the Spartan players.

And that would help them considering that they had only 2 games remaining and those against heavyweights Pulaski County and Northside, which were both vying for the district crown and were scheduled to play each other on Monday, October 24, due to a previous rain delay.[1627]

Author's note: Though I did not find anything in either the Roanoke or Salem newspapers that made mention of it, I couldn't help but think about the significance of a 0–0 tie between Salem and Glass. In my previous work, *The Team the Titans Remember*, Andrew Lewis and E. C. Glass battled to a 0–0 tie in 1963 and here in 1983—twenty years later—Salem and Glass also played to a 0–0 tie. But in 1963, an ugly melee followed the stalemate, and former Lewis players and coaches 50-plus years later recalled with specificity just how bad it was. For the details surrounding what happened, please see the aforementioned source, beginning on p. 294. Thankfully, no such brawl followed the Salem-Glass game of 1983.

With the Roanoke Valley's own version of *Monday Night Football*, the Cougars defeated the Vikings 10–7 in Dublin, which kept Pulaski County undefeated in the district and a game up over Northside.[1628]

Pulaski County (4–0 district and 6–2 overall) still had Salem and Patrick Henry to play, while Northside (3–1, 7–1) had remaining games against Cave Spring and Salem.[1629]

As anyone can glean, Salem became the common denominator between Pulaski County and Northside and situated Salem into the role of a spoiler.

Theoretically, Salem could be more than that. With district records critical to postseason play, if Salem defeated both teams, then it would tie for the district title.

Regardless of the outcome, Coach White liked the role of spoiler.

"I'm kind of enjoying it," he said. "These kids have come a long way. I'd like to be starting over in the district. We're getting a little more physical and aggressive each week. Plus, the kids are learning a little more of what I want to teach them."[1630]

Pulaski County head coach Joel Hicks had plenty of work in front of him and a short time to get there.

The Pulaski-County-versus-Northside game was originally scheduled to be played on Friday, October 21, but was delayed until

Monday, October 24, which meant Hicks had just 3 days to prepare the Cougars for the Spartans set for Friday, October 28.[1631]

Hicks thought highly of Salem's team.

"Salem has a good football team and I hope our players understand that," he said. "I'm glad I saw them against E. C. Glass last week. Now I can get the players to realize just how tough they are."[1632]

Hicks especially liked, or respected, the Salem aerial attack of Cam Young to Kevin Phipps.[1633]

He referred to Phipps as the best receiver in the district.[1634]

Game 9 (October 28): Cougars 13, Spartans 6

Salem entered this one with a solid plan: focus on stopping the quickness of Pulaski County quarterback Terry Finley and running back Ron Kimbrough.[1635]

The good news is that it worked for the most part. The bad news is that it freed up fullback Dickie Johnson to wreak havoc, and he did.[1636]

Johnson's game best 120 rushing yards were the difference.[1637]

"We had to stop Pulaski's speed," said Coach White. "Our game plan was to make the fullback beat us—and he did."[1638]

And Coach Hicks adjusted his offense accordingly.

"When [Salem] did that, we had to run Dickie out of a different set than he's used to running. He usually goes over tackle to set up the option, but this time he had to go inside over guard and center."[1639]

The game clock belonged to the Cougars.

In the first half, they held the ball for over 18 of the 24 minutes, had a 37–12 advantage in plays, a 154–40 advantage in yards, and Kimbrough broke free for a 35-yard touchdown run.[1640]

That was Pulaski's only touchdown. Its other 7 points came courtesy of Charlie Bryant, who kicked an extra point and 2 field goals, including a 33-yarder against the wind.[1641]

For Salem, which was held scoreless through 3 quarters, it got a break in the fourth when it took advantage of great field position. It all began with Salem punter James O'Quinn, whose punt was aided by the wind, and the ball was downed at the Pulaski 5.[1642]

Deep in their own territory, the Cougars failed to move the ball and were forced to punt. The Spartans took over at the Cougars' 35, and on the first play, Cam Young found Kevin Phipps on a touchdown pass that beat Pulaski safety Rickey Finley.[1643]

"I thought we had it covered," said Hicks. "I don't think our safety thought Young could throw it that far over him and he didn't get back deep enough."[1644]

Bryant and O'Quinn both punted frequently in the game. O'Quinn had 6 punts, and Bryant had 5.[1645]

With the win, Pulaski County (5–0 in the district) clinched at least a tie for the league title and would finish the regular season against Patrick Henry.

Northside (4–1) kept pace when it defeated Cave Spring (27–7) with Salem (4–4–1) up next. Even if Northside loses to Salem, it could still go to the playoffs as a wildcard team.[1646]

Going into the last week of the regular season, the top 10 ranked Group AAA teams in the state were the following:

- Hampton
- Kempsville
- T. C. Williams
- J. E. B. Stuart
- W. T. Woodson
- Hopewell.
- GW-Danville
- Pulaski County
- Northside
- Fauquier[1647]

In this, the debut season of Willis White at Salem, the Spartans would play the Vikings in the regular-season finale at Salem's Municipal Field. Win, lose, or draw, the Spartans had already won more games this season than they had since 1977 when they won 6.

Game 10 (November 4): Northside 28, Salem 0

The Spartan defense was prepared to face the Viking wishbone offense that featured quarterback Mike Ouellette and running backs Tim Boitnott and George Bruce. They expected Ouellette to routinely hand the ball off to one of the running backs. Instead, Ouellette kept the ball in his own hands for the most part and scorched the Spartans with 3 touchdown runs and a career-high 128 rushing yards.[1648]

"This was as strong as our wishbone has looked," said Northside head coach Jim Hickam. "Against Salem, that's a compliment because they're as tough as anyone defensively."[1649]

"Ouellette faked better than he had all year," said Coach White. "They're the only team [in the district] that runs the wishbone, and it always drives you crazy the first series."[1650]

For Salem's offense, it went to the air often. Quarterback Cam Young completed 13 of 24 passes for 145 yards, but he also had four interceptions.[1651]

Hickam spoke about his dream.

"I have this dream to be the smallest Group AAA school and win the state. We have 912 and [GW–] Danville has 1,800 students. We can't get much smaller."[1652]

When Northside was busy shutting out Salem, Pulaski County was doing likewise to Patrick Henry. The Cougars crushed the Patriots 33–0 and claimed the district title.[1653]

Sixteen teams from across the state qualified for the Group AAA state playoffs.

Both Pulaski County and Northside were in the bottom half of the bracket and conceivably could play each other if both won their first-round games. Pulaski County was paired against Stonewall Jackson-Manassas,[62] and Northside faced defending state champion GW-Danville.[1654]

---

[62] The geographical location of this school is designated because there are two high schools in Virginia with this name. The other is in Quicksburg of Shenandoah County.

THE SPARTAN SUCCESSION

Round 1 results: GW Danville 20, Northside 7, Pulaski County 16, Stonewall Jackson 12. The stunner: Great Bridge defeated the number 1 rated team, Hampton, 17–14.[1655]

Northside's season concluded, while Pulaski County advanced to the quarterfinals to play GW-Danville.

The Cougars hosted this game in Dublin, and late in the fourth quarter, running back Ron Kimbrough broke loose for a 72-yard touchdown run to help lift Pulaski County to a 17–7 victory.[1656]

Up next, the Cougars would host 1 of 2 semifinal games against the Majors of Mount Vernon, while the Chiefs of Kempsville would take on the Blue Devils of Hopewell in the other semifinal.

Mount Vernon ended Pulaski County's quest for a state title when the Majors scored 22 points in a 6:41 span of the fourth quarter for a 28–21 victory, while Kempsville defeated Hopewell 13–6 to set up the state final.[1657]

The championship game was played in Norfolk, and Mount Vernon shut out Kempsville 10–0 for the Group AAA state title.[1658]

Now that the state results were in, let's return to Salem and recap its season.

On this team that narrowly missed reaching the 0.500 mark, there were several Spartans that posted some impressive numbers.

In rushing, JoJo Harris led the team with 131 carries for 469 yards and 3 touchdowns.[1659]

Quarterback Cam Young attempted 152 passes and completed 71 for 1,216 yards. He threw 15 interceptions and 8 touchdown passes.[1660]

Kevin Phipps paced the receivers with 22 receptions for 508 yards, 23.1 per catch, and 5 touchdowns. Pat Keister hauled in 19 passes for 364 yards, 19.2 per catch, and Eric Pellant was next, with 17 receptions for 251 yards and 1 touchdown.[1661]

Defensively, Dickie Arnold led the team with 68 tackles and 38 assists. Tim Sutphin was next with 63 tackles, 21 assists, and 4 quarterback sacks; Grady Spradlin tallied 42 tackles and 22 assists; Frank "Tiny" Morris finished with 37 tackles, 23 assists, and 1 sack; Keister claimed 37 tackles, 17 assists, and 4 sacks; and Lee Joyner was next with 30 tackles and 17 assists.[1662]

Under first-year head coach Willis White, the Spartans finished at 4–5–1 just below the 0.500 mark, but that was still an improvement from all previous seasons except for the first; plus, the 4 wins included the defeat of Patrick Henry—White's previous team.

Remember how it all came about?

Dr. Hunt, who had replaced Frank Cosby, had immediately made finding a head football coach job one. He approached Dale Foster for his opinion as to whom to hire. Foster immediately recommended Willis White, so Hunt quickly picked up the telephone eager to get White on the line.

Whether his answer was immediate or delayed, White ultimately agreed to take the job.

Soon, time would prove that Hunt's inquisition, Foster's guidance, and White's acceptance all combined for future Spartan success.

Now *that* was the right call!

Chapter 12

1984: THE LAST IN THE SNAKE PIT

Even the tireless need water as Spartan stalwart Pat Keister decided while conferring with Coach White.

Salem's sparkplug of a running back, JoJo Harris

The new year started on a sad note for the sports community.

On January 21, 1984, one of the most well-known high school football coaches in Virginia died.

Alger Pugh died of cardiac arrest in Memorial Hospital in Danville.[1663]

Pugh, 47, had coached George Washington Danville for 20 years, and his teams had compiled a 165–43–7 record. His teams won state titles in 1968 and 1982, plus 11 district titles and 4 regional crowns during his tenure.[1664]

Born in Caroline County, he was a star halfback at Virginia Tech and led the Hokies in rushing in 1959 with 615 yards. In addition to coaching football at GW, he also helped coach track and taught government.[1665]

Salem head coach Willis White paid tribute to Pugh.

"He was totally dedicated to football. [It] was always No. 1 with him. And there's not many around like that anymore. Alger never had a fancy offense, but he always had good players. He was smart enough to recognize that and use their talents properly."[1666]

THE SPARTAN SUCCESSION

At the time of his death, Pugh had coached 2 players who were playing in the National Football League: Atlanta Falcons linebacker Buddy Curry and New York Jets running back Kenny Lewis.[1667]

* * *

At the time of Pugh's untimely passing, basketball season was well underway and fans across the nation followed their favorite collegiate and professional teams.

Eventually, on April 2, Georgetown University won the NCAA Division I men's basketball championship, and two months later, the Boston Celtics won the NBA title following their 7-game series with the Los Angeles Lakers. Game 7 was played in the Boston Garden on June 12.

Also, Major League Baseball was approaching the midpoint of the season, and the hottest team in all of baseball was the Detroit Tigers, who finished the first half of the season with a record of 57–24.[63]

As August approached, sports fans could also turn their attention to preseason football.

Since the focus of this narrative is on the Salem Spartans, how was the 1984 team shaping up?[1668]

They opened practice during the second week of August with 47 prospects.[1669]

They will be under the tutelage of Coach White and several able assistants, including newcomer Jerry Scharnus, who coached with White for 5 seasons at Patrick Henry.[1670]

"This is a great place to coach," said Scharnus. "Everyone works together and Dr. [Walter] Hunt [superintendent of Salem schools] is just terrific. I can't believe the difference here and Roanoke City. It's like night and day."[1671]

---

[63] The Tigers had a torrid start with 35 wins in their first 40 games. They led the American League East Division from start to finish and completed the 162 game-regular season with a record of 104–58. After winning the AL pennant, they faced National League champion the San Diego Padres in the World Series. The Tigers won in 5 games (www.baseball-reference.com).

335

Scharnus will coach quarterbacks and receivers, which will give John Hinkle more time to work with the backfield. "I have a lot more time to work with the secondary and it's really paying off," said Hinkle.[1672]

Salem welcomed the return of several other coaches including Steve Oliver, who coaches the defensive line; Billy Miles Jr. works with the offensive line; Danny Wheeling will once again work with the offensive backs; and Larry Bradley will coach at Andrew Lewis Middle School where he has help in Marty Yuhas and Brian Hooker.[1673]

Hinkle said, "I've been at five or six places and I've seen all kinds of programs, and this is by far the best. Coach White is a tremendous person to work for and we get more cooperation and support than anyone could expect. I hope it's the last place I coach, because I don't plan to leave. I think we've all found a home here."[1674]

Said Salem athletic director Dale Foster, "I think we have the best football coaching staff in the state of Virginia, bar none. I guarantee it. You won't find a better staff in the whole state."

The Spartans were expected to better last season's just under 0.500 mark and would open the season at Amherst County, a Group AAA Western District team.[1675]

Developmentally, Coach White reported that the offense was ahead of the defense. "That might be because we have so many skill people back," he said.[1676]

Those included veteran quarterback Cam Young, running back JoJo Harris, and wide receiver Kevin Phipps.[1677]

As for Salem's fellow members of the Roanoke Valley District, which team was deemed the forerunner to this year's crown?

At least one sportswriter gave the nod to William Fleming, which finished third in the district last year behind champion Pulaski County, and runner-up Northside, which both qualified for postseason play.[1678]

A year ago, Fleming's nemesis was Patrick Henry, which defeated Fleming twice. The two Roanoke City rivals were scheduled to face off in this year's opener, while Northside was slated to open against defending Group A state champion Parry McCluer.[1679]

Salem versus Amherst or Spartans versus Lancers

This game matched teams with nicknames that have military/warfare denotations. The Spartans of ancient history were from the Greek city state of Sparta, but what about the Lancers?

The definition of a lancer is a soldier of a cavalry regiment armed with lances, which are long weapons used by horsemen in charges.

When Salem and Amherst met on August 31, 1984, the "foot soldiers" prevailed over the "cavalry."

Final score: Spartans 16, Lancers 7.

The Spartan defense was nothing short of stifling. It limited its opponent to 31 yards on the ground, and it intercepted 4 passes, including 2 by Marvin Morris.[1680]

Salem quarterback Cam Young passed for 184 yards, including a touchdown pass to Kevin Phipps of 26 yards. That score was set up by a 57-yard pass from Young to Pat Keister on a third and 10 play. Keister caught 3 passes in the game for 90 yards.[1681]

Phipps later hauled in an 18-yard pass from Young for score, and Frank Morris ran for 1 from 1 yard out.[1682]

Around the league, defending Roanoke Valley District champion Pulaski County defeated Princeton, West Virginia, 26–10, while Patrick Henry prevailed over Alleghany, 21–7, and Northside battled E. C. Glass to a 6–6 tie.[1683]

Up next for the "infantry," a clash with a tribe of "Indians" whose hunting lands were in Blacksburg.

Game 2 (September 7): Salem 16, Blacksburg 6

The Spartans got off to a great start and led 16–0 at the intermission, mainly because the Indians coughed up 3 fumbles and threw an interception in the first half.[1684]

Kevin Phipps once again emerged to the forefront of the activity. He kicked a 23-yard field goal and surprised his head coach when he returned a punt 84 yards for a touchdown.[1685]

"For a guy who never had more than five yards (at a time) in his life, it must be nice breaking a run like that," said Spartan skipper Willis White, who referred to Phipps as a plodder.[1686]

In other games, Pulaski County kept its out-of-state schedule alive but lost on the road to West Charlotte, NC, 27–14. GW-Danville edged William Fleming, 7–0, and Cave Spring slipped past Heritage, 14–10.[1687]

Up next, Salem took on a team it has never beaten—those Knights based in southwest Roanoke County.

"Can You Just Beat Cave Spring?"

Until Willis White became the Spartan head coach, Salem—since its opening in 1977—had yet to defeat Cave Spring.

There was a time, however, when a Salem-based team had great success against Cave Spring.

As the reader might easily deduce, that period of time came when Andrew Lewis—under head coach Eddie Joyce—dominated Cave Spring.

Joyce coached the Wolverines from 1960 through 1974, or 15 seasons. Over that span of time, Lewis and Cave Spring met in 9 games. Lewis won 7, lost 1, and there was 1 tie.

Here are the results:

- 1960: the teams did not play
- 1961: Cave Spring 19, Andrew Lewis 13
- 1962: Andrew Lewis 7, Cave Spring 0
- 1963: Andrew Lewis 24, Cave Spring 6
- 1964: Andrew Lewis 47, Cave Spring 0
- 1965: Andrew Lewis 25, Cave Spring 0
- 1966, '67, '68, and '69: the teams did not play
- 1970: Andrew Lewis 14, Cave Spring 0.
- 1971: Andrew Lewis 48, Cave Spring 7
- 1972: Andrew Lewis 23, Cave Spring 13
- 1973: the teams tied, 12–12
- 1974: the teams did not play

THE SPARTAN SUCCESSION

- 1975: Mike Stevens succeeded Eddie Joyce, and the 2 teams did not play this season
- 1976: Cave Spring 7, Andrew Lewis 0.

Here are the results for Salem versus Cave Spring:

- Under head Coach Tom Kucer:
    - 1977: Cave Spring 17, Salem 14
    - 1978: Cave Spring 18, Salem 10
- Under head coach Wallace Thompson:
    - 1979: Cave Spring 28, Salem 0
    - 1980: Cave Spring 34, Salem 7
    - 1981: Cave Spring 21, Salem 12
- Under head coach Carl Richards:
    - 1982: Cave Spring 42, Salem 6
- Under head coach Willis White:
    - 1983: Cave Spring 21, Salem 14

But here, in 1984, at least one prominent sportswriter thought this would be the year the Spartans found a way to unsaddle the Knights.

Bob Teitlebaum wrote that the Spartans had big-play capability and their skill players would likely make the difference. Those included quarterback Cam Young, running back JoJo Harris, and wide receiver Kevin Phipps.[1688]

And both head coaches were keenly aware of the one-sidedness of the rivalry and the talk that preceded each game.

"I hear about it every year," said Cave Spring's Charlie Hammes. "I see something in Salem's paper."[1689]

"I've heard people mention it," said White. "I feel you approach each game the same. If you don't, you're in trouble."[1690]

But Hammes knew this year's Salem squad was better than in previous seasons.

"Last year, they didn't get the big play out of their skill people," he said. "This year, they seem to be a little bigger on the line. They have some kids well over 200 pounds."[1691]

Using the catchphrase attributed to boxing referee Mills Lane: "Let's get it on!"

Game 3 (September 14): The Drought Was Over—Salem 35, Cave Spring 7

Whoa! Not only did the Spartans win, but they did so handily.

And wide receiver Kevin Phipps scorched the Cave Spring secondary with 5 catches for 204 yards and 3 touchdowns of 67, 52, and 37 yards.[1692]

How did Phipps have such a monster game?

He exploited single coverage for most of the time, which led White to conclude: "I guess that's the last time he will see single coverage."[1693]

Phipps hauled in those passes from Cam Young, who remarked, "We took what they gave us. If they want to give us one-on-one with Kevin, I'll take it all day."[1694]

"They were playing off of me," said Phipps. "I'd go five yards, turn around, and get the ball. We call those hitches."[1695]

Charlie Hammes explained the chink in his defense's armor.

"We had the halfbacks playing the wide out. It was too much to ask them to do covering Phipps and the others."[1696]

The Knights later put 2 defenders on Phipps, which only served to open the Spartan ground game. JoJo Harris responded with 152 rushing yards.[1697]

Salem's break of the Cave Spring jinx provided a huge stepping stone to bringing back a winning football tradition in Salem.

Up next, Salem took on the preseason pick to win the Roanoke Valley District—William Fleming. The Spartans and Colonels would meet in Roanoke's Victory Stadium.

Game 4 (September 22): Salem 16, William Fleming 9

Kevin Phipps booted 3 field goals, and JoJo Harris rushed for 1 touchdown to lead the Spartans to victory.[1698]

The Spartan defense sacked Colonel quarterback Darrin Galleo 8 times.[1699]

When it was over, it appeared that these 2 teams were moving in opposite directions. Despite the preseason praise, Fleming fell to 0–4, while Salem remained unbeaten after 4 games.[1700]

"It's been a long time since we've had some respect from other people," said Spartan quarterback Cam Young.[1701]

"I wanted to establish our defense," said Coach White. "I knew we could score some points, but could we stop them? That's what worried me. I've been accused of being 'Mr. Conservative.' Defense isn't fun to watch, but it wins football games."[1702]

Around the league, Cave Spring edged E. C. Glass, 7–6, and Patrick Henry shut out Franklin County, 14–0.[1703]

Salem topped the district with a 2–0 league record and an overall mark of 4–0. Patrick Henry followed at 1–0 and 4–0.[1704]

Up next was a trip to Fieldale-Collinsville High, located in Henry County.

Game 5 (September 28): Spartans 38, Cavaliers 0

Salem won easily despite 8 penalties for 80 yards and 3 fumbles lost.[1705]

Running back JoJo Harris set a school record with 205 rushing yards on 15 carries; plus he scored 3 touchdowns on runs of 84, 18, and 3 yards.[1706]

Why such a huge game for Harris?

"I owe it all to the line," he said. "They were opening up holes you could drive an earthmover through."[1707]

Cam Young tossed 2 touchdown passes, 1 of 18 yards to Pat Keister, and the other of 76 yards to Kevin Phipps. Running back Frank Morris ran in for a score from 2 yards out.[1708]

Another highlight of this game involved Salem's Larry Wills, who intercepted a Cavalier pass and returned it 28 yards to the Fieldale-Collinsville 12, which set up a Salem score late in the first half.[1709]

In other games, Fleming notched its first win of the season when it defeated Halifax County, 15–0. Pulaski County shut out Cave Spring, 20–0, and Northside edged Franklin County, 13–12.[1710]

The Prep Poll appeared in the news on October 1. Since Salem was classified as a Group AAA team, the emphasis here is on its competition. The number 1 ranked team was T. C. Williams. GW-Danville occupied the second spot, and Patrick Henry was the topped ranked area team, coming in at number 6.[1711]

Up next for Salem was a home game against Bassett.

Game 6 (October 5): Spartans 38, Bengals 0

Salem recorded its second straight shutout and upped its unbeaten record to 6–0.

The Spartan defense limited the Bengals (2–4) to just 3 first downs and 68 yards on the ground. James O'Quinn had an interception in the game.[1712]

Salem running back JoJo Harris carried the ball 20 times for 171 yards and 3 touchdowns, and quarterback Cam Young tossed 2 touchdown passes, 1 each to Pat Keister (20 yards) and to Kevin Phipps (35).[1713]

As for Harris running roughshod again, "I thought it would be tougher (rushing this week), but the line did a terrific job as usual."[1714]

Salem takes a week off before closing the season with 4 straight Roanoke Valley District games—Franklin County, Patrick Henry, Pulaski County, and Northside.[1715]

"They'll be tough," said Coach White, "but this is just where we wanted to be."[1716]

In other games, Patrick Henry cruised past Cave Spring, 31–6; Pulaski County flattened Franklin County, 34–0; and William Fleming beat Northside, 25–6.[1717]

Roanoke Valley District games played on October 12 during Salem's bye week: Patrick Henry defeated Northside, 28–8; Pulaski County edged William Fleming in a defensive battle, 6–0; and Franklin County crushed Cave Spring, 27–0.[1718]

In the standings, Patrick Henry and Pulaski County were both 3–0 in the conference, and Salem was next at 2–0. Overall, Patrick Henry and Salem were both 6–0, and Pulaski County was 4–2. The other district teams were simply not in contention for the title.[1719]

This week's games had Franklin County at Salem, William Fleming versus Patrick Henry in Victory Stadium, and Pulaski County at Alleghany.

When the prep poll hit the news, Patrick Henry (commonly referred to in the Roanoke Valley as PH) had moved up to the third spot behind frontrunner T. C. Williams. At number 2, Robinson replaced GW-Danville, which fell to the ninth spot.[1720]

Of greater interest in this narrative, the next poll appeared nine days later. T. C. Williams, Robinson and Patrick Henry still occupied the top three spots, but guess which team now occupied the sixth spot? The answer was Salem, and it is tempting to insert an exclamation point at the end of the answer considering Salem's season records since opening in 1977.[1721]

The Spartans had not had a winning season since their debut in 1977 when they went 6–3–1.

But here in 1984, Coach White was working his second season, and the Spartans were not only unbeaten but had been tabbed the number 6 team in Group AAA. And in the section marked "Others receiving votes," Pulaski County was included in this mentioning.[1722]

As Salem (3–0 in the conference and 6–0 overall) prepared to face Franklin County (1–3, 3–4), at least one prominent sportswriter opined that the Spartans had more offensive threats than any other district team.[1723]

Running back JoJo Harris had rushed for 376 yards the last 2 weeks, and Kevin Phipps had caught 7 of Cam Young's 9 touchdown passes.[1724]

Note this too: the defense had been stellar and would soon get the acclaim it deserved.

Game 7 (October 19): Salem 19, Franklin County 3

Speaking of those offensive threats, Spartan quarterback Cam Young threw two touchdown passes to Kevin Phipps, and JoJo Harris continued his success on the ground when he tallied 110 yards on 18 carries. Salem's other points came courtesy of Pat Keister, who returned a fumble 14 yards for a touchdown.[1725]

The Salem defense limited the Eagles to crossing midfield just twice in the game. Franklin County scored its only points when Mark Poindexter booted a 32-yard field goal in the second quarter.[1726]

Phipps improved his season totals to 18 receptions for 526 yards (29.2 yards per catch) and 9 TDs, while the southpaw Young had now thrown 11 touchdown passes and was within range of a 1,000-yard season.[1727]

Now, Coach White began talking about what others had been talking about for weeks: PH.

"That's all I've heard around town," said White. "Can't wait till we play PH."[1728]

PH, White's previous team, was next on Salem's hit list which still had Pulaski County and Northside to play.

"You only get them one at a time," said White. "We got seven days rest in between. You have to keep a light heart. I used to get so tight, I couldn't sleep. Now I sleep half the time."[1729]

Here's a look at the standings: In the conference, Salem and Pulaski County were both 3–0, while Patrick Henry's only blemish was the tie to William Fleming, which put the Patriots at 3–0–1. Overall, Salem topped the list at 7–0, PH was 6–0–1, and Pulaski County was 5–2.[1730]

Two big games were slated for this week: PH at Salem, and Pulaski County at Northside.

Just before the Spartans and Patriots clashed at Municipal Field, one of Salem's key players was featured in the news—an iron man of the gridiron by the name of Pat Keister.[1731]

Keister's constant presence on the field made him the exception to the popular notion that players at Group AAA schools play either offense or defense since teams have more players from which to choose.[1732]

The question was not "When does Keister play?" but rather "When does he not?"

Answer: rarely.

He is a defensive end and tight end and is on the kickoff, kickoff return, punt, punt return, extra point, and field-goal special teams. Guess he takes a breather during timeouts and the intermission only.[1733]

After 7 games this season, Keister had caught 2 touchdown passes and returned a fumble for a TD.[1734]

Does he ever get tired?

"Oh yeah," he said, "but I suck it up. I got used to it last year… What I call getting tired is running a play, coming back to the huddle and being out of breath… My feeling is you have to get in shape at the beginning of the season [and] you'll stay in shape. Then, during the season, you can work on techniques and get yourself mentally prepared (for the games)."[1735]

That Salem is 7–0 and ranked third in the state came as no surprise to the 6-foot 1/2-inch, 185-pounder.[1736]

"We've worked hard. We haven't won by luck. We've won outright."[1737]

Against PH, Keister and his teammates have quite an assignment in Patriot running back Tim Dudley.[1738]

Last year, in the loss to Salem, Dudley rushed for 143 yards.[1739]

"What I say is that we have to contain him," said Keister. "Close him down from the outside… He's the best running back in the district. But I think he's going up against the best defense in the district… Where the battle comes down to is the line. It always does. If he hasn't got holes to run through, he won't go anywhere."[1740]

Game 8 (October 26): Salem 17, PH 7

Spartans running back JoJo Harris rushed for 104 yards and 1 touchdown, quarterback Cam Young ran for another, and Kevin

Phipps—who was shut down as a receiver—booted a 21-yard field goal to help lead Salem to victory.[1741]

For PH, Tim Dudley tallied a game best 188 rushing yards, but he and his teammates committed 6 turnovers—4 fumbles lost and 2 interceptions thrown by Patriot signal caller Ben Comer.[1742]

In fairness to Comer, both picks came during PH's last 2 possessions and were thrown in desperation.[1743]

Pulaski County kept pace when it defeated Northside, 12–7, to set up next week's showdown with the Spartans in Dublin.[1744]

Salem's victory pushed the Spartans to the number 2 spot in the Group AAA poll behind T. C. Williams and PH fell to the eighth spot. Pulaski County remained unranked.[1745]

With the district title now hanging in the balance, the matchup between the defending champion Cougars and the surprising Spartans garnered understandable attention.

As one prominent sportswriter saw it, the key matchup featured the Spartan defense against the Cougar offense led by quarterback Shane St. Clair.[1746]

Salem safety James O'Quinn was the focus in this story.

A year ago, when Coach White debuted as the Salem head coach, one of the first changes he made in the defense was moving O'Quinn from cornerback to safety.[1747]

White thought O'Quinn was too slow to play at the corner.[1748]

"I told James I could run faster than him," said White.[1749]

Apparently, White had no problem with O'Quinn's ability to play at safety.

He likened his hits to those inflicted by linebackers.[1750]

And O'Quinn thrived on the contact.

"I want people to think about where I am [on the field]," said O'Quinn. "I want people to worry about getting hit before they catch the ball."[1751]

Judging by the season O'Quinn was having, the switch to safety certainly suited him and the team just fine.

Going into the clash with the Cougars, O'Quinn shared the team lead of most interceptions with Marvin Morris, both of whom had 7 picks to their credit, which equaled 14 of the team's 20 thefts this season.[1752]

Further, the Spartan defense had not given up more than 1 touchdown in any 1 game and had recorded 14 fumbles and forced a total of 34 turnovers.[1753]

But Pulaski's defense had played awfully well, too.

Unfortunately for the Cougars, their offense had been much less consistent.

Further, considering their tradition of having good kickers, it was indeed ironic that this year's team has had to run or pass for extra points.[1754]

In analyzing the matchup, another consideration was Pulaski County's home field advantage.[1755]

Playing in Pulaski represented unique challenges to opposing teams.[1756]

Every time the home team scored, a cougar growled from the scoreboard; plus the visitors had to walk more than 100 yards from their dressing room to the field.[1757]

Coach White had experienced the disadvantages.

"The hardest part of playing at Pulaski is getting to the field from the dressing room," he said. "They haven't had good crowd control in the past, and that's made it rough on the kids. I'm going to see if I can get some of our fans to escort us in."[1758]

Pulaski head Coach Joel Hicks indicated that he would have policemen to make sure the Spartans got to the stadium and said, "They'll be no problem. I'm not sure the people hollering at them wouldn't fire a team up. I'd rather our fans not make them mad."[1759]

Another key matchup in this one featured Salem wideout Kevin Phipps versus Pulaski junior cornerback Rodney Landreth, who had 6 picks this season.[1760]

Game 9 (November 2): Pulaski 27, Salem 14

The Cougars took a 14–0 lead in the first 10:39 of play and put the Spartans in a huge hole from which they could not climb.[1761]

Led by option-running quarterback Shane St. Clair, the Cougars scored their first touchdown in just 6 plays. Running back Kenny Hampton capped the drive with an 11-yard run, the first of his 2 rushing touchdowns in the game.[1762]

St. Clair also ran for a score in the third quarter, which pushed Pulaski to a huge 27–6 lead.[1763]

And Rodney Landreth?

He had a pick 6 of 46 yards late in the third quarter.[1764]

Salem's points came when JoJo Harris rushed from 1 yard out in the third and quarterback Cam Young ran from two yards out in the fourth and then converted a 2-point play with a pass to Kevin Phipps.[1765]

The Cougars' defense held Harris to just 33 rushing yards, and Landreth limited Phipps to just 2 catches among Young's 12 completions out of 30 attempts.[1766]

St. Clair had a game best 112 yards on the ground and ran often.[1767]

"Salem was ready to take away our wide stuff," said Coach Hicks. "We couldn't get outside, so we tried to run Shane more."[1768]

Yes, to the tune of 22 times to be exact.[1769]

Of his team's combined efforts, Hicks said, "We really hit. I thought our defense was stinging. Our offensive line was coming out and knocking them [Salem's defense] off the ball the first series. We were just very up for the game."[1770]

The Cougars also forced 2 fumbles on special teams, and Coach White gave his adversary all the credit.

"They kicked our tails," he said. "We just didn't play very well. We played really flat in the first quarter. It really surprised me. I didn't think that would happen."[1771]

For Salem (4–1 conference and 8–1 overall) to make the playoffs, it had to win next week against Northside (2–3, 4–3–2) and depend on a couple of teams in the Commonwealth District to lose.[1772]

For Pulaski, the win over Salem assured it of no worse than a tie for the district. If Pulaski defeated PH next week, the Cougars would not only win the district outright but also host the first 2 rounds of the playoffs.[1773]

A look at the playoffs focuses on the Northwestern Region at this juncture in the narrative because Salem, Pulaski County, and Patrick Henry were all members of this region and vying for playoff berths.

The region included three districts: the Roanoke Valley, the Commonwealth, and the Western.

The frontrunners of those were Pulaski, Stonewall Jackson-Manassas, and Halifax County, respectively.

If all 3 won this week, the Commonwealth District runner-up Potomac would get the wild card spot over Salem and Patrick Henry.

Game 10 (November 9): Salem 27, Northside 14

It could be argued that Salem's solid defensive effort, which included a recovery of a Northside fumble by James O'Quinn that set up Salem's last touchdown, came one week too late.[1774]

"If the defense had played like this against Pulaski, we would have won," said Spartans skipper Willis White. "Last week, I felt we were patty cake."[1775]

It could also be argued that Pulaski's game plan (for example, St. Clair came out throwing long on the first play) and its hard-hitting in all facets of the game were pivotal in deciding the results.

Back to the game against Northside, Salem's first points were provided by Kevin Phipps when he kicked a 23-yard field goal. Afterward, fullback Johnny Meadows ran for 2 touchdowns, both from 1 yard out, and JoJo Harris crossed the goal line from 3 yards out.[1776]

Cam Young completed 50 percent of his passes: 7 of 14 for 44 yards and no interceptions. Phipps caught 4 of those, Harris hauled in 2, and Pat Keister, 1.[1777]

Despite the win over the Vikings, the Spartans' playoff hopes were dashed when other scores came in. Pulaski edged Patrick Henry, which played without star tailback Tim Dudley, 7–0; Potomac beat Fauquier; and Stonewall Jackson defeated James Wood.[1778]

Salem officially concluded the season with a conference record of 5–1 and an overall mark of 9–1.

More on Salem's banner year later. Now let's look at the Group AAA state playoffs.

The 16-team bracket consisted of 4 teams from each of the 4 regions. In the top half of the bracket, the first 4 teams were from the Central Region with these matchups: Hermitage versus Dinwiddie and Marshall-Walker versus Highland Springs.[1779]

Next are the 4 teams from the Northwest Region: Potomac versus Pulaski County and Halifax County versus Stonewall Jackson.[1780]

This is the bottom half: (a) from the Northern Region: Fort Hunt versus T. C. Williams and J. E. B. Stuart versus South Lakes, (b) from the Eastern Region: Booker T. Washington versus Great Bridge and Hampton versus Kellam.[1781]

The first-round winners included Pulaski, which defeated Potomac, 21–7, and Halifax, which slipped past Stonewall Jackson, 14–12.[1782]

Pulaski and Halifax met the following week in the quarterfinals, and the Cougars handed the Comets a 20–7 loss to advance to 1 of the 2 state semifinal games.[1783]

The 2 semifinal matchups included Pulaski County (number 7 seed) against T. C. Williams (number 1), and Hampton (number 6) versus Hermitage.[1784]

T. C. Williams was not only Group AAA's number 1 ranked team, but it was also ranked number 4 nationally. The Titans were led by tailback Brent Lowery, who rushed 21 times for 169 yards and 2 touchdowns in the team's win over South Lakes, 28–7, in the Northern Region championship.[1785]

Prior to the state semifinals, the Roanoke Valley District Team selections were announced.

Pulaski's Joel Hicks was named district coach of the year. Players of the year included Patrick Henry's Tim Dudley (offensive back), Cave Spring's Robert Lewis (offensive line), Pulaski's Jack Turner (defensive end), and William Fleming's Robert Majors (defensive back).[1786]

In addition, the all-state Group AAA teams were announced, and 2 Roanoke Valley District players earned first-team selections.[1787]

Salem's Kevin Phipps was chosen as a place-kicker and Majors as defensive back.[1788]

The second team included Salem quarterback Cam Young, Patrick Henry running back Tim Dudley, and Northside place-kicker George Bruce.[1789]

Here are the results from the 2 state semifinal games: T. C. Williams 13, Pulaski County 0, and Hampton 21, Hermitage 7.[1790]

Pulaski County finished the season with an overall record of 10–3. T. C. Williams would next face Hampton for the Group AAA state title.[1791]

As a parting tribute to Pulaski County, let's consider what the Cougars had accomplished in recent years.

They had simply been the best of the Roanoke Valley District. They had won 22 straight district games and 4 titles in succession. When the team showed up at W. T. Woodson High School in Fairfax to play T. C. Williams, many more of its fans made the 265-mile trip than did those of T. C. Williams, which had a much-shorter trek from Alexandria to Fairfax.[1792]

And in Joel Hicks, the Cougars had 1 of the premier head coaches in all of Virginia.

As Bill Brill of the *Roanoke Times & World-News* astutely wrote, coaches have made all the difference in bringing success to programs. In his column of December 2, 1984, his examples were proof positive. Those included Hicks, Alger Pugh at GW-Danville, Johnny Palmer at Hampton and later at E. C. Glass, Merrill Gainer in West Virginia and later at Patrick Henry-Roanoke, Eddie Joyce at Andrew Lewis, and now Willis White at Salem.[1793]

Brill opined that if T. C. Williams was the number 4 ranked team in the country, then Pulaski County was number 5.[1794]

And Hicks said, "If they're the fourth-best team in the country, then I'm Abraham Lincoln."[1795]

T. C. Williams and Hampton faced off for the Group AAA state title at Scott Stadium at the University of Virginia on December

8. The Titans' defense recorded its ninth shutout of the season and defeated the Crabbers, 10–0, for their second state title.[1796]

In Group AA, John Handley defeated Blacksburg, 28–16, and in Group A, Covington claimed the title with a 13–6 win over Central-Lunenburg.[1797]

When the All-Timesland Football Team was announced, the first team offense included 2 Spartans—quarterback Cam Young and end Kevin Phipps.[1798]

The Offensive Player of the Year went to running back Tim Dudley of Patrick Henry.[1799]

The Spartans did not have any selections to the first team defense, but end Pat Keister was named to the second team.[1800]

Robert Majors, a defensive back for William Fleming, was named Defensive Player of the Year, and the Coach of the Year honor went to John Woodrell, who coached Covington to a state crown.[1801]

Young certainly had quite a season. The senior and left-handed signal caller for the Spartans soon signed a grant-in-aid with NC State University. The only other school he visited was Virginia Tech.[1802]

"There really wasn't one advantage to one school over the other," said Young. "I think State's offense will suit me better. I'm really more of a thrower than a runner."[64, 1803]

During this '84 season, Young completed 69 of 164 passes for 1,239 yards and 11 touchdowns.[1804]

---

[64] Thanks to an article written by Randy King, a special to the *Roanoke Times*, this author learned that Young evidently had a change in plans following his graduation from Salem in 1985. Instead of playing at NC State, Young played at Virginia Tech as a backup quarterback and, in 1989, led the team to one of the biggest wins in school history—a 12–10 upset of ninth-ranked West Virginia. King's article, published on August 21, 2018, reported on Young's passion for golf. King wrote that since graduating from Virginia Tech, golf had become Young's game, and he had ascended to the top level of the state's VSGA (Virginia State Golf Association) Senior Division players. Young and his wife, Lee Ann, reside in Richmond, Virginia. The couple has two children. Son Trent is a graduate of Virginia Tech and daughter Merriet was playing soccer at Randolph-Macon. Young is employed as a regional manager for the pharmaceutical company Allergan.

And teammate William Kimbrough was named the winner of the eighth annual *Salem Times-Register* Spartan Bell award, which was presented each year to a Salem High football player. Kimbrough was a defensive end.[1805]

The award was selected by the Salem High School coaches in conjunction with the *Times-Register* and went to the player deemed to be the hardest hitter on the squad for that particular season. Kimbrough became known for his vicious hits on scrimmage plays and on specialty teams.[1806]

The previous winners were the following:

- 1977: Dale Weeks
- 1978: Dale Weeks
- 1979: Dale Weeks
- 1980: Carlton Ertel
- 1981: Larry Love
- 1982: Robert Houchin
- 1983: Tim Sutphin[1807]

* * *

As a team, the 1984 Spartans had the best season in the school's history. Their record of 9–1 easily bested last year's mark of 4–5–1, and of the nine victories, the one over Cave Spring was Salem's first ever. It signified a huge step forward in bringing back winning to the Salem community.

In fact, before the season began, Charlie Hammersley (Andrew Lewis High class of 1969) recalled that the prevailing sentiment directed toward Coach White was "Just beat Cave Spring!"[1808]

After White's team had done so, and after it had just completed the best season the program had ever had, Hammersley recalled that White's response to the Salem faithful was "Yeah, all you want me to do is beat Cave Spring! Y'all don't want me to rebuild. You want me to reload!"[1809]

Of White, Hammersley said, "He knew the Salem community would support a winner."[1810]

And winning—along with a brand-new football stadium—was clearly in Salem's forecast.

What the players and their fans did not know at the time was that the Spartans had just played their last season at Municipal Field, the dirt/grass combination that doubled as a baseball field to the city's minor league team. It had been the home to the Spartans since Salem High opened in 1977 and to Andrew Lewis High all those many years before. It was the field that former Lewis players dubbed the Snake Pit, where the Wolverines won most of the time and where many opponents dreaded to play. The Lewis teams had learned how to take full advantage of the unique geometrics and nuances of the field.

One person who was clued in to the city's plans to build a new stadium was Coach White.

In a recent telephone conversation with the former coach, he recalled what happened at the end of the 1984 season.

"I remember that for our last game the stadium [Municipal Field] was packed. There were people everywhere. [Salem City Mayor] Jim Taliaferro came up to me and said, 'The time is right for the [new] stadium.' He told me to draw up changes to the weight room and then said, 'In 1985, we *will* play in our new stadium.'"[1811]

And Taliaferro conveyed the same message to Brian Hoffman, whose conversation with the mayor on the topic of a new stadium appeared in the November 8, 1984, edition of the *Salem Times-Register*.

Hoffman wrote:

> The time is right for a new football stadium in Salem and it looks like we're going to get one…
>
> There's a need, there's an interest, and there's an influential person behind it in the person of Salem mayor Jim Taliaferro. The proposed construction will be put to a vote…at the city council meeting and the mayor thinks it would be a good idea: to say the least.

"I'm ready to be the bell cow, babe, and I don't mind one bit," said Taliaferro. "I want the plans ready in 60 days, construction to begin in late March, and a penalty clause if they don't have it ready by the first game in August; and it CAN be done."

When the stadium is built it will be the embodiment of the strong civic pride so long associated with Salem, Virginia.[1812]

It will also come at a cost—in more ways than one.

Chapter 13

1985

Part I: A Stadium of Their Own

Exactly when Jim Taliaferro first considered the building of this new stadium may not be precisely known; however, as far back as the early months of 1978, he was at least considering a modification to Municipal Field based on his concerns regarding the unsafe playing conditions for both football and baseball.

He proposed that the most economical solution was renovation of the field and turning it into a football stadium.

But at least one of his fellow Salemites disagreed.

In a letter to the editor that appeared in the February 26, 1978, edition of the *Roanoke Times & World-News*, the writer proposed that the best solution was to improve the football stadium at Glenvar and make it the permanent home of the Salem High School football team. Further, the writer asserted that Municipal Field should be used only for baseball and softball games.[1813]

Both a football and baseball supporter, the writer alluded to Salem's minor league baseball team, the Salem Pirates, which missed an opportunity to play at home during the postseason because of a football game.[1814]

What the writer did not know—and could not have known—was that four years later, Glenvar would reopen as a high school and the existing football stadium there would naturally belong to Glenvar.

And if the writer felt that baseball was taking a back seat to football, in time this matter would be rectified rather nicely.

***

Months later, Dr. Richard Fisher initiated a move to create a new football field for Salem High School. He wrote a letter to the Salem mayor, Jim Taliaferro, about the urgent need for a new field.

"There is a great need for a new football field to be used by the high school and sandlot programs…[ours] is the worst field in the state. You are well-aware that every community in which our team has played, including Shawsville, has had excellent playing surfaces. I do feel that many of the injuries that occurred at Municipal Field, particularly in the hard clay infield, would not happen in an appropriate, well kept, football field."[1815]

He suggested that the grounds of the Salem-Roanoke County Civic Center would be excellent for a permanent football facility.[1816]

"Plans could be developed for such a field at the Civic Center area as initiated before, and with local architects and help, could be built at a fraction of the cost that had been mentioned previously."[1817]

Brian Hoffman weighed in with his personal thoughts: "Memories and traditions aside, you have to admit that Salem has the worst field in the district. Pulaski has the best… It's a thing of sheer beauty. When the Spartans played there last season, I heard more than one Salemite comment, 'This is what we need in Salem.'"[1818]

"We could have a great facility like that without the cold Pulaski winds… Every time an athlete sprains an ankle on the edge of the Municipal Field infield, you hear the talk…"[1819]

***

An event that occurred in 1983 may have been a harbinger of much bigger things to come.

In a surprise move, the Roanoke County Board of Supervisors voted to give its share of the Salem-Roanoke County Civic Center to the city of Salem and to give the city $290,000.00.[1820]

Vinton supervisor Harry Nickens negotiated the agreement and indicated that the deal could save the county as much as $3 million over the next decade in operating costs for what had become a "financially strapped center."[1821]

Taliaferro said, "It remains to be voted on, but there's no reason to think it would not be approved."[1822]

Salem now faced tough decisions on operating the center because its losses had multiplied 18 times in recent years, and Salem officials were surprised by the county's offer.[1823]

"We had no idea they would go through with it because the last we heard they would not," said Taliaferro.[1824]

He also indicated that Salem would have rather kept the county as a partner, but the agreement was in the best interest of both governments because of the animosity that the situation had created.[1825]

"The center had become a piece of trivia," said Taliaferro. "It really wasn't worth all the harassment it had caused [between the two governments]."[1826]

He and Nickens agreed that the building would have a better chance of financial success if it were directed by one government.[1827]

The city's losses had grown every year, and Taliaferro said the county was wise to get out.[1828]

Nickens said that Salem was committed to operating the center for the next two years, but he would not be surprised if the building was eventually converted to a community center.[1829]

Taliaferro emphasized that no decision had been made about the future use of the building and said, "We're at base zero. And searching."[1830]

Less than a month later, Taliaferro appointed a seven-man committee to study the Salem Civic Center and make a recommendation for its future use.[1831]

The committee members included Mac Green, Glenn Thornhill Jr., Sherrill Smith, Ray Robrecht, Jack Kirby, Bob Rotanz, and Steve Mullins.[1832]

Taliaferro said the committee would examine such questions as whether the facility should continue as a civic center or become a community center or a combination of the two; whether it should be closed; and whether it should be run by a commission as it was when owned jointly by Salem and Roanoke County or operated as a Salem department as it was now.[1833]

The committee's recommendation should be ready by March 1, 1984.[1834]

Well before that date, the committee met on January 19 and decided that the facility should be retained. Further, the facility should operate as a combination community/civic center and run by a director as a city department with a joint advisory commission.[1835]

Green suggested that the committee take recommendations one step at a time and make a "wish list" to present to council on March 1.[1836]

Mullins suggested that the center incorporate a community facility for public sports activities. "Kids who want to participate in group sports have nowhere to go," he said. "I'd love to see us get something. Now we've got the chance."[1837]

The Report

The seven-member committee—comprised of five businessmen, an attorney, and a councilman—presented its report to the mayor on February 27, 1984. The committee recommended that the facility be retained, and if "economically practical," it be operated as a community/civic center. It also recommended that the facility be run as a department of the city, with the administrator reporting directly to Salem City manager William Paxton; that an assistant to the general manager be hired; that promotional efforts be upgraded; and that the center operate its own catering and food services.[1838]

These recommendations were based partly on comments made at a public hearing last October, where Salem residents suggested the center be kept open, and on recommendations made in January by James F. Oshust, managing director of the Greensboro, North Carolina, Coliseum. Oshust had suggested to committee members that areas of the center be expanded to include a facility for community activities, the "element of the city that is growing," he said earlier.[1839]

The committee endorsed Oshust's suggestion in its report and said that the combined use of the facility would embrace its present function by catering to the recreational and entertainment needs of the community.[1840]

Much of the report listed matters to be considered and listed alternatives that the city could look into. For example, the committee offered the "deletion of ice making" as an alternative operation. That would eliminate some 30 pro hockey ice dates and about 80–90 ice recreation days, providing more opportunity to rent out the arena, according to the committee's report.[1841]

Up to that date, using the ice brought in revenue of $87,000 but cost the civic enter about $77,000, according to the budget attachment included with the report.[1842]

The committee also urged the city to consider changing interests in sports and recreation and said additional development on the civic center site is something to look at in the future.[1843]

The report suggested future development of more ball fields, a swimming area, football stadium, track, and open playing fields as options that should not be dismissed.[1844]

And the mayor's response to the committee and its report?

"[They] did the best job they could with all they had to work with," said Taliaferro. "We wanted citizen input, and we got it."[1845]

His next step would be to study the report and meet with council members and the city administration staff to make final evaluations.[1846]

Up next in the batting order, so to speak, stood the Salem Planning Commission, which recommended approval for the rezoning of the Salem Civic Center property.[1847]

The city requested that the property be changed from residential classification to business, a change that city manager William Paxton said would put the 73.54 acres into the proper zoning classification.[1848]

In effect, the city-owned property would then conform to the city's zoning ordinance.[1849]

Some residents of the area expressed their concern that the rezoning would allow other businesses to be built on city property.

Paxton assured the residents that, at that time, the city had no plans to sell any of the property but may consider building a football stadium in the future.[1850]

The commission's recommendation would go before the city council at its March 26 meeting.[1851]

* * *

Remember the "Salem born and Salem bred" concept, which explains the essence of the deep and long-standing civic pride of Salem, as reported in previous chapters of this book?

And how that pride eventually set in motion and ultimately brought to fruition an independent school system after years of operating under the auspices of Roanoke County?

Well, here in 1984, Salem's civic pride was on full display.

People were talking—and some were writing—about it.

Brian O'Neill, a columnist with the *Roanoke Times & World-News*, had been following closely along with the events that were unfolding in Salem, and he was mindful enough of local history to recognize that Salem was once again on the rise.

Consider these excerpts taken from O'Neill's column, which were published on March 21.

First, he contrasts his hometown with that of Salem.

> I was brought up in what everybody says is a square-mile town. Nobody I know ever bothered to check. The population of Carle Place is about 7,000, I think, and its slammed up among Long Island (New York) villages of similar character, with nothing separating them but little green "welcome" signs. As with Salem and Roanoke, it's sometimes hard for outsiders to tell when they've moved from one place to another. But…just suggest merger with a neighboring village like the elitist Garden City. Our volunteer fire department, Brownie troops and The Wobbly Duck's

regulars would be setting up machine gun nests and barbed wire at the borders.

Salem's got the same brash confidence. Its people will set up a school system, take over a civic center, irritate an itinerant hockey team—and then go over to Brooks-Byrd Pharmacy for an orangeade.

The city's major, Jim Taliaferro, once said, "Salem is a way of life." At least I hear that's what he said. I've been trying to interview the guy for about six months, but he doesn't return my phone calls. Maybe it has something to do with the word that precedes "Times & World-News" on this newspaper's masthead. It's where I live, too. All I wanted to do was ask him, "Why is Salem like it is? The same kind of question they probably ask in advanced philosophy classes at Roanoke College… [Consider] the irony of the dove, the bird of peace, on the city's seal. How does that jibe with the Salem sucker punch, which developed into a fine art in the mid-1960s…[Back] in the days when Salem's Andrew Lewis was winning state football championships, and enemy Patrick Henry High band members were chanting, "You can take Salem out of the country, but you can't take the country out of Salem."

It's been said that the arguments between Salem and Roanoke are Old South-New South. Salem's resistant to change… Despite the changes, though, Roanoke Councilman Bob Garland said his opinion of Salem hasn't changed since he was a kid. "Salem is still separate and distinct and wants to remain that way. They want to enjoy the city of Roanoke on their own terms. I don't blame them for that. It's a nice pleasant small town on the other side of Lakeside [Amusement Park]. I don't say that in any facetious or disrespectful way."[1852]

O'Neill's column appeared under this headline: "Salem: Community pride is strong as ever, and that makes sense."[1853]

Author's take: O'Neill was correct in his assessment that the people in Salem had the courage to stand up and fight for independence and that they were once again asserting those traits.

But Salemites, irrespective of O'Neill's intent, would surely have taken exception to his choice of these words: "The Salem sucker punch, which developed into a fine art in the mid-1960s" for those cast Salem in the role of villain.

And yet it was during that decade that feelings of mistrust of the newspaper developed. Former Andrew Lewis players and coaches expressed as much during interviews this author conducted in preparation for the previous book. Generally, they felt that the Roanoke newspaper was biased against Salem and Andrew Lewis High School.

Certainly, Jim Taliaferro had read his share of articles from that news agency and likely had drawn his own conclusions. He is no longer alive to share those with us, and truly we can only speculate as to why he would not have returned O'Neill's calls.

"Show Me the Money"

If Salem's government officials were seriously contemplating the construction of a new football stadium, where was the money to finance the project?

In the summer of '84, a news article provided some promising financial figures.

Financial Director Frank Turk reported that Salem had a surplus of more than $1.4 million from the 1983–94 fiscal year.[1854]

This amount was larger than usual and attributed to the growth in the economy. Of course, officials would contemplate how to use the surplus and the city manager William J. Paxton Jr. said that the proposals included the building of a swimming pool and a football stadium.[1855]

Several months later, the city council granted Paxton authorization to seek proposals on the construction of a new football stadium and appointed a committee to study such proposals. The proposed site of the stadium is on the grounds of the Salem Civic Center.[1856]

"I think now is the time to go out and seek proposals," said Paxton. "Ten years ago we employed an architectural engineering firm to draw up plans for a new stadium. Then, the project was put on the back burner until more important things could be completed. Now, all of those things have been accomplished… The present field is not satisfactory, and it is not economical."[1857]

Paxton's comments suggest, then, that as far back as 1975, the power brokers in Salem were contemplating the building of a new football stadium.[1858]

And Taliaferro raised questions concerning the funding for the project.

"The logical way of constructing something of this issue is to go bond," said Paxton. "If we keep the bond low and the term short, we can get a low interest rate."[1859]

And for a long time, Taliaferro had been keen to some of the problems at Municipal Field, where Andrew Lewis and Salem's football teams played their home games, sometimes around the city's minor league baseball team's schedule.[1860]

"With the football and baseball overlapping so much, it's hard to make the switch," said Taliaferro. "Next year the home football season starts in August, and in past years the baseball team couldn't have playoffs here if they made it."[1861]

"Plus, you have other problems, like the chain-link backstop. We need to have that chicken wire and, if you could, roll that up for the football season. You can't take up that fence every year, so it's hard to see."[1862]

Taliaferro pinpointed two criteria: "Can we pay for it?" and "Do we need it?"[1863]

His answer was yes to both questions.[1864]

"What have we ever done for [Salem's] football team? We put our money into new stadiums at Cave Spring and Northside and Glenvar, and we didn't even have our own. We were the only school in the valley that didn't have its own stadium... We've never done anything for football, and it's time to do something... There's no doubt we need it, and I won't support anything unless it's first class, and that includes a tarp. They have a tarp at Pulaski. With as many games as would be played there, it will pay for itself."[1865]

As to any opposition to the stadium, Taliaferro said, "You have a handful of people who are going to be against everything. There're also a few people who resent success, and Salem is a success. If they don't want Salem football to succeed, they're in for a long ride, because it will succeed. It's as simple as that."[1866]

And Dale Foster opined with this: "Anyone who went to the ballgame at Pulaski County knows how much it means to the success of the program to have a nice place to play. You need a place where you can see the game."[1867]

Late in 1984, both Brian Hoffman and Robert Downey posed this question to eight random Salemites: "Should Salem build a new stadium?"[1868]

Seven—including former Spartan standout Curtis Taliaferro—answered in the affirmative, but one said no.[1869]

"I like the tradition of Lewis," said the naysayer. "I sort of like the dirt, and the opponents don't."[1870]

This person was also a former Spartan standout and a teammate of Taliaferro's.[1871]

His name was Rodney Varney, who naturally echoed the sentiments of many former Lewis players who came to understand the advantages of playing in "the snake pit."[1872]

But those who had not been players recognized that Salem deserved a new stadium, that parking had been inadequate, and that an upgrade was long overdue.[1873]

"Break on Through…"

Four companies submitted bids to build the new football stadium in Salem, and the city council awarded the contract to the lowest bidder.[1874]

And the winner was Breakell Inc., a general contracting firm of Roanoke, which was awarded the $2.2 million contract.[1875]

The three other bids were submitted by Avis Construction Co., Creative Construction and Development Corp., and Thor Inc.[1876]

Breakell will build it, but who will design it?

Answer: Kinsey, Shane and Associates. The stadium will be located on a 23-acre site at the Salem Civic Center. It will seat 8,000 people and provide parking for 1,300 cars.[1877]

What was the estimated time of completion for the new stadium?

Less than six months.

The contract was awarded on March 15, and the completion date was set for Aug. 30—the day before Salem High's first home football game.[1878]

"It is critical we get as much work done before the rains start," said company Vice President Stanley G. Breakell. "It's a pretty tough deadline, but it is achievable."[1879]

* * *

While many people have warned against the dangers of making assumption, it's a sure bet that the people of Salem would have been delighted at the prospect of the football team having its own stadium. Recall in previous narrative how important football had been in Salem for a long time. Recall, too, the independent spirit that existed among Salemites and the strong and long-standing civic pride that the town—and later the city—exhibited throughout the years.

But as has also been reported, the people in Roanoke resented Salem at times.

And in 1985, two years after Salem began its own school system, one disgruntled Roanoke County citizen voiced his dissatisfaction in a letter to the editor. It was published after some recent news about annexation, and its entire contents follow:[1880]

> With the help of a sympathetic judge, and a Board of Supervisors willing to go along, Salem has down through the years taken the county for a ride. Salem was granted land by annexation that it will not need for the next 50 years, and then overnight, to the surprise of everyone, became a city. That left the county high and dry.
>
> Then Salem voted for a civic center because Roanoke was thinking of building one. The citizens of Roanoke County did not need nor did they want this building, but the board was duped into underwriting half the cost. Of course, it had to be built in Salem, as were the new courthouse and jail. Salem would have it no other way.
>
> So when the civic center proved to be a white elephant, Salem and the Board of Supervisors refused an offer of $1 million for it. To top this, the board gave our part of the center to Salem and $250,000 of taxpayers' money to take it. No wonder my real-estate taxes were raised to such an outlandish level this year.
>
> Perhaps Vinton should become a city and annex all of the county. Then Salem would be surrounded by Vinton and Roanoke, and stew in its own juice.[1881]

* * *

Back to the promise and hope associated with the building of a new football stadium, recall that work began on this project in March of this year.

Evidently, progress continued at a satisfactory rate and the old idiom of "No news is good news" certainly held true.

But in early August, a tragic incident hit the newsstands.

A construction worker at the site of the stadium died several hours after he had been crushed by a crane.[1882]

Barry D. Williams, 24, of Roanoke, was standing behind a crane at the construction site behind the Salem Civic Center when he was crushed between the counterweight and cab of the machine.[1883]

Truly, the building of the new stadium had come with the expected monetary cost and, sadly and unexpectedly, the cost of one human life.

Tragic though his death was, construction continued with the deadline of August 30 fast approaching.

* * *

In July 1985, Brian Hoffman reported on the progress of the construction, and his report included some comments from Charlie Hammersley, who, at that time, was the director of Salem Parks and Recreation.[1884]

There was little doubt that, once completed, the stadium was going to be a source of pride for the proud citizens of Salem. It was going to be one of the best stadiums in the state for high school football.[1885]

"I've seen a lot of stadiums," said Hammersley, "and I think ours is the best I've ever seen. It's going to reflect favorably on the city as well as the high school. When someone comes from out of town and sees the stadium, they're going to be impressed."[1886]

About two weeks prior to the expected opening of the new stadium, Bob Teitlebam wrote that the new stadium, which was built to seat 8,000, "might be the best high school facility in the state. It looks as if it was designed for a Division I-AA college in the NCAA."[1887]

The first game to be played in the new stadium featured Salem versus Amherst County. In anticipation that the stadium might not be completed in time, Amherst agreed to switch the game to its field if construction was not far enough along to open.[1888]

"We'll be there [in the new stadium]. There'll be some odds and ends that won't be finished," Salem athletic director Dale Foster said.[1889]

"We might not be able to heat up hot dogs for the first game. That's what I mean about odds and ends. It should be all finished by the time we play William Fleming [in the second home game]."[1890]

* * *

In addition to reporting on the status of the stadium Teitlebaum wrote a preview of the football teams in the Roanoke Valley District. His predicted order of finish was (1) Pulaski County, (2) Northside, (3) Salem, (4) Franklin County, (5) William Fleming, (6) Patrick Henry, and (7) Cave Spring.[1891]

Pulaski County naturally seemed the best bet. The Cougars entered this season having won 21 straight district games, which led to 4 straight RVD titles either, which they claimed or shared.[1892]

Of the top challengers, Salem and Franklin County were both scheduled to host Pulaski County, while Northside would play the Cougars in Dublin.[1893]

Longtime Cave Spring head coach Charlie Hammes announced that this season would be his last.[1894]

Salem's top returning players included running back JoJo Harris and wide receiver Kevin Phipps.[1895]

But Phipps, who suffered a groin injury in practice, was listed as out for the Salem opener and probable for the following week against Blacksburg.[1896]

Salem head coach Willis White was about to coach his and the program's first-ever game in the new football stadium.

Knowing that the citizens of Salem and the football players were sure to be giddy and possibly overexcited, how did this make him feel?

"I try to stay out of that [excited celebration]," said White. "I think we're ready for the season. We'll do all right. We're further along than I thought we'd be. But the only way I can find out is to see us in action."[1897]

* * *

Though some of the grass around the stadium had still not been planted and the concession stand on the visitor side had to remain closed because it was not finished, Salem Stadium officially opened on August 30, 1985.[1898] Some in attendance who saw Salem play Amherst County bought T-shirts that read, "I was there! SALEM STADIUM 1st Football Game August 30th 1985."

Before the game, Salem Mayor Jim Taliaferro stood along the sidelines, admiring the new stadium. He may have been amazed when he considered that city council had not approved the stadium until January and grading had not begun until March, and yet there he was, in awe of what had come to fruition.[1899]

Somehow, the $2,195,000.00 stadium had been made ready for opening night, just as planned.

Taliaferro summarized how it all came about: "Workers [have] been toiling till midnight the last three nights, installing seats and lights and landscaping. This project has been a combination of city forces and the construction people. This is something the citizens and football teams had desired for a long time. Municipal Field was a poor surface for the players, and the seating for the fans was also terrible."[1900]

How was the view from the seats?

Kevin Slusher, a photographer for Salem High's newspaper *The Oracle*, said there wasn't a bad seat in the house. "Everything is dead center, not like the old field," he said.[1901]

Some politicians were also in attendance including Bill Gotchey, who opposed Salem Del. Steve Agee in the race for House of Delegates. Gotchey met with the crowd and handed out game schedules with his picture on them.[1902]

"It's great," he said. "I think it's going to be a real showcase for Salem."[1903]

Part 2: The New Era Is Complete

The view of the home bleachers and press box inside Salem Stadium

The view inside of Salem Stadium from the locker rooms

Now that the stadium had been built and football season had begun, let's check out how the Spartans did this season.

Game 1 (August 30): Salem 36, Amherst County 19

JoJo Harris scored 3 touchdowns, and Randy Foley returned an interception for one to lead the Spartans to victory.[1904]

Despite a 17-point differential, the game was close until the fourth quarter. Tied 13–13 at the start of the fourth, Harris caught a screen pass from quarterback Tooey Ondrus and ran 28 yards for his second touchdown of the game. Marvin Meadow's point after gave Salem a 20–13 lead.[1905]

The lead was short-lived because Amherst's Timmy Dempsey returned the ensuing kickoff 78 yards for a touchdown. The Lancers called a timeout to set up a 2-point try, which would give them the lead. Before the play, the Spartans also called a timeout because they only had 10 players on the field. When the action resumed, Amherst quarterback Jeff Lee rolled to his right, looking for Dempsey, but failed to hit his favorite target.[1906]

Foley gave the Spartans excellent field position when he returned the Amherst kickoff to near midfield. Eventually, the Spartans tried a 30-yard field goal courtesy of Marvin Morris, who was filling in for the injured Kevin Phipps. Morris's kick just cleared the cross bar, and Salem led 23–19.[1907]

Harris scored his third touchdown on a 29-yard run, and Foley closed out the scoring with his 31-yard pick 6.[1908]

Harris led all rushers with 182 yards on 23 carries. He also had 53 receiving yards.[1909]

"The first half was really tough," said Harris. "It's not the caliber of football that we can play."[1910]

Referring to fullback Johnny Meadows (11 carries for 50 yards), Harris said, "Johnny really did a great job of blocking for me tonight. Without his help most of what I did wouldn't have been possible. Playing in the new stadium helped out intensity and enthusiasm."[1911]

But it may have raised Coach White's blood pressure and heart rate.

"This was a typical first game," he said. "We made enough errors to last a long time, but I'm sure we'll make a lot more. It's great to be able to make a lot of mistakes and still win the football game... We were missing a lot of tackles in the first half, but except for [Dempsey's] kickoff return I thought we played much better in the second half."[1912]

Ondrus made his first appearance at quarterback and completed 5 of 9 passes without an interception for 91 yards and 2 touchdowns.[1913]

His play and demeanor impressed his coach.

"Ondrus did a good job," said White. "He handled himself well. He got hit several times, but he kept his head up and stepped back in."[1914]

"I was pretty nervous at first," said Ondrus. "The first touchdown pass, though, built up my confidence, and I felt a lot better after that."[1915]

Humble as he was, Harris became an immediate—and permanent—answer to at least one trivia question: "Who was the first player to ever score a touchdown in Salem Stadium?"

Answer: JoJo Harris.

While the Spartans were making history in their new stadium, defending Roanoke Valley District champion Pulaski County played host to Anacostia of Washington, DC. The Cougars introduced 16 new starters to their lineup but didn't miss a beat. Pulaski thumped Anacostia 42–8 in front of an audience of more than 5,000.[1916]

Up next for the Spartans was a battle with the Indians in Blacksburg.

Recall that last season the Indians were on the warpath for a Group AA state title. After winning the New River District championship, the tribe battled its way into the state finals, where it lost to John Handley High, 28–16.[1917]

As Salem and Blacksburg prepared for this season's encounter, the Indians had to factor in the addition of Spartans' receiver Kevin Phipps, who missed last week's season opener but had been given the okay to play this week.[1918]

Game 2 (September 6): Salem 14, Blacksburg 14

There was nothing misleading about the score; the game was about as evenly played as possible. The Spartans and Indians matched each other blow for blow.[1919]

"That was one good high school football game," said Salem coach Willis White. "It was well played on both sides."[1920]

"It's better than a loss," said Blacksburg chief David Crist.[1921]

And with the hard-hitting came some attrition, and Blacksburg paid the heavier toll.[1922]

Quarterback David Smart left the game in the fourth quarter after a shot to the kidney area, and linebacker Wayne Purcell injured his leg after intercepting a Tooey Ondrus pass that happened to foil Salem's final threat in the fourth.[1923]

Though Salem clearly won in the statistics department, the score had the final say.[1924]

"You don't feel bad. You just feel empty," said White. "We didn't come up here to tie."[1925]

Salem standout running back JoJo Harris had a "sensational" game. He tallied a game best 99 yards rushing and scored both of his team's touchdowns—the first on a 75-yard scamper, and the second on a 76-yard kickoff return. Kevin Phipps kicked both extra points.[1926]

The Spartans missed out on an excellent opportunity early in the fourth quarter. They pushed the ball to the Indians' 3 and went to Harris on 3 occasions, but the Blacksburg defense kept him in check and forced a fourth down. Phipps attempted a 20-yard field goal but missed, which kept the score tied.[1927]

Around the league, Franklin County beat Bassett, 41–28; William Fleming edged GW-Danville, 13–12; Pulaski County pounded Princeton (West Virginia), 41–7; Northside nudged E. C. Glass, 27–21; and Cave Spring got past Heritage-Lynchburg, 25–23.[1928]

Up next for Salem was a clash with Cave Spring, which has special meaning for this year's Spartans' quarterback.

THE SPARTAN SUCCESSION

The game between Salem and Cave Spring also marked the opener of the Roanoke Valley District matchups.

Knights' coach Charlie Hammes remembered all too well how Spartans' wide receiver Kevin Phipps blistered his team last year. Phipps hauled in 3 touchdown catches of 67, 52, and 37 yards to pace Salem to victory, 35–7.[1929]

"We have to be conscious of him, so we've made some changes," said Hammes.[1930]

For Salem signal caller Tooey Ondrus, the game against Cave Spring represented a homecoming of sorts. Last year, Ondrus was on the Cave Spring squad as a reserve and later transferred to Salem. This year, he won the starting spot at Salem.[1931]

Game 3 (September 13): Spartans 20, Knights 6

Tied 6–6 at the intermission, Salem scored a touchdown in both the third and fourth quarters to defeat Cave Spring for the second year in a row.[1932]

The Spartans scored first when William Sinkler blocked a punt and teammate Carl Young chased it down in the end zone for a 6–0 lead with just seconds remaining in the first quarter.[1933]

But the Knights took the ensuing kickoff and drove 66 yards for the tying touchdown, which came when Lance Green scored from the 3.[1934]

Salem's JoJo Harris, who led all rushers with 123 yards after 26 carries, gave his team the lead in the third quarter when he scored from 3 yards out.[1935]

And Ondrus, playing in front of many familiar people, quieted his distractors when he engineered a 76-yard scoring drive capped by his 24-yard pass to Kevin Phipps, which was Phipps's first of the year and which signaled the end of the Knights' hope.[1936]

Ondrus finished on 5 of 9 passing for 72 yards, no interceptions, and 1 TD.[1937]

Cave Spring running back Heywood Statum tallied a team best 111 yards rushing after 15 carries, but he might remember this game best for what happened when he dropped back to receive a

Salem punt. The play occurred in the third quarter, and Statum, with the ball in his sights, opted to let it hit the field and bounce. Unfortunately for him and his teammates, it zeroed in on him, and its contact made it free for the taking. Phipps made the recovery, which led to Harris's go-ahead touchdown.[1938]

While Salem was unsaddling Cave Spring, around the league, Courtland defeated William Fleming in Roanoke's Victory Stadium (9–0), Halifax County flattened Franklin County (21–7), Northside doubled up Heritage (28–14), and Patrick Henry pushed past E. C. Glass (14–7).[1939]

The defending Roanoke Valley District champions Cougars of Pulaski County had the week off.[1940]

Next week, Pulaski County continued its competition against West Virginia High Schools with a date against Bluefield, while Cave Spring visited E. C. Glass, Franklin County faced Patrick Henry at Victory Stadium, and Salem made its second appearance in its new stadium when it hosted William Fleming.[1941]

Game 4 (September 20): Spartans 6, Colonels 0

To use a current-day expression, Fleming stacked the box in an effort to stop Salem's chief offensive weapons—running back JoJo Harris and flanker Kevin Phipps.[1942]

The tactic worked, but the Colonels still lost.[1943]

Phipps used his foot to best Fleming when he booted 2 field goals to lift Salem to its second victory inside Salem Stadium and improve its overall record to 3–0–1.[1944]

Of Fleming's defensive tactics, Salem's Willis White said, "They gambled on every play and took us out of our offense, and we never could get back in it."[1945]

Harris was held to 31 rushing yards, while Phipps caught 2 of Tooey Ondrus's 5 completed passes for 56 yards.[1946]

The shutout loss represented Fleming's third of the season.[1947]

Around the league, Pulaski County bested Bluefield (West Virginia), 20–8; Patrick Henry beat Franklin County, 14–6; and E. C. Glass cruised past Cave Spring, 24–0.[1948]

THE SPARTAN SUCCESSION

Up next for the Spartans was the first-ever homecoming game in Salem Stadium. The visitors were known as the Cavaliers of Fieldale-Collinsville.

Game 5 (September 27): Spartans 49, Cavaliers 6

Salem's offense erupted and produced a season-best output of 500 yards of total offense.[1949]

Three Spartan running backs all rushed for over 80 yards. JoJo Harris topped the list with 13 carries for 139 yards and 2 TDs, Frank Morris finished with 95 yards, and Johnny Meadows tallied 87.[1950]

Kevin Phipps caught 2 touchdown passes from Tooey Ondrus and returned a punt for a touchdown.[1951]

For Fieldale-Collinsville, it took the opening kickoff and put together its only scoring drive. The Cavaliers went 68 yards on 12 plays and capped it with a 4-yard pass from quarterback Don Wigginton to Mark Thomas.[1952]

In other games, Pulaski County edged Cave Spring, 14–13; Northside beat Franklin County, 39–25; and Halifax County defeated William Fleming, 27–6.[1953]

Up next, the Spartans would battle the Bengals of Bassett.

But first, let's look at Timesland's statistical leaders at this midway point in the season.

As for the top 15 rushers in the area, Bassett's Aaron Staples topped the list and was averaging 10.4 yards per carry and 172.5 yards per game.[1954]

Salem's JoJo Harris was in the fourth spot after 97 carries for 589 yards, right at 6 yards per carry.[1955]

Among the top 15 passers, Salem's Tooey Ondrus was in the number 7 spot, and among the top 15 receivers, Kevin Phipps was number 9.[1956]

Game 6 (October 4): Salem 35, Bassett 0

Johnny Meadows, Salem's junior fullback, scored 3 touchdowns to lead the Spartans to the blowout win over the Bengals.[1957]

The area's top rusher, Aaron Staples, saw limited action for his team. He carried the ball just 8 times after having suffered a hyperextended knee and bruised eye socket in the previous week's game against Martinsville.[1958]

Meadows finished with 56 yards rushing in 13 carries and said, "The line did a super job, especially the right side. JoJo [Harris] took the pressure off me and the lanes were open all night."[1959]

Harris wasn't exactly silent. He scored Salem's other 2 touchdowns, and Kevin Phipps was 5 of 5 on PATs.[1960]

What was Coach White's take on this one?

"It was a heckuva offensive show."[1961]

In other games, Pulaski County was 3 points better than Franklin County, 17–14; Patrick Henry defeated Cave Spring 22–7; and Northside beat William Fleming, 17–7.[1962]

In the standings, 4 teams—Salem, Pulaski County, Patrick Henry, and Northside—were 2–0 against their district rivals, while 3—Northside, Pulaski County, and Patrick Henry—had perfect overall records of 5–0. Salem's only blemish was a tie, which brought the Spartans up next at 5–0–1.[1963]

Salem had next week off, while Franklin County was scheduled to play Cave Spring, Patrick Henry faced Northside, and Pulaski County squared off against William Fleming in Roanoke's Victory Stadium.[1964]

Here are those results: Franklin County 22, Cave Spring 6; Patrick Henry 19, Northside 0; and Pulaski County 28, William Fleming 6.[1965]

Up next, Pulaski County hosted Alleghany, Cave Spring traveled to Martinsville, Northside visited Western Albemarle, Patrick Henry and William Fleming clashed in Victory Stadium, and Salem returned to action when it traveled to Rocky Mount to face Franklin County.[1966]

Game 7 (October 18): Spartans 41, Eagles 0

Salem sealed the deal when it scored 4 touchdowns in the decisive second quarter.[1967]

THE SPARTAN SUCCESSION

The results were stunning. After all, the Eagles had previously lost to the likes of Northside, Pulaski County, and Patrick Henry by a combined total of only 24 points.[1968]

Salem's Johnny Meadows rushed for a game best 103 yards on 12 carries and 1 touchdown. Kevin Phipps caught 2 touchdown passes from Tooey Ondrus, Vincent Parker hauled in another, and JoJo Harris (11 carries, 68 yards) scored the team's second touchdown of the night.[1969]

The Spartan defense was nearly impenetrable. It held Mark Poindexter and Tony Montgomery—2 of Timesland's best offensive players—to 138 yards.[1970]

"You never expect to stop both of them," said Coach White. "That was just a bonus."[1971]

With the win, Salem remained unbeaten and once tied at 7–0–1 but still had not cracked the top 10 among the state's Group AAA teams.[1972]

Coach White seized the moment with a hint of sarcasm. "That's all right. We're just poor little ol' Salem. We're too small to play those big schools."[1973]

And around the league, Patrick Henry shut out William Fleming, 13–0; Northside had no problem defeating Western Albemarle, 34–6; Pulaski County pounded Alleghany, 28–0; but Cave Spring fell to Martinsville, 38–21.[1974]

Next week's schedule featured 2 key showdowns—Salem versus Patrick Henry, and Northside at Pulaski County—and all 4 were serious contenders for the coveted district crown.[1975]

* * *

Timeout "on the field" for a little reflection.

Here, in 1985, Willis White was in his third season as the head coach of the Salem Spartans. Going into the clash with PH, White's record at Salem was 19–6–2.⁶⁵ His successor at PH, Larry Carter, was 17–8–2.¹⁹⁷⁶

Carter previously coached at both Hopewell and Rockbridge County High Schools, where he developed both programs into district champions. He acknowledged that following Merrill Gainer and Willis White at Patrick Henry had been no easy task. "When you have two big names like that [to follow] it's tough. The fact that I wasn't known in the area [also] made it tough."¹⁹⁷⁷

White noted he had been primed for the change.

"I had been at PH for 14 years. That was long enough, but the challenge got for me to move."¹⁹⁷⁸

Unlike the head football coaches of the Roanoke City and County schools, White had been given a say over the junior high programs in the Salem system, and that was one of the reasons Salem had so quickly won under White.¹⁹⁷⁹

And head-to-head against his old team, White was 2–0.

Could he make it three in a row?

Game 8 (October 25): Patriots 23, Spartans 7

PH led 13–0 at the half after dominating the statistics. The Patriots ran 35 plays to just 17 for the Spartans and outgained their opponents in yardage, 197–28.¹⁹⁸⁰

But the Patriots nearly self-destructed in the third quarter.¹⁹⁸¹

Salem made it a 6-point game when Tooey Ondrus connected with Kevin Phipps for a 59-yard touchdown pass and then Phipps booted the PAT to make it 13–7.¹⁹⁸²

The Spartans threatened to cut deeper into the Patriots' lead when they later drove to the PH 3, but the Patriot defense stiffened and forced what looked like a 20-yard field goal attempt by Phipps. Though his kick was wide, that's not what bothered Coach White.

---

⁶⁵ Bob Teitlebaum, who wrote the story, listed White at 20–6–1. This author's totals are based on the sum of these records: 4–5–1 (in 1983), 9–1 (in 1984), and 6–0–1 going into the game with PH.

"It was supposed to be a fake field goal, only they missed the signal," said White.[1983]

In addition to a couple of bad snaps in the game, PH also gave up a short punt in the third quarter that gave the Spartans the ball at their own 46. But on its second play, Salem fumbled and turned the ball over to the Patriots, who then consumed over 6 minutes of the clock and capped a scoring drive with a 28-yard field goal by John Draper.[1984]

The PH defense held Salem running backs JoJo Harris and Johnny Meadows to 18 and 17 yards, respectively.[1985]

Always quick with a quip, White said, "They just whipped us up front all night. We had our moment in the sun, but we didn't score enough."[1986]

And while PH was defeating Salem, Northside pulled off the upset in Dublin against Pulaski County, 21–14. Tied 14–14 in the third quarter, Northside quarterback Scott Fisher ran for a 55-yard touchdown, which proved to be the game winner. The district loss represented Pulaski County's first after 25 straight wins.[1987]

The district standings now had Patrick Henry at 5–0 in the district and 8–0 overall, followed by Northside (3–1, 7–1), Pulaski County (3–1, 7–1), and Salem (3–1, 6–1–1).[1988]

Obviously, the last 2 games of the season would prove decisive. In the first of those, Salem would play home against Pulaski County, Northside would welcome Cave Spring, and Heritage would host Patrick Henry.[1989]

For Pulaski County and Northside, the stakes were the same; the winner could still tie Patrick Henry for the district title or earn a wild-card spot in the playoffs, while the loser would be eliminated from playoff contention.[1990]

Game 9 (November 1): Pulaski County 20, Salem 6

After a scoreless first quarter, Wayne Bruce blocked a Salem punt, and teammate Allen Martin returned the ball 16 yards for a touchdown.[1991]

Salem tied the game when Kevin Phipps hauled in a pass from Tooey Ondrus, faked a defender, and split between 2 others on a 63-yard play.[1992]

Tied 6–6 at the half, Salem fell apart after the intermission. The Spartans committed 3 second-half turnovers, and their offense sputtered.[1993]

In the third quarter, Pulaski quarterback Randy Meredith capped a 56-yard scoring drive with a 1-yard turn and later passed to James Harris for a 21-yard score.[1994]

"The blocked punt hurt," said Coach White. "It was one of those crazy nights. Anything can happen, and it did."[1995]

Recently, during a telephone conversation with White, he remembered quite well the incessant pouring rain that night when Salem and Pulaski played.

As will be seen, that dreary, rainy night was a harbinger of things to come...

Meanwhile, district rivals Patrick Henry defeated Heritage, 20–0, and Northside crushed Cave Spring, 33–0.[1996]

The 3-team race for the district title continued next week with Northside playing at Salem and Pulaski County and Patrick Henry meeting in Victory Stadium.[1997]

Though eliminated from playoff contention, Salem still found itself in the role of a spoiler. Northside had to defeat Salem to keep its playoff hopes alive.[1998]

"We really took ourselves out of the race," said Coach White. "When you score 13 points against two teams [Patrick Henry and Pulaski County], you can't expect to win. You have to score a minimum of twice and play good defense."[1999]

Patrick Henry had already clinched a tie for the Roanoke Valley District title, but Pulaski County and Northside could both claim a share of the crown if both won.[2000]

The matchup between the Spartans and Vikings featured 2 of the area's best running backs. Salem had JoJo Harris, and Northside could boast of Tim Boitnott. This Viking needed just 107 more yard to reach the 1,000 yards plateau this season.[2001]

The Flood of 1985

In the daily rush of things, it's easy to lose sight of the possibility that a natural calamity could strike at any moment and change the world as people know it.

In the Roanoke Valley, the date of November 4, 1985, will be remembered for a long time to come.

That was when the worst flooding in the valley occurred. It claimed the lives of 10 people and set new—and obviously dangerous—records. The Roanoke River crested at 23.35 feet, the rainfall total was 6.61 inches, and the property damage was listed at $200 million.[2002]

The *Roanoke Times* provided comprehensive coverage of the historic event, and the photographs taken likely left indelible images in the minds of its readers. For example, one photograph depicted the rescue of a woman in the floodwaters of Mason Creek. Without the assistance, the woman looked sure to perish. The news source's Wayne Deel captured the image, and the *Associated Press* named it the photo of the year.[2003]

Other photographs showed the extensive flooding of certain areas, including apartment complexes like Willow River in Salem, and of Roanoke's Victory Stadium, where the playing field was underwater and rendered inoperable for any upcoming games, notably the Pulaski-County-versus-Patrick-Henry showdown. As a result, the game was moved to Salem Stadium and would be played on Saturday, November 9.[2004]

Now, back to the Spartans.

Game 10 (November 8): Salem 6, Northside 6

Even a tie made Salem the spoiler of Northside's hopes. But it took some late heroics to get there.[2005]

Down 6–0 with less than 4 minutes to play, Salem drove 63 yards and capped the drive with a 2-yard run for touchdown by JoJo Harris. The drive was highlighted by a 35-yard pass from Tooey

Ondrus to Kevin Phipps, and the talented receiver provided the reporter with some play by play.[2006]

"I came out 5 yards, turned, and Tooey pumped-fake. Then I went down [field]... We sort of pulled [the play] out for this game."[2007]

Northside led early on after Tim Boitnott, who doubled as a linebacker for the team, sacked Ondrus and forced a fumble that Boitnott also recovered.[2008]

"No one picked me up," said Boitnott. "And it so happened the ball bounced to me."[2009]

Teammate Harold Hunt eventually scored on a 2-yard run.[2010]

The game story contained a twist of irony. Two accomplished kickers, Kevin Phipps and George Bruce, missed the extra points.[2011]

"I thought mine was good," said Phipps. "That's what someone on the hill [behind the goalpost] said."[2012]

"I had a different holder," said Bruce. "It was just a little left on the tee, and I hooked it a little bit."[2013]

But the outcome wasn't decided by the toe of either kicker; both teams had their chances and botched their opportunities.[2014]

Late in the second quarter, Salem drove the ball to the Northside 9 but, after 3 plays, moved the ball only to the 4, where the Spartans lined up for a field goal attempt. A bad snap forced Harris (the holder) to pick up the ball, and he was tackled on the 15-yard line.[2015]

Northside, on its last possession of the game, lined up for what would have been a 57-yard field goal try, but a delay-of-game penalty pushed the Vikings back 5 yards and out of Bruce's projected range. Head coach Jim Hickam opted for a fake punt, but it failed to get first-down yardage.[2016]

"I was going to try [the field goal]," said Hickam. "[Bruce has] kicked 60 yards in practice."[2017]

"I can't say I would have hit it, but it wouldn't [have] hurt to try," said Bruce.[2018]

The next night, Salem Stadium was the site of the big matchup between Pulaski County and Patrick Henry.[2019]

And the Patriots caged the Cougars, 28–10, in front of 9,500 fans.[2020]

THE SPARTAN SUCCESSION

The win gave PH the Roanoke Valley District title and knocked Pulaski out of contention for a playoff spot, which ended a streak of 4 years in which the Cougars had won or shared the district crown.[2021]

Except for PH, the season had concluded for the rest of the Roanoke Valley District teams.

The final district standings looked like this: Patrick Henry was a perfect 6–0 in the district and 10–0 overall. Northside was next at 4–1–1 and 8–1–1, followed by Pulaski County (4–2, 8–2), Salem (3–2–1, 6–2–2), Franklin County (2–4, 4–6), Cave Spring (1–5, 3–7), and William Fleming (0–6, 1–9).[2022]

Individually, both Tim Boitnott of Northside and JoJo Harris of Salem scored 12 touchdowns this season and were among the top scorers.[2023]

Among Timesland's top 15 statistical leaders, Tooey Ondrus finished as number 8 among passers. He completed 56 passes out of 121 attempts with 5 interceptions. He threw for 961 yards and 9 touchdowns.[2024]

Of the top 15 receivers, Kevin Phipps came in at number 10 with 26 receptions for 542 yards, 20.8 yards per catch, and 5 touchdowns.[2025]

* * *

The 16-team Group AAA playoffs featured 4 teams from both the Northwest and Northern Regions paired in the bottom half of the bracket, while the 4 from both the Central and Eastern Regions comprised the upper half of the bracket.[2026]

From the Northwest, Patrick Henry would be the home team to Osbourn Park and Gar-Field would play at Heritage-Lynchburg.[2027]

In these 2 region semifinal games, on November 15, PH defeated Osbourn Park, 7–3, and Heritage hammered Gar-Field, 27–0.[2028]

In the region finals, PH would host Heritage at Salem Stadium.[2029]

Before that game was played, the All-Roanoke Valley District team selections were named.

Three Spartans were named to the first team. Greg Wall (guard) and Kevin Phipps (flanker) were named to the first team offense, and John Dillon (tackle) made the first team defense.[2030]

Patrick Henry and Pulaski County each had 7 first team choices. Northside—like Salem—had 3, Cave Spring had 2, and Franklin County 1.[2031]

PH's David Cobb and Northside's Tim Boitnott were the only 2 players who made first team on both offense and defense.[2032]

Considering the Patriots' success this season, it likely came as no surprise that PH's Larry Carter was named the district's coach of the year.[2033]

Northwest Region Finals (November 22): PH 34, Heritage 8

The Patriots won the region title for the first time since 1979, the year they defeated Pulaski County, 14–7. Before that, PH won it in 1973 on its way to its first and only state championship.[2034]

This win in 1985 pushed PH into 1 of the 2 state semifinal games against defending state champion T. C. Williams, which defeated Herndon, 16–11.[2035]

PH and T. C. Williams would meet at Salem Stadium, and in the other state semifinal game, Hampton and Monacan would play.[2036]

Prior to those matchups, the All-Northwest Region selections were named. Among those, 8 Roanoke Valley District players made the team. Patrick Henry's David Cobb was the only player to make the first team for both offense (running back) and defense (linebacker).[2037]

Northside had 3 players named, PH and Pulaski County had 2 each, and Salem had 1.[2038]

By now, the reader can deduce what Spartan player made the squad.

Yes, that would have been Kevin Phipps.[2039]

When the results for the *Associated Press*'s All-Group AAA football team were announced, 3 Roanoke Valley District players had been named.[2040]

Pulaski County's Rodney Landreth and Patrick Henry's Donald Crenshaw, both defensive backs, made the list, and the high-flying flanker from Salem, Kevin Phipps.[2041]

Three RVD players earned second team honors: defensive end Jerome Stephens of Patrick Henry, defensive lineman Nick McCrary of Pulaski County, and linebacker Tim Boitnott of Northside.[2042]

In the postseason, the All-Timesland team was announced.

Patrick Henry paced the field with 4 selections, and Blacksburg had 3. The 4 Patriots were David Cobb (running back), Trae Dickson (defensive back), Don Crenshaw (defensive back), and Jerome Stephens (defensive end).[2043]

The 3 Indians included linebacker Darwin Herdman, who was also named Defensive Player of the Year, and teammates James Craig (defensive lineman) and Lucian Zelazny (defensive back).[2044]

The first team offense included Phipps. His offensive teammates included Martinsville quarterback Shawn Moore, who was named the Offensive Player of the Year. Moore completed 83 of 156 passes for 1,478 yards and 22 touchdowns.[2045]

Herdman was a beast from his linebacker position. He was in on 90 tackles, had 4 interceptions, and blocked 4 punts.[2046]

Larry Carter of Patrick Henry was named Coach of the Year.[2047]

As part of the praise bestowed to Carter, he was credited in game situations with "not waiting until his team was behind to pull out new players in desperation."[2048]

Two other coaches were mentioned for their achievements this season. Dave Crist again established Blacksburg as a state power, and Norm Lineburg led Radford to the Region IV title game against Blacksburg.[2049]

Among the second team selections, Salem's Rob Vaughan, a lineman, was named.[2050]

Group AAA state semifinal results (November 30)

At Salem Stadium, T. C. Williams blanked Patrick Henry, 10–0, to once again advance to the state championship game and end PH's quest for a state crown.[2051]

The Patriots played without the services of 2 of their starting defensive backs, including all-state performer Donald Crenshaw (knee) and Stephen Waskey (broken ankle). Waskey watched the game from the sideline, and Crenshaw watched from a wheelchair just inside the Patriots' dressing room.[2052]

In the other semifinal game, Hampton shutout Monacan, 18–0.[2053]

The Crabbers' Sam Crayton made his first start at tailback and carried the ball 28 times for 209 yards.[2054]

The state title games would be played on December 7.

In Group AAA, the Titans and Crabbers would meet at W. T. Woodson High in Fairfax; in Group AA, Blacksburg will take on Courtland; and in Group A, Lunenberg Central would play Powell Valley.[2055]

The Group AAA final featured a rematch of last year's finals, during which the Titans beat the Crabbers 10–0.[2056]

Here are the results:

- Group AAA: Hampton 16, T. C. Williams 0
- Group AA: Courtland 13, Blacksburg 6
- Group A: Powell Valley 28, Lunenburg Central 27[2057]

* * *

Now, let's refocus on the Salem Spartans and look at where they had been and where they had come.

Individually, Kevin Phipps finished his career with 72 receptions.[2058]

JoJo Harris tallied 868 rushing yards this season and finished his career with 2,576 yards.[2059]

Salem's defense had several steady performers. Linebacker Larry Wills led the team in tackles with 120. William Sinkler was second with 112, including 6 sacks. Jonathan Dillon finished with 95, Marvin Morris with 88, Davey Thomas with 87—including 8 sacks. Frank "Tiny" Morris finished with 80, Carl Young with 78, and Todd Smith with 76.[2060]

Defensive back Randy Foley led the Spartans with 5 interceptions.[2061]

In December, Johnny Meadows made Spartan history. He was the first offensive player named as the recipient of the Spartan Bell Award, which was annually presented by Brian Hoffman of the *Salem Times-Register* at the sports awards banquet.[2062]

In the 8 previous years the award had been given, 6 had gone to linebackers and 2 to defensive linemen.[2063]

Of Meadows, White said, "He'll stick ya. He hit a boy from Amherst right in the ear hole and that's something to see on film. That kid just spun around and collapsed right there. I wish you [Hoffman] could show that film before you present the award."[2064]

In Hoffman's customary comprehensive coverage of Salem sports, this article included a photograph of Meadows running with the football and leveling a would-be tackler with a stiff arm.[2065]

Hosted by the Salem Sports Foundation, the annual awards banquet was held in mid-December.

In addition to the Spartan Bell Award presented to Meadows, they included the following:

- Top offensive back: JoJo Harris
- Top defensive back: Randy Foley
- Top offensive lineman: Rob Vaughan
- Top defensive lineman: Jonathan Dillon
- Most Improved: Brad Braxton
- The J.W. Burress Most Valuable Substitute: Bert Sumpter
- Special Award: Kevin Phipps, for being a two-time first-team all-state selection[2066]

Coach White provided this author with an assessment of his first 3 seasons at Salem.

In 1983, he inherited a team that was not very talented.

"We had one tailback, one fullback, and I could have put other kids in, but we would have gone way downhill. By the end of the year, the kids were buying into the program. You have to change the culture, and you're not going to do it overnight. You want people to do stuff because *they* want to do it."[2067]

Things changed in 1984.

"They bought in," said White. "We went 9–1, and the only game we lost was to Pulaski. [Salem] had never beaten Cave Spring, and we beat them by 3 or 4 touchdowns. We hadn't beaten PH, and we beat PH. We beat Fleming. We beat everybody around except Pulaski."[2068]

But here in 1985, the team did not duplicate the feats of '84, and according to White, some folks had already given up on him.

"People wanted to fire me. They had a petition up to fire me."[2069]

As for the '85 squad, "they didn't have as much talent," explained White. "They had a lot of want-to, but when you play people with talent want-to is not enough some time."[2070]

After the '85 season, Coach White's record at Salem was 19 wins, 8 losses, and 3 ties.

Against its district foes, Salem was unbeaten against Franklin County at 3–0 and 2–1 against Cave Spring, William Fleming, and Patrick Henry.

It had played Northside on even terms at 1 win, 1 loss, and 1 tie.

But the downside was that Salem was winless in 3 games against Pulaski County.

And if Salem was ever going to compete in the postseason, it would have to figure out a way to beat Pulaski, for it seemed that the road to the playoffs always went through Dublin.

Next consideration: the 1985 season marked the beginning of the Spartans playing their home games in Salem Stadium—indeed, a true marvel among high school football stadiums in Virginia.

THE SPARTAN SUCCESSION

It is this author's contention that the establishment of Salem Stadium provided the final link in the evolutionary process that ushered in the completion of a new era in Salem football.

Consider these previous steps: The Wolverines of Andrew Lewis High brought gridiron acclaim to Salem under the tutelage of Eddie Joyce and his assistants. Recall that Lewis won state titles in 1962 and 1964 and finished as runner-up in 1966, 1967, and 1971.

Next, Joyce resigned after the '74 season, and Mike Stevens coached the Wolverines during their final two seasons of '75 and '76. The following year, Salem High opened and welcomed the student bodies of both Andrew Lewis and Glenvar, and those 2 previous high schools became junior highs.

In 1982, Glenvar reopened as a high school and, along with Salem, operated under the auspices of Roanoke County.

But Salem broke away from the county and formed its own school system and began independent operations in 1983.

That was also the year that Willis White became the head coach of the Spartans, who still played their home games at Municipal Field, which, as the reader can recall, was also the home to the minor league baseball team in Salem and which former Lewis players dubbed the Snake Pit.

The Spartans played their last games on this combination of dirt and grass in 1984 and, in 1985, began play in a stadium that would make many high school teams envious and many college teams proud.[66]

---

[66] As noted in this chapter, Breakell Inc. was the contracting company that built Salem Stadium. The company had a solid reputation, which it maintained throughout the years, but in 2013, the company ceased operations. According to an article published in *The Roanoke Times* on January 4 of this year and written by Laurence Hammack, the company made this decision after fifty years of building in the Roanoke Valley. It not only felt the effects of a lackluster economy, but the year before, a former project manager was charged with cheating the company out of more than $1 million. This person was later convicted in federal court and sentenced to serve three years and five months and to make restitution of $1.05 million to Breakell and of $240,000 to Great American Alliance Insurance Company. It was truly unfortunate because the company had established a stellar reputation in Southwest Virginia in handling govern-

All events considered, a new era was fully complete.

The only thing missing was a championship, or at least an opportunity to play for one.

Thankfully, the Spartans and their fans would not have to wait long.

Just next season, the Spartans would battle their way to a place no other Salem-based team had gone since 1971—a trip to the Group AAA state finals—exactly fifteen years later.

---

ment, commercial, industrial, and private building projects. The company had been involved in high-profile construction projects over the years, and in 2009, Stanley Breakell was named Roanoke City's Citizen of the Year. The CEO of a prominent competitive company praised the company for its reputation: "They were good competitors. They did good work. But they had problems that were not of their own making."

Chapter 14

LEST WE FORGET

Burgess Garnett King was known to family and friends as "BG" The photo was provided courtesy of his daughter, Nancy King Porter.

Who is the man described as the common denominator in both Andrew Lewis's and Salem's football success?

He's Dale LeRoy Foster, born on November 6, 1936, in Botetourt County, Virginia, to the marital union of Roy Foster and Ruby Eller Foster. He grew up on a 200-acre cattle farm, which had much to do with developing his solid work ethic at a young age.[2071]

He attended public schools within Botetourt County and played three sports: football, basketball, and track. After graduating from the former Colonial High School, he attended Bridgewater College and majored in physical education and economics and played three sports. He was a quarterback and defensive halfback on the football team and a guard on the basketball squad, and he competed in the broad jump and ran the 440 in track.[2072]

After graduation from Bridgewater, he took his first coaching job in 1960 as the head football coach at James River High School in Buchanan. He was there only a year when he decided to go to law school. He attended the T. C. Williams School of Law at the University of Richmond for a year but soon decided that it was not for him; he wanted to coach. He next coached at Midlothian High in Richmond but only briefly.[2073]

Then, whether by fate or divine intervention, he attended a high school state basketball tournament in Richmond whose teams included Andrew Lewis. While there, he reconnected with Dick Miley, the head basketball coach at Lewis and a former basketball teammate of Foster's at Bridgewater. Miley told him about a coach's position open at Lewis.[2074]

In 1962, Foster became an assistant football coach, junior varsity basketball coach, and the assistant track coach at Lewis. He became the head track coach in 1964 when Fred Hoback, who became a lawyer and judge, resigned.[2075]

From the beginning and throughout his time at Lewis, Foster was always on the go and always looking to make the players/athletes he coached better.[2076]

In 1963, the Lewis football team installed the slanting monster defense.[2077]

In addition to helping install this type of defense at Lewis, Foster also coached the offensive backs, the defensive secondary, and the monster man position; plus, he graded films and taped shoulders and ankles.[2078]

He became such an expert on this particular defensive set that he wrote a book about it. *The Slanting Monster Defense in Football* was published in 1970 by Parker Publishing Company of West Nyack, New York.

"Someone wanted to know how many books were sold," he said. "Advertisement went to all high school and college football programs throughout the country and to some foreign countries. A total of 3,500 books were sold that first month just to coaches, thanks to Coach Doug Dickey, the head football coach at the University of Tennessee, who wrote the foreword for the book. He had just won a national championship, one of six national championships won at the University of Tennessee.[2079]

"A few books were sold in foreign countries. The Andrew Lewis High School Wolverines became known all throughout the country and outside the country."[67, 2080]

And at least one famous collegiate coach relied upon its contents. His name was Pat Dye. He is best remembered for his head coaching days at the University of Auburn, where he coached for twelve seasons, 1981–1992.[2081]

He led the Tigers to four Southeastern Conference (SEC) titles and was named as the SEC Coach of the Year three times. He was inducted into the College Football Hall of Fame in 2005. He also served as Auburn's athletic director (1981–2001); and on November 19, 2005, the playing field at Auburn was named in his honor: Pat Dye Field.[2082]

He and Foster share a birthday.

Patrick Fain Dye was born on November 6, 1939, in Blythe, Georgia. He went on to play football at the University of Georgia, where he graduated and then played for three years in the Canadian Football League as a linebacker for the Edmonton Eskimos.[2083]

---

[67] The book can still be purchased at www.amazon.com or at www.alibris.com, which has the most selections. To order the original edition, order the 1970 edition by Dale Foster.

On September 10, 2008, an article was published about Dye's office and his bookshelf, which included several great works of literature. "One book, however, was front and center. Its pages were frayed, many of them dog-eared, and there were notes scattered on and in it." This description was a reference to Foster's book, *The Slanting Monster Defense in Football*, and "Pat Dye was a disciple."[2084]

Further, Foster's book also won some acclaim in a movie. *Radio*, released in 2003, starred Cuba Gooding Jr. and Ed Harris. Harris played the role of Coach Harold Jones at T. L. Hanna High, just outside Anderson, South Carolina. Less than five minutes into the movie, Harris can be seen watching game film in his home office. Foster's book is located on his desk within proximity of the film projector, and the camera stays focused on the book easily long enough for viewers to take notice.

Now, back to Foster's days at Andrew Lewis.

Foster described a whole different culture back then. "After the home games, we would get together at the homes of different people. We had food. My wife baked up chicken and everything. Football games were more of a formal occasion back then. Coach Joyce's wife, JoAn, and my wife, Fran, were good friends. JoAn and Fran went to the ball games together. They sat in the same seats in Salem. They wore corsages. People kind of dressed up then."[2085]

Foster, who earned a bachelor's degree at Bridgewater and a master's degree at Virginia Tech, stayed on at Andrew Lewis through the '71 football season and then was offered an administrative position at Salem Intermediate School. He accepted and served from 1972 through 1977. That year, he became the athletic director at Salem High School during its first year. He served in this position until 1990, for thirteen years. At one time, he served as athletic director, assistant principal, and assistant football coach. He was also offered the job as head coach of the football team at Salem High, which he declined.[2086]

Foster retired in 1996, but beginning that year and through 2001, he ran the summer school program as the principal for the high school and middle school in Salem. His wife, the former Fran

Firebaugh, became sick and was in the hospital nineteen times in the 1990s. She suffered a brain stroke and died on October 30, 2014.[2087]

Losing his wife to illness dealt Foster one of the two major blows he has sustained over the course of his life. The other blow is discussed in Volume 2.[2088]

When he thought about the great memories he shared with his wife and the Joyce family, two other people came to mind as prominent Salemites whom he, to this day, consider as the top supporters of both Andrew Lewis and Salem football.[2089]

He began with Jim Taliaferro.

"It was 1967, the date of the first Super Bowl. Because he had a color television set, Jim invited me over to his house to watch the Super Bowl. Just the two of us watched that game in his living room that afternoon.[68] Jim would come to the coach's office and watch game film with us. He also came to a lot of our practices. He even drove Coach Joyce and myself to Bluefield, West Virginia, when we were scouting E. C. Glass on a Saturday night in 1965.[69, 2090]

"In 1986, when Salem played four straight away playoff games, Jim came by my office and laid a $10,000 check on my desk. He said, 'Take care of the football team, the band, and the cheerleaders.' He had a heart of gold. He would not accept free reserved seats at the new stadium, even though he built it. He was always first in line to buy his two reserved seats for his wife, Rixine, and himself.

"As mayor of Salem [1974–1996] he built the football stadium just for football. It opened for the its first football game in 1985. He had told me many times that he was going to install the playing surface inside the stadium that would be narrow enough so that *only* football could be played on it. It was to be a football stadium *only*. He also added on to the field house and built the football practice fields. Salem football would not be what it is today if Jim had not

---

[68] Foster is correct about the first Super Bowl. This author remembers watching the game as well. It featured the Green Bay Packers against the Kansas City Chiefs.

[69] Scouting Glass was something that Foster had the ability to do most seasons because Glass played its home games on Saturdays, and in 1965 Glass had numerous players who were considered as Division I prospects.

taken such a tremendous interest in Andrew Lewis football during the Eddie Joyce era of the 1960s and early 1970s."[2091]

Foster was emphatic when he said, "If it hadn't been for Jim, we wouldn't have Salem Stadium today."[2092]

The reader can take notice of how impressive this stadium is simply by viewing the pictures, especially when one considers that this stadium was built for a *high school football team*. It is impressive enough; in fact, from 1993 through 2017, the Division III college championship game, also known as the Alonzo Stagg Bowl, was played here.

Back to Foster, he next lauded the contributions of B. G. King. "BG was in charge of the two-week, preseason football camp. That was quite a job until 1983 when Coach Willis White discontinued it after twenty-three years of camps. I had a sixteen-millimeter projector and screen in my basement where Coach Wallace Thompson and myself would grade the past Friday night's Andrew Lewis game film.[70, 2093]

"BG was a neighbor of mine. On some Saturdays, BG would come over while we were grading the film. I would give him my list of players, and I would tell him to put a plus or minus beside the player's name. He really enjoyed doing that, and it helped me out. Each player was graded on every play that he participated in. That's the reason it took the biggest part of the day to grade game film. The grades were posted in the locker room on Monday before practice. The player that had the lowest grade would receive the Baby Doll Award." With a small chuckle in his voice, Foster said, "This is still a much-talked subject among the Wolverines."[2094]

He continued, "BG also came to a lot of our practices. He was a very intelligent person, and he loved football. He was a player at one time at Andrew Lewis. He also had lost sight in one eye. It was unbelievable the good eyesight he did have with one eye. He and his

---

[70] The reference to football camps pertain to the annual, two-week preseason camps that the Lewis players attended. Coach Eddie Joyce began sending players to a secluded camp in 1961 and continued this tradition throughout the remainder of his fifteen seasons as the head coach.

THE SPARTAN SUCCESSION

wife, Grace, would take my wife, Fran, and Coach Joyce's wife, JoAn, to all the away games."[2095]

"He was also a member of the first Salem School Board and he and Jim Taliaferro were best of friends."[71, 2096]

* * *

Both King and Taliaferro would live long enough to see their efforts and commitments come to impressive fruition: not only an impressive football stadium but a host of other sports facilities that would be part and parcel of the pride of all that is Salem.

And with the aid of Foster's "dedications," the folks in Salem should never forget their huge impact and contributions.

---

[71] Both Taliaferro and King are deceased. Beginning with Taliaferro, his obituary was published in the *Roanoke Times* soon after he passed away. Some of its contents read as follows: "James Edward Taliaferro, Sr., of Salem, Virginia, passed away Saturday, August 3, 2002. He was born on February 12, 1936, in Wabun, Virginia. After attending Andrew Lewis High School, Jim served in the 101st Airborne as a paratrooper for three years. Following his time in the armed services, Jim worked for several years for the Norfolk and Western Railroad, and then became a salesman for the Shelton-Witt Equipment Company. In 1965, he formed Salem Contracting, Inc. with a partner and entered the construction business. Jim operated the company continuously until his death. He entered politics in 1972 by successfully winning election to the Salem City Council. Two years later, he was named mayor, a position he held for twenty-two years until 1996, the year of his retirement... In lieu of flowers, please make donations to the National D-Day Memorial...Bedford, Virginia...in honor of Jim and all our nation's veterans..."

[King] preceded Taliaferro in death. Known as BG, Burgess Garnett King, 76, "a lifelong resident of Salem, passed away Thursday, February 3, 2000. He was preceded in death by his wife Grace Baugess King...The family suggest memorial may be made to the Salem Sports Foundation, Salem Educational Foundation, or Salem Rescue Squad." Source: Electronic mail provided by Mr. Jonathan Stilwell, funeral director at John M. Oakey & Son Funeral Home and Crematory in Salem, Virginia.

SOURCES FOR THE SPARTAN SUCCESSION

Books used as sources include the following:

- *The Slanting Monster Defense in Football* by Dale Foster, published in 1970 by Parker Publishing Company Inc., West Nyack, NY.
- *The Team the Titans Remember* by Mark A. O'Connell, published in 2017 by Page Publishing, Inc., New York, NY.

As for yearbooks, I've used the last two editions of the *Pioneer* from Andrew Lewis High School and numerous editions of the *Laconian* from Salem High School. Some of those editions were found in the Logan Library of the Salem Museum.

As I reported in the previous publication, it would not have been possible to write the history of any team without the reliance upon the sports articles and game stories written by sportswriters for several newspapers. I believe that each article is duly credited (source, author, and date of publication). The Alderman Library at the University of Virginia is where Michell Capozzoli and I viewed voluminous editions of the *Roanoke World-News* and the *Roanoke Times*. She also reviewed the combined editions published as the *Roanoke Times & World-News*, which came into being in September of 1976 as a weekend edition.

After Ms. Capozzoli's relocation, I assumed that responsibility coupled with occasional reviews of several editions of the *Salem*

Times-Register, which I found either in the Virginia Room of the Roanoke City Library or at the Salem Museum.

The staff at the Alderman Library offered consistent and friendly assistance to ensure that I had access to the microfilm readers. This is true also for the staff at the Salem Museum and at the Virginia Room at the Roanoke County library. I conducted interviews with former coaches and players, and those are noted in the appropriate places.

The internet proved a valuable resource, and I included information from these websites:

- www.roanoke.com/sports/columns
- www.virginia-24e-lions.org
- www.lyricsmode.com
- www.fchs.wythe.k12.va.us
- Google Maps
- www.profootballhof.com
- www.careertrend.com
- www.songfacts.com
- www.johnoakey.com
- www.huskers.com
- www.hswv.postperfectonline.com
- www.thepeoplehistory.com
- www.bobborst.com
- www.vasportshof.com
- www.camdenmilitary.com
- www.britannica.com.
- www.findagrave.com.
- www.bing.com
- www.vhsl.org
- www.morgangriffith.house.gov
- www.wisek12.org
- www.salemtimes-register.com
- www.history.com.
- www.virginiapreps.com
- www.virginia.gov
- www.chancecrawford.org

- www.raycralle.com
- www.visitroanokeva.com
- www.amazon.com
- www.imdb.com
- www.amhistory.si.edu
- www.maxpreps.com
- www.gwfootball.com
- www.pcpatriot.com
- www.espn.com
- www.baseball-reference.com
- www.memorials.johnoakey.com
- www.saturdaydownsouth.com
- www.encylopediaofalabama.org

INDEX

A

Acree, Reid 157
Adams, David 231
Adams, Jerry 286
Agee, Steve 370
Allen, Bruce 162
Allen, Keith 203
Alls, Jay 87, 97
Andrews, M. Carl 121, 123, 424
Armstrong, Fred 152
Arnold, Dickie 318, 331
Avis Construction 366
Awad, Abraham 168

B

Baby Doll Award 35, 398
Bailey, Charles 40
Bailey, W. Perry Jr. 288
Baker, Scott 226
Ballentine, Jay 95
Ballou, Ernest W. 45
Barnard, Paul 191
Barnett, Robert Lee 49, 220
Barrett, Jeff 195
Bates, Carl 88, 96
Batten, Frank Jr. 438
Beach, Richard 40
Bean, Jimmy 278
Beckner, Tim 157
Belcher, Sharon Gale 303
Benson, Donnie 91
Berry, Lawrence 80
Bessell, Mark 201
Bevins, Ron 201, 219
Bier, Peggy 416
Bill Brown Field 320
Billys Barn 282
Bishop, Jim 167
Bland, Curtis 200, 219
Blankenship, Joe 201
Blomberg, Chris 96, 142, 147, 151, 156, 157, 158
Bogaczyk, Jack 75, 76, 420
Boitnott, Tim 330, 382, 384, 385, 386, 387
Boone, Herman 33
Boorman, Mark 430, 435
Booth, Donald 92
Bostian, Allen 88
Bradford, Vince 31
Bradley, Larry 310, 316, 336
Bradley, Lawrence 316
Brailey, Junior 79
Brammer, Steve 232
Brancati, Mike 50
Brancati, Vic 157
Braxton, Brad 389
Breakell Inc. 366, 391
Britts, Bill 70
Brock, Jay 195, 196, 198, 199

Brooks, Greg 218
Brooks, Larry 71
Brooks, Ralph 90, 93, 95, 97
Brubeck, William 263
Bruce, George 330, 351, 384
Bruce, Wayne 381
Brugh, Bobby 126
Bryant, Charlie 319, 328
Bryant, Mike 92
Burress, J. W. 389
Burton, Arnold 42, 238
Burton, Steve 157
Butcher, Jimmy 81

C

Caldwell, Clarence P. Jr. 256
Caldwell, Greg 277
Campbell, Earl 161
Campbell, Keith 157
Capozzoli, Michelle 12
Carr, Phil 150
Carter, Larry 380, 386, 387
Carter, Mike 89
Casey, Carey 178, 233
Catron, Billy 225, 232
Chamberlain, Jack 42, 180, 253, 258, 416, 423, 425, 432, 436, 442
Cheatwood, Charles 146
Childress, Dot 214
Childress, William 90
Chinault, Bud 305
Clark, Gary 200
Cline, R. S. 238
CMT sporting goods 43
Cody, Robert 281
Cole, Alan 197
Coleman, Mike 194
Collie, David 196, 199
Collie, Kevin 142, 156, 162, 166, 170
Collier, Benjie 164
Comer, Ben 346
Conner, Scott 79
Coombs, Fran 127, 424, 442

Cooper, Robert 272
Cosby, Frank A. 239, 241
Craig, James 387
Cralle, Ray 222
Crawford, Chance 163, 164, 169, 195, 196, 198, 199, 206, 208, 209, 210, 211, 215, 217, 220, 221, 267, 439
Crawford, Danielle C. 223
Crawford, Gary E. 212
Crawford, Janice 216
Crawford, Kelly 87, 88, 92, 95, 97
Crayton, Sam 388
Creative Construction and Development Corp. 366
Crenshaw, Donald 387, 388
Crist, David 374
Cromer, Jim 256
Crotty, Butch 90
Curry, Buddy 335

D

DAddurno, David 81
Dalton, John 56
Dame, Bobo 147, 149, 168
Daulton, Donald 37
Davidson, Geoff 195
Davis, Dale 157
Deal, Mike 96
Deane, Kim 218
Delaney, Shannon 306, 311
Dempsey, Timmy 372
Dewilde, Lyle 129
Dickey, Doug 395
Dillon, Jonathan 389
Dillon, Tony 216
Dishon, Tillow 318
Dooley, Hugh 274
Doughty, Doug 209, 437, 449, 455, 458
Dowe, Mike 209
Downey, Robert 265, 365, 446, 460
Draper, John 381

Drew, Dwayne 171
Dudley, Tim 323, 345, 346, 349, 350, 351, 352
Duffy, David 157
Dutton, Glenn 87, 91, 96, 141, 149, 157

E

Eanes, Chuck 83
Earp, James 263
East, Dean 89, 186
Eastrom, Kent 59
Echols, Steve 72
Edwards, Cecil 151
Edwards, J. R. 268
Edwards, Robert 167
Eichenberger, Bill 207, 437, 438
Ellis, Brian 318
Emick, Dudley J. 239
Ergle, William 244, 247, 249, 254, 259
Ertel, Carlton 197, 353
Eubank, Bryon 211

F

Farlow, Blake 200
Farris, Duane 79, 97, 125, 141, 142, 143, 146, 151, 158
Fencik, Gary 161
Ferguson, Brian 227, 274
Ferguson, Paul 318
Ferguson, Roger 164, 195
Ferrum College Field 325
Finley, Rickey 329
Finley, Terry 231, 279, 319, 328
Finnerty, John 142
Fisher, Jimmy 96, 150, 162, 164, 168
Fisher, Richard 215, 262, 357
Fisher, Scott 381
Foley, Alan 275
Foley, Randy 372, 389
Forbes, Lee 212

Ford, Robert 324
Foster, Dale 8, 11, 15, 17, 20, 49, 52, 65, 137, 142, 144, 151, 173, 176, 191, 193, 199, 208, 211, 240, 267, 268, 282, 294, 308, 332, 336, 365, 369, 395, 415, 425, 432, 437, 439, 449, 450, 465
Foster, Fran Firebaugh 397
Foster, Roy 394
Foster, Ruby Eller 394
Fourqurean, Larry 203
Fox, Pete 317
Fracker, Roger 232
Francisco, Joey 78, 92, 97
Frederick, Daniel 206
French, Greg 70, 73, 74, 77, 79, 80, 82, 105
Fulton, Tim 272, 321

G

Gainer, Merrill 49, 160, 172, 210, 304, 314, 351, 380
Galleo, Darrin 341
Garber, Elaine Estella 268
Garland, Bob 362
Garnett, Tom 326
Garrett, Bob 143
Garst, Rusty 162, 163, 166, 168, 169, 195, 199, 202, 210, 214, 216, 219, 220
Gaston, Harry 72, 73, 74, 78, 79, 80, 82, 85, 105
George, George 59, 85
Gilmore, Gary 71
Gladden, Kelly 157, 161, 171, 173
Glaspie, Enos 157
Gotchey, Bill 370
Graham, Chris 141, 145, 162
Graham, Ricky 226, 271
Graybill, Jack 291
Gray, Mike 318
Green, W. Mac 238

Gregory, Trey 318
Gresham, Jim 157
Gresham, Van 288
Griffith, Morgan 114, 120, 121
Gunter, Charlie 144, 160, 162, 168, 171, 172

H

Hall, Todd 195, 198, 199
Hall, Wayne 40
Hammersley, Charlie 11, 29, 38, 220, 282, 310, 353, 368, 449, 459
Hammerstrom, Dick 43, 416, 417, 426
Hammes, Charlie 165, 172, 320, 339, 340, 369, 375
Hankis, Lanksford 324
Harley, Robert 210
Harris, George 78
Harris, James 382
Harris, JoJo 276, 280, 318, 323, 324, 331, 336, 339, 340, 341, 342, 343, 344, 345, 348, 349, 369, 372, 373, 374, 375, 376, 377, 379, 381, 382, 383, 385, 388, 389
Harrison, Allen 162, 196
Harrison, David 318, 326
Harrison, Tommy 70
Harris, Russell 28, 317
Harris, Tim 217
Harvey, Jeff 170
Harvey, King 201, 218
Hawkins, Lorenzo 276
Hayes, Ralph 324
Hayocks, Gavin 271
Heller, Richard 318
Hensley, Dick 277
Henson, Bo 279
Herdman, Darwin 387
Hickam, Jim 96, 152, 157, 169, 201, 232, 330, 384
Hicks, Joel 203, 219, 277, 319, 327, 347, 350, 351
Hicks, T. J. 319
Highfill, Jeff 268
Hill, Mark 194
Hinkle, John 310, 316, 336
Hoback, Fred 40, 394
Hoback, Kirk 162
Hodge, Joe 170
Hodson, Randy 153
Hoffman, Brian 12, 78, 134, 142, 145, 151, 156, 160, 172, 178, 183, 195, 225, 283, 354, 357, 365, 368, 389
Hoffman, Randy 420, 422, 426, 429, 432, 434, 437, 440, 442, 453, 456, 459, 465
Holland, Tommy 230
Holliday, Todd 197
Hooker, Brian 96, 141, 142, 143, 149, 151, 154, 155, 157, 158, 317, 336
Hopkins, Charles 70, 72, 76, 77, 79, 80, 105
Hopkins, Herbert 262
Hopper, Jeff 126, 424
Horne, Brian 143, 158, 162, 166, 168
Hostetter, Butch 87, 88
Houchens, Robert 229
Houchin, Robert 353
Houston, Richard 198
Hudgins, Mike 156
Huffman, Neil 91
Hunt, Harold 384
Hunt, Walter A. 112
Hutchinson, Lynwood 318
Hyer, Steve 136, 213

I

Irvin, Robbie 70, 74, 77, 79, 80, 84, 85, 105
Ives, Mike 129, 425

J

Jackson, James 208, 227, 228, 231, 272, 280
James, Mark 196
Janoskie, Tony 214
Jefferson, Dennis 276
Jenkins, Derek 199
Jenkins, Dwayne 152
Jennings, Kurt 322
Johnson, Dickie 319, 328
Johnson, Hal Jr. 82, 89
Johnson, Sheldon 232
Jonas, Bill 83
Jones, Brian 275
Jones, Darryl 146, 167
Jones, David 218
Jones, Don 318
Jones, George 61
Jones, Paul 214
Jones, Sidney 213, 215, 267
Jones, Tim 320
Jones, Timmy 203
Jordan, Melinda 126, 424
Joyce, Charles 318
Joyce, Eddie 8, 11, 16, 18, 20, 24, 25, 27, 36, 39, 44, 49, 50, 54, 59, 64, 89, 100, 105, 135, 151, 166, 176, 177, 183, 187, 188, 191, 204, 209, 220, 237, 238, 256, 267, 273, 282, 283, 288, 293, 314, 338, 339, 351, 391, 398
Joyner, Lee 318, 331

K

Keister, Pat 318, 325, 326, 331, 337, 341, 342, 344, 349, 352
Keller, Ted 97
Kelly, Tony 164
Kerkhoff, Blair 270, 271, 273, 292, 293, 294, 440, 447, 449, 450, 455, 459
Keys, Greg 194
Kimbrough, Ron 319, 328, 331
Kimbrough, William 318, 322, 353
King, B. G. 115, 119, 177, 238, 398
Kinsey, Roy Jr. 217
Kinsey, Roy Sr. 112
Kinsey, Shane and Associates 112
Kinzer, Chris 231, 277, 279, 280, 281, 319
Kirby, Jack 358
Kirchner, Jimmy 157
Kreider, Kurt 71
Krupft, Chad 278
Kucer, Tom 91, 132, 133, 134, 135, 136, 137, 140, 141, 142, 143, 144, 145, 146, 147, 149, 150, 151, 152, 153, 154, 155, 156, 157, 161, 162, 164, 165, 166, 167, 168, 170, 174, 175, 176, 182, 186, 237, 291, 293, 314, 339, 425

L

Lambert, Joe 85
Lampros, John 42, 43, 45, 47, 48, 55, 58
Landreth, Rodney 347, 348, 387
Laury, Dennis 167
Lawrence, Jeff 162
Lawrence, Tony 201, 231
Lawson, Allen 324
Layne, David 157, 158
Lee, Don 73, 89
Lee, Jeff 372
Lee, Larry 95
Leftwich, John 126
Lewis, Kenny 335
Lewis, Robert 350
Lewis, Ronnie 232
Light, David 94, 95, 162, 165, 229, 231
Light, Larry 226, 230
Lilly, Tony 166, 197

Lineburg, Norman 183, 387
Lipscomb, Robert 136, 174, 264, 291, 292, 297, 309
Long, June 246
Love, Larry 225, 353
Lowery, Brent 350

M

Mackey, Chico 88
Majors, Robert 350, 352
Mallis, Jimmy 275
Manns, D. D. 275
Manuel, Robey 95
Markham, Kevin 276
Marrazzo, Larry 70
Martin, Dean 74, 91
Martin, Kirk 163
Martin, Roger 270
Martin, Waymon 320
Mayes, Daryl 229
Mayo, Archie 145
McBride, Oliver 213
McClelland, Jeff 201
McCrary, Nick 387
McGillamy, John 210
McGregor, John 89, 137, 209, 232, 273
McLelland, Bob 23, 24, 37, 49, 70, 73, 90, 95, 96, 120, 133, 134, 136, 137, 140, 141, 143, 154, 174, 182, 183, 186, 189, 191, 192, 193, 217, 415, 417, 419, 420, 421, 422, 423, 425, 426, 428, 432, 433, 434, 441
Meadows, Johnny 349, 372, 377, 379, 381, 389
Meredith, Randy 382
Miles, Billy Jr. 9, 59, 225, 273, 282, 309, 310, 316, 317, 323, 325, 336, 452
Miley, Dick 394
Miller, George 59
Miller, Gus 230

Milton, Lynn 78
Mitchell, Buddy 147
Moles, Kelly 88
Montgomery, John 285
Moore, Doug 318
Moore, John 246, 285
Moore, Shawn 387
Morgan, Richard 271, 274, 277
Morgan, Travis 208
Morris, Frank 322, 337, 341, 377
Morris, Marvin 337, 346, 372, 389
Mountcastle, Steve 94
Mountcasttle, Tommy 143, 151
Moyer, James 180, 188
Mullins, Steve 358
Mumper, Matt 218
Murphy, David 317
Murphy, Terry 222
Muscaro, Jim 84
Mutter, Price 141, 150, 157, 158
Myers, Billy 231, 279

N

Natt, Edward A. 127
Neal, Lewis 78, 84
Neese, Greg 154, 171, 173, 201
Neese, Vernon 70
Nester, Paul 89, 90, 157
Nichols, Perry 70, 71, 72, 73, 74, 76, 77, 78, 79, 80, 82, 84, 85, 87, 105
Nickens, Harry 358
Noftsinger, Dabo 74
Nowlin, Gary 318
Nowlin, Melvin 157, 158
Nuckolls, Will 272

O

Oakes, Don 73, 80, 82, 83, 185, 191
Obenchain, E. B. 274
ODell, Nathan 321
Oliver, Steve 310, 316, 325, 336

Olverson, Randy 170
Ondrus, Tooey 372, 373, 374, 375, 376, 377, 379, 380, 382, 384, 385
ONeill, Brian 361, 363, 460
OQuinn, James 318, 323, 325, 328, 329, 342, 346, 349
Oshust, James F. 359
Otey, Eddie 96, 155, 156, 157
Ouellette, Mike 330
Overfelt, Mark 226
Overstreet, Tim 232
Overton, Billy 168

P

Pace, John 91
Packett, Howard 288
Packett, John 317
Page, Paul 277
Palmer, Bruce 59
Parker, Scott 152
Parrett, John 81
Paxton, David 89
Paxton, William 238, 359, 360
Peacock, Steve 129, 216
Peck, Ralph 143, 157
Peery, Jay 144
Pellant, Eric 324, 325, 326, 331
Pence, Wilbur 111
PEPPER 119
Phelps, Gary 163
Phillips, Charles B. 43
Phipps, Kevin 318, 319, 320, 321, 322, 323, 324, 326, 328, 329, 331, 336, 337, 338, 339, 340, 341, 342, 343, 344, 346, 347, 348, 349, 351, 352, 369, 372, 373, 374, 375, 376, 377, 378, 379, 380, 382, 384, 385, 386, 387, 388, 389
Phlegar, Richard 228
Pickle, Bobby 226
Pickle, Mike 94, 97, 141, 143, 150, 157, 158
Plank, Doug 161
Plunkett, Randy 232, 280
Poff, Benjie 92
Poindexter, Mark 344, 379
Price, Billy 211
Pugh, Alger 37, 281, 334, 351
Purcell, Wayne 374
Purdue, Kevin 87, 97
Putt, Cap 230

R

Reaser, Dennis 136
Redding, Dave 164
Reed, Eddie 50, 77
Reed, Mickey 70, 77, 105
Revercomb, Randy 81
Reynolds, Clarence 80
Rhodes, Barry 142, 146, 152, 164
Richards, Bob 268
Richards, Carl Jr. 267, 270, 271, 275, 282, 287, 288, 291, 292, 295, 309, 314, 317, 339
Richardson, Price 221
Riddle, Tommy 230
Riley, Eddie 226, 227, 229, 233, 276, 281, 321
Riley, Edwina 288
Riley, James 318, 323, 325, 326
Ripley, Paul 59
Roadcap, Jerry 198
Roberts, Bryan 153
Robertson, Jeff 217
Robertson, Mike 72
Robinson, Churchill 81
Robinson, Darryl 209
Robinson, Rodney 324
Robrecht, Ray 56, 57, 358
Rosborough, Darryl 322
Rosenthal, David 443
Ross, Donnell 91, 149
Rotanz, Bob 358
Roth, Tom 142

Rowland, Randy 163
Russo, Don 60, 89

S

Salem Planning Commission 238, 360
SALT 114, 115, 117, 119, 126
Sample, Billy 27
Sampson, Mike 207
Sanders, Bernie 277
Saunders, Jack 95
Sayres, Melinda 126
Scarangella, Dave 436
Scharnus, Jerry 335
Scott, Mike 226
Scott, R. J. 212, 229
Sease, Jody 225, 233
Semones, Howard 177
Shaw, Billy C. 52
Shelton, Glenn 325
Sheppard, Chris 274
Shue, Ronnie 74
Simmons, Jay 207
Sinkler, William 375, 389
Sisson, Jeff 214
Slanting Monster Defense 18, 35, 282, 395, 396, 415
Slusher, Kevin 370
Smart, David 374
Smith, Alex 446
Smith, Arthur 45
Smith, Dan 50, 75, 77, 80, 94, 125, 134, 417, 419, 420, 421, 424
Smith, Eddie 325
Smith, F. LaGard 55, 417
Smith, Fred 89
Smith, Jay 208
Smith, Larry 70, 72, 73, 74, 76, 77, 78, 80, 82, 83, 84, 104, 105
Smith, Martha 263
Smith, Randy 196, 200
Smith, Sherrill 358
Smith, Todd 318, 389
Snyder, William G. 136

Spartan Bell Award 353
Spradlin, Grady 318, 331
Sprinkle, Grant 95
Stamus, Tony 93, 422
Staples, Aaron 324, 377, 378
Statum, Heywood 375
St. Clair, Shane 105, 346, 348, 349
Stebbins, Charles 44, 416, 423, 443, 444
Steede, Warren 166
Stephens, Jerome 387
Stevens, Brian 67, 90, 91, 93, 94, 96, 143, 163, 166, 167, 169, 171, 172, 173, 195
Stevens, Mike 16, 62, 64, 65, 74, 84, 97, 100, 134, 191, 293, 311, 314, 339, 391, 418, 423, 425
Stevenson, Ralph 152, 153, 157
Stevens, Sharon Littreal 67, 135
Stevens, Todd 67, 226, 272
Stickney, Red 59, 171, 172, 183, 198
Stratton, Robert 226
Summers, Deke 47, 52, 59
Summers, George Jr. 39
Sumpter, Bert 389
Surber, Roger 59, 209
Sutphin, Tim 278, 318, 325, 331, 353

T

Taborn, Tony 232
Tait, Mike 226
Taliaferro, Curtis 226, 227, 229, 230, 232, 233, 365
Taliaferro, James 180, 246
Taliaferro, Rixine 397
Talley, David 210
Tarpley, Carl E. Jr. 238
Tarpley, Ned 88, 90, 91, 92, 93, 94, 96, 125, 142, 157
Tate, Bob 84, 193
Taylor, Bobby 230
Taylor, Henry 226
Teitlebaum, Bob 59, 85, 177, 206,

207, 277, 339, 369, 380, 436,
448, 453, 455, 456, 457, 458,
459, 461, 462, 463, 464, 465
The Oracle 370
Thomas, Davey 389
Thomas, Kent 224
Thomas, Mark 377
Thompson, Blair 198, 208, 211
Thompson, Blanche Boyd 184
Thompson, Drew 318
Thompson, Ernest 184
Thompson, Harriett 184
Thompson, Jimmy 208, 214
Thompson, John Wallace 184
Thompson, Wallace 82, 83, 188, 191,
194, 201, 206, 209, 213, 227,
231, 232, 233, 238, 266, 291,
293, 314, 339, 398, 433, 446
Thor Inc. 366
Thornhill, Glenn 252
Timberlake, Otis 75, 91, 137
Tingler, Malcolm 220, 221
Tolliver, Arthur 167
Tota, Frank 287, 312
Towler, Zach 89, 143, 150, 156
Trail, Curtis 201
Trammell, Gene 221
Trent, Richard 46
Turk, Frank 363
Turner, David 167
Turner, Jack 319, 350
Turner, Jeff 230
Turner, Steve 90, 143, 157, 158
Turpin, Brian 279
Tyree, Dale 70, 76, 87, 90, 97

U

Unitas, Johnny 299

V

Valvano, Jim 314
Varney, Rodney 209, 211, 214, 225,
226, 229, 230, 232, 233, 275,
276, 365
Vaughan, Rob 318, 387, 389
Venable, Timmy 154
Viars, Ted 173, 195, 196, 197, 200,
203
Virginia Hunters 59

W

Wade, Ruth 176
Walker, John 199
Wall, Greg 386
Ward, Darrell 203
Warren, Bill 317
Waskey, Stephen 388
Webb, Mike 151, 156
Weeks, Dale 150, 160, 164, 197, 198,
203, 353
Weeks, David 70, 72
Weinbarger, Jerry 208
Wesley, Greg 207
Wheeling, Danny 84, 142, 193, 225,
310, 317, 336
White, Joe 149
White, JoJo 320
White, Macel Jordan 297
White, Willis 8, 18, 160, 172, 210,
277, 291, 292, 295, 296, 308,
309, 314, 316, 322, 324, 326,
329, 332, 334, 338, 339, 349,
351, 369, 374, 376, 379, 380,
391, 398, 450, 451, 459, 465
Wigginton, Don 377
Wiley, Allan 320, 321, 323
Williams, Barry D. 368
Williams, Bobby 70, 105
Williams, Mark 76, 87, 88, 91, 97
Willis, David 81
Wills, Larry 341, 389
Wilson, Bayes 42, 128, 133, 148, 233,
240, 249, 254, 255, 257, 262,
265, 270
Wingfield, Mark 96, 170

Winter, Bill 59, 63, 84, 142
Wiseman, Tim 207
Withers, Bo 230
Witt, John 56, 57, 58, 215, 399, 418, 438
Woodrell, John 352
Woodrum, Allan 143
Woolwine, Dickie 95
Word, Barry 196
Wright, Alan 163, 167, 169

Y

Young, Anthony 154
Young, Cam 271, 274, 275, 276, 278, 318, 319, 321, 322, 324, 325, 326, 328, 329, 330, 331, 336, 337, 339, 340, 341, 342, 343, 344, 345, 348, 349, 351, 352
Young, Carl 375, 389
Young, Chuck 226
Yuhas, Marty 310, 317, 336

Z

Zelazny, Lucian 387

NOTES

Chapter 1: The Last Years of Joyce

Part 1: Cementing a Legacy

1. *The Pioneer*, Andrew Lewis High School yearbook for the year 1973.
2. From the records chronicled in *The Team the Titans Remember*, published by Page Publishing Co. in 2017, by Mark A. O'Connell.
3. *The Pioneer*, Andrew Lewis High School yearbook for the year 1973.
4. *The Pioneer*, Andrew Lewis High School yearbook for the year 1974.
5. *The Pioneer*, Andrew Lewis High School yearbook for the year 1975.
6. Bob McLelland, *Roanoke Times & World-News (RTWN)*, unspecified date in 1974.
7. Written article authored, modified, and revised on several occasions by Dale Foster and provided by electronic email.
8. Dale Foster, *The Slanting Monster Defense in Football* (New York: Parker Publishing Company Inc., 1970).
9. Written article by Foster and provided by electronic mail.
10. Ibid.
11. O'Connell, *The Team the Titans Remember* (New York: Page Publishing Inc., 2017).

Part 2: The Fall from Grace

12. Personal interview with Dale Foster on January 5, 2018.
13. Personal interview with George Summers on February 11, 2018.
14. Ibid.
15. Ibid.
16. Ibid.
17. Ibid.
18. Football program for the Sandlot Benefit Game, published on September 23, 1960.
19. Personal interview with Summers on February 11, 2018.
20. Ibid.

21. Ibid.
22. Ibid.
23. Ibid.
24. Ibid.
25. Ibid.
26. Jack Chamberlain, *Roanoke Times & World-News (RTWN)*, August 15, 1974.
27. Ibid.
28. Ibid.
29. Ibid.
30. Ibid.
31. Ibid.
32. Ibid.
33. Ibid.
34. Ibid.
35. Ibid.
36. Ibid.
37. Ibid.
38. Ibid.
39. Ibid.
40. Ibid.
41. Ibid.
42. Dick Hammerstrom, *RTWN,* August 15, 1974.
43. Ibid.
44. Ibid.
45. Ibid.
46. Charles Stebbins, *RTWN,* August 16, 1974.
47. Ibid.
48. Ibid.
49. Ibid.
50. Hammerstom, *RTWN,* August 7, 1975.
51. Ibid.
52. Hammerstrom, *RTWN,* August 27, 1975.
53. Ibid.
54. Ibid.
55. Hammerstrom and Peggy Bier, *RTWN,* August 28, 1975.
56. Ibid.
57. Ibid.
58. Ibid.
59. Ibid.
60. Ibid.
61. Ibid.
62. Ibid.
63. Ibid.

64. Personal interview with Summers on February 11, 2018.
65. Hammerstrom and Bier, *RTWN*, August 29, 1975.
66. Ibid.
67. Ibid.
68. Ibid.
69. Ibid.
70. Hammerstrom and Bier, *RTWN*, August 30, 1975.
71. Ibid.
72. Ibid.
73. Ibid.
74. Ibid.
75. Unnamed author, *RTWN*, August 29, 1975.
76. Bob McLelland, *RTWN*, November 15, 1974.
77. Ibid.
78. Ibid.
79. Ibid.
80. Ibid.
81. Dan Smith, *RTWN*, exact date unknown.
82. Ibid.
83. Ibid.
84. Personal interview with Summers on February 11, 2018.
85. Ibid.
86. Unnamed author, *RTWN*, September 11, 1975.
87. Hammerstrom, *RTWN*, September 30, 1975.
88. Ibid.
89. Ibid.
90. Ibid.
91. Unnamed author, *RTWN*, December 19, 1975.
92. Unnamed author, *RTWN*, January 1, 1976.
93. Personal interview with Summers on February 11, 2018.
94. Ibid.
95. Ibid.
96. Ibid.
97. Ibid.
98. Ibid.
99. Ibid.
100. Ibid.
101. Ibid.
102. Ibid.
103. Ibid.
104. F. LaGard Smith, *The Daily Bible* (Oregon: Harvest House Publishers, 1984), 672.
105. Unnamed author, *RTWN*, July 9, 1976.

106. John Witt, *RTWN,* January 9, 1979.
107. Ibid.
108. Ibid.
109. Ibid.
110. Ibid.
111. Senate Document No. 2, January 6, 1979, to January 9, 1980.
112. Witt, *RTWN,* April 3, 1979.
113. Personal interview with Summers on February 11, 2018.
114. Ibid.
115. Ibid.
116. *The Team the Titans Remember,* page 726.

Chapter 2: A Legend's Successor

Part 1: Extra Large Shoes to Fill

117. www.metrolyrics.com.
118. Personal interview with George Summers on February 11, 2018.
119. Ibid.
120. Ibid.
121. Ibid.
122. Ibid.
123. Ibid.
124. Ibid.
125. Ibid.
126. Ibid.
127. Ibid.
128. Ibid.
129. Ibid.
130. Ibid.
131. www.thepeoplehistory.com.
132. www.famousbirthdays.com.
133. www.boborst.com.
134. Ibid.
135. Personal interview with Mike Stevens on April 6, 2018.
136. Ibid.
137. Ibid.
138. Unnamed author, *RTWN,* September 29, 1961, and personal interview with Stevens on April 6, 2018.
139. Unnamed author, *RTWN,* September 29, 1961.
140. Personal interview with Stevens on April 6, 2018.
141. Ibid.
142. Ibid.
143. Ibid.

144. Ibid.
145. Ibid.
146. Ibid.
147. Ibid.
148. Ibid.
149. Ibid.
150. Ibid.

Part 2: 1975

151. Bob McLelland, *RTWN*, August 28, 1975.
152. Ibid.
153. Ibid.
154. Ibid.
155. Ibid.
156. Ibid.
157. Ibid.
158. Unnamed author, *RTWN*, September 9, 1975.
159. Ibid.
160. Ibid.
161. Ibid.
162. Unnamed author, *RTWN*, September 13, 1975.
163. Ibid.
164. Ibid.
165. Ibid.
166. Ibid.
167. Dan Smith, *RTWN*, September 20, 1975.
168. Ibid.
169. Ibid.
170. Ibid.
171. Ibid.
172. Ibid.
173. Ibid.
174. Bob McLelland, *RTWN*, September 25, 1975.
175. Ibid.
176. Ibid.
177. Ibid.
178. Ibid.
179. Unnamed author, *RTWN*, October 4, 1975.
180. Ibid.
181. Ibid.
182. Unnamed author, *RTWN*, October 7, 1975.
183. Ibid.

184. Ibid.
185. Ibid.
186. Dan Smith, *RTWN*, October 9, 1975.
187. Ibid.
188. Ibid.
189. Jack Bogaczyk, *RTWN*, October 11, 1975.
190. Ibid.
191. Ibid.
192. Dan Smith, *RTWN*, November 15, 1975.
193. David Heath, Andrew Lewis High School class of 1973.
194. Smith, *RTWN*, November 15, 1975.
195. Ibid.
196. Ibid.
197. Ibid.
198. Unnamed author, *RTWN*, October 20, 1975.
199. Ibid.
200. Brian Hoffman, *Salem Times-Register (STR)*, October 23, 1975.
201. Ibid.
202. Ibid.
203. Ibid.
204. Smith, *RTWN*, October 25, 1975.
205. Ibid.
206. Ibid.
207. Ibid.
208. Ibid.
209. Smith, *RTWN*, November 1, 1975.
210. Ibid.
211. Ibid.
212. Ibid.
213. Ibid.
214. Ibid.
215. Ibid.
216. Ibid.
217. Ibid.
218. Ibid.
219. Ibid.
220. Ibid.
221. McLelland, *RTWN*, November 7, 1975.
222. Ibid.
223. Smith, *RTWN*, November 15, 1975.
224. Ibid.
225. Ibid.
226. Smith, *RTWN*, November 8, 1975.

227. Ibid.
228. Ibid.
229. Unnamed author, RTWN, November 11, 1975.
230. Ibid.
231. Ibid.
232. Unnamed author, *RTWN*, November 14, 1975.
233. Ibid.
234. Ibid.
235. Unnamed author, *RTWN*, November 15, 1975.
236. Ibid.
237. Virginia High School League (VHSL) record book, page 29.
238. McLelland, *RTWN*, November 27, 1975.
239. Ibid.
240. Ibid.
241. BobTeitlebaum, *RTWN*, November 27, 1975.
242. Ibid.

Part 3: The Last Wolverines (1976)

243. Bob McLelland, *RTWN*, August 30, 1976.
244. Ibid.
245. Ibid.
246. Ibid.
247. Ibid.
248. Ibid.
249. Unnamed author, *RTWN*, September 4, 1976.
250. Ibid.
251. Ibid.
252. Ibid.
253. John Markon, *RTWN*, September 11, 1976.
254. Ibid.
255. McLelland, *RTWN*, September 18, 1976.
256. Ibid.
257. Ibid.
258. Ibid.
259. Dan Smith, *RTWN*, September 22, 1976.
260. Ibid.
261. Ibid.
262. Ibid.
263. Ibid.
264. Mark A. O'Connell, *The Team the Titans Remember*, page 510.
265. McLelland, *RTWN*, September 25, 1976.
266. Ibid.

267. Ibid.
268. Ibid.
269. Ibid.
270. Ibid.
271. Ibid.
272. Ibid.
273. Ibid.
274. McLelland, *RTWN*, September 30, 1976.
275. Ibid.
276. Brian Hoffman, *STR*, October 7, 1976.
277. Ibid.
278. Ibid.
279. Ibid.
280. Hoffman, *STR*, October 14, 1976.
281. Ibid.
282. Ibid.
283. Ibid.
284. Ibid.
285. Ibid.
286. Ibid.
287. Ibid.
288. Ibid.
289. Tony Stamus, *RTWN*, October 16, 1976.
290. Ibid.
291. Ibid.
292. Ibid.
293. Ibid.
294. Smith, *RTWN*, October 23, 1976.
295. Ibid.
296. Ibid.
297. Ibid.
298. Ibid.
299. Ibid.
300. Ibid.
301. Hoffman, *STR*, November 4, 1976.
302. Ibid.
303. McLelland, *RTWN*, November 3, 1976.
304. Ibid.
305. McLelland, *RTWN*, November 5, 1976.
306. Ibid.
307. Ibid.
308. Ibid.
309. Ibid.

310. Ibid.
311. McLelland, *RTWN*, November 16, 1976.
312. Ibid.
313. Ibid.
314. McLelland, *RTWN*, November 23, 1976.
315. Ibid.
316. McLelland, *RTWN*, December 6, 1976.
317. Ibid.
318. Ibid.
319. McLelland, *RTWN*, May 3, 1977.
320. Unnamed author, *RTWN*, June 8, 1977.
321. Personal interview with Mike Stevens on February 11, 2018.
322. Ibid.
323. Ibid.
324. Ibid.
325. Ibid.

Chapter 3: Fire Left

326. The entire contents of this chapter taken from an article written by Charles Equi and provided to this author via electronic mail.

Chapter 4: One Tribe of Salemites

Part 1: The Resistance

327. Charles Stebbins, *Roanoke Times & World-News (RTWN)*, October 1, 1974.
328. Ibid.
329. Jack Chamberlain, *RTWN*, October 9, 1974.
330. Ibid.
331. Letter to the editor, *RTWN*, November 5, 1975.
332. Ibid.
333. Ibid.
334. Ibid.
335. Ibid.
336. Unnamed author, *RTWN*, November 7, 1975.
337. Ibid.
338. Ibid.
339. Ibid.
340. Ibid.
341. Ibid.
342. Ibid.
343. Ibid.
344. Ibid.

345. Letter to the editor, *RTWN*, November 12, 1975.
346. Ibid.
347. Ibid.
348. Ibid.
349. Letter to the editor, *RTWN*, November 13, 1975.
350. Ibid.
351. Letter to the editor, *RTWN*, November 15, 1978.
352. Ibid.
353. Ibid.
354. Ibid.
355. Ibid.
356. Letter to the editor, *RTWN*, November 15, 1975.
357. Ibid.
358. Ibid.
359. Weekly Forum Section of *The Roanoke World-News*, November 20, 1975.
360. Letter to the editor, *Roanoke World-News (RWN)*, November 21, 1975.
361. Ibid.
362. Unnamed author, *RWN*, January 14, 1976.
363. Ibid.
364. Ibid.
365. Ibid.
366. Ibid.
367. Unnamed author, *RWN*, February 10, 1976.
368. M. Carl Andrews, *RWN*, July 9, 1976.
369. Ibid.
370. Letter to the editor, *RWN*, July 14, 1976.

Part 2: We Shall Be One
371. Dan Smith, *Roanoke Times (RT)*, October 20, 1976.
372. Ibid.
373. Jeff Hopper and Melinda Jordan, *Roanoke Times & World-News (RTWN)*, June 8, 1977.
374. Ibid.
375. Ibid.
376. Ibid.
377. Ibid.
378. Fran Coombs, *RTWN*, June 24, 1977.
379. Ibid.
380. Unnamed author, *RTWN*, June 28, 1977.
381. Ibid.
382. Ibid.
383. Ibid.
384. Ibid.

385. Jack Chamberlain, *RTWN*, August 5, 1977.
386. Ibid.
387. Chamberlain, *RT*, August 29, 1977.
388. Ibid.
389. Ibid.
390. Mike Ives, *RTWN*, September 1, 1978.
391. Ibid.
392. Ibid.
393. Ibid.
394. Ibid.
395. Ibid.

Chapter 5: Kucer Named King of the Spartans

396. Bob McLelland, *Roanoke World-News (RWN)*, January 20, 1977.
397. Ibid.
398. Ibid.
399. Ibid.
400. Ibid.
401. Ibid.
402. Ibid.
403. Ibid.
404. McLelland, *RWN*, January 20, 1977.
405. Personal interview with Mike Stevens on February 11, 2018.
406. Ibid.
407. Ibid.
408. Ibid.
409. Ibid.
410. Ibid.
411. Ibid.
412. Ibid.
413. Ibid.
414. Ibid.
415. McLelland, *RWN*, January 20, 1977.
416. Ibid.
417. From one of several personal interviews with Dale Foster.
418. Ibid.
419. McLelland, *RWN*, March 1, 1977.
420. Ibid.
421. Ibid.
422. Ibid.
423. Ibid.

Chapter 6: The First Two Battle Waves

Part 1: 1977

424. Bob McLelland, *Roanoke Times & World-News (RTWN)*, August 9, 1977.
425. Ibid.
426. Ibid.
427. Ibid.
428. Dick Hammerstrom, *RTWN*, August 8, 1977.
429. McLelland, *RTWN*, August 23, 1977.
430. Ibid.
431. Ibid.
432. Ibid.
433. Brian Hoffman, *Salem Times-Register (STR)*, August 11, 1977.
434. Hoffman, *STR*, September 1, 1977.
435. Hoffman, *STR*, September 8, 1977.
436. Ibid.
437. Ibid.
438. Ibid.
439. Ibid.
440. McLelland, *RTWN*, September 8, 1977.
441. Ibid.
442. Ibid.
443. Ibid.
444. Ibid.
445. Hoffman, *STR*, September 15, 1977.
446. Ibid.
447. Ibid.
448. Ibid.
449. Ibid.
450. Ibid.
451. Ibid.
452. Ibid.
453. Ibid.
454. Ibid.
455. Ibid.
456. Unnamed author, *RTWN*, September 16, 1977.
457. Ibid.
458. Ibid.
459. Ibid.
460. Ibid.
461. Hoffman, *STR*, September 20, 1977.
462. Ibid.
463. Ibid.

464. Ibid.
465. Ibid.
466. Ibid.
467. Ibid.
468. Unnamed author, *RTWN*, September 20, 1977.
469. Ibid.
470. Hoffman, *STR*, September 27, 1977.
471. Ibid.
472. Ibid.
473. Ibid.
474. Ibid.
475. Ibid.
476. Ibid.
477. Ibid.
478. Ibid.
479. Ibid.
480. Unnamed author, *RTWN*, October 6, 1977.
481. Ibid.
482. Comedian Bill Engvall's Debut Comedy Album, Warner Brothers, 1996.
483. Unnamed author, *RTWN*, October 10, 1977.
484. Ibid.
485. Unnamed author, *RTWN*, September 30, 1977.
486. Ibid.
487. Ibid.
488. Ibid.
489. Ibid.
490. Hoffman, *STR*, October 13, 1977.
491. Ibid.
492. Ibid.
493. Ibid.
494. Ibid.
495. Ibid.
496. Ibid.
497. Ibid.
498. Ibid.
499. Ibid.
500. Ibid.
501. Ibid.
502. Ibid.
503. Hoffman, *STR*, October 20, 1977.
504. Ibid.
505. Ibid.
506. Ibid.

507. Ibid.
508. Ibid.
509. Unnamed author, *RTWN*, October 18, 1977.
510. Ibid.
511. Ibid.
512. Ibid.
513. Hoffman, *STR*, October 27, 1977.
514. Ibid.
515. Ibid.
516. Ibid.
517. Ibid.
518. Ibid.
519. Ibid.
520. Ibid.
521. Ibid.
522. Ibid.
523. Ibid.
524. Hoffman, *STR*, November 3, 1977.
525. Ibid.
526. Ibid.
527. Ibid.
528. Ibid.
529. Unnamed author, *RTWN*, November 1, 1977.
530. Ibid.
531. Ibid.
532. McLelland, *RTWN*, November 4, 1977.
533. Ibid.
534. Ibid.
535. Ibid.
536. Ibid.
537. Ibid.
538. Ibid.
539. Ibid.
540. Hoffman, *STR*, November 10, 1977.
541. Ibid.
542. Ibid.
543. Ibid.
544. Ibid.
545. Ibid.
546. Ibid.
547. Ibid.
548. Ibid.
549. Ibid.

550. Unnamed author, *RTWN*, November 22, 1977.
551. Ibid.
552. Ibid.
553. Ibid.
554. Ibid.
555. Hoffman, *STR*, December 8, 1977.

Part 2: 1978
556. Unnamed author, *Roanoke Times & World-News (RTWN)*, September 1, 1978.
557. Ibid.
558. Brian Hoffman, *Salem Times-Register (STR)*, August 31, 1978.
559. Ibid.
560. Ibid.
561. Ibid.
562. Ibid.
563. Ibid.
564. Ibid.
565. Ibid.
566. Ibid.
567. Ibid.
568. Ibid.
569. Ibid.
570. Ibid.
571. Ibid.
572. Ibid.
573. Ibid.
574. Hoffman, *STR*, September 7, 1978.
575. Ibid.
576. Ibid.
577. Unnamed author, *RTWN*, September 8, 1978.
578. Ibid.
579. Hoffman, *STR*, September 14, 1978.
580. Ibid.
581. Ibid.
582. Ibid.
583. Hoffman, *STR*, September 21, 1978.
584. Ibid.
585. Ibid.
586. Ibid.
587. Ibid.
588. Ibid.
589. Hoffman, *STR*, September 28, 1978.

590. Ibid.
591. Ibid.
592. Ibid.
593. Ibid.
594. Unnamed author, *RTWN*, September 26, 1978.
595. Hoffman, *STR*, October 5, 1978.
596. Ibid.
597. Ibid.
598. Ibid.
599. Ibid.
600. Mark Boorman, *RTWN*, October 6, 1978.
601. Ibid.
602. Ibid.
603. Hoffman, *STR*, October 12, 1978.
604. Ibid.
605. Ibid.
606. Ibid.
607. Ibid.
608. Ibid.
609. Ibid.
610. Unnamed author, *RTWN*, October 10, 1978.
611. Ibid.
612. Ibid.
613. Ibid.
614. Hoffman, *STR*, October 19, 1978.
615. Ibid.
616. Ibid.
617. Ibid.
618. Unnamed author, *RTWN*, October 17, 1978.
619. Ibid.
620. Ibid.
621. Hoffman, *STR*, October 26, 1978.
622. Ibid.
623. Ibid.
624. Ibid.
625. Ibid.
626. Ibid.
627. Ibid.
628. Boorman, *RTWN*, October 27, 1978.
629. Ibid.
630. Ibid.
631. Ibid.
632. Ibid.

633. Ibid.
634. Ibid.
635. Ibid.
636. Hoffman, *STR*, November 2, 1978.
637. Ibid.
638. Ibid.
639. Ibid.
640. Ibid.
641. Ibid.
642. Ibid.
643. Hoffman, *STR*, November 9, 1978.
644. Ibid.
645. Ibid.
646. Ibid.
647. Ibid.
648. Ibid.
649. Ibid.
650. Unnamed author, *RTWN*, November 21, 1978.
651. Ibid.
652. Unnamed author, *RTWN*, April 24, 1979.
653. Unnamed author, *RTWN*, November 21, 1978.
654. Ibid.
655. Ibid.
656. Ibid.
657. Ibid.
658. Ibid.
659. Ibid.
660. Ibid.
661. Ibid.
662. Ibid.
663. Ibid.
664. Ibid.
665. Ibid.
666. Hoffman, *STR*, November 23, 1978.
667. Ibid.
668. Ibid.
669. Ibid.
670. Ibid.
671. Ibid.
672. Ibid.
673. Ibid.
674. Ibid.
675. Ibid.

676. Ibid.
677. Bob McLelland, *RTWN*, April 3, 1979.
678. Ibid.
679. Ibid.

Chapter 7: Can Thompson Rally the Spartans?

680. Steve Haner, *Roanoke Times & World-News (RTWN)*, April 20, 1979.
681. Ibid.
682. Ibid.
683. Brian Hoffman, *Salem Times-Register (STR)*, 1979, exact edition not known.
684. Ibid.
685. Ibid.
686. Ibid.
687. Ibid.
688. Ibid.
689. Ibid.
690. Haner, *RTWN*, April 20, 1979.
691. Ibid.
692. Jack Chamberlain, *RTWN*, May 4, 1979.
693. Ibid.
694. Ibid.
695. Ibid.
696. Chamberlain, *RTWN*, May 24, 1979.
697. Ibid.
698. Ibid.
699. Ibid.
700. Chamberlain, *RTWN*, May 25, 1979.
701. Ibid.
702. Ibid.
703. Ibid.
704. Ibid.
705. Personal interview with Dale Foster.
706. Margie Fisher, *RTWN*, June 28, 1979.
707. Personal interview with Dale Foster.
708. Ibid.
709. Ibid.
710. Bob McLelland, *RTWN*, May 31, 1979.
711. Ibid.
712. Hoffman, *STR*, May 24, 1979
713. Ibid.
714. Chamberlain, *RTWN*, June 19, 1979.
715. Hoffman, *STR*, June 7, 1979.

716. Personal interview with Wallace Thompson by telephone on March 14, 2018.
717. Ibid.
718. Ibid.
719. Ibid.
720. Ibid.
721. Ibid.
722. Ibid.
723. Ibid.
724. Ibid.
725. Ibid.
726. Ibid.
727. Ibid.
728. Ibid.
729. Ibid.
730. Ibid.
731. Ibid.
732. Ibid.
733. Ibid.
734. Ibid.
735. Mark A. O'Connell, *The Team the Titans Remember* (New York, New York: Page Publishing Co., 2017), and personal interview with Thompson on March 14, 2018.
736. O'Connell, *The Team the Titans Remember*.
737. Personal interview with Thompson.
738. Ibid.
739. Ibid.
740. McLelland, *RTWN*, June 1, 1979.
741. Ibid.
742. Ibid.
743. Ibid.
744. Chamberlain, *RTWN*, June 1, 1979.
745. Ibid.
746. Ibid.
747. Ibid.
748. Ibid.
749. Ibid.
750. Ibid.
751. Ibid.
752. Ibid.
753. Ibid.
754. Ibid.
755. Ibid.

756. Ibid.
757. Ibid.
758. McLelland, *RTWN*, June 1, 1979.

Chapter 8: His Trio

Part 1: The Beleaguered (1979)
759. Bob McLelland, *Roanoke Times & World-News (RTWN)*, July 3, 1979.
760. Ibid.
761. Ibid.
762. Ibid.
763. Ibid.
764. Ibid.
765. Ibid.
766. Ibid.
767. Ibid.
768. Ibid.
769. Ibid.
770. McLelland, *RTWN*, July 31, 1979.
771. Ibid.
772. Ibid.
773. Brian Hoffman, *Salem Times-Register (STR)*, August 16, 1979.
774. Ibid.
775. Ibid.
776. Ibid.
777. Ibid.
778. Ibid.
779. Hoffman, *STR*, September 13, 1979.
780. Ibid.
781. Ibid.
782. Hoffman, *STR*, September 20, 1979.
783. Ibid.
784. Ibid.
785. Hoffman, *STR*, September 27, 1979.
786. Ibid.
787. Ibid.
788. Ibid.
789. Ibid.
790. Ibid.
791. Ibid.
792. Ibid.
793. Ibid.
794. Hoffman, *STR*, October 4, 1979.

795. Ibid.
796. Ibid.
797. Mark Boorman, *RTWN*, October 4, 1979.
798. Ibid.
799. Ibid.
800. Ibid.
801. Ibid.
802. Ibid.
803. Ibid.
804. Ibid.
805. Ibid.
806. Ibid.
807. Ibid.
808. Ibid.
809. From staff reports, *RTWN*, October 13, 1979.
810. Ibid.
811. Ibid.
812. Hoffman, *STR*, October 18, 1979.
813. Ibid.
814. From staff reports, *RTWN*, October 20, 1979.
815. Ibid.
816. Hoffman, *STR*, October 25, 1979.
817. Ibid.
818. Ibid.
819. Ibid.
820. Dennis Latter, *RTWN*, October 27, 1979.
821. Ibid.
822. Ibid.
823. Ibid.
824. Ibid.
825. Ibid.
826. Ibid.
827. Ibid.
828. Ibid.
829. Ibid.
830. Ibid.
831. Hoffman, *STR*, November 8, 1979.
832. Ibid.
833. Ibid.
834. Ibid.
835. From staff reports, *RTWN*, November 4, 1979.
836. Ibid.
837. Ibid.

838. Hoffman, *STR*, November 8, 1979.
839. Ibid.
840. Ibid.
841. Ibid.
842. Ibid.
843. Ibid.
844. Ibid.
845. Ibid.
846. Ibid.
847. Ibid.
848. Ibid.
849. Ibid.
850. Ibid.
851. Ibid.
852. Ibid.
853. Ibid.
854. Hoffman, *STR*, November 29, 1979.
855. Ibid.
856. Boorman, *RTWN*, December 11, 1979.
857. Ibid.
858. Ibid.
859. Ibid.
860. Ibid.
861. Ibid.
862. Ibid.
863. Ibid.

Part 2: The Nearly Crushing Blow (1980)
864. Jack Chamberlain, *Roanoke Time & World-News (RTWN)*, April 25, 1980.
865. Ibid.
866. Chamberlain, *RTWN*, July 1, 1980.
867. Ibid.
868. Ibid.
869. Ibid.
870. Ibid.
871. Ibid.
872. Dave Scarangella, *RTWN*, July 22, 1980.
873. Ibid.
874. Ibid.
875. Ibid.
876. Ibid.
877. Ibid.
878. Bob Teitlebaum, *RTWN*, September 6, 1980.

879. Bill Eichenberger, *RTWN*, Septmber 13, 1980.
880. Ibid.
881. Ibid.
882. Ibid.
883. Ibid.
884. Ibid.
885. Ibid.
886. Mark A. O'Connell, *The Team the Titans Remember* (New York: Page Publishing Inc., 2017), 35 and 46.
887. Ibid.
888. Ibid.
889. Ibid.
890. Doug Doughty, *RTWN*, October 5, 1980.
891. Ibid.
892. Ibid.
893. Ibid.
894. Ibid.
895. Ibid.
896. Ibid.
897. Ibid.
898. Ibid.
899. Ibid.
900. Doughty, *RTWN*, September 26, 1980.
901. Ibid.
902. Ibid.
903. Ibid.
904. Ibid.
905. Ibid.
906. From staff reports, *RTWN*, October 5, 1980.
907. From one of several personal interviews with Dale Foster.
908. Ibid.
909. From staff reports, *RTWN*, October 5, 1980.
910. Ibid.
911. Ibid.
912. Ibid.
913. Ibid.
914. Ibid.
915. Ibid.
916. From staff reports, *RTWN*, October 7, 1980.
917. Ibid.
918. Ibid.
919. Brian Hoffman, *STR*, October 7, 1980.
920. Ibid.

921. Ibid.
922. Ibid.
923. Ibid.
924. Ibid.
925. Ibid.
926. Ibid.
927. Frank Batten Jr., *RTWN*, October 10, 1980.
928. Ibid.
929. Ibid.
930. Ibid.
931. Ibid.
932. Chamberlain, *RTWN*, October 10, 1980.
933. Ibid.
934. Ibid.
935. From staff reports, *RTWN*, October 11, 1980.
936. Ibid.
937. John Witt, *RTWN*, October 11, 1980.
938. Ibid.
939. Ibid.
940. Ibid.
941. Ibid.
942. Witt, *RTWN*, October 12, 1980.
943. Ibid.
944. Ibid.
945. Ibid.
946. Ibid.
947. Ibid.
948. From staff reports, *RTWN*, October 18, 1980.
949. Ibid.
950. .
951. .
952. .
953. .
954. O'Connell, *The Team the Titans Remember.*
955. Bill Eichenberger, *RTWN*, October 25, 1980.
956. Ibid.
957. Ibid.
958. Ibid.
959. Ibid.
960. Ibid.
961. Ibid.
962. Ibid.
963. Ibid.

964. Ibid.
965. From staff reports, *RTWN*, November 1, 1980.
966. Ibid.
967. Ibid.
968. Ibid.
969. Ibid.
970. From staff reports, *RTWN*, November 8, 1980.
971. Ibid.
972. Ibid.
973. Ibid.
974. From one of several interviews with Dale Foster.
975. Ibid.
976. Ibid.
977. From a personal interview with Chance Crawford on August 27, 2018.
978. Ibid.
979. Ibid.
980. Ibid.
981. Ibid.
982. Ibid.
983. Ibid.
984. Ibid.
985. Ibid.
986. Ibid.
987. Ibid.
988. Ibid.
989. Ibid.
990. Ibid.
991. Ibid.
992. Ibid.
993. Ibid.
994. Ibid.
995. Ibid.
996. Ibid.
997. Ibid.
998. Ibid.
999. Ibid.
1000. Ibid.
1001. Ibid.
1002. Ibid.
1003. From one of several interviews with Foster.

Part 3: Little Fun in Eighty-One

1004. Blair Kerkhoff, *Roanoke Times & World-News (RTWN)*, August 30, 1981.
1005. Ibid.
1006. Ibid.
1007. Ibid.
1008. Ibid.
1009. Ibid.
1010. Brian Hoffman, *Salem Times-Register (STR)*, September 3, 1981.
1011. Ibid.
1012. Ibid.
1013. Ibid.
1014. Ibid.
1015. Ibid.
1016. Ibid.
1017. Ray Cox, *RTWN*, September 5, 1981.
1018. Ibid.
1019. Ibid.
1020. Ibid.
1021. Randy King, *RTWN*, September 12, 1981.
1022. Ibid.
1023. Ibid.
1024. Ibid.
1025. Ibid.
1026. Ibid.
1027. Ibid.
1028. Ibid.
1029. Ibid.
1030. High School Football Roundup, *RTWN*, September 20, 1981.
1031. Kerkhoff, *RTWN*, September 22, 1981.
1032. Kerkhoff, *RTWN*, September 26, 1981
1033. Ibid.
1034. Ibid.
1035. Ibid.
1036. Ibid.
1037. Ibid.
1038. Letter to the editor, *RTWN*, September 29, 1981.
1039. From staff reports, *RTWN*, October 3, 1981.
1040. Ibid.
1041. Ibid.
1042. From staff reports, *RTWN*, October 10. 1981.
1043. Ibid.
1044. Ibid.
1045. Ibid.

1046. Ibid.
1047. Ibid.
1048. From staff reports, *RTWN*, October 17, 1981.
1049. Ibid.
1050. Ibid.
1051. Ibid.
1052. From staff reports, *RTWN*, October 25, 1981.
1053. Ibid.
1054. Ibid.
1055. Ibid.
1056. Ibid.
1057. Ibid.
1058. King, *RTWN*, October 31, 1981.
1059. Ibid.
1060. Ibid.
1061. Ibid.
1062. Ibid.
1063. Ibid.
1064. Ibid.
1065. Ibid.
1066. Ibid.
1067. From staff reports, *RTWN*, November 7, 1981
1068. Ibid.
1069. Ibid.
1070. Ibid.
1071. Ibid.
1072. Ibid.
1073. Ibid.
1074. Ibid.
1075. Jack Bogacyzk, *RTWN*, November 7, 1981.
1076. From staff reports, *RTWN*, November 9, 1981.
1077. From staff reports, *RTWN*. November 16, 1981.
1078. From staff reports, *RTWN*, November 19, 1981.
1079. Ibid.
1080. Ibid.
1081. Ibid.
1082. Hoffman, *STR*, December 17, 1981.
1083. Ibid.
1084. Bob McLelland, *RTWN*, December 16, 1981.
1085. Ibid.
1086. Ibid.
1087. Ibid.
1088. Ibid.

1089. Ibid.
1090. Ibid.

Chapter 9: A Secession of Sorts

1091. Fran Coombs and Steve Haner, *Roanoke Times & World-News (RTWN)*, April 30, 1979.
1092. Ibid.
1093. Ibid.
1094. Ibid.
1095. Ibid.
1096. Ibid.
1097. Brian Hoffman, *Salem Times-Register (STR)*, June 28, 1979.
1098. Ibid.
1099. Ibid.
1100. Haner, *RTWN*, August 16, 1979.
1101. Ibid.
1102. Ibid.
1103. Hoffman, *STR*, November 22, 1979.
1104. Ibid.
1105. Jack Chamberlain, *RTWN*, August 5, 1980.
1106. Ibid.
1107. Ibid.
1108. Ibid.
1109. Ibid.
1110. Ibid.
1111. Ibid.
1112. Ibid.
1113. Ibid.
1114. Ibid.
1115. Ibid.
1116. Ibid.
1117. Ibid.
1118. Ibid.
1119. Ibid.
1120. Unnamed author, *RTWN*, August 8, 1980.
1121. Ibid.
1122. Ibid.
1123. Ibid.
1124. Ibid.
1125. Chamberlain, *RTWN*, November 30, 1980.
1126. Ibid.
1127. Ibid.

1128. Ibid.
1129. Ibid.
1130. Ibid.
1131. Ibid.
1132. Ibid.
1133. Ibid.
1134. Ibid.
1135. Ibid.
1136. David Rosenthal, *RTWN* Salem Bureau, December 5, 1980.
1137. Ibid.
1138. Ibid.
1139. Ibid.
1140. Ibid.
1141. Ibid.
1142. Rosenthal, *RTWN*, December 9, 1980.
1143. Ibid.
1144. Ibid.
1145. Ibid.
1146. Ibid.
1147. Rosenthal, *RTWN*, January 13, 1981.
1148. Ibid.
1149. Ibid.
1150. Ibid.
1151. Ibid.
1152. Ibid.
1153. Ibid.
1154. Ibid.
1155. Ibid.
1156. Rosenthal, *RTWN*, February 2, 1981.
1157. Ibid.
1158. Ibid.
1159. Ibid.
1160. Ibid.
1161. Ibid.
1162. Charles Stebbins, *RTWN*, February 6, 1981.
1163. Ibid.
1164. Ibid.
1165. Ibid.
1166. Ibid.
1167. Rosenthal and Jere Atkin, *RTWN*, February 5, 1981.
1168. Ibid.
1169. Ibid.
1170. Rosenthal, *RTWN*, February 6, 1981.

1171. Ibid.
1172. Ibid.
1173. Ibid.
1174. Ibid.
1175. Ibid.
1176. Ibid.
1177. Ibid.
1178. Ibid.
1179. Ibid.
1180. Chamberlain, *RTWN*, March 16, 1981.
1181. Ibid.
1182. Ibid.
1183. Ibid.
1184. Chamberlain, *RTWN*, March 26, 1981.
1185. Ibid.
1186. Chamberlain, *RTWN*, April 1, 1981.
1187. Ibid.
1188. Ibid.
1189. Chamberlain, *RTWN*, April 9, 1981.
1190. Ibid.
1191. Ibid.
1192. Ibid.
1193. Stebbins, *RTWN*, April 5, 1981.
1194. Ibid.
1195. Ibid.
1196. Ibid.
1197. Ibid.
1198. Ibid.
1199. Chamberlain, *RTWN*, May 13, 1981.
1200. Ibid.
1201. Ibid.
1202. Ibid.
1203. Chamberlain, *RTWN*, May 15, 1981.
1204. Ibid.
1205. Ibid.
1206. Ibid.
1207. Unnamed author, *RTWN*, June 5, 1981.
1208. Ibid.
1209. Ibid.
1210. Ibid.
1211. Chamberlain, *RTWN*, June 12, 1981.
1212. Ibid.
1213. Ibid.

1214. Ibid.
1215. Ibid.
1216. Ibid.
1217. Ibid.
1218. Ibid.
1219. Ibid.
1220. Ibid.
1221. Editorial, *RTWN*, June 15, 1981.
1222. Ibid.
1223. Chamberlain, *RTWN*, June 18, 1981.
1224. Ibid.
1225. Ibid.
1226. Ibid.
1227. Ibid.
1228. Ibid.
1229. Ibid.
1230. Ibid.
1231. Ibid.
1232. Ibid.
1233. Ibid.
1234. Ibid.
1235. Ibid.
1236. Letter to the editor, *RTWN*, June 19, 1981.
1237. David Rosenthal, *RTWN*, June 24, 1981.
1238. Ibid.
1239. Ibid.
1240. Ibid.
1241. Chamberlain, *RTWN*, July 1, 1981.
1242. Ibid.
1243. Ibid.
1244. Chamberlain, *RTWN*, July 2, 1981.
1245. Ibid.
1246. Ibid.
1247. Ibid.
1248. Ibid.
1249. Ibid.
1250. Chamberlain, *RTWN*, "Salem Declares Independence," July 10, 1981.
1251. Ibid.
1252. Ibid.
1253. Ibid.
1254. Ibid.
1255. Ibid.
1256. Ibid.

1257. Ibid.
1258. Ibid.
1259. Ibid.
1260. Ibid.
1261. Victoria Brown, *RTWN*, July 28, 1981.
1262. Editorial Section, *RTWN*, November 11, 1981.
1263. Ibid.
1264. Ibid.
1265. Ibid.
1266. Ibid.
1267. Chamberlain, *RTWN*, November 10, 1981.
1268. Ibid.
1269. Ibid.
1270. Ibid.
1271. Ibid.
1272. Chamberlain, *RTWN*, November 6, 1981.
1273. Ibid.
1274. Ibid.
1275. Chamberlain, *RTWN*, August 26, 1982.
1276. Ibid.
1277. Ibid.
1278. Ibid.
1279. Hoffman, *STR*, August 11, 1983.
1280. Ibid.
1281. Chamberlain and Mike Hudson, *RTWN*, September 1, 1981.
1282. Ibid.
1283. Ibid.
1284. Ibid.
1285. Ibid.
1286. Ibid.
1287. Alex Smith, News Editor, *STR*, March 19, 1984.
1288. Ibid.
1289. Ibid.
1290. Ibid.
1291. Robert Downey, *STR*, August 1984 (specific date not recovered).
1292. Ibid.
1293. Ibid.

Chapter 10: 1982: We Shall Not Kick

1294. Personal interview with Wallace Thompson by telephone on March 14, 2018.
1295. Ibid.

1296. Ibid.
1297. Ibid.
1298. Ibid.
1299. Ibid.
1300. Ibid.
1301. Ibid.
1302. Ibid.
1303. Ibid.
1304. Ibid.
1305. Ibid.
1306. Blair Kerkhoff, *Roanoke Times & World-News (RTWN)*, February 12, 1982.
1307. Ibid.
1308. Ibid.
1309. Ibid.
1310. Ibid.
1311. Ibid.
1312. Ibid.
1313. Kerkhoff, *RTWN*, August 26, 1982.
1314. Ibid.
1315. Ibid.
1316. Ibid.
1317. From staff reports, *RTWN*, September 4, 1982.
1318. Ibid.
1319. Ibid.
1320. Ibid.
1321. Ibid.
1322. Ibid.
1323. Ibid.
1324. Ibid.
1325. Ibid.
1326. Ibid.
1327. Ibid.
1328. Ibid.
1329. Kerkhoff, *RTWN*, September 11, 1982.
1330. Ibid.
1331. Kerkhoff, *RTWN*, September 17, 1982.
1332. Ibid.
1333. Kerkhoff, *RTWN*, September 18, 1982.
1334. Ibid.
1335. Ibid.
1336. Ibid.
1337. Ibid.
1338. Ibid.

1339. Ibid.
1340. Randy King, *RTWN*, September 23, 1982.
1341. Ibid.
1342. Ibid.
1343. Ibid.
1344. Ibid.
1345. From staff reports, *RTWN*, October 1, 1982.
1346. Ibid.
1347. Ibid.
1348. Ibid.
1349. Ibid.
1350. Ibid.
1351. From staff reports, *RTWN*, October 9, 1982.
1352. Ibid.
1353. Ibid.
1354. Ibid.
1355. Ibid.
1356. Ibid.
1357. Bob Teitlebaum, *RTWN*, October 12, 1982.
1358. Ibid.
1359. Ibid.
1360. Ibid.
1361. Ibid.
1362. Ibid.
1363. Ibid.
1364. Teitlebaum, *RTWN*, October 26, 1982.
1365. Ibid.
1366. Ibid.
1367. Ibid.
1368. Ibid.
1369. Ibid.
1370. Ibid.
1371. Ibid.
1372. Ibid.
1373. Ibid.
1374. Ray Cox, *RTWN*, October 30, 1982.
1375. Ibid.
1376. Ibid.
1377. Ibid.
1378. Ibid.
1379. From staff reports, *RTWN*, November 6, 1982.
1380. Ibid.
1381. Ibid.

1382. Ibid.
1383. Kerkhoff, *RTWN*, November 6, 1982.
1384. Ibid.
1385. Sports Briefs, High School Football Pairings, *RTWN*, November 17, 1982.
1386. Ibid.
1387. From staff reports, *RTWN*, November 13, 1982.
1388. Doug Doughty, *RTWN*, November 20, 1982.
1389. Virginia High School League Record Book, Page 28.
1390. From staff reports, *RTWN*, December 16, 1982.
1391. Ibid.
1392. Ibid.
1393. From one of several interviews with Charlie Hammersley.
1394. Ibid.
1395. Ibid.
1396. From one of several interviews with Dale Foster.
1397. From one of several interviews with Hammersley.
1398. Ibid.

Chapter 11: 1983

Part 1: The Trap Block
1399. Steve Haner, *Roanoke Times & World-News (RTWN)*, February 9, 1983.
1400. Ibid.
1401. Ibid.
1402. Ibid.
1403. Ibid.
1404. Ibid.
1405. Ibid.
1406. Ibid.
1407. Ibid.
1408. Ibid.
1409. Editorial, *RTWN*, February 10, 1983.
1410. Ibid.
1411. Ibid.
1412. Ibid.
1413. Ibid.
1414. Haner, *RTWN*, February 10, 1983.
1415. Ibid.
1416. Ibid.
1417. Ibid.
1418. Ibid.
1419. Ibid.
1420. Ibid.

1421. Ibid.
1422. Haner, *RTWN*, February 23, 1983.
1423. Ibid.
1424. Ibid.
1425. Ibid.
1426. Ibid.
1427. Ibid.
1428. Ibid.
1429. Ibid.
1430. Ibid.
1431. Ibid.
1432. Ibid.
1433. Ibid.
1434. Ibid.
1435. Ibid.
1436. Ibid.
1437. Haner, *RTWN*, February 24, 1983.
1438. Editorial, *RTWN*, February 25, 1983.
1439. Letter to the editor by Kaye Sellers, *RWN*, March 19, 1983.
1440. Haner, *RTWN*, "Willis White to Be Named Salem Coach," April 7, 1983.
1441. Ibid.
1442. Ibid.
1443. Ibid.
1444. Ibid.
1445. Ibid.
1446. Ibid.
1447. Ibid.
1448. Blair Kerkhoff, *RTWN*, "Salem Didn't Give Richards a Fair Chance," April 12, 1983.
1449. Ibid.
1450. From one of several personal interviews with Dale Foster.
1451. Ibid.
1452. Ibid.
1453. Ibid.
1454. Ibid.
1455. Kerkhoff, *RTWN*, May 7, 1983.
1456. Ibid.
1457. Ibid.
1458. Ibid.
1459. Ibid.

Part 2: A Country Boy Named Willie
1460. Personal interview with Willis White on January 19, 2018.
1461. Ibid.
1462. Ibid.
1463. Ibid.
1464. Ibid.
1465. Ibid.
1466. Ibid.
1467. Ibid.
1468. Ibid.
1469. Ibid.
1470. Ibid.
1471. Ibid.
1472. Ibid.
1473. Ibid.
1474. Ibid.
1475. Ibid.
1476. Ibid.
1477. Ibid.
1478. Ibid.
1479. Ibid.
1480. Ibid.
1481. Ibid.
1482. Ibid.
1483. Ibid.
1484. Ibid.
1485. Ibid.
1486. Ibid.
1487. Ibid.
1488. Ibid.
1489. Ibid.
1490. Ibid.
1491. Ibid.
1492. Ibid.
1493. Ibid.
1494. Ibid.
1495. Ibid.
1496. Ibid.
1497. Ibid.
1498. Ibid.
1499. Ibid.
1500. Ibid.
1501. Ibid.

1502. Ibid.
1503. Ibid.
1504. Ibid.
1505. Ibid.
1506. Virginia High School League (VHSL) Record Book, page 28.
1507. Personal interview with White on January 19, 2018.
1508. Ibid.
1509. Ibid.
1510. Ibid.
1511. Ibid.
1512. Ibid.
1513. Ibid.
1514. Ibid.
1515. Ibid.
1516. Ibid.
1517. Ibid.
1518. Ibid.
1519. Ibid.
1520. Ibid.
1521. Ibid.
1522. Ibid.
1523. Ibid.
1524. Ibid.
1525. Personal interview with Billy Miles in March of 2018.
1526. Personal interview with White on January 19, 2018.
1527. Ibid.
1528. Ibid.
1529. Ibid.
1530. Ibid.
1531. Ibid.
1532. Ibid.
1533. Ibid.
1534. Ibid.
1535. Ibid.
1536. Ibid.
1537. Ibid.
1538. Ibid.
1539. Ibid.
1540. Ibid.
1541. Ibid.

Part 3: Now *That* Was the Right Call!

1542. Brian Hoffman, *Salem Times-Register (STR)*, September 1, 1983.
1543. Ibid.
1544. Ibid.
1545. Ibid.
1546. Ibid.
1547. Ibid.
1548. Ibid.
1549. Ibid.
1550. Ibid.
1551. Ibid.
1552. Ibid.
1553. Ibid.
1554. Ibid.
1555. Ibid.
1556. Ibid.
1557. Ibid.
1558. Ibid.
1559. Ibid.
1560. Ibid.
1561. Ibid.
1562. Ibid.
1563. Dan Callahan, November 10, 2002, www.patriot.com.
1564. Ibid.
1565. Ibid.
1566. Unnamed author, *Roanoke Times & World-News (RTWN)*, August 25, 1983.
1567. Ibid.
1568. Ibid.
1569. Ibid.
1570. Ray Cox, *RTWN*, September 1, 1983.
1571. Ibid.
1572. Ibid.
1573. Ibid.
1574. Ibid.
1575. Ibid.
1576. Ibid.
1577. Ibid.
1578. From staff reports, *RTWN*, September 1, 1983.
1579. Ibid.
1580. Ibid.
1581. Bob Teitlebaum, *RTWN*, September 9, 1983.
1582. Ibid.
1583. Teitlebaum, *RTWN*, September 10, 1983.

1584. Ibid.
1585. Ibid.
1586. Ibid.
1587. Ibid.
1588. From staff reports, *RTWN*, September 17, 1983.
1589. Ibid.
1590. Ibid.
1591. Ibid.
1592. Football scores, *RTWN*, front page, September 17, 1983.
1593. From staff reports, *RTWN*, September 24, 1983.
1594. Ibid.
1595. Ibid.
1596. Ibid.
1597. Ibid.
1598. Ibid.
1599. Ibid.
1600. Ibid.
1601. From staff reports, *RTWN*, October 2, 1983.
1602. Ibid.
1603. Ibid.
1604. Ibid.
1605. Ibid.
1606. Ibid.
1607. Ibid.
1608. Prep Standings, *RTWN*, October 2, 1983.
1609. From staff reports, *RTWN*, October 8, 1983.
1610. Ibid.
1611. Ibid.
1612. Ibid.
1613. Ibid.
1614. Ibid.
1615. Ibid.
1616. From staff reports, *RTWN*, October 13, 1983.
1617. From staff reports, *RTWN*, October 16, 1983.
1618. Ibid.
1619. Ibid.
1620. Ibid.
1621. Ibid.
1622. Ibid.
1623. Ibid.
1624. From staff reports, *RTWN*, October 22, 1983.
1625. Ibid.
1626. Ibid.

[1627]. Ibid.
[1628]. Teitlebaum, *RTWN*, October 25, 1983.
[1629]. Ibid.
[1630]. Teitlebaum, *RTWN*, October 28, 1983.
[1631]. Ibid.
[1632]. Ibid.
[1633]. Ibid.
[1634]. Ibid.
[1635]. Teitlebaum, *RTWN*, October 29, 1983.
[1636]. Ibid.
[1637]. Ibid.
[1638]. Ibid.
[1639]. Ibid.
[1640]. Ibid.
[1641]. Ibid.
[1642]. Ibid.
[1643]. Ibid.
[1644]. Ibid.
[1645]. Ibid.
[1646]. Teitlebaum, *RTWN*, October 30, 1983.
[1647]. Blair Kerkhoff, *RTWN*, November 1, 1983.
[1648]. Teitlebaum, *RTWN*, November 5, 1983.
[1649]. Ibid.
[1650]. Ibid.
[1651]. Ibid.
[1652]. Ibid.
[1653]. Doug Doughty, *RTWN*, November 5, 1983.
[1654]. Prep Sports, *RTWN*, November 8, 1983.
[1655]. Playoff Winners, *RTWN*, November 12, 1983.
[1656]. Teitlebaum, *RTWN*, November 19, 1983.
[1657]. Prep Playoffs, *RTWN*, November 27, 1983.
[1658]. From staff reports, *RTWN*, December 4, 1983.
[1659]. Final Football Statistics, Hoffman, *STR*, December 1, 1983.
[1660]. Ibid.
[1661]. Ibid.
[1662]. Ibid.

Chapter 12: 1984: The Last in the Snake Pit

[1663]. From staff reports, *Roanoke Times & World-News (RTWN)*, January 23, 1984.
[1664]. Ibid.
[1665]. Ibid.
[1666]. From staff reports, *RTWN*, January 24, 1984.

1667. Ibid.
1668. Ibid.
1669. Brian Hoffman, *Salem Times-Register (STR)*, August 16, 1984.
1670. Ibid.
1671. Ibid.
1672. Ibid.
1673. Ibid.
1674. Ibid.
1675. Bob Teitlebaum, *RTWN*, August 31, 1984.
1676. Ibid.
1677. Ibid.
1678. Ibid.
1679. Ibid.
1680. From staff reports, *RTWN*, September 1, 1984
1681. Ibid.
1682. Ibid.
1683. Ibid.
1684. From staff reports, *RTWN*, September 7, 1984.
1685. Ibid.
1686. Ibid.
1687. Ibid.
1688. Teitlebaum, *RTWN*, September 14, 1984.
1689. Ibid.
1690. Ibid.
1691. Ibid.
1692. Teitlebaum, *RTWN*, September 15, 1984.
1693. Ibid.
1694. Ibid.
1695. Ibid.
1696. Ibid.
1697. Ibid.
1698. Mike McCall, *RTWN*, September 22, 1984.
1699. Ibid.
1700. Ibid.
1701. Ibid.
1702. Ibid.
1703. Standings, *RTWN*, September 22, 1984.
1704. Ibid.
1705. From staff reports, *RTWN*, September 29, 1984.
1706. Ibid.
1707. Ibid.
1708. Ibid.
1709. Ibid.

THE SPARTAN SUCCESSION

1710. Standings, *RTWN*, September 29, 1984.
1711. Prep Poll, *RTWN*, October 1, 1984.
1712. From staff reports, *RTWN*, October 6, 1984.
1713. Ibid.
1714. Ibid.
1715. Ibid.
1716. Ibid.
1717. High School Football, *RTWN*, October 6, 1984.
1718. High School Football Standings, *RTWN*, October 13, 1984.
1719. Ibid.
1720. Prep Poll, *RTWN*, October 9, 1984.
1721. Prep Poll, *RTWN*, October 16, 1984.
1722. Ibid.
1723. Teitlebaum, *RTWN*, October 19, 1984.
1724. Ibid.
1725. Teitlebaum, *RTWN*, October 20, 1984.
1726. Ibid.
1727. Ibid.
1728. Ibid.
1729. Notes 'N' Quotes, *RTWN*, October 23, 1984.
1730. Standings, *RTWN*, October 20, 1984.
1731. Teitlebaum, *RTWN*, October 24, 1984.
1732. Ibid.
1733. Ibid.
1734. Ibid.
1735. Ibid.
1736. Ibid.
1737. Ibid.
1738. Ibid.
1739. Ibid.
1740. Ibid.
1741. Teitlebaum, *RTWN*, October 27, 1984.
1742. Ibid.
1743. Ibid.
1744. District Scores, *RTWN*, October 27, 1984.
1745. Polls, *RTWN*, October 30, 1984.
1746. Teitlebaum, *RTWN*, October 30, 1984.
1747. Ibid.
1748. Ibid.
1749. Ibid.
1750. Ibid.
1751. .
1752. Ibid.

1753. Ibid.
1754. Ibid.
1755. Ibid.
1756. Ibid.
1757. Ibid.
1758. Ibid.
1759. Ibid.
1760. Ibid.
1761. Teitlebaum, *RTWN*, November 3, 1984.
1762. Ibid.
1763. Ibid.
1764. Ibid.
1765. Ibid.
1766. Ibid.
1767. Ibid.
1768. Ibid.
1769. Ibid.
1770. Ibid.
1771. .
1772. Associated Press, *RTWN*, November 7, 1984.
1773. Ibid.
1774. Doug Doughty, *RTWN*, November 10, 1984.
1775. Ibid.
1776. Ibid.
1777. Ibid.
1778. Teitlebaum, High School Sports, *RTWN*, November 13, 1984.
1779. Ibid.
1780. Ibid.
1781. Ibid.
1782. From staff reports, *RTWN*, November 17, 1984.
1783. Teitlebaum, *RTWN*, November 24, 1984.
1784. Ibid.
1785. High School Football, *RTWN*, November 25, 1984.
1786. From staff and wire reports, *RTWN*, November 24, 1984.
1787. From staff and wire reports, *RTWN*, November 29, 1984.
1788. Ibid.
1789. Ibid.
1790. Wire reports, *RTWN*, December 2, 1984.
1791. Ibid.
1792. Bill Brill, *RTWN*, December 2, 1984.
1793. Ibid.
1794. Ibid.
1795. Ibid.

THE SPARTAN SUCCESSION

1796. High School Football, *RTWN*, December 9, 1984.
1797. Ibid.
1798. Teitlebaum, *RTWN*, December 18, 1984.
1799. Ibid.
1800. Ibid.
1801. Ibid.
1802. Blair Kerkhoff, *RTWN*, January 30, 1985.
1803. Ibid.
1804. Ibid.
1805. Hoffman, *STR*, December 20, 1984.
1806. Ibid.
1807. Ibid.
1808. From one of several personal interviews with Charlie Hammersley.
1809. Ibid.
1810. Ibid.
1811. Personal conversation with Coach Willis White by telephone, date not recorded.
1812. Hoffman, *STR*, November 8, 1984.

Chapter 13: 1985

Part 1: A Stadium of Their Own
1813. Letter to the editor, *Roanoke Times & World-News (RTWN)*, February 26, 1978.
1814. Ibid.
1815. Brian Hoffman, *Salem Times-Register (STR)*, December 13, 1979.
1816. Ibid.
1817. Ibid.
1818. Ibid.
1819. Ibid.
1820. Roland Lazenby, *RTWN*, September 28, 1983.
1821. Ibid.
1822. Ibid.
1823. Ibid.
1824. Ibid.
1825. Ibid.
1826. Ibid.
1827. Ibid.
1828. Ibid.
1829. Ibid.
1830. Ibid.
1831. Belinda Anderson, *RTWN*, October 25, 1983.
1832. Ibid.

1833. Ibid.
1834. Ibid.
1835. Leslie Taylor, *RTWN*, January 20, 1984.
1836. Ibid.
1837. Ibid.
1838. Taylor, *RTWN*, February 9, 1984.
1839. Ibid.
1840. Ibid.
1841. Ibid.
1842. Ibid.
1843. Ibid.
1844. Ibid.
1845. Ibid.
1846. Ibid.
1847. From staff reports, *RTWN*, March 15, 1984.
1848. Ibid.
1849. Ibid.
1850. Ibid.
1851. Ibid.
1852. Brian O'Neill, "Salem's Community Pride As Strong As Ever, and That Makes Sense," *RTWN*, March 21, 1984.
1853. Ibid.
1854. Taylor, *RTWN*, March 28, 1984.
1855. Ibid.
1856. Mary King, *STR*, November 15, 1984.
1857. Ibid.
1858. Ibid.
1859. Ibid.
1860. Hoffman, *STR*, November 29, 1984.
1861. Ibid.
1862. Ibid.
1863. Ibid.
1864. Ibid.
1865. Ibid.
1866. Ibid.
1867. Ibid.
1868. Hoffman and Robert Downey, *STR*, December 6, 1984.
1869. Ibid.
1870. Ibid.
1871. Ibid.
1872. Ibid.
1873. Ibid.
1874. Taylor, *RTWN*, March 16, 1985.

1875. Ibid.
1876. Ibid.
1877. Ibid.
1878. Ibid.
1879. Ibid.
1880. Letter to the editor by W. Randolph Abshire, *RTWN*, July 20, 1985.
1881. Ibid.
1882. Unnamed author, *RTWN*, August 6, 1985.
1883. Ibid.
1884. Hoffman, *STR*, July 25, 1985.
1885. Ibid.
1886. Ibid.
1887. Bob Teitlebaum, *RTWN*, August 18, 1985.
1888. Ibid.
1889. Ibid.
1890. Ibid.
1891. Teitlebaum, *RTWN*, August 28, 1985.
1892. Ibid.
1893. Ibid.
1894. Ibid.
1895. Ibid.
1896. Unnamed author, *RTWN*, August 29, 1985.
1897. Teitlebaum, *RTWN*, August 30, 1985.
1898. Terrence Samuel, *RTWN*, August 31, 1985.
1899. Ibid.
1900. Ibid.
1901. Ibid.
1902. Ibid.
1903. Ibid.

Part 2: The New Era Is Complete
1904. Wade Kendrick, *Roanoke Times & World-News (RTWN)*, August 31, 1985.
1905. Ibid.
1906. Ibid.
1907. Ibid.
1908. Ibid.
1909. Ibid.
1910. Ibid.
1911. Ibid.
1912. Ibid.
1913. Ibid.
1914. Ibid.
1915. Ibid.

1916. Ray Cox, *RTWN*, August 31, 1985.
1917. Bob Teitlebaum, *RTWN*, September 6, 1985.
1918. Ibid.
1919. Cox, *RTWN*, September 7, 1985.
1920. Ibid.
1921. Ibid.
1922. Ibid.
1923. Ibid.
1924. Ibid.
1925. Ibid.
1926. Ibid.
1927. Ibid.
1928. High School Football, *RTWN*, September 7, 1985.
1929. Teitlebaum, *RTWN*, September 13, 1985.
1930. Ibid.
1931. Ibid.
1932. Teitlebaum, *RTWN*, September 14, 1985.
1933. Ibid.
1934. Ibid.
1935. Ibid.
1936. Ibid.
1937. Ibid.
1938. Ibid.
1939. High School Football, *RTWN*, September 14, 1985.
1940. Ibid.
1941. Ibid.
1942. Wade Kendrick, *RTWN*, September 21, 1985.
1943. Ibid.
1944. Ibid.
1945. Ibid.
1946. Ibid.
1947. Ibid.
1948. High School Sports, *RTWN*, September 21, 1985.
1949. Howard Wimmer, *RTWN*, September 28, 1985.
1950. Ibid.
1951. Ibid.
1952. Ibid.
1953. High School Football, *RTWN*, September 28, 1985.
1954. Statistical leaders, *RTWN*, October 1, 1985.
1955. Ibid.
1956. Ibid.
1957. From staff reports, *RTWN*, October 5, 1985.
1958. Ibid.

1959. Ibid.
1960. Ibid.
1961. Ibid.
1962. Scores and standings, *RTWN*, October 5, 1985.
1963. Ibid.
1964. Ibid.
1965. High School Football, *RTWN*, October 12, 1985.
1966. Ibid.
1967. Teitlebaum, *RTWN*, October 19, 1985.
1968. Ibid.
1969. Ibid.
1970. Ibid.
1971. Ibid.
1972. State poll, *RTWN*, October 19, 1985.
1973. Ibid.
1974. Ibid.
1975. Ibid.
1976. Teitlebaum, *RTWN*, October 23, 1985.
1977. Ibid.
1978. Ibid.
1979. Ibid.
1980. Teitlebaum *RTWN*, October 26, 1985.
1981. Ibid.
1982. Ibid.
1983. Ibid.
1984. Ibid.
1985. Ibid.
1986. Ibid.
1987. Ray Cox, *RTWN*, October 26, 1985.
1988. High School Football, *RTWN*, October 26, 1985.
1989. Teitlebaum, *RTWN*, November 1, 1985.
1990. Ibid.
1991. High School Football, *RTWN*, November 2, 1985.
1992. Ibid.
1993. Ibid.
1994. Ibid.
1995. Ibid.
1996. High School Football, *RTWN*, November 2, 1985.
1997. Ibid.
1998. Teitlebaum, *RTWN*, November 8, 1985.
1999. Ibid.
2000. Ibid.
2001. Ibid.

[2002]. Kevin Myatt, "Flood of 1985 Slowly Flows from Memory to History," Weather Channel, published on November 3, 2015, www.roanoke.com.
[2003]. Ibid.
[2004]. Ibid.
[2005]. Teitlebaum, *RTWN*, November 9, 1985.
[2006]. Ibid.
[2007]. Ibid.
[2008]. Ibid.
[2009]. Ibid.
[2010]. Ibid.
[2011]. Ibid.
[2012]. Ibid.
[2013]. Ibid.
[2014]. Ibid.
[2015]. Ibid.
[2016]. Ibid.
[2017]. Ibid.
[2018]. Ibid.
[2019]. Teitlebaum, *RTWN*, November 10, 1985.
[2020]. Ibid.
[2021]. Ibid.
[2022]. Final Football Standings, *RTWN*, November 12, 1985.
[2023]. Final Statistical Leaders, *RTWN*, November 12, 1985.
[2024]. Ibid.
[2025]. Ibid.
[2026]. High School Closeup, High School Football Pairings, *RTWN*, November 12, 1985.
[2027]. Ibid.
[2028]. Teitlebaum, *RTWN*, November 16, 1985.
[2029]. Ibid.
[2030]. Sports Briefs, *RTWN*, November 18, 1985.
[2031]. Ibid.
[2032]. Ibid.
[2033]. Ibid.
[2034]. High School Closeup, *RTWN*, November 23, 1985.
[2035]. Ibid.
[2036]. Ibid.
[2037]. Unnamed author, *RTWN*, November 26, 1985.
[2038]. Ibid.
[2039]. Ibid.
[2040]. From staff reports, *RTWN*, November 28, 1985.
[2041]. Ibid.
[2042]. Ibid.

2043. Teitlebaum, *RTWN*, December 17, 1985.
2044. Ibid.
2045. Ibid.
2046. Ibid.
2047. Ibid.
2048. Ibid.
2049. Ibid.
2050. Ibid.
2051. Teitlebaum, *RTWN*, December 1, 1985.
2052. Ibid.
2053. High school playoffs from staff and wire reports, *RTWN*, December 1, 1985.
2054. Ibid.
2055. Ibid.
2056. Ibid.
2057. High school football playoffs, *RTWN*, December 8, 1985.
2058. Brian Hoffman, *Salem Times-Register (STR)*, November 21, 1985.
2059. Ibid.
2060. Ibid.
2061. Ibid.
2062. Hoffman, *STR*, December 19, 1985.
2063. Ibid.
2064. Ibid.
2065. Ibid.
2066. Ibid.
2067. From a personal interview with Coach Willis White on January 19, 2018.
2068. Ibid.
2069. Ibid.
2070. Ibid.

Chapter 15: Lest We Forget

2071. From one of several personal interviews with Dale Foster.
2072. Ibid.
2073. Ibid.
2074. Ibid.
2075. Ibid.
2076. Ibid.
2077. Ibid.
2078. Ibid.
2079. Ibid.
2080. Ibid.
2081. Richard Scott, Birmingham, Alabama, January 30, 2009, www.encylopediaofalabama.org.

2082. Ibid.
2083. Ibid.
2084. http://patdyefield.blogsport.com/2008/09/slanting-monster.html, October 25, 2019.
2085. From one of several personal interviews with Foster.
2086. Ibid.
2087. Ibid.
2088. Ibid.
2089. Ibid.
2090. Ibid.
2091. Ibid.
2092. Ibid.
2093. Ibid.
2094. Ibid.
2095. Ibid.
2096. Ibid.

ABOUT THE AUTHOR

Salem native Mark A. O'Connell resides in Somerset of Orange County, Virginia. He has previously authored three books: *Criminal Minds in Real Time*, *Justice Denied*, and *The Team the Titans Remember*. Since 1998 he has served as both a freelance sports correspondent for a couple of newspapers in central Virginia and has provided the play-by-play commentary for the television broadcasts of high school football and lacrosse games.

Contact him by email at takedownnews@ao.com. Visit his Facebook page, @authorOConnell, or his website, www.markaoconnell.com.

CPSIA information can be obtained
at www.ICGtesting.com
Printed in the USA
LVHW090205180720
661047LV00001B/2